RELIGION IN COLONIAL AMERICA

Religion
In Colonial America

by

William Warren Sweet

COOPER SQUARE PUBLISHERS, INC.
NEW YORK
1965

Copyright 1942 by Charles Scribner's Sons

Published 1965 by
Cooper Square Publishers, Inc.
59 Fourth Avenue, New York, N.Y. 10003

Printed in the United States of America

Library of Congress Catalog Card Number: 65-17183

To our three sons

Paul Robinson Sweet
William Warren Sweet, Jr.
Richard Williams Sweet

Preface

THE PURPOSE of this volume is to place religion in its proper perspective in American colonial history. Religion has been the most neglected phase of American history. The average college student could pass a better examination in Greek mythology than on American Church history, and is better informed on the Mediaeval popes than he is on the religious leaders of America. It is hoped that this volume and the others that are to follow will help to remedy this lamentable situation. The present volume tells the story of the beginnings of organized religion in America; of the struggle for survival of the transplanted religious bodies; of their gradual growth and expansion, and of their increasingly important part in the developing life of the American people. A knowledge of this story is essential if the soul and spirit of America is to be understood.

The early chapters of the volume deal with the transplanting to the colonies of a cross-section of western European religion as it existed in the seventeenth century. To 1660 the dominant religious groups in America were the offshoots of the dominant religious bodies of Protestant Europe, representing the conservative wing of the Protestant Reformation. This resulted in the bringing over of the European tradition of Church-State relationship, and it was put into operation in all the colonies established up to that time, except in Rhode Island and Maryland. After 1660, however, a whole new set of liberalizing influences began to operate, which by the end of the colonial period had completely changed the entire situation. From this time forward the right wing bodies became less and less important while the left wing religious groups, finding in Anglo-America for the first time a chance to develop, waxed stronger and stronger. In the seventeenth century there was little in the way of religion that could be called distinctively American; in the eighteenth century America began to turn its back more and more upon European influence, with the result that a distinctively American religious scene began to appear.

In the last two chapters the principal theme is the Americanization of Christianity. The eighteenth century saw American religion more and more democratized and, in the Great Colonial Revivals, for the first time religion reached down to the masses. In the process the old European Church-State relationship was gradually changed, and with independence came the opportunity to bring to a successful completion the century-and-a-half struggle for religious freedom and the separation of Church and State.

How this, the greatest of all of American contributions both in the realm of religion and politics, was achieved cannot be understood unless the course of colonial religious development is carefully followed.

The growing interest in American cultural history renders a larger understanding of the religious development of America a necessity. The attempt to appraise American culture apart from religion is a contradiction in itself, for culture has to do with the moral and religious as well as the intellectual life of a society. Until recent years this phase of American history, outside New England, was not only neglected, it was minimized and even despised by some who liked to think of themselves as trained historians. For the last generation and more a majority of our historians have been economic determinists, and consequently stressed our materialistic development to the neglect of those matters which have to do with the mind and the spirit. No nation of the world has had its political and economic life so fully analyzed as has ours; on the other hand, no great people of modern times have been so neglectful of the spiritual and idealistic phase of their development.

A generation ago a doctor's dissertation on an American Church history subject was unheard of in an American university. If such a thing had been proposed the student, doubtless, would have been told that it could not be accepted, since objectivity was impossible to achieve with such subjects. Fortunately that attitude toward the study of organized religion as a phase of American history has been greatly modified, and it is now entirely respectable in every major American university to choose such a field of interest. Because that is true it is now possible to write the history of religion in America undergirded by the research of many capable scholars, some of whom I have had the privilege of advising in their undertakings. To them and to many others I am deeply indebted in the preparation of this volume, as I will be also in the preparation of the two volumes that are to follow. These two additional volumes will take the subject up to present times.

A nine-months leave of absence granted me by the University of Chicago in 1940–41 permitted me to spend three months at the Huntington Library in San Marino, California, where, under delightful conditions and aided by the friendly and efficient staff of that institution, I was able to make more progress in the preparation of this volume than could have been done otherwise. My thanks are due to Doctor Paul R. Sweet of Bates College and to my colleague, Doctor Sidney E. Mead, for reading parts of the manuscript. Doctor Mead has also rendered a great service in lending his assistance in the arduous task of proofreading.

WILLIAM W. SWEET

Swift Hall
The University of Chicago
May 18, 1942

Contents

RELIGION IN COLONIAL AMERICA

I

Religious Motives
in American Colonization

THE YEAR 1578 marks the beginning of English colonization of America. In that year Queen Elizabeth granted to Sir Humphrey Gilbert *Letters Patent* "for the inhabiting and planting of our people in America," the first such English document to mention colonization. While numerous charters had been granted previously to English trading companies, none had contemplated the planting of Englishmen permanently beyond the seas. Acting under these *Letters Patent* Sir Humphrey attempted the establishment of a colony on the Island of Newfoundland (1583–84). He took possession of the island in the name of the Queen and landed a few nondescript men to hold his claim while he set forth with the remainder to find a better location for his enterprise. In that attempt he was lost at sea and the colony proved a failure. The colonizing schemes thus begun were taken over by Sir Walter Raleigh, the half-brother of Sir Humphrey Gilbert, who turned his attention to a more hospitable clime, and in 1584 sent out ships to what are now the coasts of Virginia and the Carolinas to locate a suitable place for his intended colony. Others also were beginning to show an interest in colonization; but the Queen, who was accustomed to have her subjects serve her and the state at their own expense, was not yet won over to the enterprise, at least to the extent of being willing to furnish funds for its encouragement and promotion.

It was in order to secure the Queen's support that Sir Walter Raleigh obtained the assistance of Richard Hakluyt, the young chaplain of the English embassy at Paris, to prepare a discourse setting forth the advantages to the English nation which might accrue through the planting of colonies in America. The discourse which Richard Hakluyt prepared in 1584 on "Western Planting" sets "forth in full, as if once and for all," the case for expansion, and although the work lay hidden for nearly three centuries, and so was robbed of its deserved influence, yet it furnishes an indispensable record of the motives and intentions of the early colonizers. The arguments for colonization here found were to be used over and over again by the promoters of such enterprises to the very end of the first colonizing period.[1]

Richard Hakluyt graduated from Christ Church in Oxford in 1574 and began at once the study and teaching of cosmography. To aid him in his study he began the collection of those records of English voyages which have made his name immortal. In 1584 he published *Divers Voyages touching the Discovery of America and the Islands adjacent to the same, made first of all by our Englishmen, and afterwards by the Frenchmen and Britons.*[2] The year following he left Oxford to become the chaplain of the English ambassador in Paris. Though young in years he had earned already a deservedly high reputation as a student of maritime affairs and was known as an authority on colonization. It was to young Richard Hakluyt that Sir Walter Raleigh turned, to prepare the arguments which he hoped would convince the

---

[1] George Bruner Parks, *Richard Hakluyt and the English Voyages.* New York; American Geographical Society, 1928. (Special Publication No. 10.)

Hakluyt built a complete and rounded argument for colonial expansion, in a document unique in its time, which spreads before the historian the full scope of the movement overseas. The now familiar case for expansion is here set forth in full outline, as if once and for all. The attractions of the purse are here, assembled from the shelves of experience which are heaped to profitable past experiences; a full statement of policy, to sound the national appeal; a glowing prospectus, to sound the private appeal. Had the work not lain hidden for nearly three centuries, it would have proved a guidebook in colonial theory. It did remain unknown until the last century and so was robbed of its deserved influence. As it is, it affords an indispensable record of the motives and intentions of the first colonizers. Chapter vii, p. 98.

[2] The title page of the Discourse reads: "*A Particular discourse concerning the great necessitie and manifolde commodyties that are like to growe to this Realme of Englande by the Western discoueries lately attempted, written in the year 1584, by Richarde Hackluyt of Oxforde, at the request and direction of the right worshipfull Mr. Walter Rayhly, nowe Knight, before the coming home of his twoo barkes, and is divided in XXI chapiters, the titles whereof followe in the next leafe.*" The Discourse evidently was not written for the press, but for the eye of the Queen and such as she might call in to advise her. It was first published in *Documentary History of the State of Maine,* Vol. ii. Cambridge: 1877. For an account of the discovery of the manuscript see *Ibid.,* Introduction, pp. xxiii-lxi.

Queen of the value to the English nation of the colonization of America.

I

HAKLUYT'S DISCOURSE ON WESTERN PLANTING

IN THE first chapter of the *Discourse* the author shows "that this westerne discoverie will be greatly for the inlargement of the gospill of Christe, whereunto the princes of the refourmed relligion are chiefly bounde, amongst whome her majestie ys principall." The fact that religious reasons were mentioned first indicates that the expansion of Protestantism was prominently in the minds of Englishmen as one of the important factors to be considered in a period when Catholic Spain was gaining such large conquests for the Catholic faith in America. Thus Hakluyt argued:

Nowe the Kinges and Queenes of England have the name of Defendours of the Faithe. By which title I thinke they are not only chardged to Mayneteyne and patronize the faithe of Christe, but also to enlarge and advaunce the same. Neither oughte this to be their laste worke, but rather the principall and chefe of all others, according to the commandemente of our Saviour, Christe, Mathewe 6, Firste seeke the kingdome of God and the righteousnes thereof, and all other things shall be mynistred unto you.

He noted how both the Spaniards and the Portuguese had established bishoprics and "colledges" in their colonies to train up the youth of the "infidells," "of which acte they more vaunte in all their histories and chronicles than of anythinge els that ever theuy achieved." If therefore the Spaniards and Portuguese,

in their superstition by means of their plantinge in those partes, have done so great things in so shorte a space, what may we hope for in our true and syncere relligion, proposinge unto ourselves in this action not filthie lucre nor vain ostentation, as they indeede did, but principally the gayninge of the soules of millions of those wretched people, the reducinge of them from darknes to lighte, from falsehoodde to truthe, from dumbe idolls to the lyving God, from the depe pitt of hell to the highest heaven.

"America," the young author maintained, "crye oute unto us, their nexte neighboures, to come and helpe them, and bringe unto them the gladd tidinges of the gospell." Another reason why he thought Protestant princes should take this matter in hand is "because the papistes confirm themselves and drawe other to theire side, showinge thet they are the true Catholicke churche because they have bene the onely converters of many millions of infidells to Christianitie. Yea, I myselfe," he stated, "have been demanueded of them, how many infidells have been by us converted." And to this question he "was not able to name one infidell by them [Protestant ministers] converted." The first chapter closes with,

Nowe therefore I truste the time is at hande when by her Majesties forwardness in this enterprise, not only this objection and suche like shalbe aunswered by our fruitfull labor in Godds harvest among the infidells, but also many inconveniences and strifes at home, in matters of ceremonies, shalbe ended. For those of the clergye which by reason of idleness here at home are now alwayes coyninge of newe opynions, havinge by this voyadge to set themselves on worke in reducinge the savages to the chief principles of our faithe, will become less contentious, and be contented with the truthe in relligion alreadie established by authoritie. So that they shall beare the name of Christians shall shewe themselves worthye of their vocation, so shall the mouthe of the adversarie be stopped, so shall contention amongst brethren be avoyded, so shall the gospell amonge infidells be published.

Though the other sections of the Discourse deal principally with political and economic arguments for colonization, there are repeated references to religious considerations. In chapter two it is shown that all other English trade has grown "beggerly or dangerous," especially in the dominions of the King of Spain, where the English traders are compelled "to flinge their bibles and prayer bookes into the sea" and renounce their religion and conscience in order to carry on trade. The covetous merchants in England know full well this situation, but they keep it secret.

They devoutly take the communion in England and send their sons into the Spanish dominions to hear mass. Further he contended that America would yield all the commodities to be obtained in Europe, Africa, and Asia, and by its development all of England's wants could be supplied. Another consideration was that the development of western trade and colonization would give employment to idle men and thereby remove the danger of revolt against settled government as well as relieve England of numerous criminals, since "all the prisons of the lande are daily pestered and stuffed full of them, where either they pitifully pyne away or els at lengthe are miserably hanged, even xx^{ti} at a clappe oute of some one jayle."

The bitter enmity that Englishmen felt toward Spain and the Spaniards is clearly indicated in Hakluyt's argument that one of the principal ways to combat Spain was to fortify certain islands near Florida where Spanish ships returning from the Indies might be waylaid. He also advocated making alliances with the savages, or at least providing them with arms—"as the Spaniardes arm our Irishe rebells"—which would trouble the king of Spain more than "he hath or can trouble us in Ireland, and holde him at suche a bay as he was never yet helde at." Seven chapters are devoted to the various ways in which England might cripple the power of Spain, for at this particular time Spanish dominance of western Europe and the rapid development of her empire was an ever-present menace to English trade and expansion. Spanish claims to all of the New World, based upon the Papal Bull of Demarcation of 1493 and the Treaty of Tordesillas of the following year, by which the whole unoccupied world, east as well as west, was divided between the two Catholic powers, Spain and Portugal, were stoutly denied and resisted by the statesmen of Elizabethan England.

The cruelties of the Spanish conquerors as related in the writings of the great Bartolome de Las Casas were well known to Hakluyt, as well as the unspeakable barbarities which the Spaniards had practiced in Holland and other places in Europe. For these reasons, he states, the whole world hates the Spaniard, and he asks, "what nation, I pray you, of all Christendome loveth the Spaniardes, the scourge of the worlde . . .?" For this reason and also because the King of Spain, Philip II, would die without leaving any "fitt yssue to wealde so greate a governmente," he predicts the speedy dissolution of the Spanish kingdom and empire. He closes this section with,

In fine, there is almoste no nation of Europe that may not say againste the Spaniarde with the poet: Distuleratque graues in idonea tempora poenas ("but she had put off her vengeance until a fitting time"); and so, Eum multos metuere necesse est quem multi metuunt ("He whom many fear must be afraid of many."); and, Multorum odiis nulla respublica stare, diu potest ("Under the hatred of many men no state can long endure.").

Another argument advanced by Hakluyt was that distant trade and colonization would be a means of training Englishmen to the sea and at the same time provide shipbuilding supplies, of which England had become more or less denuded.

It is the longe voyadges . . . that harden seamen, and open unto them the secretes of navigation; the nature of the windes; the currentes and settinge of the sea; the ebbinge and flowinge of the mayne ocean; the influence of the sonne, the moone, and of the rest of the celestiall planetts. . . .

To emphasize the importance of such training he noted the fact that the Emperor Charles Fifth of Spain had created a school of navigation and had "ordeyned" that no man was to take charge of a ship to the West Indies who had not passed a due examination. Indeed, he states, Sir Humphrey Gilbert's death was due to the fact that "such grosse and insufficient felowes" were in charge of the ship.

England's claim to the West Indies or at least to that part from Florida to the Arctic Circle, the author asserted, "is more lawful and righte than the Spaniardes, or any other Christian Princes." This claim he based on the fact that Cabot discovered the mainland in the year 1496 (1497), whereas the Spaniards did not touch the mainland (firme) until 1498. Nor, he asserted, has the Pope's Bull giving all the West Indies to the Kings of Spain any validity since "no Pope had any lawfull authoritie to give any such donation at all." True, the Popes had deposed Emperors and transferred empires from one people to another, but they never gave that which was in their actual possession. "It is an easie matter to cutt large thonges, as we say, of other men's hides, and be liberall of other men's goodds . . . but he that will be in deede and truthe liberall, he muste give of his owne, and not of other men's." Hakluyt produced six reasons why the Pope's donation was invalid and ended his argument by saying that the Kings of Spain never made any great account of the Pope's donation anyhow, but used it simply to "blinde the eyes of the worlde with the sea of Rome." But if England is to take advantage of her "luckye westerne discoveries" she must do so speedily, for if she procrastinates the French, the Normans, the Britons or the Dutch will take possession. To suffer "Papistes" to plant "rounde aboute us . . . and let them inriche themselves under our noses" would cause great danger and inconvenience.

Finally there are summarized under twenty-three heads the arguments that had been advanced, while others were added to the list. Among these is one suggesting that the English colonies once planted in America would become a religious refuge for people throughout the world persecuted for conscience. Thus he stated:

Wee shall by plantinge there inlarge the glory of the gospell, and from England plante sincere religion, and provide a safe and a sure place to receive people from all parts of the worlde that are forced to flee for the truthe of Gods worde.

The young author doubtless had little conception of the great significance of this suggestion for the future. To him this seems to have been more or less an afterthought. For the fierce fires of religious persecution had not yet been fully lighted in England, but on the continent they had been burning since the days of the Peasants' Revolt and the Wars in the Low Countries, and already there were men and women seeking a refuge from religious intolerance. It was these Europeans that he doubtless had in mind, though the time was soon to come when in Great Britain an

increasing host of people persecuted for conscience were to turn
their eyes longingly toward America as a haven of refuge.

II

THE CRUSADE AGAINST CATHOLICISM

THE POLICY instituted by the crown in separating the English
Church from the Papacy was eventually to mean that religion was
to be a major motive in laying the foundations of empire. The
call of the mission field and the conversion of the heathen were
given lip service by all the early writers on colonization, but it
produced little immediate fruit. The Elizabethan seamen were
Protestants of the Protestants when it came to hating Roman
Catholicism, but their personal religion was a strange compound
of "fervid patriotism, a varied assortment of hates, a rough code
of morals, and an unshaken trust in the providence of God. To
the heathen they brought not peace but a sword. To the Pope,
whom they named with the Turk and the Devil, they wished
destruction. For Queen and country they would go anywhere and
attempt anything." [3] The Spanish conquest of South and Central
America has been called the last of the crusades and the Spanish
Conquistadores the last of the crusaders. With equal appropriateness the Elizabethan Sea Dogs might be termed Protestant
crusaders. But instead of warring against the infidel, their crusad-
ing zeal was aimed primarily at Roman Catholicism and their
particular venom was saved for Spanish Catholicism and all its
works.

There arose among Englishmen interested in trade and colonization the notion that England had a particular Christian mission to perform, which was to give the Gospel to the Gentiles.
But, "this scheme for the evangelization of the heathen had no
history." It was little more than "a stock weapon in the argu-
mentative armoury of determined explorers." All Elizabethan

---

[3] Walter Raleigh, *The English Voyages of the Sixteenth Century.* In Vol. XII,
Principall Navagations, Voyages, Traffiques and Discoveries of the English Nation, by
Richard Hakluyt. Glasgow: James Maclehose and Sons, 1905, p. 34.

writers on colonization refer to the religious mission of England, but "in cursory fashion, or plead for it like sharp Christian attorneys, without sincerity."[4] Although there were a few devoted and successful missionaries like John Eliot, the Mayhews and the Moravian Brethren, Colonial Protestantism as a whole was little interested in the Christianization of the "infidel," and their missionary record was much less impressive than that of the Catholic missionaries in the Spanish and French colonies.

The same antipathy to Spain and Spanish Roman Catholicism, which the Elizabethan Sea Dogs and colonizers possessed to such a fanatical degree, is evidenced also as one of the powerful motives in determining Cromwell's colonial policy. He justified the attack upon the Spanish West Indies in 1655-56 on the ground of Spanish outrages against English traders and colonists. "The Spaniard," he asserts, "is your enemy; and is your enemy naturally . . . by that antipathy that is in him 'and also' providentially. . . . You could not . . . have an honourable Peace with him. . . ." Later in the same speech he declared:

the plain truth is Make any peace with any state that is Popish and subjected to the determination of Rome and "of the Pope himself,"— you are bound and they are loose. . . . And it is as true, and it hath been found by common and constant experience, That Peace is but to be kept so long as the Pope saith Amen to it.

Further justification for war against Spain is the fact that:

The Papists in England,—have been accounted, ever since I was born, Spaniolized. . . . Spain was their patron. . . . Therefore I must needs say, this "Spanish" interest at home is a great piece of your danger.

Thus Cromwell returned to the policy of the Elizabethans and utilized Elizabethan arguments in its support. The Spaniards, he continued, "appropriate to themselves the sole signory of the new world," which is based on "no other or better right or title than that of the Pope's donation," "whereas," he stated, "we have

---

[4] *Ibid.*, p. 32. Sir Walter Raleigh (Professor of English at Oxford) characterizes Sir George Peckham's treatise of *The Western Planting,* Hakluyt's *Voyages,* Vol. VII, as an example of "the too familiar compound of avarice, self-righteousness and hypocrisy." P. 32, Note 1.

colonies in America as well in islands as upon the continent upon as good and a better title than the Spaniards have any, and have as good a right to sail in those seas as themselves," yet,

without any just cause or provication . . . they have notwithstanding continually invaded in a hostile manner our colonies, slain our contrymen, taken our ships and goods, destroyed our plantations, made our people prisoners and slaves, and have continued so doing from time to time till the very time that we undertook the expedition against them.[5]

This anti-Spanish and anti-Catholic motive in colonization continued active down to the end of the Colonial period. The intercolonial wars covering nearly a century, from King William's War (1689–97) through the French and Indian War (1756–63), were in a sense a struggle between Protestantism and Roman Catholicism for empire in the New World. The British accused the Catholic missionaries of blessing "the Indian's tomahawk and scalping knife, and bade him God-speed in the work of destroying heretics." [6] The English expedition against Spanish Florida in 1702 was justified not only on the ground of protecting the Carolinas against Spanish aggression, but also on the ground of religion, to protect Protestant truth from Catholic superstition. The patriotic sermons of the eloquent Samuel Davies of Virginia, preached during the French and Indian War, and heard by the youthful Patrick Henry, abound in references to the ravaging of the frontiers by "merciless savages" and the murder of "our fellow subjects . . . with all the horrid arts of Indian and Popish torture." [7] In a sermon on "The Curse of Cowardice," preached at a general muster on May 8, 1758, Davies spoke of the "barbarities

---

[5] *The Letters and Speeches of Oliver Cromwell with Elucidations,* by Thomas Carlyle. Edited by S. C. Lomas etc., London: Methuen and Company, 1904. Vol. II, pp. 507–557, Cromwell's speech before Parliament Sept. 17, 1656. See also Samuel R. Gardiner, *History of the Commonwealth and Protectorate, 1649–1660.* London: Longmans, Green and Company, 1901, Vol. III, pp. 400–405.

[6] Sister Mary Augustina, (Ray), *American Opinion of Roman Catholicism in the Eighteenth Century,* New York: Columbia University Press, 1936, pp. 217 ff.

[7] From the sermon preached to Captain Overton's Independent Company of Volunteers, raised in Hanover County, Virginia, August 17, 1755. *Sermons on Important Subjects* etc., by Samuel Davies. Seventh edition in Four Volumes. London: 1815, Vol. III, pp. 375 ff. The sermon is entitled "Religion and Patriotism, the Constituents of a Good Soldier."

and depredations" perpetrated upon our frontiers by a "mongrel race of Indian savages and French Papists." [8]

The colony of Georgia, the last of the thirteen to be established, was motivated not only by direct humanitarian and religious considerations, but by the prospect of imperialistic and mercantile advantage.[9] Its promoters, as well as the members of Parliament who spoke in favor of granting money to aid in its establishment, thought of it in terms of a buffer colony fortifying their frontiers against Spanish claims and aggressions. It was widely advertised as a refuge for Protestants all over the world, and its chief promoters were active in their hostility to the Church of Rome. The "Georgia Sermons" which were delivered annually before the Trustees of the colony abound in indictments of Catholicism and enmity toward Roman Catholic Spain.

The increasing French activity behind the seaboard colonies throughout the first half of the seventeenth century, and particularly the growing French influence over the Indians, was to the New Englander especially a serious menace. The French Catholic missionaries were accused of teaching the Indians that the Mother of Jesus was a French lady and that those who crucified Him were Englishmen, and that it was therefore a meritorious thing to destroy the English nation.[10] In an election sermon of May 29, 1754, Jonathan Mayhew pleaded that the red man be rescued from the "various artifices of the Romish missionaries, to convert them to their wicked religion, which among other things teaches that it is the duty of Catholics to butcher and scalp Protestants." [11] In eloquent phrase he pictured the dreadful prospect if the French should be victorious:

Do I behold these territories of freedom, become the prey of arbitrary power? . . . Do I see the slaves of Lewis with their Indian allies, dispossessing the free-born subjects of King George, of the inheritance

---

[8] *Ibid.*, p. 427.

[9] V. W. Crane, *Promotion Literature of Georgia*, in "Bibliography Essays: A Tribute to Wilberforce Eames," Cambridge: 1929. See also Ray, *op. cit.*, pp. 219 ff.

[10] Cotton Mather, *Magnalia Christi Americana* etc., Hartford: 1920, Vol. I, p. 195. See also Hannah Swanton, *The Casco Captive: Or the Catholic Religion in Canada and its Influence on the Indians in Maine.* Mass. Sabbath School Society, Boston: 1837.

[11] Sermon preached before Gov. Shirley, May 29, 1754. (Boston, 1854.)

received from their forefathers, and purchased at the expense of their ease, their treasure, their blood! . . . Do I see a protestant, there taking a look at his Bible, and being taken in the fact and punished like a felon! . . . Do I see all liberty, property, religion, happiness, changed, or rather transsubstantiated, into slavery, poverty, superstition, wretchedness!

The vast output of this type of propaganda in the colonies is almost unbelievable.[12] The great efforts put forth by the several colonies, particularly by New England and Virginia, in furnishing troops and contributing funds for the carrying on of the war furnish irrefutable proof of its effectiveness. The clergy thundered from the pulpit, "pamphlets poured from the press, while the newspapers, the broadsides and the almanacs made their contributions"; collections of patriotic verse, the fulminations of college presidents, the commencement orations of the graduates all united in one universal warning that France and Roman Catholicism must be driven from American soil in order to protect the dearly bought liberties of the colonies.[13]

Thus from the beginning of the agitation for English colonization of America to the very outbreak of the War for Independence the Protestant crusade against Roman Catholicism was a major motive in projecting, in planting, and in extending the English colonies in America. To what extent this motive brought individual colonists, however, is another question, and perhaps impossible to appraise accurately. The prospect of economic advantage was undoubtedly the cause of bringing the great majority of individual colonists, but tied in with this economic urge was the growing attractiveness of America as a religious refuge "to people from all partes of the worlde that are forced to flee for the truth of Gods worde," to repeat the prophetic words of Richard Hakluyt in his *Western Planting.*

---

[12] The extent of this type of material may be visualized by simply looking through the footnotes of Sister Mary Augustina (Ray's) book, *op. cit.*, Chapter VI, "Tradition in Action," pp. 212–261.

[13] *Ibid.*, pp. 228–229.

III

CONTRIBUTIONS OF THE GERMAN REFORMATION

THE DIVISIONS and controversies created in almost every country of western Europe by the religious upheavals of the sixteenth and seventeenth centuries furnished a large proportion of the leadership in the establishment of England's colonies in America as well as a considerable proportion of colonists. Religion and economics gave America William Bradford, John Winthrop, Thomas Hooker, Roger Williams, Cecil Calvert, and William Penn, certainly among the most conspicuous social and political architects of colonial America.

The three leading movements of the Reformation were Lutheranism, Calvinism, and Anabaptism. Lutheranism was adopted and defended by a large number of the German princes. This meant that Lutheranism found political security to a large extent where it took root. There was therefore little Lutheran migration to the New World as a result of persecution. The Peace of Augsburg established the principle that the religion of the Prince determined the religion of the subject, and thus in many German principalities Lutheranism became the religion of the State. Lutheranism also became established as the State religion in the Scandinavian countries; Norway and Denmark in 1527 and in Sweden in 1593. The Lutherans, however, living in the province of Salzburg in Austria were an exception. There they were bitterly persecuted by the Catholic Archbishop and as a consequence a considerable number of them eventually came to America. But as a whole Lutherans did not come to America because of persecution, but rather for economic advantage.

Of far greater significance for colonial America were the spiritual children of the Genevan Reformer, John Calvin. It has been suggested that one of the principal contrasts between Lutheranism and Calvinism was due to the fact that Luther began life as a monk and Calvin as a lawyer. Calvinism was not only a creed but a system of government. Calvinism implied a partnership between religion and government, the State serving as the protecting arm of the Church. Lutheranism, on the other hand, had grown up under a situation in Germany in which religion was recognized as occupying a separate sphere from that of the State. Luther, it is true, taught that the State had the duty of protecting the true religion, but it was a negative duty. Calvinism, on the other hand, taught this function as a positive duty. In Lutheranism the duty of the Church was to establish the kingdom of God on earth; in Calvinism that was the duty of Church and State working intimately together. For these reasons Lutheranism had little influence in shaping the political ideas of colonial America. On the other hand, the Calvinists of one kind or another— the Puritans and the Scotch-Irish particularly—furnished a good share of the constructive leadership as well as a large proportion of the colonists.

It has been suggested that Luther should have been the leader of the peasants, instead of Münzer and Carlstadt, since he had come from a peasant family and well understood their sad economic plight. He knew well the tyranny of the nobility and was in agreement with the "Twelve Articles," the peasants' charter of revolt. He even had warned the landlords of their danger unless they mitigated their unjust demands upon their tenants, but to no avail. The peasants likewise turned a deaf ear to his appeal to submit to authority, no matter how unjust that authority might be. The slaughter and turmoil of the peasants' uprising, together with their indiscriminate looting, turned Luther against them and in a terrible pamphlet he hounded the princes to crush the revolt. Not only were fifty thousand peasants destroyed, but their lot under the Lutheran princes was even worse than it had been before. Luther was now tied to the princes, thereby insuring his own safety and that of Lutheranism, but at the expense of liberty. From that time forward Lutheranism in Germany became more and more a department of the State, which has been a major factor in bringing it to its present pathetic situation.

These events divided the German Reformation into two separate religious camps. The Lutheran Reformation which had started as a national movement, now became middle-class in its orientation, while the peasant movement tended to break up into many fragments, all gathered under the name Anabaptist.[14] By the latter sixteenth century there were some forty different Anabaptist sects representing a yariety of religious opinions. After 1640 they came to be known more and more as Mennonites, after Menno Simons, a Dutch priest, who in 1536 renounced the Catholic faith and threw in his lot with the peaceful wing of the Anabaptists, becoming their most active and respected leader. Throughout the whole colonizing period the Mennonites or the Anabaptists were outlawed in practically every country of western Europe except Holland. They were always unprotected, always exposed to persecution, always on the defensive. Their radical leadership had passed away with the crushing of the Peasants' Revolt, leaving only the non-resisting wing of the movement. Their refusal to bear arms or take an oath brought misunderstanding and persecution. In 1520 the Diet of Spires provided that all Anabaptists should be executed without a trial, for they were considered by the Reformers and the Catholics alike as traitors—"disloyal, heretical, rebellious, and untrustworthy subjects of the state." [15] It has been estimated that some five thou sand of them died a martyr's death. With little opportunity in their native land for the cultivation of their religious life and with declining economic opportunity as well, these generally humble people constituted an increasing body of prospective colonists for the New World. When the time came, they were ready for the joyful opportunity which America afforded.

IV

ENGLISH RELIGIOUS MINORITIES

THE COURSE of the Reformation in England, at least from the standpoint of its general influence upon the colonization of

---

[14] M. Christoff Erhardus, *Wahrhaftige Historia von den Muensterischen Brüdern und Widdertäuffern*, 1589, gives the number as forty. Heinrich Bullinger, writing in 1561, places the number at sixteen. See C. H. Smith, *The Mennonite Immigration to Pennsylvania in the Eighteenth Century*, Norristown: 1929, p. 37.

[15] Ernst H. Correll, *Das Schweizerische Täufer-Mennoniten*, Tüebingen: 1925, pp. 10 ff.

America, followed much the same general pattern as that in Germany. Here too it resulted in the rise of several distinct movements. At the center were the Anglicans, the State Church, though at the time of its establishment it was in no sense a Protestant Church.[16] In fact the only change made by the Act of Supremacy (1534) was the transfer of final authority from the Pope to Henry VIII. In doctrine and worship the English Church remained Catholic. It is true that the King abolished the monasteries and the chantries and confiscated their lands and rich endowments, but it was not for the purpose of reform, or for the transforming of the English Church into a Protestant body. During the brief reign of Edward VI (1547–53) the English Church was purged of most of its Catholicism; Confession was abolished and celibacy of the clergy abandoned. Latin gave way to English in the services. The Zwinglian interpretation of the sacrament replaced the doctrine of transubstantiation. Mary Tudor reestablished Catholicism during her five-year reign (1553–58), but with Elizabeth's coming to the throne Anglicanism was as easily restored as Catholicism had been under Mary.

The English Reformation was carried forward by political rather than by religious leaders, and in the close relationship between Church and State which resulted the State became the dominating partner. This dominance of the State over the Church was displeasing both to the Catholic-minded Anglicans and to the growing number of Calvinists or Puritans. But the Anglican Church was Catholic enough to satisfy the moderate Catholics and Protestant enough to satisfy the moderate Protestants, and combined they made up a large majority of the English people. Thus there came to be in England three distinct religious parties. In the center were the Anglicans established by law and closely

---

[16] While this statement is in general true, as a matter of fact a number of changes in doctrine and worship were made through the Ten Articles of 1536 and the injunctions issued by Thomas Cromwell, Henry VIII's Vicar General. "The doctrine of purgatory and worship of the saints were greatly modified in the direction of Protestantism. The cults of relics, images, and pilgrimages were discouraged. Most of the old religious ceremonies were retained, but the people were to be taught their meaning. They were also to have access to the Bible in their own language." Marshall M. Knappen, *Tudor Puritanism: A Chapter in the History of Idealism*. Chicago: The University of Chicago Press, 1939, p. 51.

tied in with the government. To the right were the Roman Catholics made up largely of the landed gentry whose wealth and position made them naturally conservative. On the left were the Puritans, or the extreme Protestants, constituting people holding differing shades of religious opinion, but all agreeing in their dissatisfaction with the English Establishment. The presence of these dissatisfied groups in seventeenth century England and the political and religious agitation which they precipitated profoundly influenced the whole course of English colonization.

On Elizabeth's accession to the throne she declared that "she would not allow her people to swerve to the right hand or the left from the religion established by law." Although in the main the Queen succeeded in her determination, she, like many another ruler, was to learn that "even the will of a king may break against the rock of religious conviction." The contest with the Catholics became increasingly critical as Elizabeth's reign wore on, and the laws against Catholics were accordingly made more severe. When Mary Queen of Scots fled to England from her Protestant subjects in Scotland she became the center of Catholic plots to place her on the English throne. And when the Pope deposed Queen Elizabeth in 1570 and placed England under the interdict, the nation was alarmed for the Queen's safety and new savage treason laws were hurried through Parliament. The efforts of the Jesuits to convert Protestant nations and their alarming success in numerous instances caused new anti-Catholic enactments, and by the time James I came to the throne Catholicism had been outlawed in England.

The Catholic hope that the son of Mary Queen of Scots would favor milder treatment of their co-religionists was blasted soon after his reign began by the Gunpowder Plot (1605), which once more stirred anti-Catholic feeling to fever heat. Even if James had desired to inaugurate a milder policy toward Catholics, he would have had to oppose an overwhelming public opinion, and for that he was too timid. Consequently, anti-Catholic legislation became even more severe. It was not strange, therefore, that English Catholics began to consider the possibility of finding a refuge in the New World, and before the reign of James came to its close a Catholic gentleman, Sir George Calvert, soon to become the first Lord Baltimore, had obtained a charter for the establishment of a colony in Newfoundland. So ambiguously worded was the charter that it would be possible to take out under it both Catholic settlers and priests. Later (1632) this was exchanged for the Maryland charter under which the only English colony, founded as a refuge for Catholics, was established.

The number of English Catholics to come to America, however, was relatively insignificant compared to the left-wing religious bodies which sought refuge in the New World. In America the term "Puritan" has come to apply only to those who planted Congregationalism in America. But in the period of colonization it had a far wider significance. Then it signified an attitude of mind toward religion, and included all those who desired to "purify" the Church of all those practices and ceremonies which they considered anti-Christian, the accretions of the intervening centuries since apostolic times. And, just as the name Anabaptist was a generic term applied to all the left-wing bodies of the continental Reformation, so the term "Puritan" came to mean all those left-wing elements in the English Reformation.

These radical Reformation groups, whether Anabaptists in Europe or Puritans in England, had little chance to come to their full development in their native lands in the face of the bitter laws which everywhere were instituted against them. But the New World furnished to both the opportunity which the Old World denied. In America the small, radical, and despised sects found the opportunity for the application and promulgation of their principles. All the great freedoms for which American democracy stands today—the freedom of conscience, individual rights, self-government, separation of Church and State, freedom of speech and of the press—all have their roots in the principles of these left-wing bodies which came to full fruition on American soil.[17]

---

[17] Ernest Sutherland Bates, in his *American Faith* (New York: W. W. Norton & Co., 1940) classes all Calvinistic bodies as belonging to the right wing of the Reformation. I am using the term "Puritan" not simply to designate the Calvinistic bodies in the English Reformation, but to mean all extreme Protestants, which would include the early Puritan elements and also the Baptists and later the Quakers and Methodists.

The term "Puritan" first was applied to the Marian exiles on their return to England after the death of Mary Tudor. At its rise Puritanism was a movement to escape from formalism; it grew out of an aspiration for greater spirituality. Outwardly this was expressed in Puritan opposition to clerical vestments, mediaeval ceremonies, and the whole Catholic system of Church government. Such practices as making the sign of the cross in baptism, keeping of holy days, the wearing of the surplice by the priest were to the Puritans "rags of Antichrist" which must be discarded so that the simplicity of the primitive ages might be restored. So long as Puritanism meant only this, it found support even among some of the bishops and many of the leading clergy. In the churches of the European exiles during Mary's reign there were five bishops and five deans of the English Church, besides more than fifty doctors of divinity.[18] But Queen Elizabeth had little liking for the exclusion from Christian worship of everything pleasing to the aesthetic taste, and soon placed herself in opposition to the Puritan party.

A second phase of Puritanism was its attack on evils in personal conduct. It was this phase of its history which gave to the name Puritan a new and higher meaning, for to the reform in manners and morals wrought by this movement the English people are indebted eternally to Puritanism. For "it is only by the religious ferments infused successively by new sects and movements" such as the preaching friars, the Lollards, the Puritans, the Quakers, the Methodists, and in our own time the Salvation Army and the "Holy Rollers" that religion reaches down to the lowest levels of society, and the "great unleavened mass of men is rendered less sodden." [19]

It was inevitable that Puritans would develop cleavages among themselves, and during the Commonwealth period particularly they divided and redivided into numerous sects with myriad opinions. The earliest division resulted in the emergence of Sepa-

---

[18] See the Census of Exiles in Christina Hallowell Garrett, *The Marian Exiles*. Cambridge University Press: 1938.

[19] Edward Eggleston, *The Beginners of a Nation*. New York: Appleton Co., 1900, Book II, Chapter 1, p. 121. The four chapters on Puritan Migration, pp. 98–219, show unusual insight.

ratism, which soon developed its own divisions. Its origin as an organized movement has been attributed to Robert Browne (1581–1586), but it undoubtedly existed before his time in little gatherings of devout Puritans who came together to sing a psalm and "to talk of God's word." Gradually through the latter years of Elizabeth's reign the number of Separatists increased. In 1593 Sir Walter Raleigh estimated their number at twenty thousand—doubtless an exaggeration. London was the principal center of the movement, and it was there that they began to pronounce the Church of England as anti-Christian, so corrupt as to be past all hope of reformation. There they developed a system of Church polity, a mixture of independency and Presbyterianism, which has come to be known as Barrowism, after their first leader Henry Barrow. Their extreme views soon brought persecution upon them, and their leaders, Henry Barrow and John Greenwood, were hanged at Tyburn, and others met a similar fate. Migration to Holland, where toleration was to be found, was the natural consequence; and by the close of Elizabeth's reign Separatism had been almost extirpated from England.[20] There remained, however, one congregation, that at Scrooby in Nottinghamshire, whose migration to Holland in the early years of the seventeenth century and thence to America constitutes one of the notable epics in English colonization.

So far the persecution of Puritans had been confined largely to the Separatists, the most radical element. But at the beginning of his reign King James had said of the Puritan party within the Established Church at the Hampden Court Conference (1604): "I shall make them conform themselves or I will harry them out of the land, or else do worse," and in a letter to a friend he boasted that he had "peppered the Puritans soundly." It was this foolish policy of a foolish king that drove the growing party of more conservative Puritans into opposition both to his religious and governmental policies, which eventually sealed the fate of his son, the doom of his dynasty, and led to the peopling of New England. At the beginning of his reign the Puritans had been primarily a religious party stressing strict morals, rigid Sabbath observance,

---

[20] M. M. Knappen, *op. cit.*, Chapter xv, "Separatism."

and Calvinistic dogmatism in opposition to the growing Arminian influence among High Church Anglicans; by the end of his reign Puritanism had become in addition a political party. To the religious Puritans were now added political Puritans whose interest in religion was secondary to their desire to limit the growing absolutism of the King.

King Charles First was an even greater enemy of Puritanism than was his father, and in William Laud, who was elevated to the Arch-episcopal See of Canterbury, the King found an ideal instrument for carrying out his anti-Puritan policy. Laud's predecessors in Canterbury had contented themselves with suppressing the Separatists, but the new Archbishop began to lay his plans at once to strike at the powerful Puritan party within the Church of England. Laud has been ironically called the "father of New England," which is not out of place when it is recalled that the great Puritan migration to New England began soon after he came to office, waned as he declined in power, and ceased altogether with his fall.

The Puritans who had remained in the Church of England had been sustained through the years by the hope that they might eventually rid the Church of those who oppressed and defiled her. Eventually they expected to gain power, and then they would "winnow the chaff from the wheat." But the coming of William Laud to office and the policy instituted by him in his relentless use of the Courts of the Star Chamber and High Commission in bringing Puritan leaders to trial and punishment, together with the growing fear that the Stuart House was tending in the direction of a return to Roman Catholicism, brought gloom and disappointment to many influential Puritans.

A project for planting in the wilds of America "a particular Church" as they termed it, now began to be whispered about among the clan of East Anglia Puritans of whom John Winthrop, head of a well-to-do family in Suffolk and a former student at Trinity College, Cambridge, was the recognized leader. The whispering soon eventuated in the formation of the great Massachusetts Bay Company among the Puritan clan of East Anglia, and in the year 1630 seventeen ships left England for New England carrying more than a thousand passengers. Thus the great Puritan migration began which within ten years was to bring more than twenty thousand colonists to America. More important than any other single motive in bringing these comfortably situated people in England to dwell in poor cabins in a wilderness was their consuming desire to establish what they considered the true Church. They were convinced that the European Churches had come to desolation and ruin, and their coming to the New World was to avoid "the Plague when it is foreseene & not to tarry . . . till it overtake us." [21]

During the period of the Commonwealth (1649-60) England was overrun with dissatisfied men and women and every institution in both State and Church was under criticism. As a consequence new religious sects in bewildering numbers arose—for it is always easy in times when old standards and old authorities are disintegrating for the prophets of new gospels to gain a following. Among the numerous new movements which emerged during the middle years of the seventeenth century were the Quakers. The founder of the movement, George Fox, started forth in the year 1647-48 to be the apostle of a new and complete reformation. He had become convinced, through several years of spiritual searching, that there is a direct illumination from God within every man's inner being. To the Calvinistic theory that there is a seed of sin in every new-born child, he countered by asserting that there was a seed of God in every soul. Since, therefore, religion rests on man's inner being there was no need for what he termed "hiriling priests" nor for the outward sacraments to bring religion to man, since its seed was already there.

From the start of the movement Fox and his helpers met mob violence and abuse. On various grounds he was arrested and imprisoned. Sixty times he was brought before magistrates and was imprisoned eight times. By 1652, however, he had begun to find able helpers, especially in the northern counties; and the movement spread rapidly. In the early years the Quakers were indefatigable missionaries, perhaps unequalled in modern times, with the possible exception of the Jesuits and the Moravians. "No one was too high to be spoken to, and no one too low to be con-

[21] Charles M. Andrews, *The Colonial Period of American History: The Settlements.* New Haven: 1934, Vol. I, pp. 344-399.

sidered." [22] The Pope was visited in Rome, while to the Sultan of Turkey went Quaker enthusiasts. Their missionary zeal, to say nothing of their refusal to take an oath, made them conspicuous; while their custom of wearing hats on almost all occasions when others took theirs off made them even more conspicuous. For these and other reasons Quakers suffered persecution. It has been estimated that at least 21,000 suffered fines and imprisonments, many of them more than once, and at least 450 died either in prison or soon afterward as its result.

Independents, Presbyterians, and Church of England leaders alike were aroused to fury by the Quaker tenets. Their teaching that neither the Church nor the Bible was the basis of authority, but rather the inevitable conviction within every soul, seemed to be a direct contradiction of the basic Protestant position that the Scriptures contained all things necessary for God's own glory and men's salvation, "Unto which nothing at any time is to be added, whether by new Revelations of the Spirit, or Traditions of Men," as the Westminster Confession puts it. In spite of the limited toleration proclaimed by Cromwell's Instrument of Government many Quakers were imprisoned during the period of his rule. But under the many acts against dissenters passed in the early years of Charles II's reign, the Quakers bore the brunt of an even more fearful time of persecution. Their preachers suffered more than any other dissenting group, because they refused to be driven under ground. It was out of this background of suffering that the Quakers began to look to America as a land where they might hope to live in peace, and from 1675 to 1689 the Quaker leaders were active in promoting colonizing schemes in the New World.

V

CONTRIBUTIONS OF CONTINENTAL CALVINISM

ALTHOUGH THE Puritans among the Calvinists made the principal contribution to American colonization, the Dutch, German, French, Scotch and Scotch-Irish Calvinists also exercised a very

[22] A. Neave Brayshaw, *The Quakers: Their Story and Message.* New York: Macmillan Company, 1927, Chapter VII, "The Quaker Worship."

important influence. Of these several groups religion played a major rôle in bringing to America only the Germans of the Palatinate and the French Huguenots. The Palatinates, as well as the Mennonites and the Dunkers, were primarily the victims of the ambition of Louis XIV to annex the Rhine region to his empire. Between the years 1674 and 1704, in a series of devastating invasions, the Rhine provinces were laid waste again and again. In one awful year (1689) the cities of Worms, Mainz, Speyer, Mannheim, and Heidelberg, besides many towns and villages, were burned. The great castle of Heidelberg, the principal residence of the Electors of the Palatinate, was destroyed and its ruins stand today as a memorial of that terrible time. Fields were laid waste, the vineyards on the hillsides were cut down, and thousands of people were driven from their homes in the midst of winter. Many died of exposure and starvation. Thousands found refuge in Switzerland and in Holland. Queen Anne's sympathy for the suffering Palatinates led her to extend an invitation for them to seek a home in America, and in 1709 some thirty thousand of them were encamped near London clamoring for transportation to the colonies. During these years German immigration to America became a mighty stream, threatening to depopulate the Rhine region. War and religious persecution were responsible for this vast popular movement which eventually brought more than 150,000 colonists of many religious complexions to the land of hope.

During the last quarter of the seventeenth century and the first half of the eighteenth, thousands of persecuted Huguenots fled from France to find new homes in America. This great Huguenot exodus has been estimated at from 300,000 to 1,000,000, and they found their way to every part of the world where any degree of religious toleration prevailed. The story of this great migration of French Protestants from the land of their birth revolves about the revocation of the Edict of Nantes in 1685. The Edict had been issued (1598) as the final confirmation of various treaties and agreements concluded between Catholics and Protestants after a long period of bitter struggle, and when it was proclaimed it was heralded as "a star of promise and the beginning of a new era of historical development and religious toleration." Almost from the beginning, however, the Edict was practically a dead letter in every region where Catholic authority was dominant; proselyting, persecution, and outrages continued as before. Long before its revocation hundreds of Protestant families were leaving France, and the annulling of the Edict only stimulated what already was under way.[23]

As early as 1555 Admiral Gaspar de Coligny, a Huguenot nobleman and the recognized leader of the Protestant party in France, began the promotion of Huguenot colonies in America. The first was that in Brazil under the leadership of an adventurer, Durand de Villegagnon. It is interesting that this colony had the indorsement of John Calvin. Villegagnon's conversion to Catholicism led to his betrayal of the colony, and in 1558 it was destroyed by the Portuguese. A second attempt was made in Florida (1662-1665), which at first gave promise of success. But Spanish vengeance destroyed the Huguenot fort at the mouth of the St. John's River, and a little later a fierce hurricane completed the destruction. Lack of support from the French government was one of the reasons for the dismal failures of these early attempts at Huguenot colonization. It was the failure of the French Protestants to find a refuge that finally led them to seek a haven in the English colonies. Negotiations for the establishment of Huguenots in the English colonies actually had begun as early as 1629 and continued at intervals throughout the seventeenth century. It was not, however, until 1680 that the first large group found a foothold in South Carolina. The revocation of the Edict of Nantes greatly increased Huguenot emigration which continued to flow until the end of the colonial period.

VI

THE SCOTCH-IRISH

FROM ABOUT 1720 onward to the beginning of the War for Independence, the largest part of the emigration to the English colonies in America came from north Ireland. This emigration,

---

[23] Arthur H. Hirsch, *The Huguenots of Colonial South Carolina.* Durham: Duke University Press, 1928, Chapter i.

made up largely of the descendants of the lowland Scotch who had been colonized in north Ireland as a result of the policy instituted by Elizabeth and James I, was caused chiefly by economic discontent. Economically Ireland was treated by the English Parliament not as an integral part of the kingdom, but as a colony, and Irish trade and manufacturing were restricted for the benefit of England in accord with the economic delusion of the time. The most famous of these restraining measures was the Woolens Act of 1699 which utterly destroyed the manufacturing of Irish woolens and caused great distress and discontent. Although an attempt was made to encourage the linen industry, and a subsidy was granted to this end, it was many years before it was fully established. Besides the distress caused by these unwise enactments, there were recurring crop failures with resulting famine. Added to their economic discontent were very real religious grievances. The first was the necessity of paying tithes to support the Irish Established Church, and another was the barring of Presbyterian students from the colleges of the Irish Establishment.

John Fiske makes the statement that at the opening of the eighteenth century there was probably a smaller percentage of illiteracy in Ulster than was to be found anywhere else in the world. This was due to the fact that there were more than a million Presbyterian Scotch inhabiting that region, a type comparable to that which colonized Massachusetts and Connecticut. As a result of England's illiberal economic and religious policy more than half the Presbyterian population of Ireland came to America during the middle years of the eighteenth century.

VII

THE TOLERATION ACT

THE PASSAGE of the Toleration Act (1689) [24] in the first year of the reign of William and Mary marked the end of an era. For

---

[24] George M. Trevelyan, *England Under Queen Anne,* Vol. I, *Blenheim.* London: Longmans, Green and Co., 1930, pp. 4, 52, 53–62.

nearly two centuries Catholic and Protestant, Puritan and Anglican had been engaged in bitter and often bloody rivalries, and
the nation had become heartily tired of persecution. The new
Dutch king had no interest in the old religious controversies;
besides, he personally disliked persecution and intolerance. His
primary reason for accepting the English crown was to gain
English support in his struggle against the mighty Louis, for that
required a united nation. For two hundred years religion had
divided the nation into warring camps; now growing trade was
exercising a unifying influence. "The Bible had now a rival in
the Ledger," and the zeal of both High Churchman and dissenter
was being tempered by economic and patriotic considerations.
For old times' sake they still called one another hard names, but
more and more people of varying religious views were able to
unite in the promotion of political and economic projects. This
brought to an end the religious motive in American colonization
as far as England was concerned, but to people persecuted for
conscience in other parts of the world America continued to be
a haven of refuge.

II

Transplanting Anglicanism

Of all the religious bodies which were brought from the Old World to the New during the entire colonial period, none received so much assistance from the mother country in gaining a foothold in America as did the Church of England. It came to occupy the most privileged position in six of the colonies and in all of the others attempts were made at various times by royal governors and other English officials to further its interests. Under the circumstances this official concern for the welfare of the Anglican Church in the colonies was only natural. But in spite of official favor which would seem to have given it the advantage over all other religious bodies which came to the colonies, the Church of England failed to gain either the numbers or support which under the circumstances might have been expected. In the long run the special privileges which it enjoyed proved a handicap rather than an advantage. Generally speaking, people of Anglican attachment lacked the strong emotional urge in coming to America which was so manifest among the Puritans, the Quakers, the Germans and the Scotch-Irish. America to them was not primarily a religious refuge. It was not necessary for them to leave their native land in order to secure freedom of worship, but whether they remained in England or came to America, in either case they were a privileged class as far as religion was concerned.

If the English government may be said to have had any ecclesiastical policy relative to her colonies it was to obtain the establishment of the Church of England as widely as possible. But the possibility of securing an establishment in colonies founded by those seeking to escape from establishment at home was slight, and in such colonies efforts were made to secure its toleration. In none of the thirteen colonies, however, was the Anglican Church completely established, since in none was there ever a bishop or an ecclesiastical court. Nor were the establishments alike in the several colonies—there were as many kinds of establishments as there were colonies possessing them. For that reason it will be necessary to trace the steps by which establishment was brought about in each of the several colonies where it was achieved.[1]

I

ANGLICAN ESTABLISHMENTS IN AMERICA
VIRGINIA

IN VIRGINIA, the oldest of the Anglican colonies, the process of establishment was gradual. The first charter (1606) provided that "the true word, and service of God and Christian faith be preached, planted and used" within the several "colonies and plantations," not only for the benefit of the colonists but also "amongst the salvage people which doe or shall adjoine unto them." [2] The charter of 1609 required all persons going out to the colony to take the Oath of Supremacy, the charter stating that since the principal purpose of founding the colony was to convert the natives to "the true worship of God and the Christian religion" it was therefore of importance to keep out all those who were "suspected to effect the superstitions of the Church of Rome." The members of the first Assembly were likewise required to take the Oath of Supremacy,[3] and among their first enactments were regulations regarding the duties of clergymen. They were to reprove persons guilty of drunkenness, to record christenings, burials and marriages:

"to read the service, and exercise their ministerial functions according to the Ecclesiastical Lawes and orders of the church of Englande." On

---

[1] Elizabeth H. Davidson, *The Establishment of the English Church in Continental American Colonies*, Durham, N. C.: 1936, is a recent competent study. W. W. Manross, *A History of the American Episcopal Church*, New York and Milwaukee: 1936, contains an informing general account.

[2] William Walker Hening, *The Statutes at Large being a Collection of all the Laws of Virginia from the First Session in the Year 1619*, etc., New York: 1923, Vol. I, pp. 68–69. The several changes in the status of the Established Church in Virginia may be traced in succeeding volumes of Hening's *Statutes*.

[3] *Ibid.*, I., 97–98.

Sundays they were to "Chatachize suche as are not yet ripe to come to Com[munion]." [4]

In its session of 1623-24 the Assembly placed a requirement upon every plantation to provide a place of worship; fixed penalties for non-attendance on divine worship and for disparaging a minister. Likewise a penalty "forfeiting half his means" was placed upon a minister absenting himself "above two months in all the year" from his church. [5]

As long as the Virginia Company was in control the only clergy in the colony were the chaplains approved and sent over by the company. [6] In 1618 among the instructions to the governor was one providing that one hundred acres of land be set aside toward the support of the several ministers in the colony, and that other provisions be made "so as to make the living of every minister two hundred pounds sterling or more." [7] In 1621-22 the Virginia Assembly passed an enactment that each clergyman was to receive from his parishioners 1500 pounds of tobacco and sixteen barrels of corn. Ten pounds of tobacco and one bushel of corn was the utmost that any individual could be compelled to pay, and every male of sixteen years and over was liable for assessment. The law concludes with the statement that should the levy fail to produce the desired two hundred pounds the minister was to be content with less. The enactment of this provision and the creation of glebes may be considered to mark

---

[4] *Colonial Records of Virginia*, II, pp. 20, 26-27.

[5] Hening, I, 122, 124.

[6] An example of the action taken by the Company in sending over a clergyman is that of Rev. William Leate (June 10, 1622): "We send over Mr. William Leate, a minister recommended unto us for sufficiencie of learning and integrity of life: if he be entertained by any private Societie we shall expect the charge of 26s 1d which the Comp. hath laid out for him, to be returned by the first in good Tobacco 18d pld. . . ." Edward D. Neill, *History of the Virginia Company of London*, etc., Albany: 1869, pp. 309-310.

[7] When Sir Edwin Sandys became the treasurer of the Virginia Company in 1619 he drew up elaborate plans for the advancement of the Company, covering almost every phase of the colony's organization and life. Among his schemes were the apportionment of unoccupied lands for public uses, among them being that of providing glebes for the clergy. Charles M. Andrews, *The Colonial Period of American History: The Settlements*, Vol. I, New Haven: 1934, pp. 136-137; 150-153. See also Philip Alexander Bruce, *Institutional History of Virginia*, 2 vols. New York: 1910, I. Chapter xv, "The Clergy, Glebes and Parsonages," 163-176. *Virginia Company Records*, I, pp. 266-271; 389-399.

the beginning of the establishment of the Church of England in America.[8] The process of completing the establishment in Virginia, or at least as far as it was to go, was brought about soon after the colony became a royal province (1624).

John Harvey, appointed royal governor in 1629, received instructions from the Privy Council to "Suffer noe Innovation in matters of religion, and be careful to appoynt sufficiant, and conformable Ministers to each Congregation that may Chatechise and instruct them in the grounds and principles of Religion." [9] Turning the pages of the Laws of Virginia one is impressed with the amount of attention given to religious matters by the early legislators. In September 1696 the Virginia Assembly enacted the following provision fixing ministers' salaries which was to remain in force until the Revolution.

. . . That all and every minister or ministers in all and every parish and parishes in this dominion . . . shall have and receive for his or their maintenance the sume of sixteen thousand pounds of tobacco besides their lawful perquisites. . . .[10]

The Assembly did not pass an act providing for vestries until 1641, but it is probable that there were vestries in Virginia before there was any legal requirement for them, since the vestry is an essential feature of Anglican organization. The number of vestrymen was fixed at twelve and they were chosen by the voters of the parish. After the Restoration (1660) the vestries became self-perpetuating,[11] a provision which meant that thereafter the vestries were to be composed of the upper class, socially and economically. Among the duties of the Virginia vestries was that of

---

[8] Francis L. Hawks, *Contributions to the Ecclesiastical History of the United States of America*. New York: 1836, pp. 35–36. At this time there were five clergymen in Virginia.

[9] *Acts of the Privy Council of England. Colonial Series*. I, p. 127.

[10] Hening, III, pp. 151–153.

[11] The following is the wording of the Act providing for the self-perpetuating vestries: ". . . in the case of death of any vestry man, or his departure out of the parish, that the said minister and vestry make choice of another to supply his room, and be it further enacted that none shall be admitted to be of the vestry that doe not take the oath of allegiance and supremacy to his majesty and subscribe to be conformable to the doctrine and discipline of the church of England." Hening, II, pp. 44–45.

selecting the minister and presenting him to the Governor for induction.

In England the selection of ministers of parishes lay with the patron, who might be either a person or a corporation, such as one of the colleges of Oxford or Cambridge. There was a long-drawn-out dispute between the vestries, the Governor and, in the eighteenth century, with the Commissaries, over this question. The historians of the Episcopal Church have generally taken the view that the vestry's control over the Virginia clergy was detrimental to the well-being of the colonial Church. Generally, it is true, the vestries refused to present their ministers to the Governor for induction, since by so doing they would lose their control over them. The transfer to America of the English freehold tenure would have made every clergyman independent of his local vestry.

Those who made the bitterest complaint of the vestries' treatment of the clergy were those who wanted to see the English system fully introduced. Since induction gave the minister a life tenure in his pulpit he would thus have become independent of his congregation's favor or disfavor. There is no doubt but that in many instances the vestries' control over the clergy was used in a manner detrimental to the best interests of the Church, as the uncertainty of tenure doubtless prevented many clergymen of superior talents from coming to Virginia, and those who did come many times found small inducement to remain. On the other hand, to have given the average Virginia clergyman, who too often was a second-rate man, a life tenure in his pulpit without effective episcopal supervision, would have created a situation that might have proven even more deplorable than that which obtained.[12] From a worldly point of view the Virginia clergy were better off than the usual run of the rural clergy in England. The success with which the Virginia vestries maintained their control over the parishes throughout the entire colonial period was a factor of large political as well as ecclesiastical significance. For

---

[12] For a summary of the disadvantages of the system of vestry control as seen through the eyes of Commissary James Blair see Blair's *Memorial* concerning Governor Andros, 1697, in William S. Perry (Ed.), *Historical Collections Relating to the American Colonial Church*, Vol. I, *Virginia*, 1873, p. 15. For arguments favorable to the Virginia system see Bruce, I, *op. cit.*, pp. 141–142.

one thing it helps to account for the unanimity with which leading churchmen of Virginia supported the War for Independence.

MARYLAND

THE RELIGIOUS background of Maryland differed from that of any other colony. Its Proprietor was a Catholic nobleman and his main purpose in its establishment was to provide a place of refuge for his coreligionists. But from the beginning Lord Baltimore welcomed Protestants to his colony and warned the Catholic settlers to avoid offending their Protestant neighbors. Baltimore, however, was unable to prevent frequent conflicts between the several religious groups, especially after 1640 when the Puritan element began to increase rapidly, and in order to strengthen and preserve his policy of toleration he pressed through the Assembly the Toleration Act of 1649. Although the Catholics were in control of the government of Maryland in the early years, there was never anything like a legal establishment of Catholicism. In fact such a thing would have been an impossibility even if Lord Baltimore had desired it, which he did not, and any such attempt surely would have lost to him his proprietaryship. Nor was there a chance for any English colony anywhere to remain long under Catholic control in the face of what was taking place in the English religious scene from 1640 to 1660. Baltimore was attempting to establish toleration in Maryland on a broader basis than was to be found anywhere else in the world, except in Rhode Island, but he soon found it impossible for a Catholic even to administer toleration in the face of the bitter anti-Catholicism being engendered in England.

The agitation for the establishment of Anglicanism in Maryland dates from 1676, when the Rev. John Yoe, one of three Anglican ministers then in the colony, sent a petition to the Archbishop of Canterbury urging that steps be taken to bring about an establishment. He reported that in the ten or twelve counties of the colony there was a total of some twenty thousand inhabitants; that there were only three Church ministers, but numerous irregular preachers; and that the Quakers were especially active and had numerous "speakers" for their conventicles. When referred to the

Privy Council Lord Baltimore was summoned before them and questioned about the situation. He stated that at least three fourths of the inhabitants were dissenters and that it would be impossible under such conditions to secure an establishment of any one church. The Anglican party, however, persisted in their demands, and found a powerful ally in Henry Compton, Bishop of London, who was interested in promoting closer relations between the English Church and the colonies.

The overthrow of James II in 1688 brought a revolt in Maryland against the Catholic Proprietor, and the province was transformed into a royal colony under the immediate control of the Assembly made up of Protestants. Immediately the toleration policy inaugurated by Lord Baltimore came to an end and steps were soon taken to bring about the establishment of the English Church.[13] In 1692 and again in 1696 the Assembly passed acts of establishment, but both were disallowed by the Board of Trade and Plantations. A third act, largely inspired by Dr. Thomas Bray who had just arrived in Maryland as the Bishop of London's Commissary, was passed (1700) and through the influence of Dr. Bray, who now returned to England to urge it before the Board, it was approved and became law in 1702.[14]

The Act of establishment provided that each parish was to elect a vestry of six members, the two serving longest to be dropped each year to give place to two newly chosen members. The vestry was to choose each year two church wardens who were not considered vestrymen. Unlike the Virginia vestry the duties of Maryland vestries were largely confined to business matters and did not include the selection of ministers. As in Virginia, salaries of ministers were paid in tobacco, which was at first fixed

---

[13] The steps in the establishment of the Church of England in Maryland may be traced in *The Archives of Maryland, Proceedings and Acts of the General Assembly,* 1637–64; 1684–92; 1693–97; 1700–04, and in the *Proceedings of the Council of Maryland* for the same years. For the text of the Act of 1700, see *Proceedings and Acts,* 1700–1704, pp. 91–98.

[14] "In his effort to live up to his principles and perhaps to weaken the Jesuits by admitting Puritans to settle within his province, Baltimore had opened the doors to a powerful body of religious insurgents, who were determined to nullify all his efforts to organize his government on the broad basis of toleration and justice to all. Though successful in his struggle with the Jesuits, he now went down to defeat at the hands of the Puritans." Andrews, *op. cit.,* Vol. II, p. 314.

at forty pounds a poll and was levied on all freemen over sixteen, all male servants and all slaves of both sexes over sixteen. The presentation of ministers was vested in the proprietor, but during the period in which Maryland was a royal colony the Governor performed this duty.

The most active opponents to the establishment were the Quakers and the Catholics. The Quakers, constituting about one twelfth of the population, according to the Council of Maryland, were the most obnoxious in their opposition. The Council asserted that if this law for establishment were disallowed both sects (Catholic and Quakers) would increase, for they "are daily insinuating their doctrines into other of his Majesty's good subjects & imploying their utmost endeavours to pervert them from their Religion. . . ."[15]

NEW YORK

NEW YORK was the only state north of Maryland where there came to be any semblance of a Church of England establishment and this was brought about by a peculiar set of circumstances. Previous to the taking over of the colony by the English (1664), the Dutch Reformed Church was recognized as the only legal religion by the Dutch West India Company which controlled the colony. All dissenting groups were prohibited by law, and in some instances there was actual persecution.[16] When New Netherland passed into English hands the proprietor, the Duke of York, later to become James II, displayed a tolerant spirit toward the Dutch, and the Duke's Laws of 1665,[17] among other provisions gave special recognition to the Reformed religion, it being the only religion mentioned by name. The laws, however, were so worded

---

[15] *Proceedings of the Council of Maryland,* 1698–1731. Baltimore: 1905. Letter of the Council to the "Comsrs. of Trade and Foreign Plantations," dated June 27, 1700. Pp. 91–94.

[16] Frederick J. Swierlein, *Religion in New Netherland 1623–1664.* Rochester: 1910. See Chapters II "Church and State"; VI and VII "Persecution of Lutherans"; "Persecution of Quakers." "There was . . . in all New Netherland, except the South River territory, an absolute prohibition of non-conforming religions outside the family."

[17] *Ecclesiastical Records of the State of New York.* (Hugh Hastings, State Historian) Albany: 1901. Vol. I, pp. 570–572. The Duke's Laws are dated February 28, 1665 and were applicable only to Long Island and Staten Island until 1674.

as to give governmental recognition to all Protestant bodies, though in order to prevent "ignorant pretenders" from "intruding themselves" upon the people every minister was required to present his credentials showing that he had received ordination from a properly accredited authority. It was not until his status had been thus fully vouched for that the Governor was permitted to induct a minister into his parish. Thus the continuation of a kind of Dutch establishment was provided for under English rule.

This generous treatment of the Dutch by their English rulers established friendly ecclesiastical relations between them from the start, and the English chaplain was soon conducting Anglican services in the Dutch chapel within the fort at Dutch invitation. The toleration of all Protestant bodies inaugurated under the new regulations was unusual for the seventeenth century, but the great variety of religious groups which the English found in New Netherland helps explain the necessity for this liberality.

James II ascending the throne in 1685 and, anxious to secure toleration for Catholics, appointed in 1686 a Catholic governor, Thomas Dongan. Dongan, an honest and broad-minded man, received secret instructions from James to further the interests of the Anglican Church, but at the same time he was to permit "all persons of what Religion soever quietly to inhabit within your government without giving any disturbance or disquiet soever for or by reason of their differing opinions in matters of religion Provided they give no disturbance to ye public peace, nor doe molest or disquiet others in the free exercise of their religion."[18] This broad toleration, intended of course to include Catholics, came to an end with the overthrow of James II.

Governor Slaughter, the first governor sent over by the new sovereigns, William and Mary, was instructed to secure an act of establishment of the Church of England. The first step in this direction was the introduction of the Test Act (1691) which had been annulled by James II on his ascension to the throne. Both Governor Slaughter and his successor, Governor Fletcher, attempted to secure the passage of a ministry act, but it was not

---

[18] Secret instructions sent by James II to Governor Dongan, of New York, 1686, May 29. *Ecclesiastical Records of the State of New York*, Vol. II, pp. 915–916.

until 1693 that the Assembly, dominated by Dutchmen, succumbed and passed a measure entitled "Act for Settling a Ministry, and raising a Maintenance for them in the City of New York, County of Richmond, Westchester and Queens' county."[19] The Governor, not satisfied with the act as passed, demanded an amendment providing that all ministers be presented to him for collation. This the Assemblymen refused to enact, whereupon the irate Governor informed them that whether they enacted the amendment or not he intended to exercise the power of appointing or suspending any minister within the government. The Governor's state of mind may be easily imagined from the following communication he addressed to them:

Gentlemen:
There is also a Bill for settling a ministry in this city and some other counties of the government. In that you have shown a great deal of stiffness. You take upon you as if you were dictators. I sent down to you one amendment of three or four words in that Bill, which, though very immaterial, yet was positively denied. I must tell you it seems very unmannerly. There never was an amendment yet desired by the Council Board but was rejected. It is a sign of stubborn ill temper, and [but] this [I] have also passed [overlooked]. But, gentlemen, I must take leave to tell you, if you seem to understand by these words that none [ministers] can serve without your collation or establishment, you are mistaken; for I have the power of collating or suspending any minister in my government by their Majesties letters patent, and whilst I stay in the government I will take care that neither heresy, sedition, schism nor rebellion be preached amongst you, nor vice and profanity encouraged. It is my endeavor to lead a virtuous and pious life and to give you a good example, I wish you all to do the same. You ought to consider that you have but a third share in the legislative power of the government and ought not to take all upon you, nor be so peremptory. You ought to let the Council have a share. . . .[20]

This act secured with so much difficulty was later interpreted by the Governors as establishing the Church of England in the

---

[19] *Ibid.*, pp. 1076–79.
[20] *Ibid.*, pp. 1075–76.

counties named in the act. That the Assembly so intended is highly doubtful. It has been pointed out that the phrase "sufficient Protestant minister" in English legal usage meant a minister of the Establishment, a fact with which we may be reasonably sure the Dutch Assemblymen were not familiar. On the surface it looks as though the Governor was attempting to get the desired legislation by hook or crook and took advantage of Dutch unfamiliarity with English legal usage.

The Church of England is not mentioned in the act. The six parishes named were each to be supplied with "a good sufficient Protestant minister," and were to be supported by an annual tax. The freeholders in each parish were to elect a vestry of ten men and two church wardens, who with the assistance of the county justices were to levy the tax. The clergy were to be chosen by the vestry and the wardens. The salaries of the ministers in the several parishes were to be as follows:

For the City and County of New York, One Hundred Pounds; for the two Precincts of Westchester, One Hundred Pounds, for each Fifty Pounds, to be paid in Country Produce, at Money Price; for the County of Richmond, Forty Pounds, in Country Produce, at Money Price; and for the two Precincts of Queen's County, One Hundred and Twenty Pounds, to each Sixty Pounds, in Country Produce, at Money Price.[21]

The attempt to secure an Anglican minister for New York under this act was not successful until 1696. In the first two elections a majority of dissenters were chosen vestrymen, who accordingly favored a dissenting minister. It was not until the Dutch Church in New York secured a charter that the present Trinity Parish was formed.[22] Under the charter obtained by the Dutch Church in 1696 it was provided that instead of a vestry the church was to be governed by four deacons and four elders. The following year Trinity Church also received a charter. The Dutch, now placated by the receipt of their own liberal charter, made no

---

[21] *Ibid.*, p. 1077.

[22] For materials relating to the incorporation of the Dutch and Anglican churches in New York City, see, *Ibid.*, 1112–1115; 1116–1117; 1133–1134. A new act passed in 1705, amending that of 1693, gave larger powers to the church vestry and limited the county vestry to the collection of funds. *Ibid.*, pp. 1595–1596.

objection. In the other counties covered by the Ministry Act there was little attempt to found Anglican churches until after the formation of the Society for the Propagation of the Gospel in 1701.

THE CAROLINAS

THE OUTSTANDING figure in the establishment of the Carolinas was Sir Anthony Ashley Cooper, a Presbyterian who had been prominent in both the Commonwealth and Protectorate. He was liberal, tolerant in religious matters, with a flair for philosophic idealism. His former relationship to the Commonwealth made him suspect, and colonies, and with the return of the King to power the promotion of foreign plantations became his most absorbing interest. His former relationship to the Commonwealth made him suspect, and in order to gain the royal favor for his colonial projects it was necessary to secure the backing of men whose place at court was recognized. This accounts for most of the eight proprietors to whom a royal patent was granted in 1663 for lands south of Virginia under the name of Carolina.[23]

The charter provided for religious toleration, despite "the unity and uniformity established in this nation," but gave to the proprietors the "patronage and advowsons of all churches," while all church buildings were to be dedicated according to the ecclesiastical laws in force in England.[24] John Locke, an intimate friend of Ashley Cooper and living in his family, prepared, probably with Ashley's assistance, the Fundamental Constitutions (1669) and although they were never put into operation in the colony they doubtless expressed the views of the proprietors, or at least of Ashley, on religious toleration. Among the provisions on religion was that, "Noe person whatever shall disturbe, molest or persecute another for his speculative opinions in Religion or his way of Worship." They also provided that the Church of England alone should receive public support, but that any seven persons of the same religious belief might form a church under any name

---

[23] Chapters v and vi in Andrews, *op. cit.*, Vol. III, are devoted to an account of Carolina beginnings. Pp. 182–267.
[24] *Colonial and State Records of North Carolina*, I, pp. 20–33; II, pp. 202, 857.

they should choose, provided they acknowledged the existence of God and their purpose to worship Him. Such ideas as were here set forth were widely current and from this time onward toleration in religious matters was granted to all colonies that were established.

NORTH CAROLINA

North Carolina particularly attracted colonists of many religious opinions.[25] The Quakers, who early became especially numerous, resisted strenuously all attempts to establish the English Church. Aroused by the growing Quaker influence, the Anglicans, who were in the majority in the Assembly, succeeded in passing a Vestry Act in 1701. Disallowed by the Proprietors because of the united opposition of the dissenters, particularly the Quakers and Presbyterians, a second act was passed in 1705, the exact terms of which are not known. Political disturbances, precipitated by the religious parties, prevented the carrying out of the provisions of the act and it became a dead letter. Finally in 1715 another establishment Act was passed, largely through the activity of the S. P. G. missionaries who were now active in the colony. This law won the acceptance of the Proprietors. It provided for the division of the colony into five parishes, each with a vestry of twelve members. Two church wardens were to be chosen by the vestry from among their own members, each vestryman to serve a year as warden in turn. The levy for ministerial support was not to exceed five shillings per poll, the levy to be on all persons subject to tax, including slaves over sixteen years of age. Other laws pertaining to an Established Church were enacted, but all were more or less dead letters, due to lack of support as a result of the growing number of dissenters.[26] It was not until 1765 that an act of establishment was passed which met the approval of the home authorities. This law placed the minister's salary at £133.0.8, placed the right of presentation in the Governor, and in fact gave

---

[25] Andrews, *op. cit.,* Vol. III, pp. 260–261; also S. B. Weeks, *The Religious Development in the Province of North Carolina.* Johns Hopkins Univ. Studies. Tenth Series, V-VI. Baltimore: 1892.

[26] Davidson, *op. cit.,* Chapter IV, pp. 47–57.

the Governor more or less complete control. This rendered the act unpopular, causing parishes to resist receiving ministers presented, and in fact the act did the Church more harm than good.

SOUTH CAROLINA [27]

THE TYPE of colonists in South Carolina differed widely from the heterogeneous character of the North Carolina settlers. From the beginning the English Anglicans were prominent and not only possessed the largest share of the wealth but controlled the offices. As a consequence the establishment of the Church of England was accomplished more quickly. Huguenots began to arrive in 1680 and after the revocation of the Edict of Nantes the flow of immigration from France sharply increased. They soon came to constitute about ten percent of the population, numbering perhaps five hundred. Altogether they formed seven churches. The tendency to intermarry with the English and to merge with the Anglicans threw their influence on the side of the Established Church party.[28] There were also groups of Presbyterians, Congregationalists, Baptists, and Quakers, the latter constituting in 1710 about two and a half percent of the population. The whole body of dissenters about equalled the Anglicans. Any attempt to secure an act of establishment therefore would be certain to lead to a struggle between these groups.

In 1704 "by dint of political trickery" a Church Act was passed by the Assembly, and, though later disallowed, the measure is important since practically the same provisions were written into the Act of 1706 which became the basis for the South Carolina Church establishment. The provisions of the act differed radically from other colonial establishments. It did not require that ministers be certified to by the Bishop of London as in all the other colonies; selection of ministers was by vote of the parish-

---

[27] For the first time in 1710 North and South Carolina were put on an equal footing by the appointment of Edward Tynte as Governor of South Carolina and Edward Hyde as Governor of North Carolina. Both became royal colonies in 1728. The pretext for voiding the proprietary charter and erecting them into royal colonies was bad government.

[28] Arthur Hirsch, *The Huguenots of Colonial South Carolina.* Durham: Duke University Press, 1928. See especially Chapter III, "The French-Protestant Churches," and IV, "The Assimilation of the Huguenots."

ioners, not by the vestry; ministers' salaries were to be paid by the
government; a vestry of seven members, of whom the minister
was considered one, were to supervise the records of the parish,
select the clerk and sexton, while the church wardens, who were
to be elected annually with the vestry, were to pay all parochial
charges and keep the church in repair out of fines collected for
law violations. The most radical provision was the creation of a
self-perpetuating commission of twenty laymen, whose duties
were to make purchases of land for glebes and churches and
receive all voluntary contributions.[29] Though the minister of the
parish was chosen by vote of the parishioners, the vestry usually
provided the candidates, which was frequently done by appealing
to the Society for the Propagation of the Gospel or to the Bishop of
London.

GEORGIA

GEORGIA [30] was a philanthropic enterprise with twenty-one trustees
of whom five were Anglican clergymen. The three most active lay
members of the board, the Earl of Egmont, James Vernon, and
James Oglethorpe, were high churchmen yet their humanitarian
interests made them more eager to alleviate human misery than
to further a particular religious body. This not only led to their
granting freedom of worship to the colonists, but they even
assisted in securing ministers and meeting-houses for the several
dissenting groups. The Church of England, however, was most
favored by them.

The religious complexion of the early Georgia colonists was
varied. Of the first 116 who sailed for the colony in November
1632 it is only known that they had convinced the Trustees that
they were Protestants. On the southern frontier an original colony
of 175 Highlanders was settled. From the continent of Europe
came small groups of French and Swiss and larger numbers of

---

[29] *Colonial Records of North Carolina*, II, pp. 870–882; see also Davidson, *op. cit.*,
Chapter v.

[30] Reba Carolyn Strickland, *Religion and the State in Georgia in the Eighteenth
Century*, New York: Columbia University Press, 1939, is a recent study of this aspect of
early Georgia history. See especially Chapter III, "The Royal Government and Religion,"
pp. 100–138.

German Palatinates, the latter coming largely as indentured servants. The largest body of German Protestants, however, to came to Georgia were the Salzburgers, driven from their homes in the province of Salzburg by the intolerance of the Catholic Archbishop. They began to arrive in 1733 and others continued to come for the next ten years until some 200 or more had settled in the vicinity of their town of Ebenezer. Some Moravians from the great estate of Count Zinzendorf in Saxony began to arrive in 1734. And perhaps strangest of all came a considerable number of Jews, most of whom were refugees from Portuguese persecution.[31]

With the expiration of the proprietary charter, Georgia became a royal province in 1752, with a royal Governor appointed by the crown and a representative assembly. Almost at once an attempt was made, following the example of the other southern provinces, to bring about the establishment of the Anglican Church. An establishment bill was passed in 1755 which was, however, rejected by the appointive Council, probably because they feared it would stop the flow of settlers to the colony. In 1758, in spite of the fact that all the members except two of the upper house were dissenters and there was but one Anglican Church with a minister in the colony, a law was passed to establish the Church of England.[32] The law provided for the division of the colony into eight parishes; commissioners were appointed to build churches and parsonages and to acquire land for glebes, cemeteries and churches; all freeholders were entitled to vote for vestrymen, and the vestry was empowered to levy a tax within each parish to provide for repairing church, paying the salaries of sexton and clerk, and caring for the poor; church wardens were to look after the recording of births, burials, and marriages. The law said nothing as to how ministers were to be secured, but the royal

---

[31] Leon Huhner, "The Jews of Georgia in Colonial Times," Am. Jewish Hist. Soc., Pub. X, Baltimore: 1902, 66–70.

[32] For the text of the bill see the *Colonial Records of Georgia,* XVIII, pp. 258–272. The law is entitled "An Act for constituting and dividing the several Districts and Divisions of this Province into Parishes, and for establishing of Religious Worship therein according to the Rites and Ceremonies of the Church of England; and also for impowering the Church Wardens and Vestrymen of the Respective Parishes to assess Rates for Repair of Churches, the Relief of the Poor, and other Parochial Services."

instructions to the Governor gave him the right of collation when parishes became vacant. In spite of such favorable legislation the Church of England in Georgia remained weak throughout the colonial period, there being rarely more than two Church ministers in the colony at the same time. The vestry, however, became the principal organ of local government. The dissenters continued to increase as population pushed in from colonies to the north and soon the combined membership of the Congregationalists, Presbyterians, Baptists, Quakers, Lutherans and Catholics far outnumbered the members of the Church of England.[33]

A question which immediately arises in considering these several Acts of Establishment is, How was it possible to secure the passage of such enactments in colonies where Anglicans were definitely in the minority? This would seem to have been the case in all the colonies where such acts were passed with the exception of Virginia. One of the factors which sheds some light upon this question is the fact that the Anglicans doubtless constituted the most influential social and political groups in each of the colonies where establishment was secured. In Maryland,[34] where influence of the Catholics had been strong in the early years, the political and religious revolution after 1640 brought to them complete political eclipse. In New York where the Dutch were in the majority throughout the colonial period, a semblance of an establishment, as we have seen, was secured more or less by subterfuge. In North Carolina the several acts of establishment were all to a large degree dead letters, and the indifference of dissenter opinion to such legislation was evidently based upon their certain knowledge that the acts could not and would not be enforced. In South Carolina the Established Church party came nearer representing a majority than anywhere else except in Virginia, but even here the dissenters outnumbered the Anglicans, and establishment was secured by manipulation of the proprietors in placing Anglicans in the principal offices and in juggling the

---

[33] Strickland, *op. cit.*, Chapter III, "The Royal Government and Religion"; also Davidson, *op. cit.*, Chapter VI, "The Church in Georgia."

[34] For a summary of anti-Catholic legislation in Maryland see Sister Mary Augustina (Ray), *American Opinion of Roman Catholicism in the Eighteenth Century*, New York, Columbia University Press, 1936, pp. 58–60.

elections to the Assembly.[35] In Georgia establishment seems to have been achieved as a natural consequence of the fact that it had been from the beginning an Anglican benevolent enterprise.

Of significance in understanding the passage of the Acts of Establishment in the Southern colonies is the fact that parish organization in England was not solely a church affair, but the vestry was an organ of local government. In New England the town was the unit of local government; in the Southern colonies the parish became the local governmental unit. It was the system to which they had been accustomed in England, and its transfer to the colonies, where the Anglican element was relatively strong, was but natural. Illustrations of the colonial vestries exercising secular functions might be numerously cited. Vestries in Virginia were charged with the duty of looking after the poor.[36] In Maryland the vestries administered the Tobacco Acts of 1730 and 1747, the purpose of which was to regulate the production and improve the quality of the tobacco crop.[37] In Georgia the vestry of Christ Church were charged with protecting the town against fire, and were to see that rubbish, ashes and dung were not dumped in the lanes and squares.

Still another factor was the influence of English officialdom, together with the activities of the missionary and benevolent agencies created to further the interest of the Established Church in the colonies. The Bishops of London and the Archbishops of Canterbury, who bore the responsibility for supervising the church clergy in the colonies, found ways and means of putting pressure on colonial officials to favor the Church. With the exception of Virginia all the colonial establishments were created after the restoration, when the influence of the Established Church was definitely in the ascendant, a fact which has a bearing on what was taking place in colonial America.

---

[35] Andrews, *op. cit.*, III, pp. 242–244.

[36] For a discussion of poor relief as carried on in Virginia see M. W. Jernegan, *Laboring and Dependent Classes in Colonial America, 1607–1783*. Chicago: University of Chicago Press, 1931, Chapter xii, "Public Poor Relief in Virginia." See also numerous references in Hening's *Statutes*.

[37] *Archives of Maryland, Proceedings of the Assembly,* 1730–32, p. 140; *Ibid.,* 1745–47, pp. 599, 612. Strickland, *op. cit.*, pp. 109–110.

II

New England

He that stirs a nest of Hornets, will have a confused din about his ears, and if not well guarded against invenom'd stings, be severly wounded and tormented by those angry insects: Noe better treatment must I expect from those waspish creatures of N. E. for laying them open to the world, and publishing their wicked designs & unwarrantable practices. . . .

THESE ARE the opening words of *An Account of the Colony and Provinces of New England in General, More particularly that of Massachusetts,* a document found among the manuscripts in Lambeth Palace, prepared after the overthrow of Governor Andros in 1689. It has little good to say of New Englanders in general and none at all of Massachusetts, and the reason is not far to seek.[38] On May 15, 1686 the Reverend Robert Ratcliffe landed in Boston with instructions to establish an Anglican Church in that stronghold of New England Congregationalism. Since the restoration, the House of Stuart had been attempting to reduce New England to ecclesiastical and political obedience. In a reply to a loyal address which Massachusetts sent to King Charles II, hoping thereby to ward off threatened danger, the King had reminded them that the foundation of their charter was freedom of conscience, and demanded that the Church of England be permitted to carry on its worship within their bounds. In 1664 a royal Commission was dispatched to Massachusetts which attempted to secure a modification of that colony's religious restrictions, but with small success. Finally after repeated failures to obtain toleration for Anglicans, the King began an attack on the Massachusetts charter through the courts on *quo warranto* proceedings, and on October 3, 1684 the charter was forfeited. The same proceedings were now instituted against the other charter and proprietary colonies, and of them all Pennsylvania alone

---

[38] Perry, *op. cit.,* Vol. III, *Massachusetts,* pp. 39–53.

was able to retain her original charter.[39] The King's agent in carrying out these proceedings was Edward Randolph, who in 1678 had been appointed the collector of customs for New England.[40] A loyal but bigoted churchman, Randolph was unpopular with New Englanders on several counts, but particularly because of his activity in attempting to put a stop to the widespread violation of trade restrictions. Such were the events immediately preceding the arrival of the Reverend Robert Ratcliffe, the first minister of the first permanent Anglican parish in Massachusetts.

The year Ratcliffe arrived in Boston a royal government was set up over Massachusetts under Joseph Dudley, a native of the colony and a graduate of Harvard, who later conformed to the Church of England. He was soon succeeded by Edmund Andros, a devoted servant of the reigning house who arrived in Boston on December 25, 1686. On the very day of his arrival Andros sought to make arrangements with the Puritan ministers for the use of one of their meeting houses for Anglican worship. This request soon brought the answer that the ministers "could not with a good conscience consent y^t our Meeting House should be made use of for ye Common Prayer worship." The Churchmen of Boston, therefore, were under the necessity of continuing their services at the Town-House where they had been held since the coming of Ratcliffe. Finally on March 22, 1687, Andros inspected three Puritan Meeting Houses in Boston for the purpose of choosing one to be used for Anglican worship, and on Good Friday an Anglican service was held at the South Meeting House. On Easter Sunday the Governor and his retinue met in the Meeting House at eleven o'clock, but it was two o'clock before the long service ended. Meanwhile the regular congregation had gathered and were milling about the street. A *modus vivendi* was finally

---

[39] *Quò warranto* proceedings had first been inaugurated against the charters of cities and was found to be a good way to secure money for the crown. This was one of the motives for its extension to the colonies.

[40] Randolph had come to New England in 1675–76 under royal instructions to report on conditions in the colonies. He was given scant courtesy by the Massachusetts government and as a result gained a lifelong dislike of New Englanders. His several reports on colonial affairs are filled with denunciations and he became a hated figure in America. V. F. Barnes, *The Dominion of New England*, New Haven: 1923.

arranged and both congregations continued to use the Meeting House until the completion of King's Chapel.[41]

The construction of King's Chapel began in October of the following year (1688), but before its completion news reached Boston that William of Orange had landed in England and that King James was a fugitive on the continent. This was the signal for a local revolution. Randolph and Andros were imprisoned. Ratcliffe, though escaping imprisonment, was closely watched and was obstructed in the performance of his duties. "Scandalous pamphlets" were published vilifying the liturgy, while members of the Church were "daily called Papists, Doggs and Rogues to their Faces," and "Plucking down the Church was threatened." Increase Mather thought this a good time to publish "a most scandalous pamphlet" on the "Unlawfulness of the Common Prayer Worship." Fortunately the Church escaped with broken windows only.

The Massachusetts leaders were hopeful that their old charter would be restored and dispatched Increase Mather to England to work to that end. Unable to secure the return of the old charter Mather accepted a compromise, among the new provisions being one forbidding religious tests for the suffrage. This new provision gave Church of England people equal opportunity with the Congregationalists in the government of the colony, property ownership being the test rather than religious affiliation. By 1722 there had come to be so many Church of England people in Boston that a second church was formed and its first minister was Timothy Cutler, the late president of Yale College, whose conversion to Anglicanism had taken place that very year. Within a few years Christ Church had a membership of seven or eight hundred, and in 1729 a third Anglican parish, Trinity, was formed in the capital of New England Congregationalism.

Though Maine [42] and New Hampshire were originally settled by churchmen, there were no permanent parishes formed there

---

[41] William Perry, *The History of the American Episcopal Church*, Boston: James Osgood & Co., 1885, Vol. I, Chapter x.

[42] Edward Ballard, *The Early History of the Protestant Episcopal Church in the Diocese of Maine.* Collection of the Maine Historical Society. Portland: 1859. Vol. VI, pp. 171–202.

until well along in the eighteenth century. The beginning of Anglicanism in Connecticut and Rhode Island was likewise delayed until the opening of the new century. In the general overthrow of the charters, noted above, only Connecticut and Rhode Island, among the New England colonies, had escaped. Both had been frightened into a temporary surrender, but with the overthrow of Andros they were allowed to resume their liberal charters, which they succeeded in retaining until the end of the colonial period. Thus neither was ever subjected to a royal governor and both escaped the unfortunate experience of having the Anglican Church forced upon them.

The growth and development of the Anglican Church in colonial New England throughout the eighteenth century is so closely related to the activities of the Society for the Propagation of the Gospel that it will be treated under that head. The beginnings of the Church in Connecticut, however, demand separate treatment. Here the Church found deeper rootage than anywhere else in New England because of the peculiar circumstances which marked its early years. The first parish to be established in Connecticut was that at Stratford in 1706. Colonel Caleb Heathcote, the proprietor of a large estate in Westchester county, New York, and an ardent Churchman, was largely responsible for its formation. Three years later Rev. Timothy Cutler, a graduate of Harvard College, with a reputation of being one of the best preachers in New England, was ordained over the Congregational Church in Stratford.[43] Here he remained until he was called to the presidency of Yale College in 1719. Previous to Cutler's coming the College had followed a precarious course, divided between New Haven, Wethersfield and Saybrook, but under Cutler's leadership it was permanently located in New Haven.[44]

It has been suggested that Cutler already was leaning toward

---

[43] E. E. Beardsley, *The History of the Episcopal Church in Connecticut*, etc., New York: 1865, Chapters II, III, and IV.

[44] For a concise and illuminating account of the early years of Yale College and of the presidency of Timothy Cutler see Ola Elizabeth Winslow, *Jonathan Edwards, 1703–1758*, New York: 1940, Chapter III. Jonathan Edwards was a student at Yale during the first year of Cutler's presidency and returned to the college as a tutor immediately after Cutler's defection to Anglicanism.

Anglicanism before his coming to Yale College, having been under the influence of John Checkley, an ardent advocate of the Apostolic origin of Episcopacy.[45] Both Cutler's father and mother were critical of what had taken place in Boston on the overthrow of Andros, and Cutler was seemingly always hospitable toward non-Congregational points of view. The deciding factor in bringing about the conversion of Cutler and the Yale tutors to Anglican views was the gift of a thousand books to the college library, gathered in England by Jeremy Dummer, the Massachusetts agent in London. Among them were several volumes relating to church polity, and in their perusal of them, Rector Cutler, Tutor Brown and several neighboring Congregational ministers were convinced that the Church of England and not Congregationalism was the lineal descendant of the Church of the Apostles.

Meanwhile they were in touch with the Anglican missionary at Stratford, Rev. George Pigot, and finally decided openly to declare for episcopacy. Besides Timothy Cutler and Daniel Brown, of Yale College, Samuel Johnson, a former tutor of the college, but now minister of the West Haven Congregational Church, and James Wetmore with three other Congregational ministers were involved in the defection. The announcement of their decision was made to the astonished trustees the day after the commencement in September 1722. The trustees were taken completely by surprise, for they had not the slightest inkling of what was taking place.[46] For such defection to occur among the trusted guardians of Connecticut orthodoxy was a blow hard to take, and the Congregational ministers throughout the colony "were amazed and filled with darkness." One writing to the Mathers in Boston of the affair added this lament: "How is the gold become dim! and the silver become dross! and the wine mixed with water!"

But if the New England Congregationalists were filled with

---

[45] John Checkley was a native of Boston, born of English parents and partly educated in England. As keeper of a bookshop in Boston he gained a reputation as an advocate of Anglicanism and published several books and pamphlets assailing Congregationalism. See E. F. Slater, *John Checkley* (Prince Society, 2 vols., 1897), *Dictionary of American Biography*, IV, p. 46.

[46] For the sources bearing on this episode see Perry, *Historical Collections*, Vol. III, *Massachusetts*, various references under Cutler. See also Beardsley, *op. cit.*, pp. 28–60; Manross, *op. cit.* pp. 102–104.

dismay at this occurrence, the Anglican leaders both in New England and in England may be forgiven for any evidence of elation which they displayed, for the story of these happenings was not only "news" in New England, but was printed in the London papers and was read with deep satisfaction by the clergy and loyal churchmen generally. Within a week after the announcement of their conversion to Anglicanism, Cutler, Brown and Johnson were on their way to England to seek ordination at the hands of the English bishops. They sailed October 23, 1722. Once in England the highest Anglican officials, including the archbishops, vied with one another in showering attention upon them. In March (1723) they were confirmed, and ordained deacons and advanced to the priesthood. In April Brown died of smallpox. By this time Wetmore had arrived and was also admitted to orders. Before sailing for home Oxford and Cambridge conferred the doctorate on Cutler and the Master of Arts on Johnson.

The new Christ Church congregation in Boston had requested that Cutler be their minister, and on his return he immediately began his work in that parish, where he remained until the end of his life (d. 1765). Samuel Johnson became the S. P. G. missionary at Stratford where he remained until called to the presidency of King's College on the opening of that institution in 1754. Westmore became the missionary at Rye, New York, where he served faithfully until his death of smallpox in 1760. In spite of the efforts of Congregational leaders in Connecticut to keep Yale orthodox by requiring the rectors and tutors thereafter to subscribe to the Saybrook Platform and to give satisfaction as to the soundness of their faith, conversions of Yale students to Anglicanism continued, and by 1733 eight had professed conversion, and in the ten years following 1722 more than one out of every ten graduates of Yale entered the priesthood of the Church of England.[47]

---

[47] Perry, *The History of the American Episcopal Church*, Vol. I, pp. 253-255.

III

In the Quaker Colonies

No RELIGIOUS group suffered physical persecution in the Quaker colonies, yet among all the religious bodies in colonial America the Quakers were the most active in combating Anglican attempts to secure a foothold. The original charter of Pennsylvania (Section XXII) contained the requirement that,

if any of the inhabitants of the said province to the number of twenty, shall at any time hereafter be desirous, and, shall by any writing, or by any person deputed by them, signify such their desire to the Bishop of London . . . that any preacher or preachers, to be approved by the said Bishop, may be sent among them, for their instruction; that such preacher or preachers, shall and may reside within the said province, without any denial, or molestation whatsoever.

It was not, however, until 1694–95 that any attempt was made to introduce Anglican worship into Pennsylvania. That the progress of the Anglican parish in Philadelphia (Christ Church) was rapid is indicated by a letter written in 1700 to the Archbishop of Canterbury, by Rev. Thomas Clayton, the first Church clergyman there. He states that "in less than four years' space from a very small number her community consists of more than five hundred sober and devout souls in and about this city." After Clayton's death in the great pestilence which swept Philadelphia at the end of the century, the Rev. Evan Evans, a Welshman, was sent out (1700) by the Bishop of London. He not only served Christ Church in Philadelphia, but itinerated widely, preaching in surrounding communities. Before 1707 churches had been built at Oxford, Chester and Newcastle in Pennsylvania, and Evans' ability to preach in Welsh kept numerous Welsh settlers in the vicinity from leaving the Church and joining non-conformist bodies. In 1707 Evans was commissioned by the S. P. G. as a missionary to the Welsh settlers in America. In 1718 he left Pennsylvania and became the rector of a Maryland parish.[48]

The zeal of the early Pennsylvania clergy to convert the Quakers

---

[48] Perry, *Historical Collections*, Vol. II, *Pennsylvania*, p. 16.

to the Anglican Church was largely due to the Keithian controversy which had divided the Quakers around Philadelphia into contending factions. In a report to the S. P. G. in 1707, Rev. Evan Evans thus summarizes his early labors in and around Philadelphia:

> And God was in a little time pleased to prosper my labors to that degree, as that I had, in less than three years after my arrival, a very numerous congregation, consisting for the most part of persons brought over from the Quakers, and other sectaries, to the Church of England; and the true religion (by the frequent resort of persons from remote parts to Philadelphia) did so spread, and the numbers of converts did increase so fast, that I was obliged to divide myself among them so often and as equally as I could, till they were formed into proper districts, and had Ministers sent over to them by the Venerable Society.[49]

It sometimes has been erroneously stated that the Church of England was established in New Jersey.[50] It is true that when the first royal Governor of New Jersey, Lord Cornbury, assumed power in 1702, his instructions from Queen Anne authorized him to "collate any person, or persons, to any churches Chappells, or other Ecclesiastical Benefices within our said Province . . ." and he was to have care that "God· Almighty be devoutly and duly served" and that the "book of common prayer, as by law established, [be] read each Sunday and holy day." At the time there was not an Established Church in the province, nor had the provincial assembly enacted any measure of establishment. The Queen may have thought that establishment could be provided for by her instructions to the royal Governor, but if so she was decidedly mistaken. For, as was brought out in the Francis Makemie trial in 1707, the Queen's instructions may have been law for Lord Cornbury but for no one else.[51]

---

[49] Earnest Hawkins, *Historical Notices of the Missions of the Church of England in the North American Colonies; previous to the independence of the United States: chiefly from the MS. Documents of the Society for the Propagation of the Gospel in Foreign Parts.* London: 1845, p. 108.

[50] George Bancroft, *History of the United States.* 8 Vol. Edition, Boston: 1864. Vol. II, pp. 355–357. Carl Zollman, *American Church Law,* St. Paul: West Pub. Co., 1933, p. 3, lists New Jersey among the Established Church colonies.

[51] Sanford H. Cobb, *The Rise of Religious Liberty in America,* New York: Macmillan Co. 1902, pp. 399–418, gives a full account of these incidents relating to the Established Church in New Jersey.

The first period in the history of the Anglican Church in the colonies ends with the seventeenth century, and a new period opens with the formation of the great missionary agency, the Society for the Propagation of the Gospel in Foreign Parts in the year 1701. The following is a contemporary description of the status of the Anglican Church in the colonies as it entered upon the new century.

In *South Carolina* there were computed seven thousand souls, besides negroes and Indians, living without any minister of the Church of England, and but few dissenting teachers of any kind, above half the people living regardless of any religion. In *North Carolina,* above five thousand souls without any minister, or any religious administration used; no public worship celebrated, neither the children baptized, nor the dead buried in any Christian form. *Virginia* contained about forty thousand souls, divided into forty parishes, but wanting near half the number of clergymen requisite. *Maryland* contained about twenty-five thousand, divided into twenty-six parishes, but wanting also half the number of ministers requisite. In *Pennsylvania* [says Colonel Heathcote] there are at least twenty thousand souls, of which, not above seven hundred frequent the Church, nor have they more than two hundred and fifty communicants. The two *Jerseys* contain about fifteen thousand, of which, not above six hundred frequent the Church, nor have they more than two hundred and fifty communicants. In *New York* Government we have thirty thousand souls, of which about one thousand two hundred frequent the Church, and we have about four hundred and fifty communicants. In *Connecticut* colony in New England there are about thirty thousand souls, of which when they have a minister among them, about one hundred and fifty frequent the Church, and there are about thirty-five communicants. In *Rhode Island* and *Narragansett,* which is one government, there are about ten thousand souls, of which about one hundred and fifty frequent the Church, and there are thirty communicants. In *Boston and Piscataway* Government, there are about eighty thousand souls, of these about six hundred frequent the Church, and one hundred and twenty the sacrament. In *Newfoundland,* there are about five hundred families constantly living in the place, and many thousand of occasional inhabitants, and no sort of public Christian worship used. This is the true though melancholy state of our Church in North America; and whoever sends any other accounts more in her favor are certainly under mistakes; nor can I take them (if they do it knowingly) to be friends of the Church; for if the distemper be not rightly known and understood, proper remedies can never be applied.[52]

IV

THE COMMISSARIES

THE ONLY episcopal supervision which the American Episcopal Church enjoyed during the entire colonial period was the long-distance jurisdiction exercised by the Bishop of London. This had come about in the course of time as a result of a series of incidents in the management of the affairs of Virginia. The Virginia Company in 1620 had asked the Bishop of London to appoint suitable ministers for the colony, and about the same time Bishop King had shown an interest in the colony by raising money for a school for Indian youth. He was also a member of the Company.

The real beginnings of the Bishop of London's authority over the colonial Church dates from Bishop Laud's incumbency of that See. Anxious to˙ save the Church from Calvinistic infection, he proposed to the Privy Council in 1632 that measures be taken to extend and enforce uniformity and conformity to the national Church among British subjects outside the British Isles. Accordingly the Privy Council gave to the Bishop of London jurisdiction over English subjects beyond the seas, to see that the Liturgy and the Discipline were properly enforced. The fact that London was the center of foreign trade and would naturally have closer contact with colonial affairs made the See of London seem the most appropriate one to exercise such supervision. A further step was taken in legalizing the Bishop of London's authority in the colonies when Henry Compton became the Bishop of that See in 1675. At his request instructions were issued to the colonial governors, requiring that no minister be received in the colonies without a certificate from the Bishop of London; the same require-

---

[52] The above summary is based on reports sent to the Secretary of the S. P. G. by Joseph Dudley, Colonel Morris and Colonel Caleb Heathcote. David Humphreys, *An Historical Account of the Incorporated Society for the Propagation of the Gospel in Foreign Parts*, etc. London: 1730; reprinted, New York: 1853, pp. 17–24.

ment was made for schoolmasters. It was Bishop Compton also who was responsible for the appointment of the first Commissaries and it was during his occupancy of the See of London that the great missionary agencies, the S. P. G., the S. P. C. K. and the Associates of Dr. Bray, were formed.[53]

There are certain essential functions in the Anglican Church which a bishop alone can perform, the most important being confirmation and ordination. Neither of these can be delegated to another. Other functions such as supervision and administering discipline could be delegated. It was Bishop Compton who began the practice of delegating these functions to officials called commissaries. The first such official appointed (1689) was James Blair for the colony of Virginia. Blair, a native of Scotland, was educated at Aberdeen and Edinburgh and had entered the Anglican Church in Scotland where for a time he had held a parish. Later employed in the office of the Master of the Rolls in London, he was prevailed upon by Bishop Compton to accept an appointment as a missionary to Virginia. He became the rector of Henrico Parish in 1685 and four years later became the Bishop of London's Commissary for Virginia, which position he occupied until his death in 1743. That he was an effective commissary is shown by the fact that in 1700 more than half the parishes were vacant while at his death there were but two parishes without ministers. The second commissary appointed by Bishop Compton was Thomas Bray for Maryland, and though he spent less than a year in the colony his was the major influence in creating the great benevolent and missionary agencies mentioned above, all of which had large significance for colonial Anglicanism.[54]

---

[53] Episcopal jurisdiction in the colonies is treated in Arthur Lyon Cross, *The Anglican Episcopate and the American Colonies.* New York: Longmans, Green, 1902.

[54] Samuel R. Mohler, *Commissary James Blair, Churchman, Educator and Politician of Colonial Virginia.* (Typed Ph.D. thesis, The University of Chicago, 1940.)

Aside from James Blair and Thomas Bray the names of the colonial commissaries are little known. In Virginia, William Dawson, professor of Theology at William and Mary, succeeded Blair; and he in turn was followed by his brother Thomas Dawson. In 1761 when William Robinson succeeded to the office the Commissary's power had largely evaporated. In Maryland after Bray's departure the Commissaryship amounted to little. In 1716 two were appointed, one Christopher Wilkinson for the eastern shore and Jacob Henderson for the western shore. In 1730 Henderson became Commissary over the whole colony. Gideon Johnson was the first commissary for the Caro-

V

The S. P. G.

WE COME now to a consideration of the great missionary agencies whose colonial activities are the chief glory of the Church of England during the eighteenth century. If we were entirely dependent upon official accounts for our knowledge of the founding of the greatest of these agencies, the Society for the Propagation of the Gospel in Foreign Parts, we would be under the necessity of giving credit to a long list of Lord Archbishops, and Lord Bishops, Deans and Archdeacons, Professors of Divinity at the ancient seats of learning, Earls, Viscounts and Knights, for they are all duly listed in the charter granted in 1701. But the one chiefly responsible for its formation was Thomas Bray, whose name appears inconspicuously past the middle of the long list of incorporators.

Thomas Bray's appointment as the first Commissary for Maryland already has been noted. A graduate of All Souls College, Oxford (1678), he served conscientiously several English parishes. His publication of the first volume of *Catechetical Lectures* made him well known in London, and in response to the request of Governor Nicholson and the Assembly of Maryland to send a commissary to that colony he was appointed to that post in 1696. In trying to secure recruits for Maryland parishes he found that the only ones interested were poor men, unable to buy books. It was this discovery which started him on his course as the organizer of the three societies whose activities have persisted to this day. His first object was to raise funds for the buying of libraries for missionaries going out to the colonies. Securing the support of both archbishops and five, and later twelve, bishops, he extended his plan to establish libraries in every deanery in England and

---

linas (1707–16), and was succeeded by William T. Bull (1716–29), and he in turn by Alexander Garden (1729–49), whose chief distinction arises from his attempt to discipline George Whitefield. Other Virginia commissaries were James Horricks (1771–72) and his successor John Camm. Roger Price was appointed Commissary for New England in 1730. William Vesey served as Commissary of New York and New Jersey from 1714 to 1746.

Wales. This led to larger projects, resulting in the formation of the Society for the Promotion of Christian Knowledge, which held its first meeting March 8, 1698/9. Before sailing for Maryland, Bray had sent £2,400 worth of books into the plantations, and libraries were eventually established in Boston, New York, New Jersey, Pennsylvania and Charleston, while thirty libraries were placed in Maryland, the largest being at Annapolis, consisting of more than a thousand volumes.[55]

Compelled to pay the cost of his voyage to America, Bray sold his personal effects and borrowed money on credit. He sailed in December 1699 and arrived in the colony in March 1700. Francis Nicholson, who had been Governor of the colony since 1694, had done much to promote the interest of the Church. In fact it was largely through his influence that a commissary had been appointed for Maryland. Both the Church of England and the cause of education were primary interests of Governor Nicholson and in the five colonies where he served as either Governor or Lieutenant Governor he gave these two objects much attention.[56] With his accustomed energy Bray made a visitation of the several Maryland parishes, attempted to discipline some of the most notoriously incompetent of the clergy, and was largely responsible for pushing through the Maryland Assembly an Act of Establishment. He then hurried back to England to secure its approval by the Board of Trade and Plantations.

Arriving in England, Bray published a report on the state of religion in the colonies, calling particular attention to the shortage of ministers, and urged that each diocese in England take upon itself the obligation of raising funds for sending ministers to the colonies. With this suggestion in mind the Convocation of Canterbury on May 13, 1701 appointed a committee to consider methods of furthering the cause of Christianity in the British colonies. Meanwhile the newly formed Society for the Promotion of Christian Knowledge was considering the same matter. Encouraged by

---

[55] Bernard G. Steiner, "Rev. Thomas Bray and his American Libraries," in *American Historical Review*, Vol. II, October 1896, pp. 59–75.

[56] *Dictionary of American Biography*, XIII, pp. 499–502. For his activities for the Church of England see Perry, *Historical Collections*, Vol. I, *Virginia*. Governor Nicholson's personal life and temper belied his interest in religion. On his death he left most of his estate to the S. P. G., of which he had been a member since its formation.

these expressions of interest, Bray, with the support of Thomas Tenison, Archbishop of Canterbury, and Henry Compton, Bishop of London, petitioned the King for a royal charter.[57] The purpose of the Society as set forth in the charter, dated June 16, 1701, was to provide for the "better support and Maintenance of an Orthodox Clergy in Forreigne Parts," since so "many of the King's Loveing Subjects doe want the Administration of God's Word and Sacraments, and seem to be abandoned to Atheism and Infidelity." Though the main object of the Society was to advance the cause of religion among emigrant English settlers in the British colonies, it also had in mind from the start the conversion of the natives and negro slaves.

Before starting its work in America the Society determined to make a survey of the situation in the colonies, and for that purpose commissioned George Keith. No better man could have been secured for this duty. A recent convert from Quakerism to the Church of England he was full of zeal for its expansion, while a previous residence in the colonies further fitted him for his task. Accompanying Keith was Rev. Patrick Gordon going out as a missionary to Long Island, the first in the long line to be sent out, but he died of smallpox eight days after his arrival.[58] The chap-

---

[57] Archbishop Tenison contributed twenty guineas toward the cost of obtaining the charter. The charter may be found in full in Humphreys, *Historical Account*, pp. 1–8; also in Hawkins, *Historical Notices*, etc., Appendix A, pp. 415–421. Also see the first anniversary sermon preached by the Dean of Lincoln, February 20, 1702, quoted in Hawkins, *op. cit.*, p. 19.

[58] George Keith was a Scotchman, educated at Aberdeen for entering the ministry of the Church of Scotland. His conversion to Quakerism in 1664 brought him in contact with all the early Quaker leaders. He was soon recognized as one of the most effective of the Quaker apologists, and in 1677 accompanied George Fox, William Penn and Robert Barclay on their missionary tour to Holland and Germany. Appointed surveyor-general of New Jersey (1685) he ran the boundary line between East and West Jersey and a few years later settled in Philadelphia, where he became the master of the School which became the famous William Penn Charter School. Here he soon came in conflict with the Pennsylvania Quaker leaders, whom he attacked on the ground that the *inner light* was insufficient for salvation. He also advocated the Lord's Supper as a Love Feast. The controversy became increasingly bitter, largely due to Keith's contentious temper, and eventually he was disowned by the Philadelphia Yearly Meeting (1692). Keith, however, succeeded in drawing off a considerable Quaker following who became known as Keithian Quakers. Returning to London Keith continued to propagate his ideas, and in a rented hall was accustomed to administer the sacraments in Quaker garb. In 1700 he entered the Anglican Church and two years later was on his way to America with a commission as Missionary at large for the Society for the Propagation of the Gospel in Foreign Parts (Rufus M. Jones, *The Quakers in the American Colonies*, pp. 437–458, New York: 1910).

lain of the ship, the *Centurian,* on which Keith sailed was John Talbot, a graduate of Christ's College, Cambridge, and was in orders. So impressed was he with the importance of Keith's mission that on reaching Boston he joined him as his assistant, and spent the remainder of his life in the colonies.[59]

Keith and his companions landed in Boston July 28, 1702, and from that moment until he sailed for England from the James River in Virginia on June 8, 1704, Keith was busy propagating Anglicanism. He has left us a sprightly *Journal* [60] of his American itinerary, a good share of which is taken up with accounts of his debates with the Quakers. These debates he deliberately sought by attending Quaker meetings uninvited, often taking several Church of England people with him to lend him moral support. That it was a sorry way to propagate Christian truth will be recognized, but it was seemingly effective in winning numerous converts to the Anglican Church.[61] John Talbot centered most of his energies in Pennsylvania and New Jersey. At Burlington (New Jersey) he laid the cornerstone of St. Mary's Church on March 25, 1703, and in 1704 consented to become the rector of that parish. Talbot was an ardent advocate of a bishop for America,[62] and made two visits to England to urge that object before the Anglican authorities. Archbishop Tenison at his death left a legacy for the support of an American bishop, the income of which was first assigned to Talbot. There is a tradition that on his second visit to England Talbot received consecration clandestinely at the hands of non-juring bishops. This is based, however, on questionable evidence. Accused of Jacobite sympathies, Talbot was dismissed as a missionary of the S. P. G. in 1724.

Writing from Philadelphia February 24, 1703 to Dr. Bray, Keith stated:

---

[59] Edgar L. Pennington, *Apostle of New Jersey, John Talbot, 1645–1727* (Church Hist. Soc. Pub., No. 10). Philadelphia: 1938.

[60] *A Journal of Travels from New Hampshire to Caratuck, on the Continent of North America,* by James Keith, A.M., Late Missionary from the Society for the Propagation of the Gospel in Foreign Parts; and now Rector of Edburton in Sussex. London: 1706. Reprinted in the *Collections of the Protestant Episcopal Historical Society,* 1851. New York: 1851.

[61] Keith's activity at Newport, Rhode Island, is typical of his methods in propagating Anglicanism among the Quakers. See *Journal,* August 6, 9, 10, 14 (1702), pp. 13–22.

[62] Pennington, *op. cit.,* Chapter VI, pp. 66–79.

There is a mighty cry and desire, almost in all places where we have traveled, to have ministers of the Church of England sent to them in these northern parts of America . . . some well affected to the Church have desired me to write to my Lord of London and to you that if a Minister be not sent with the first conveniency, Presbyterian Ministers from New England would swarm into those countries and prevent the increase of the Church.

The following month (September 3, 1703) in a letter to the Secretary of the Society he reports that the Keithian Quakers in East and West Jersey received him kindly and above a hundred came over to the Church, and "they greatly desire that good and able ministers may be sent among them." In many places his coming, Keith stated, was "as the sowing of the Seed and Planting"; in other places it was "a watering to what had been formerly sown and planted," and everywhere he reported "good materials prepared for the building of Church, of living stones, as soon as, by the good Providence of God, Ministers shall be sent among them." [63]

Even before Keith's return to England S. P. G. missionaries began to arrive in the colonies. Rev. Samuel Thomas reached Charleston, South Carolina, on Christmas Day 1702; Rev. John Blair made his appearance in North Carolina in 1704; Rev. N. Nichols was the first S. P. G. appointee to Pennsylvania where he arrived in 1704, and the same year Rev. J. Honyman came to labor at Newport in Rhode Island. As has been noted, Talbot accepted an invitation to remain at Burlington, New Jersey, also in 1704. From 1702 to 1783 fifty-four missionaries labored in South Carolina; thirty-three in North Carolina; forty-seven in Pennsylvania; eighty-four in New England; forty-four in New Jersey; fifty-eight in New York; two only in Virginia; five in Maryland and thirteen in the new colony of Georgia. The total number of missionaries sent to the thirteen colonies was three hundred and nine, while the Society assisted two hundred and two central mission stations, all at a total cost of £227,454.[64]

---

[63] Keith, *A Journal of Travels*, etc., pp. xxii–xliii. See also C. F. Pascoe, *Two Hundred years of the S. P. G.*, and Humphreys, *Historical Account* . . . 1701–1900. London: 1901. Pp. 1–12.

[64] Pascoe, *op. cit.*, pp. 86–87.

The Venerable Society, as it soon came to be called, was largely supported by contributions from its English friends, but it also received gifts from several of the colonial Governors and other interested colonials. Governor Wentworth of New Hampshire was an enthusiastic supporter of the S. P. G. The missionary at Portsmouth writing to the Society in 1751 stated that the Governor "purposes to interest the Society in every one of the new Towns that he shall grant from time to time," while in 1769 the Governor proposed a scheme by which the Church of England might be established in the "Province upon a permanent system." [65] Sir William Johnson, the Indian Commissioner among the Iroquois, was an energetic member of the Society and gave it his full support in its work among the Indians under his supervision.[66]

These are but examples of the type of cooperation given the Society by colonial officials. Taken as a whole the long line of missionaries serving in America maintained a good reputation both from the standpoint of character and devotion to their work. This is borne out by the testimony of Governor Hunter of New York who wrote to the Society's secretary in 1711, "We are happy in these provinces in a good set of missionaries, who generally labor hard in their functions and are men of good lives and ability." [67] There were, however, few men of outstanding ability among them. Charges against missionaries were carefully investigated by the Society, and there were some dismissals. In fact it has been stated that the Society "erred on the side of strictness rather than leniency." Though without authority to deprive a missionary of his ministerial office, the Society could and did dismiss men from its service.[68]

Some of the Society's most able missionaries labored in Massachusetts, many of whom had come from the Congregational

---

[65] Library of Congress Transcripts: See S. P. G. Correspondence, Series B. Vol. 19, pp. 63–64; Arthur Browne to Gov. Wentworth Nov. 20, 1751; also Wentworth to Jos. Harrison Sept. 24, 1769; Fulham MSS. New Hampshire, No. 6.

[66] "Sir William Johnson and the Society for the Propagation of the Gospel, 1749–1774" by Arthur J. Klingberg. *Hist. Mag. of the Prot. Epis. Church,* Vol. VIII, 1939, pp. 5–37.

[67] Pascoe, *op. cit.,* p. 62.

[68] Manross, *op. cit.,* p. 56.

ranks. Of this number Timothy Cutler of Christ Church, Boston, and Edward Bass of Newburyport are perhaps the best known.[69] The Church in Connecticut likewise was manned largely by native New Englanders, many of whom were graduates of Yale College. In 1748, nine Episcopal clergymen were present at the Yale commencement at which Samuel Seabury, Jr., later to become the first American Episcopal bishop, and the youngest son of Samuel Johnson, William Samuel Johnson, were graduated.[70] In the colonies where Congregationalists were the dominant religious body there was constant bickering over the legal restraints imposed. Frequently town treasurers refused to surrender money contributed for the support of the Episcopal minister, or members of the Episcopal Church were fined and sometimes imprisoned for failure to pay for the support of the Congregational minister. Cutler was a high Tory and was particularly arrogant in his attitude toward his former Congregational brethren, and among other presumptuous claims attempted to gain a seat as an Overseer of Harvard College, claiming that he was a "teaching elder" as required by the college charter. On the other hand, Cutler, as well as other Anglican clergymen, complained constantly of the ungenerous treatment afforded them by the "Standing Order" clergy. Writing on February 3, 1727/28 Cutler complained that:

. . . all possible art consistent with safety & secrecy is used at that college [Harvard] to suppress any good inclination in the Students towards our Excellent Church. . . .[71]

Anglican Church beginnings in New York cannot be told apart from the activities of Colonel Caleb Heathcote. This "able, geniel and shrewd" gentleman had come to New York in 1692 from Scarsdale in Derbyshire and was soon recognized as one of the

---

[69] Others in Massachusetts were Henry Caner of King's Chapel, Mather Byles of North Church, Boston; Ebenezer Thompson of Scituate; John Wiswall of Falmouth and Joshua Weeks of Marblehead.

[70] Beardsley, *op. cit.*, p. 159.

[71] From 1703 to 1779 thirty-two missionaries were supported wholly or in part in Massachusetts and there were thirteen Episcopal churches in that colony in the latter year. "The S. P. G. and the Colonial Church in Massachusetts," by Sir Edward Midwinter. *Hist. Mag. of the Prot. Epis. Church,* Vol. IV, pp. 100–115.

leading men in the colony. Appointed a member of the Governor's Council almost at once, he continued active in New York politics throughout his life. At the same time he engaged in extensive land speculation and carried on numerous business enterprises. The last manor to be granted in the British Empire was his Scarsdale Manor in Westchester county, erected in 1701. He was mayor of New York City 1711–13; Colonel of the Westchester militia and judge of the county court. Beside all this he was an active and enthusiastic churchman.

. . . if this man of steady purposes had one determination more sharply marked than any other, it was that the Church of England should follow the English flag, a safe, well-ordered polity, the decentist if not the only road to heaven.[72]

He gave full support to Governor Fletcher in his attempt to secure the establishment of the Church in New York, and it was largely through his clever manipulation that the Episcopal Church got its start in New York City.

As has been noted above, the first attempt to secure an Anglican minister in New York under the *Ministry Act* was defeated when a majority of dissenters were chosen vestrymen. Instead of an Anglican minister they selected William Vesey, a native of Massachusetts, a graduate of Harvard and a Presbyterian. Hardly had he begun his ministry in New York before Caleb Heathcote persuaded him to conform to the Church of England, and he at once departed for England to secure Episcopal orders. This act of Vesey's, however, was not as unusual as it might appear at this distance. The leading Presbyterians in England at this time were generally willing to accept the Low-Church Episcopalianism of the Archbishop Usher model and there was little difference in the polity of Low-Church Episcopalianism and High-Church Presbyterianism. It is, however, true that Vesey was offered better support by Colonel Heathcote if he would consent to come over into the Church. Vesey's conversion was complete and he became an ardent churchman. The year of his ordination (1697) Trinity

---

[72] Dixon Ryan Fox, *Caleb Heathcote, Gentleman Colonist, 1666–1721*. New York: 1926.

Church was organized. "By easy methods," to use Heathcote's words, "the people were soon wrought into good opinion of the church" in other communities in the vicinity of New York, and before the Colonel's death (1721) Episcopal worship had been established at Westchester, Rye, New Rochelle, Eastchester and Yonkers. This was accomplished through the full cooperation of the S. P. G., for the Venerable Society had no more enthusiastic supporter than the Westchester Colonel.[73]

VI

AGITATION FOR AN AMERICAN BISHOP

No ONE will dispute the fact that the Episcopal Church was greatly handicapped in performing its work in the colonies by the absence of bishops. Since the bishop was the only ordaining authority young colonials who desired to enter the Church were compelled to journey to England. That this involved grave risk the long list of those who died on the way of smallpox alone is ample proof.[74] Any church without an effective means of administering discipline, especially on a crude and rough frontier, is bound to acquire an unsavory reputation. This was the situation which the Church of England faced in the American colonies, deprived of the supervisory and disciplinary authority of bishops. It is not surprising, therefore, that there should have been continuous efforts to secure colonial bishops on the part of those who had the interests of the Church at heart. To one unacquainted with all the facts in the case the whole situation seems an anomaly. In the Spanish and Portuguese colonies an entire hierarchy of the Roman Catholic Church was soon established and by the end of

---

[73] Charles A. Briggs, *American Presbyterianism, its Origin and Early History* (New York: 1885), pp. 143–152, tells the story from the Presbyterian angle.

[74] One of the arguments used for American bishops was that so many young men who had gone to England for ordination died on the journey. Samuel Johnson wrote in 1766 "ten valuable lives have been lost for want of ordaining powers here, out of the 51 (nigh one in five) that have gone from hence within the compass of my knowledge in little more than forty years; which is a much greater loss to the church here in proportion than she suffered in the times of the persecution in England." (Johnson to Seker, May 2, 1766.) Lambeth Palace MS., Library of Congress Transcripts.

the eighteenth century there were seven archbishops and forty-
one bishops in Spanish and Portuguese America. What were the
reasons which hindered the Church of England from doing likewise? It was established by law in the mother country and occupied the most privileged position in six of the colonies, and yet
it was prevented from transplanting some of its most essential
machinery to America.

The first important fact to bear in mind in answering this question is that the great majority of the colonists were dissenters from
the Established Church, or at least had no great love or veneration
for it. The peaceful establishment of bishops in America with all
temporal and ecclesiastical powers which they possessed in England would, therefore, have been an impossibility. Even in Virginia, where for the first hundred years at least the Anglicans
were in the undoubted majority, there would have been insuper-
able objections to bishops. There were also objections on the part
of commercial and landed interests who objected to bringing
bishops to the colonies on the ground that by so doing the colonies
would be less attractive to the kind of people upon whom they
depended for the success of their enterprises. With the coming
of the Whigs to power in England political objections were
added. The uncertainty of the Hanover tenure of the English
throne caused the ministers who controlled the government to
advocate the Walpole policy of letting-well-enough-alone.
The dissenters made up an important element in the coalition
upon which the stabilization of the throne depended, and any
move that might alienate dissenter opinion was liable to bring
disaster even to the extent of the overthrow of the reigning house.
Colonial politics also played a part in the episcopal controversy
and in the seventeen sixties and seventies merged with other issues
to help form the state of mind which eventually brought on the
American Revolution.

Active and persistent agitation for an American bishop dates
from the beginning of the eighteenth century and arose out of the
new interest created by the formation of the Society for the
Propagation of the Gospel. In fact Dr. Bray himself made an
earnest plea in behalf of colonial bishops, while John Talbot, one

of the first missionaries as we have seen, was untiring in his agitation of the question from the beginning of his American residence. In 1706 he made a journey to England to urge the cause. This early agitation in the Society resulted in the appointment of a committee to formulate a plan for American bishops. As finally submitted the plan provided for four American bishops, two in the West Indies and one each in Williamsburg, Virginia, and Burlington, New Jersey, where Talbot resided. The question as to how they were to be supported was left more or less in the air. This scheme was submitted to Parliament, but the Queen's death (1715) put a stop to the whole procedure. When the same plan was submitted to George I and his ministers it fell on deaf ears. This was the nearest success ever obtained by any plan to secure colonial bishops. The agitation continued, however, in one form or another to the very end of the colonial period.[75]

The three bishops of London most active in furthering the colonial episcopate were Henry Compton (1675–1713), Edmund Gibson, (1723–48), and Thomas Sherlock, (1748–61). As has been noted, Gibson was the first Bishop of London to secure legal jurisdiction over the colonial Church and manifested his interest in the colonies by securing detailed information in regard to every American parish through elaborate questionnaires which he caused to be sent out in 1724.[76] The very year he entered upon his duties as Bishop of London he presented a memorial favoring colonial bishops, and twenty-two years later, near the end of his life, he made an offer of £1000 toward the support of a colonial bishop, provided one should be sent during his lifetime. Sherlock, however, was far more active. Immediately on assuming office he presented to the King a memorial on the state of the Church in the colonies and urged the need of a resident bishop. He also sent an agent to America to sound out colonial opinion. In 1749–50 he prepared a document entitled "Considerations relating to Ecclesiastical Government in his Majesty's Dominions in America"

---

[75] Cross, *op. cit.*, is the standard treatment of this question. W. W. Manross, *op. cit.*, Chapter viii, is an excellent recent summary.

[76] Perry, *op. cit.* Vol. I, pp. 261–334; Vol. II, pp. 136–137; Vol. III, pp. 147–155; Vol. IV, pp. 190–232. The above dates represent the period of incumbency of the See of London.

and entered into an extensive correspondence on the subject with some of the principal ministers of state. As a consequence of his activity rumors began to float about in America that bishops were soon to be sent over. The attitude of the King's ministers, however, that has been noted, rendered such an outcome an impossibility.[77]

In America agitation for bishops began first among the S. P. G. missionaries in the Middle Colonies, especially centering in the missionary at Burlington, New Jersey, John Talbot. With the rise, however, of a native clergy in New England, following the conversion to the Church of Timothy Cutler and his associates in 1722 a new phase of the agitation began. Samuel Johnson and Timothy Cutler never missed an opportunity in their correspondence with English Church officials to urge the matter upon them. Cutler especially displayed great arrogance and his assumption of superiority, which was more than the Congregational clergy could bear, did more harm than good to the cause.

Writing to the Bishop of London on April 24, 1751, Cutler stated, that with the Church of England "compleated by the Residence of a Bishop" its "increase would be out of the societies of the Dissenters, perhaps to the breaking up of some of them." With such an attitude it is easy to understand the bitter pamphlet warfare between the New England Anglican and Congregational clergy which began in the seventeen thirties and continued until the end of the colonial period. The Congregational clergy naturally resented the sending of the S. P. G. missionaries among them, implying a low state of religion and morals in New England.[78] The two leading Congregational ministers in Boston, Jonathan Mayhew and Charles Chauncy, became the flaming leaders of New England's opposition to an American episcopate. The excitement caused by the passage of the Stamp Act (1765) and the resistance

---

[77] The objections to colonial bishops in America held by the Whig ministers are summarized in a letter of Horatio Walpole, a member of the Privy Council and a brother of Robert Walpole, to Thomas Seker, at that time Bishop of Oxford and later Archbishop of Canterbury, dated January 2, 1750–51. (Cross, *op. cit.*, pp. 118–122.)

[78] The manuscripts in the London residence of the Bishop of London, Fulham Palace, and in the Lambeth Palace, the residence of the Archbishop of Canterbury contain many letters and documents bearing on this controversy. Transcripts of much of this material may be found in the Library of Congress.

it aroused set off the Anglicans from their fellow New Englanders politically, since nearly all the Anglican missionaries urged non-resistance to the act and took pains to point out to the English authorities that their work in America enhanced the power of the crown in the colonies.[79]

In the Middle Colonies the controversy was between the Anglicans and the Presbyterians. There too a pamphlet and newspaper war was begun, and continued until the outbreak of the Revolution. William Livingston, a Presbyterian lawyer in New York, led the attack, and was ably supported by two associates in the law, John M. Scott and William Smith, Jr. All were graduates of Yale College. The controversy over the King's College charter was but a phase of the larger issue of the growing Anglican influence in the colonies and the agitation for a colonial episcopate. Here too it merged with political issues after 1765. Thomas B. Chandler, a S. P. G. missionary in New Jersey, led the Anglican forces. In connection with the Stamp Act controversy he asserted that "the best security in the colonies does and must arise from the Principles of Submission and Loyalty taught by the Church."

Resolutions and Memorials adopted by a series of clerical conventions in New England and the Middle Colonies were another means used by the missionary clergy in attempting to secure colonial bishops. All of them stressed the loyalty of the colonial churchmen to the Crown and the mother country as a reason why their requests for bishops should be heeded. They could not understand, in the light of their record of loyalty to the Crown, why the home officials could not see the political expediency of strengthening the colonial Church as much as possible.

Another thing which greatly troubled the New England and

---

[79] The latter phases of the Episcopal controversy are elaborately treated by Richard J. Hooker, *The Anglican Church and the American Revolution.* (Typed Ph.D. thesis, University of Chicago, 1942.)

The death of the S. P. G. missionary at Braintree, Massachusetts, was the occasion for an attack upon the S. P. G. missionaries in New England by a writer in the *Boston Gazette,* Feb. 21, 1767 (quoted in Hooker). Ironically he pictured the unspeakable hardships endured by the missionaries in their travels "about the rugged wilderness and Lakes of Braintree, and from cottage to cottage, with incredible toil, endeavouring to turn the miserable Barbarians from darkness to Light and from the powers of Satan etc. . . ."

Middle Colony clergy was the indifference of the southern clergy
to the whole question. Samuel Johnson in a letter to the Rector of
Trinity Parish (New York) in 1765 bemoans the fact that "the
southern clergy, as far I [he] can [could] learn" were totally
averse to bishops. "They are now," he says, "their own masters,
quite independent of the people, and therefore do not chuse a
Master! Besides," he remarks, "its too notorious that no bishop,
unless a very abandoned one, would put up with the lives they in
general lead. . . ." In a letter the following year to the Bishop of
London (Oct. 8, 1766) he makes the same complaint, adding that
the very fact that in some of the colonies where the Church is
established they are "insensible of their miserable condition" is one
of the "strongest reasons for sending the bishops." "Never having
had any Ecclesiastical order . . . the cause of religion for want of
it, is sunk and sinking to the lowest ebb . . ."

The low opinion of religious conditions in Virginia during the
eighteenth century has doubtless been partly due to such disparaging remarks as those contained in the letters to the Anglican
authorities in England on the part of the more zealous New
England and Middle Colony missionary clergy. The Virginia
gentlemen who dominated the Church vestries and controlled
the clergy were often men who had a real religious concern. This
interest in religion is revealed in the large number of religious
books which made up a considerable portion of the libraries of
the great tobacco planters. It was not uncommon to find that
more than a third of the books in many of these gentlemen's
libraries were of a religious nature, including books of devotion
such as Allestree's *The Whole Duty of Man,* Taylor's *The Rule
and Experience of Holy Living* and its companion volume *The
Rules and Experience of Holy Dying.* Nor were the books entirely
confined to works by Anglican authors, for such Puritan works
as those of William Ames and Calvin's *Institutes* as well as the
Quaker Barclay's *Apology* frequently found a place. The Virginia
planter looked upon religious books as an essential part of his
reading. Though their outward effect upon his life may have been
less in evidence than might be desired, nevertheless he had a real
respect for religion and looked upon it as an essential part of the
civilization he was helping to build.

The religious attitude of one great Virginia planter, Robert Carter, is revealed in the following extract from a letter to his London agent in 1720 giving the latter instructions as to his desires for his sons who were in school in England.

Let others take what courses they please in the bringing up of their posterity, I resolve the principles of our holy religion shall be instilled into mine betimes; as I am of the Church of England way, so I desire they shall be. But the high-flown up notions, and the great stress that is laid upon ceremonies, any farther than decency and conformity, are what I cannot come into the reason of. Practical godliness is the substance—these are but the shell.[80]

All this would indicate that some of the Anglican lay leaders in Virginia were not as benighted as the S. P. G. missionaries would have us believe.

In attempting to secure support for their enterprise, a New York and New Jersey convention in 1771 deputed two of their members to go to Virginia for that purpose. They succeeded in securing a vote of approval from a thinly attended Virginia clerical convention. The net result proved a boomerang, however, for two Virginia clergymen openly protested the action and received a vote of thanks from the Virginia House of Burgesses for their resistance to it. The plain fact in the matter was that the Maryland and Virginia clergy were opposed to a colonial episcopate and on the same grounds as the Presbyterians and Congregationalists. In other words, they looked upon a colonial bishop as "just another agency of British tyranny."

The series of aggressive Anglican conventions noted above was one of the factors which brought together the Connecticut Congregationalists and the Middle Colony Presbyterians in a series of conventions which met annually from 1766 to 1775. Their main purpose was to resist the demand for colonial bishops. One of the means adopted by them was to enter into correspondence with the influential Dissenter Committee in London which in turn

---

[80] Louis B. Wright (ed.), *Letters of Robert Carter, The Commercial Interests of a Virginia Gentleman,* San Marino, California. The Huntington Library, 1940. Also Louis L. Wright, "Pious Reading in Colonial Virginia," *The Journal of Southern History,* Vol. VI (1940), pp. 383–392.

intervened with the ministers of state. They professed to have no objection to "harmless and inoffensive Bishops" whose function would be solely religious and ecclesiastical, but they apprehended the introduction into America of bishops with political as well as ecclesiastical authority. If Parliament, they argued, could create dioceses and appoint bishops, nothing could hinder them from establishing tithes, forbidding the performing of marriages and funerals by dissenting ministers. In fact they might forbid dissent entirely, make schism a crime and impose penalties even to the forfeiture of life and property.[81]

---

[81] *Minutes of the General Convention of Delegates appointed by the Synod of New York and Philadelphia and the General Association of Connecticut, 1766–1775.* William H. Roberts (Ed.), Philadelphia: 1904. Bound with the *Records of the Presbyterian Church in the United States of America etc. 1706–1788.*

III

The Swarming of the Puritans

THE GREAT VOGUE which the economic interpretation of history has had these past forty years and more has been particularly hard on the Puritans. In fact, for many historians of the last generation any stick has been good enough with which to beat the Puritans. Yet any attempt to interpret from a purely economic angle what happened in New England in the seventeenth century is bound to misunderstand, if it does not miss entirely, the basic element in early New England history.[1]

I

TYPES OF ENGLISH PURITANS

THE CORE of the early Puritan movement was a body of leaders who desired to replace the Anglican Establishment with the ecclesiastical system which John Calvin had perfected in Geneva, and which had been successfully transplanted to Scotland. In other words, English Puritanism was in its beginning predominately Presbyterian; both in doctrine and polity it was Calvinistic and aimed at displacing the episcopal government of the

---

[1] Samuel Eliot Morison in refuting the statement made by James Truslow Adams in his *Founding of New England* (p. 121) that the people of early Massachusetts, as a whole, were not Puritans, and that "four out of five" had no sympathy with the Puritan Church concludes that "religion, not economics nor politics, was the center and focus of the Puritan dissatisfaction with England, and the Puritan migration to New England." (Appendix, p. 246.) Perry Miller in his *Orthodoxy in Massachusetts* (Foreword) takes a like view when he states that "In the sixteenth and seventeenth [centuries] certain men of decisive character took religion seriously . . . they often followed spiritual dictates in comparative disregard to all ulterior considerations," and it was predominately men of this stamp who led the great migration to Massachusetts and who laid the foundation for New England.

James Truslow Adams, *The Founding of New England,* Boston: 1921; Samuel Eliot Morison, *Builders of the Bay Colony,* Boston: 1930; Perry Miller, *Orthodoxy in Massachusetts,* Cambridge: 1933.

Church of England with the Presbyterian system of polity—the prelate to give place to the presbytery. The sharp rejection by King James at the Hampden Court Conference of their proposal to make the Established Church Presbyterian was a bitter disappointment to them, and led them to seek Parliamentary support against the King and the bishops. And yet the Presbyterians did not repudiate the kingly authority over the Church, nor the idea of a national uniformity of religion. In their view of the Church they were in agreement with the Anglicans, that it (the Church) is composed of all those who honor the ministry of the Word, and the administration of the Sacraments. Since it was impossible to tell in every case who were of the elect, and since unity required that all should be subject to church discipline, the non-elect as well as the elect are to be accounted members of the Church.[2]

Nevertheless the question as to what constituted a true Church divided English Puritanism and gave rise to Congregationalism. And the same question, in turn, divided Congregationalism into Separatist and non-Separatist bodies. A Young Puritan, Robert Browne, was the first (in 1581) to advance the view that only persons who could prove that they were of the elect could be true Church members, and that any Church containing the non-elect was therefore not a true Church.[3] To qualify for membership in the true Church, the Congregationalists contended, a person must give sure evidence of Christian character, and relate a satisfactory conversion experience before the congregation. To form a true Church a group of "proved saints" must come together voluntarily, make a confession of their faith, bind themselves by a covenant of allegiance to Christ as king and prophet, and promise to obey his laws. A second essential of the true Church was its self-sufficiency.

Thus every church was a separate unit, independent of all outside control; hence all directing bodies, as synods, presbyteries

---

[2] The Calvinistic ideal was a Church composed of the elect only, but Calvin concluded, for the purposes of an imperfect world, that this was impossible of achievement. Calvin's *Institutes of the Christian Religion,* Sixth Am. edition, 2 vols. Philadelphia: 1928, Book IV, Chapter 1, Parts 7–9.

[3] See extracts from Browne's *Booke which Sheweth the Life and Manner of All True Christians,* 1582, in Williston Walker's *Creeds and Platforms of Congregationalism,* New York: 1905, pp. 18–27.

and bishops or hierarchical officials were unscriptural and unnecessary. This, they believed, was definitely set forth in the Scriptures and therefore obligatory, and all other Churches holding to other systems, whether Presbyterian or Anglican, were wrong and therefore not true Churches. Those holding such views found it necessary to withdraw from the Established Church, since it contained within its folds the non-elect. Such were the Separatists. Though withdrawing from the national Church, they did not thereby reject the idea of national uniformity in religion, nor seek to destroy the ruler's authority over the Church; rather they would only shut him out of the internal affairs of particular Churches, since no intermediary could come between God and His chosen.

Toward the close of Elizabeth's reign still another group of Puritans arose, agreeing with the Separatists in restricting Church membership to the proved elect and in the independence of each congregation, but refusing to accept their conclusion that the Church of England was not a true Church. They held to the fiction that unbeknown to bishops and government there always had been some true saints in every Church of England congregation, and that they carried on the Congregational essentials even unknown to themselves, and that therefore there had been preserved a kernel of truth "in the husks of corruption." They preserved the voluntary principle by stating that if earnest Christians came to the services voluntarily, the reprobate who came under compulsion should be disregarded. Thanks to their genius for sophistry, following the lead of William Bradshaw and William Ames, the principal Puritan casuists, these non-Separatist Congregationalists could assert their loyalty to the Scriptural polity of the Separatists and at the same time avow their loyalty to the Church of England, and also to the principle of compulsory uniformity. Though just as emphatic as were the Separatists in their condemnation of the Presbyterians, at the same time they repudiated Separatism and avowed themselves in communion with the Established Church.[4]

---

[4] For this discussion of the Puritan groups I am principally indebted to Perry Miller's *Orthodoxy in Massachusetts*, a fresh and understanding study based on a whole reading of the sources.

This pathetic attempt of the non-Separatist Congregationalists to prove their loyalty to the Church of England undoubtedly was due partly to the fact that as a class they had much more to lose than had the Separatists by an open break with the Establishment, with all it meant in the way of social and political prestige. Their better economic and social position made them the more timid. But in the long run, open and avowed separation proved the wiser course, for the reasons advanced by the non-Separatists to prove their loyalty to the national Church convinced no one, not even themselves. It is not surprising, therefore, that in the reign of Charles First, as John Cotton claimed, the Separatists were better treated by the authorities than were the non-Separatists. This fact Roger Williams explains with the penetrating statement that "It is a principle in nature to prefer a professed enemy before a pretended friend."

It is necessary to keep in mind the essential differences between these several groups of sixteenth and seventeenth century Puritans if the part taken by each of them in the colonization of New England is to be understood.[5]

II

PLYMOUTH

THIS IS not the place to recount the story, so often told, of the flight of the Separatists in 1608, from the counties of East Anglia to the hospitable shores of Holland. Nor will it be necessary here to enumerate the several factors which were responsible for causing that little company of humble Englishmen, after some ten fairly successful years in Leyden, to look with longing eyes across the broad Atlantic to the New World. The forming of a partnership with Thomas Weston and seventy London adventurers was the fortunate circumstance which enabled the Pilgrims to hire the *Mayflower* and secure the necessary supplies for the long voyage. Weston had obtained a patent to settle lands in Virginia and with that in hand he had hurried to Leyden to interest the Sep-

---

[5] For an illuminating discussion of the term "Puritan" see Adams, *op. cit.,* p. 65.

aratists in entering into a partnership with him and his associates. After some delay an unincorporated joint-stock company had been formed, in which Weston and his associates were to furnish the money and supplies for the founding of a colony in America, while the Leyden Pilgrims were to furnish nothing but themselves and their capacity to work. It was the already widespread reputation of the American fisheries which lured Weston to this undertaking and furnished the Pilgrims their chief prospect of repaying the seven thousand pounds the London partners were to furnish. Thus was set the stage for the establishment of the first Puritan colony in America.[6]

On August 5, 1620 two little vessels set sail from Southampton; the *Speedwell* of sixty tons burden had been purchased by the Pilgrims from the proceeds of the sale of their Leyden property, to bring them from Holland to Southampton; the *Mayflower,* hired by Weston, was a sturdy, hundred and eighty ton ship, square-rigged, double-decked and slow sailing. The smaller of the ships, after two starts, was found entirely unseaworthy and it was regretfully decided that she must be left behind and the *Mayflower* was to go on alone with as many colonists as could be crowded in her.

Of the one hundred and forty-nine on board, forty-eight were officers and crew; of the one hundred and one prospective colonists, sixty-six were from London and Southampton and only thirty-five from Leyden. Nor were they all Separatists. Of the thirty-one .children on board at least seven of them were not the children of any of the passengers, and it has been conjectured that they might have been waifs being sent out to Virginia by the City of London, a practice which became increasingly common as colonization proceeded. At least nine of the company were indentured servants or hired artisans of one sort or another. It is definitely known that five of the adults, including John Alden and Myles Standish, were not Separatists. Alden was a cooper

---

[6] Charles M. Andrews, *The Colonial Period in American History: The Settlements,* New Haven: 1934, Vol. I, Chapters xiii to xviii and xx and xxi, is the most recent account of the establishment of the Puritan colonies in America, and these chapters are among the best in his monumental work. See also R. P. Stearns, *Congregationalism in the Dutch Netherlands,* Chicago: Am. Soc. of Church History, 1940.

employed at Southampton to look after the beer hogsheads, and Standish was a soldier of fortune who had served in the Low Countries and was employed by the Pilgrims to accompany them. Alden, instead of returning to England, as doubtless he had intended, remained in the colony, probably because of Priscilla Mullens, and later became a member of the Church. There is some doubt as to whether Standish ever became a member of Pilgrim Church. The majority of those on board were undoubtedly affiliated with the Church of England, but the Pilgrim minority was a homogeneous group, and since they had instituted the whole enterprise they naturally furnished political as well as religious leadership, though their chief concern was the maintenance of their religion.

As the *Mayflower* came to land not in the territory provided for in their patent, but within the bounds of New England, the Pilgrims were compelled the next year to secure a new patent from the Council of New England. It used to be thought that the *Mayflower's* coming to Cape Cod was an act of treachery on the part of the Captain, who was supposed to have had a secret agreement with the Council of New England to bring the ship to their territory, but this view has been completely discredited and the good character of the *Mayflower's* captain, Christopher Jones of Harwich, has been fully established. But whatever may have been the set of circumstances which brought the Pilgrims to New England instead of Virginia, it was a fortunate turn of affairs for them. For Anglican Virginia had little love for Puritans and even less for Separatists, and the Pilgrim Church would have fared no better there than it had in the mother country.

Since the primary purpose of the Pilgrims' coming to America was to preserve their peculiar type of church polity, which they believed was the only kind sanctioned by the Bible, they subordinated all their interests to that one concern. Among the non-Separatists on board ship discontent and near mutiny had already appeared; it might easily develop into open rebellion after landing. The Pilgrim leaders fully realized that if their religious integrity was to be preserved they must keep control of the affairs of the colony, once it had been established. The Mayflower Compact, based on the Scrooby Church Covenant, was the immediate result of this realization. Until Plymouth was incorporated as a part of Massachusetts the *Compact,* signed by forty-one adults in the cabin of the ship, remained the basis of government although it was later supplemented by the patents received from the Council of New England.[7]

For several years after the Pilgrims had established themselves at Plymouth they were without a minister, since it was thought best that their beloved pastor, John Robinson, should remain at Leyden with the major portion of the congregation, while to Elder Brewster was committed the spiritual leadership of the "remnant who had braved the hardships of colonization." The merchant-partners in London were anxious that young men should be added to the colony, since they would be more effective as fishermen and fur gatherers. They therefore showed little inclination to aid in the bringing out of the remainder of the Leyden congregation. Least of all were they interested in bringing John Robinson, for his reputation as a dangerous radical might well injure the plantation in the eyes of the British authorities.

Finally in 1624 the London partners sent out John Lyford as the Pilgrims' minister. Lyford was a Church of England clergyman who professed an interest in Puritan principles, but was evidently a "canting hypocrite, a sort of lascivious Uriah Heep," as Adams calls him. Being unordained Brewster had not presumed to administer the Sacraments, and thus the colonists had been without means of securing either baptism or the Lord's Supper for a period of four years. Though anxious for the Sacraments, the Pilgrims soon discovered that Lyford was an Anglican "snake in the grass" who soon was plotting with the hot-headed trader, John Oldham, to set up not only a rival colony but a rival Church as well. To the Pilgrims this was nothing short of treason against the principles which had brought them to the New World,

---

[7] The Mayflower Compact was the first example of the "Plantation Covenant" which was to be used over and over again "in the land of covenants, ecclesiastical and civil." H. L. Osgood, *The American Colonies in the Seventeenth Century,* New York: 1930, Vol. I, p. 291.

and there was nothing to be done but to bring the traitor to trial. He was•expelled from the colony.[8]

The dissolution of the partnership with the London merchants, soon after Lyford's expulsion, was not entirely to the credit of the Plymouth leaders. From the beginning Plymouth had resented any attempt on the part of their merchant-partners to take any active part in the control of the colony, and the Lyford affair brought things to a crisis. Discouraged over the prospect of receiving any adequate returns from their partnership with such religious fanatics, the merchants sought a way to end their agreement. The arrangement finally made was that the colony was to purchase the interest of the London merchants for £1,800 to be paid in nine annual installments, and also to assume the £600 indebtedness due the company's creditors. This business arrangement and the forming of a holding company of eight of the Plymouth leaders to meet these obligations is the earliest example of Yankee business acumen, and its successful conclusion was to them, no doubt, a clear indication of the Lord's favor.

One of the immediate results of the buying out of their London partners and of thus becoming their own masters was their determination to bring out the remainder of the Leyden congregation. This was done within the next few years. John Robinson, however, was never to set foot on American soil. He died in Holland in 1626. Nevertheless his was undoubtedly the most potent influence in shaping the ideas and ideals of this first body of Puritans to establish a colony on American soil.

Meanwhile other emigrants began filtering into the region of the Plymouth settlement. Some were helpful neighbors, others were most undesirable. The most notorious of them all was the Thomas Morton colony, Merry Mount, located in what is now the town of Quincy. Though Governor Bradford's account of the "goings on" at Merry Mount doubtless was colored by his Puritan spectacles, yet there was much to justify Plymouth's interference beside the famous May Pole and the dancing, such as selling arms to the Indians and the sexual looseness which went on with the Indian squaws. James Truslow Adams uses the May Pole inci-

---

[8] Andrews in his account of this affair more or less whitewashes Lyford. *Op. cit.*, I, p. 276.

dent as a text for moralizing on the evil consequences of the whole Puritan opposition to gaiety and amusement, the suppression of which, he thinks, only served to foster the grosser form of vice; but it seems that at Merry Mount the grosser forms flourished to an even greater extent than the lesser ones.

It was not until 1629 that the Pilgrims' church secured a satisfactory minister in Ralph Smith. Toward the close of the summer of 1631 Roger Williams began a two years' residence at Plymouth, and while there served as an assistant to Ralph Smith, though he actually held no office and received no pay. The following is a description of a service held in the Plymouth church in 1632 on the occasion of a visit to the colony of Governor Winthrop and Rev. John Wilson of Boston as recorded by Winthrop:

On the Lord's day there was a sacrament, which they did partake in; and in the afternoon, Mr. Roger Williams propounded a question to which the pastor Mr. Smith, spoke briefly; then Mr. Williams prophesied; and then the governor of Plymouth spoke to the question; after him the elder, Brewster; then some two or three more of the congregation. Then the elder desired the governour of Massachusetts and Mr. Wilson to speak to it, which they did. When this was ended, the deacon, Mr. Fuller, put the congregation in mind of their duty of contribution; whereupon the governour and all the rest went down to the deacon's seat, and put into the box, and then returned.

Here is an example of freedom and democracy in worship which constituted the basic cause of the Pilgrims' coming to the New World.

In the successful establishment of the Pilgrims' colony at Plymouth the way was charted for the great migration which was to bring some twenty thousand Puritans to America between the years 1628 and 1640.

III

THE GREAT MIGRATION

WHEN THE great Puritan migration to America began the English had already established numerous successful colonies, not alone on the mainland of the American continent, but also on the islands of the West Indies. Indeed in 1640 there were more Englishmen on the three islands of Nevis, St. Kitts and the Barbadoes than were to be found in all the several mainland colonies. In other words, by the end of the first third of the seventeenth century colonization was no longer in the experimental stage. Recent careful historians have been at pains to set forth the economic background of the great Puritan migration, and no one will or can dispute the great importance of the economic motives. It has been pointed out that in the very region in England where Puritanism had taken its strongest hold economic and financial difficulties, due to an immediate crisis in the cloth trade, were causing unrest among all classes. Among those economically affected in East Anglia was a group of well-to-do and influential Puritans, who, Andrews states, "formed a veritable clan, knit by ties of blood, marriage, propinquity and personal friendship, and by common loyalty to religious ideals." [9]

An important figure in this group was John Winthrop, a Puritan squire of Suffolk, who was of an influential family and had attended Trinity College, Cambridge. He had long been interested in colonization, having sent one of his sons to the Barbadoes to establish a plantation, and was fully aware of other colonizing activities. In addition to the fact that his economic interests had not prospered, he was saddened by the growing corruption of English life. He deplored the degraded condition of the schools and universities and was indignant at the treatment meted out to the Puritan clergy. The increasing acceptance of Arminianism among the Established Church clergy he considered fatal to vital religion, and the King's policy of carrying on the government without Parliament brought gloom and disappointment to all sincere Puritans.

In the latter sixteen twenties certain colonizing organizations, which were to be the instruments in bringing out the great body of Puritans, were in process of formation. The Massachusetts Bay Company, chartered March 4, 1628/29, was to be the principal

---

[9] Andrews, *op. cit.*, I, p. 383.

Puritan colonizing agency. It was preceded by the Dorchester Company, a semi-religious corporation formed under the leadership of Rev. John White, a Presbyterian Puritan, to combine fishing with religion. Made up of merchants, small traders and clergymen, largely from the southwest counties, it soon proved a failure and was merged in 1628 into the New England Company, and the New England Company in turn into the Massachusetts Bay Company. In the process of change the western county members gave place to a body of non-Separatist Congregational Puritans from the eastern counties. This new company concerned itself with maintaining the settlement at Salem, which had been begun in 1626 by a few nondescript settlers sent over by the Dorchester Company. Two years later (1628) it was taken over by a new body of colonists representing the Massachusetts Bay Company under the leadership of stubborn, narrow-minded John Endicott.[10]

To Salem in the spring of 1629 came two non-Separatist Puritan clergymen, Francis Higginson and Samuel Skelton, and on July 10th of that year the Salem church was formed on an independent, congregational basis. It was founded on a mutual agreement or compact, by which the members bound themselves to the Lord by an indissoluble covenant. Skelton and Higginson were chosen pastor and teacher, respectively, and although both had been episcopally ordained, the congregation, through some of its "gravest members" proceeded to set them apart by the laying on of hands. This was the first non-Separatist Congregational Church in America, and the mother of a long line of similar churches to be organized in New England.

Until recent years the principal reason assigned as to why the Salem church became Congregational in polity was the influence exerted by the Plymouth church, especially through the kindly ministrations of deacon-doctor Fuller, who had been loaned to Salem by Plymouth during the first sickly winter. The studies of Perry Miller, however, have completely overthrown this view. He has shown that the Puritans who established the Massachusetts

---

[10] James D. Phillips, *Salem in the Seventeenth Century*, Boston: 1933; *Salem in the Eighteenth Century*, Boston: 1937.

Bay colony were already Congregationalists of the non-Separatist variety, which accounts for the oft-quoted farewell speech of Francis Higginson in which he called the Church of England their "dear mother." [11] The Salem church and the other Massachusetts Bay churches which followed the Salem model, did not therefore adopt Congregational polity primarily because of the influences coming out of Plymouth, but would have proceeded along the same lines even if there had never been a Plymouth church or a Plymouth colony. Both Plymouth and Salem were equally Congregational, but the former was rigidly Separatist, the latter non-Separatist. Both opposed the use of the Prayer Book, Salem equally with Plymouth, as shown by the expulsion of John and Samuel Browne who had attempted to inaugurate an Anglican service in Salem, although both were freemen and men of influence and were members of Governor Endicott's Council. [12]

The difference between Pilgrim and Puritan attitudes toward the Church of England and the royal authority may thus be summarized: The Pilgrims repudiated the Church of England in all its parts, but recognized the King as their royal master; the Puritans desired to build a state without a king, and rejected as far as they dared the royal authority, but the English Church they recognized as their "dear mother" in all things spiritual and never forbade their people when in England from attending services in the parish churches. [13]

It would be difficult to overestimate the importance of the adoption of the Congregational form of Church polity by the New England churches, in terms of the future of democracy. It is true that the democratic seed here planted was of slow development, but there was no other soil in the world so well adapted to its full unfolding as was that of the American frontier. The oft-quoted statement by Gooch, that "democracy is the child of the Reformation, not the Reformers," suggests a similar generalization that New England democracy was the child of Congre-

---

[11] For relatively recent statements of the old view see Adams, *op. cit.*, pp. 131–132, and W. W. Sweet, *The Story of Religion in America*, New York: 1939, pp. 72–74.

[12] Miller, *op. cit.*, Chapter v, especially pp. 127–128.

[13] Andrews, *op. cit.*, I, p. 372.

gationalism, not of the Congregational leaders.[14] To the Puritan leaders in New England, democracy was a dangerous thing in a government such as theirs, pledged to carry out God's will; for, they asked "How could ungodly rulers know the will and purposes of God?" Thus they felt under the necessity of keeping the godly minority in control. Winthrop argued that there was no democracy in Israel, and that among civil states it was the meanest form of government.

From these, as from many similar statements that might be cited, it can be seen plainly that the New England fathers were not in the least interested in the setting up of a democratic state. Rather they conceived it to be their task to rebuild God's true Church in the New World, where it might serve as an example to the mother Church in the Old. To do this they were willing and even glad to meet seemingly unsurmountable difficulties. Nor would they tolerate any form of opposition, whether religious or political, in carrying out their holy endeavor. In ridding their churches of what they considered sin, idolatry and error they were forced to use what seemed to outsiders harsh and inhuman methods. But to them the cause justified the action and rendered it a holy duty.

On August 26, 1629 a momentous meeting convened, in that ancient university center, Cambridge. It was made up of twelve of the leading members of the Massachusetts Bay Company who there entered into an agreement to be

ready in our persons and with such of our families as are to go with us and such provisions as we are able conveniently to furnish ourselves withal to embark for the said plantacion (Massachusetts Bay) by the first of March next [1630], at such port or ports of this land as shall be agreed upon by the Company, to the end to passe the Seas (under God's protection) to inhabite and continue in New England Provided always that before the last of September next the whole government together with the Patent for the said plantacion bee first by an order of Court legally transferred and established to remayne with us and others which shall inhabit upon the said plantacion.[15]

---

[14] G. P. Gooch, *The History of English Democratic Ideas in the Seventeenth Century,* Cambridge: 1898. Adams, *op. cit.,* pp. 84, 144.

[15] *Massachusetts Hist. Soc. Proceedings,* Vol. 62, pp. 279–280. As to the legality of the transfer of the charter see Andrews, *op. cit.,* I, pp. 390–393.

The importance of this plan to remove the charter from England to America becomes evident when it is understood that the company was an open corporation and therefore new members might come into it and change its whole character and purpose. The transfer of the charter thus prevented this possibility. With the successful accomplishment of this plan on October 29, 1629, the flood-gates of Puritan emigration to America were opened. It also marks the beginning of John Winthrop's leadership in the New England colonization enterprise.

"The greatest exodus that England has known in the entire history of her colonizing activities" was begun when the first contingent of the Winthrop fleet of eleven vessels, brought together at Southampton, sailed on March 29, 1630. During the course of that year seventeen vessels, carrying a thousand passengers, left England for New England. Of these seventeen ships the *Arabella* carried the most historic cargo, for on her were the Winthrops and the Charter. The possession of this instrument gave the New England Puritans the right to govern themselves practically as they pleased. Here was a state in the making

dominated by a powerful conviction as to its place in the divine scheme. It was led by the largest and most important group of men that ever at any time came over the seas to New England; men of wealth and education, of middle-class origin with a quantum of political training, hard headed and dogmatic. . . . They looked upon themselves as commissioned of God to create a purer church and a cleaner social order than those which prevailed at home and were mastered by the idea of the "saving remnant" whom God had elected to do his will.[16]

Though not all those who found their way to New England during the years of the great migration were Puritans, yet the leaders were, and the strength of the colony lay not so much in the number of colonists as in the strength and ability of its leaders.

The swarming of the Puritans on the New England coast led to the rapid formation of new churches, each of them following

---

[16] Andrews, *op. cit.* I, p. 395.

the congenial pattern set by Salem and Plymouth.[17] Walker makes out a strong case for Plymouth influence during these formative years, showing that Plymouth was consulted constantly as well as Salem. By 1645 twenty-three churches had been gathered in Massachusetts, but the total membership was small in comparison with the total population. These years are also notable because of the coming of a whole galaxy of Puritan ministers, destined to furnish the principal leadership in the colony in its formative stage. With Winthrop had come Rev. John Wilson and Rev. George Phillips, the first soon to be chosen teacher, and the latter minister of the Boston church. In 1631 Roger Williams arrived, and then in rapid succession came Thomas Shepard, Thomas Welde, John Cotton, Samuel Stone, Thomas Hooker, Richard Mather, Hugh Peter and numerous others. All were university trained, two thirds of them at Cambridge. Between 1630 and 1641 sixty-five ministers arrived in Massachusetts. Because of the belief held by their flocks that they were divinely inspired, great deference was given their views and judgments, tending to make them opinionated and determined to have their own way. Charles Francis Adams has characterized the first two generations of the New England clergy as theologically learned, highly moral, imbued with a sense of the dignity and duty of their calling, with strong and narrow minds; as a consequence they were bigoted and to the last degree intolerant; "for all men," he says, "are intolerant who in their own conceit know they are right; and upon this point doubt never entered the minds of the typical divines of that generation." [18]

To the Puritan the Scriptures were the source of guidance in both religious and secular affairs, but to interpret them and apply them to any given case was the function of the minister. This, as Adams states, was simply substituting the "Lord Brethren" for the "Lord Bishop"; setting up many local popes for the one at Rome. The Old Testament constituted their fundamental law;

---

[17] Details on the forming of these early churches will be found in Williston Walker's *The History of the Congregational Churches in the United States,* New York: 1894, pp. 109–114.

[18] *Three Episodes in Massachusetts History,* 2 vols., Boston: 1893, I, pp. 383–384; 387–389; 391–392.

the clergy were the supreme court set up rightly to interpret it. Behind every decision was the *Word;* behind the *Word* was God. Religion to the Puritan was an everyday affair, and it must be applied to every interest and every concern of life.[19]

On May 18, 1631 the Massachusetts General Court reached the momentous decision that:

Noe man shalbe admitted to the freedom of this body polliticke, but such as are members of some of the churches within the limits of the same.[20]

Their justification for so limiting the suffrage to church members, which was a flagrant violation of their charter, was that "the body of the commons may be preserved of honest and good men," or in other words, in order to keep the government in the hands of the godly. By this act the government came under the indirect control of the clergy, since their influence in the admission of members to the church was decisive. Previously (October 19, 1630) a change in the method of choosing the Governor and Deputy Governor had been enacted providing that they should be elected by the Assistants from among their own number, and they with the Assistants were to make the laws and select the officers to enforce them. This was in full accord with Winthrop's idea that the power should be kept "in the hands of those whose Christian calling is to govern and that their number should remain as small as possible." [21]

It is often stated that seventeenth century Massachusetts was a theocracy, yet that assertion does not coincide with the facts, if by

---

[19] An extreme Biblicism underlay the Puritan's intolerance. He argued that (1) The Scriptures are definitive for doctrine, polity and government. (2) They are so plainly written that "he that runneth may read." (3) Dissenters are those who misinterpret or misunderstand the Scriptures, and are in error for that reason. (4) It is the duty of the minister to show dissenters where they are in error. Hence the first step in proceeding against a dissenter was to appoint a minister to answer his arguments and point out his errors. (5) Then, if the dissenter still failed to agree, it was not because the Scriptures were not plain enough, but because he willfully persisted in error against the light of his own conscience. Thus John Cotton held that it was wrong to persecute a man against conscience, but argued that no man's conscience compelled him to reject the truth, and therefore to force the truth upon him was no violation of conscience. *Cf.* Perry Miller, *The New England Mind,* New York: 1939, numerous references under "Bible."

[20] *Massachusetts Colonial Records,* I, p. 87.

[21] *Massachusetts Historical Society Collections* (Winthrop Papers), I, p. 5.

a theocracy is meant a government by ecclesiastics. The part played by the Massachusetts clergy in the government was entirely unofficial. They held no political office, though they did express opinions. But their opinions carried weight. On the other hand the Governor and the Assistants were appropriately called "the nursing fathers of the churches," for they concerned themselves with the internal affairs of congregations, settling disputes of many sorts whether of doctrine or polity, and punishing such infractions of the commandments as swearing and Sabbath breaking. They likewise looked into the fitness of ministers, determined where newly arrived ministers should be located, and concerned themselves with heresy charges. They called Synods and ordered the ministers to formulate a confession of faith and a form of discipline. In short it can be said with truth that the Massachusetts clergy had a lesser part in the control of civil government than the civil government had in the control of the Church. Or to use a technical term, Massachusetts was more Erastian than it was theocratic, which is to say that the Church was indirectly concerned in government, but that the government was directly concerned with the affairs of the Church.

IV

The Massachusetts Rebels and the Dispersion of the Puritans

Massachusetts intolerance was one of the principal reasons for the formation of other New England colonies. With the exception of New Haven all the other New England colonies established after Massachusetts Bay owe their origin in a greater or less degree to the clash of religion and politics in the Bay colony. The undercurrent of discontent in Massachusetts from the beginning was much stronger than appears on the surface, and the desire to get beyond her boundaries and outside her control was great enough to cause many to brave anew the hardships of forming new settlements in the wilderness. On the other hand Massachusetts showed an equal willingness to be rid of those out of harmony with her ideas of Church and State. This is succinctly expressed in Nathaniel Ward's remark that, "all Familists, Anabaptists and other enthusiasts shall have free liberty to keepe away from us." Thus Connecticut's, New Hampshire's and Rhode Island's beginnings were the direct result of rebellion in Massachusetts, and to a limited degree rebellion contributed to the peopling of the northern shore of Long Island and northern New Jersey. Some were expelled from Massachusetts as were John Wheelwright, Anne Hutchinson and Roger Williams; others left of their own accord as did Thomas Hooker and the Watertown congregation.

The founders of Rhode Island were only the most conspicuous of the Massachusetts rebels. From the beginning the Massachusetts leaders had adopted the policy of ridding themselves of troublemakers, such as rigid Separatists and Anabaptists, both of whom they considered especially dangerous to the welfare and even the safety of the colony.

Roger Williams and his wife arrived in Massachusetts in February 1631, and were warmly welcomed, for Williams' reputation as a Godly minister had gone before him. In fact, it was expected that he would succeed Mr. John Wilson as teacher of the Boston Church. Williams' refusal of the call, on the ground that the Boston Church was not fully separated from the Established Church, centered the attention of the colonial authorities upon him, and from then on he was under suspicion. Though but twenty-eight years of age, Williams had already reached a position diametrically opposed to the fundamental ideas upon which Massachusetts had been established, and was determined to stand by his views with all the courage and enthusiasm of youth. When a call came to him from the Salem church to the office of teacher to succeed Higginson, who had died, the Boston leaders hurried to send in their protest. It was at this juncture—the autumn of 1631—that Williams took refuge at Plymouth. Here for two years he resided, earning his living by farming and trading with the Indians, at the same time serving as the assistant to Ralph Smith, the minister.

At the end of his Plymouth residence he returned to Salem as teacher of that church. Here was an opportunity of giving wide publicity to his views, and he made the most of it. As a rigid Separatist he refused to have communion with the Boston Church, finally withdrawing from the Salem Church on the ground that it also was not completely separated. At the same time he renounced communion with all New England churches for the same reason. Nor was the question of separation the only one on which he clashed with the Massachusetts authorities. Another was the legality of their right to the land, since they had not purchased it from the Indians, the rightful owners. He also questioned the Church-State relationship in the colony and the right of the State to enforce uniformity or to collect taxes for the support of the ministers, while the King and the charter came in for a share of denunciation.[22]

In a situation such as that which prevailed in Massachusetts, where intolerance was "ingrained in her institutions and the prevailing way of life," Williams' trial and conviction was a foregone conclusion. The outcome was his banishment, which was put into execution in January 1636, in the dead of a New England winter. With snow to his knees and swift rivers to wade, he made his way to Narragansett Bay. His former friendly relations with the Indians of that region, during his Plymouth residence, now stood him in good stead, for they afforded him shelter, food and clothing, and in the spring a grant of land was made to him. Here it was that Williams began his plantation as a "shelter for persons distressed for conscience." From that time forward to the end of his life in 1683, Roger Williams was busily engaged in putting his theories of State-Church relationship into practice in what was to become the colony of Rhode Island.[23]

[22] Miller maintains that the nub of Massachusetts' quarrel with Williams was the non-Separatist position of the colony. *Orthodoxy in Massachusetts*, pp. 157–158.

[23] A number of fresh treatments of Roger Williams have appeared in recent years. The latest, Samuel Hugh Brockunier, *The Irrepressible Democrat Roger Williams*, New York: 1940, is a specialized study of Williams' career as an exemplification of "the democratic upthrust in the seventeenth century." James Ernst, *Roger Williams: New England Firebrand*, New York: 1932, is somewhat vitiated by careless mistakes and failure to annotate the numerous quotations, often inaccurately copied, but based on new sources. Charles M. Andrews, *op. cit.*, Vol. I, pp. 470–476; II, pp. 1–66; V. L. Parrington, *The Colonial Mind, 1620–1800*, New York: 1927, and John M. Mecklin, *The Story of American Dissent*, New York: 1927, are largely interpretative. W. W. Sweet, *Makers of Christianity from John Cotton to Lyman Abbott*, New York: 1937, pp. 47–61, is a brief running account.

Hardly had the Williams case been disposed of before a far more serious affair began to disturb the little Boston community of some two thousand souls. The chief actors in the drama known as the Antinomian controversy were three in number. Anne Hutchinson, who had sat under John Cotton's preaching in Boston, England, arrived with her husband and children in 1634. Henry Vane, son of an English knight of the same name, a generous-minded and honest youth of twenty-three, and an enthusiastic Puritan, arrived in 1635 in the midst of Williams' trial, in time to express sympathy for Williams' views. The Rev. John Wheelwright, a brother-in-law to Mrs. Hutchinson, arrived with his family in 1636.

Within two years of her arrival in Boston Mrs. Hutchinson began to gather the neighbor women into her home or the homes of her acquaintances, at first simply to relay to them the sermon she had heard the previous Sabbath. Soon she was adding her own comment and criticism on the discourse, and it was not long until, as Winthrop states, "she had more resort to her for counsell about matters of conscience than any minister in the country." No wonder the ministers, accustomed to have their discourses accepted as oracles, viewed with alarm the criticisms of this "nimble witted, clever tongued woman." Rev. John Wilson of the Boston Church seems to have been the butt of her sharpest comments, and on one occasion she even left the church as he arose to preach. Thus it is easy to see how she gained ministerial dislike, and likewise, no doubt, it was her boldness and skill in argument which made her popular with the people of Boston. Her greatest mistake seems to have been in playing favorites among the ministers. This she did when she boldly stated that only John Cotton and her brother-in-law John Wheelwright preached a covenant of Grace; all the other ministers, a covenant of works. By that she meant that persons under the covenant of Grace were Christians not because of any "works" they might have performed, but by virtue of the divine spirit prevailing in them. All other so-called Christians lacked that indwelling spirit, and therefore were Christians in name only.

Mrs. Hutchinson's singling out of John Cotton and John

Wheelwright for her approval put them both "on the spot" in the theological tempest which now followed. Wheelwright was already under a cloud as being disputatious and doctrinally unsound. Increased attention was centered upon him by the proposal that he be chosen assistant teacher of the Boston Church. This brought opposition from Winthrop and the proposal was defeated. He then became the minister at Mt. Wollaston—present-day Quincy. Invited to preach the fast day sermon in the Boston Church in January 1637, he took advantage of the occasion roundly to denounce all those who walked in a covenant of works. This open siding with Mrs. Hutchinson, and in John Wilson's own pulpit at that, led the Boston authorities to bring him to trial for sedition. Wheelwright, however, was not without supporters. When it became known that he was to be brought to trial, a petition signed by some forty Boston Church members begged the magistrates to open the trial to the public, whereas it had been begun in secret. The result was Wheelwright's conviction for sedition and contempt of authority, though it was by a bare majority. The feeling in Boston had become so inflamed, however, that sentence was postponed until after the next election for Governor.

This brought the whole sorry affair into politics. Young Henry Vane had been elected Governor in May 1636, eight months after his arrival, and from the start had openly sided with the views of Mrs. Hutchinson and Wheelwright as he had with Williams. If he were reelected both would be safe, at least for another year. Pitted against young Henry Vane was John Winthrop, the candidate of the conservatives. The campaign waxed bitter with personal dislikes and religious antipathies playing their part. The outcome was Vane's defeat. In August the somewhat bumptious youth left the colony, never to return, to play a much larger rôle in the affairs of Cromwell's Commonwealth.

The next turn in affairs was the call of a Synod, the first general Council to be held in New England. It was composed of all the ministers of Massachusetts, with Thomas Hooker and Samuel Stone from Connecticut—some twenty-five in all—together with the body of magistrates. Expenses of the delegates

were met out of the general treasury, an indication of its official
character. The matter to be settled was the whole question of
heresy in the colony. The Synod lasted twenty-four days and
unearthed eighty-two errors entertained by the Hutchinson-
Wheelwright party, or that could be deduced from their teaching.
One of the important results of the Synod was the winning over
of John Cotton to Winthrop's side, leaving the accused entirely
without ministerial support. They were not without friends, however, from among the most influential citizens of the colony.
William Coddington and William Aspinwall, members of the
General Court from Boston, were on their side, as were also John
Coggeshall and Captain John Underhill. The net result of the
Synod's work was the setting up of definite standards of orthodoxy
for the colony, which were to serve as a theological net in which
to catch all those disagreeing with the party in control. And that
it had a political as well as a religious purpose is plainly evident.
With the Synod's work completed, the next meeting of the
General Court in November disposed of Wheelwright and Mrs.
Hutchinson in summary fashion and both were sentenced to
banishment—Wheelwright to become one of the founders of
New Hampshire, Mrs. Hutchinson a co-founder of Rhode
Island.[24]

In their dealing both with the Williams and Anne Hutchinson
cases the Massachusetts leaders desired to make the religious
element involved in them seem of slight importance and placed
the emphasis upon their civil and political significance. Thus they
wanted it to appear that it was not heresy that had exiled Wheelwright and Williams, but sedition. Winthrop spoke for the
leaders in reply to John Coggeshall during the latter's trial.
Coggeshall argued that the charges against him amounted only

---

[24] The classic account of the Antinomian controversy is that of Charles Francis
Adams, *op. cit.,* Vol. I. Andrews' account, *op. cit.,* I, pp. 477–486, is a model of brevity
and clarity. George E. Ellis' *The Puritan Age and Rule in the Colony of Massachusetts,
1629–1685,* New York: 1888, remains the fullest and best treatment. See also Charles
Francis Adams (ed.), *Antinomianism in the Colony of Massachusetts Bay 1636–1638,*
Boston: 1894, which contains the *A Short Story of the Rise, reign, and ruine of the
Antinomians, Familists & Libertines, that infected the Churches of New England,* docu-
ments relating to the examination and trial of Mrs. Hutchinson, and extracts from John
Cotton's *The Way of the Congregational Churches Cleared.*

to difference of opinion, and he knew of no example in Scripture where a man was banished for his judgment. To which Winthrop replied that if the prisoner

had kept his judgment to himself, so as the public peace had not been troubled or endangered by it, we would have left him to himself, for we do not challenge power over men's consciences, but when seditious speeches and practices discover such a corrupt conscience, it is our duty to use authority to reform both.[25]

Massachusetts' relationship to the English government was extremely precarious at the time, and any movement threatening internal unity in the colony was a real danger. But religion was the real issue on both sides. Any admission of Anne Hutchinson's claim that she had direct leadings from the Almighty, not only might lead to a dangerous fanaticism, but it was also an absolute denial of one of the fundamental tenets of Calvinism, that the Scriptures contained all things necessary for man's salvation, and to them nothing was to be added either by "new revelations of the Spirit, or traditions of men." This was to be also the basic reason for Puritan opposition to the Quakers when they were to appear in the colony a generation later. Ten years after the disposal of the Williams, Wheelwright and Hutchinson controversies, the question as to the toleration of other forms of church organization was to arise. This was brought to a head by attempts to form Presbyterian churches at Newbury (1643) and at Hingham (1645), under the leadership of Dr. Robert Child. Since these were the years of Presbyterian dominance in the English government the Massachusetts authorities were given some anxious moments in dealing with this new threat to their control.[26]

Restless Plymouth traders, particularly Edward Winslow and John Oldham, were responsible for making the Connecticut valley known to the Puritan settlers; religious, economic and political discontent led to the mass migration to Connecticut and the formation of that colony. Those who are today familiar with the

---

[25] C. F. Adams, *Three Episodes*, II, p. 564, quoting Winthrop.
[26] George Lyman Kittredge, "Dr. Robert Child the Remonstrant," in the *Publications, The Colonial Society of Massachusetts*, XXI, is fully adequate.

thinness of the soil in the vicinity of Boston, can well understand the scarcity of desirable pasturage and meadow which developed with the rapid increase of population during the great migration, a population to a large degree dependent upon live stock and agriculture. Reports of the broad, rich level meadows along the Connecticut River were inducement enough to draw many from Massachusetts to that region. For such men as John Haynes and Roger Ludlow, men of education and property, who had served in the highest positions in the Bay colony, Massachusetts was beginning to be an uncomfortable place in which to live. This was due not alone to its oligarchic government, but also because there was little chance there for them to exercise the influence which they desired, and they doubtless looked forward to the possibility of building their own little world in a new locality. Rev. Thomas Hooker, the most eloquent of the Bay clergy and the minister of the Newtown congregation, was, as Adams calls him, a "born democrat," and many things in the Massachusetts system of government were displeasing to him. Theologically, also, he was not in full agreement with John Cotton, "the unmitred pope" of Boston. These, and other causes more obscure, account for the movement into Connecticut which began in 1635 and became a veritable exodus the following year, when the Newtown and Dorchester congregations, with their ministers Thomas Hooker, Samuel Stone and John Warham, made their way overland to Connecticut.

Religiously Connecticut and Massachusetts saw eye to eye, that is as far as creed and Church polity were concerned, but in the relation of the Church to the State there were some significant differences. In Connecticut Church membership was not a requirement for the exercise of the suffrage. Hooker held that authority was based on the free consent of the people and that the choice of magistrates belonged to the people. The term "the people," however, as interpreted in the Fundamental Orders of Connecticut, has not the connotation we generally attach to the term, and the result was a considerably restricted democracy. In fact the Connecticut founders had the same general purpose in mind in setting up their government as had the Bay leaders, that is, to keep the best and wisest people in control. In the towns, any man with a competent estate, a good character and a believer in religion, might vote for local officials and for deputies to the colonial assembly, whether a church member or not. But the general colonial affairs were in the control of "freemen," persons chosen to "freemanship" by the general court; these, constituting not more than a third of the adult males, were the real rulers of the colony. Though far from what we mean by democracy today, it was a step ahead of Massachusetts in that direction.

The last of the Puritan colonies to be established was New Haven, begun, as Andrews states, in the vestry of St. Stephen's Church in London, where the Rev. John Davenport was the vicar. The membership of this church was made up of people engaged in mercantile pursuits, strongly imbued with Puritan principles. Davenport, after a residence of several years in Holland where he had fled to escape persecution on the coming of Laud to power, determined to follow his friends, John Cotton and Thomas Hooker, to America. Returning to London in disguise, he set to work to interest his former parishioners in accompanying him. He found in Theophilus Eaton, a former schoolmate and parishioner and now a wealthy merchant, his most enthusiastic supporter and soon a large company were gathered for the American enterprise. In April 1636 two hundred and fifty prospective colonists sailed for Boston, where they probably intended to remain and become a part of that colony. But a two-months stay in the Massachusetts colony, then in the throes of the Anne Hutchinson excitement, was enough to convince the leaders that another location outside the Massachusetts jurisdiction would be best for their future development and happiness. After considerable exploring of prospective locations they finally fixed on what is now New Haven, where a settlement was begun. Like the Plymouth colony, New Haven had no patent of any kind, so the free settlers, numbering some seventy in all, gathered on June 4, 1639 to form a government and organize a church. Both government and Church took Massachusetts as their model, the government being based on a Church-member suffrage, thus assuring the control of the godly. In the founding of other towns in the vicinity of New Haven ministerial leadership was a conspicuous factor. Gradually New Haven developed into a loose confederation of towns, held together by a central General Court, until its amalgamation with Connecticut in 1665.

V

THE PURITAN THEOLOGY

To THE New England Puritans, whether clergy or laity, theology was far more than an exercise in dialectics; rather it was a matter of prime importance in their daily lives. To them God was an everyday reality, even though He was unknowable and His activities beyond and above all understandable laws. But this fact did not deter the Puritan theologian, any more than it does the modern scientist, from trying to explain the world which he continually confesses that he does not understand. The Puritan held, however, that there could be pieced together certain attributes of God in such terms as human intelligence could grasp. And of these attributes the sovereignty of God was the most emphasized. God was not only the designer and creator of the universe, but He is continuously creating, and exercising over all His creation continuous sovereignty. To God nothing can happen outside His knowledge or contrary to His purpose and plan. What He has created He controls, and in ways beyond man's comprehension. All that men can know is that God has ordered things as they are. That God's acts are arbitrary they recognized as a fact of experience. But they believed that the arbitrary acts of God are necessarily good, for God's will is just and right because He is the source of all justice— "what flows from goodness must be good."

A second cardinal principle of Puritan faith was that the Bible was the inspired word of God, and contained all discoverable truth. Nothing essential was to be learned or could be learned outside revelation. Consequently the Puritan must support every proposition by chapter and verse. The Bible, however, was not the ultimate authority; behind it—God's declared will—is God's secret will. It was this space between "the revealed will and the secret will," to use the words of Perry Miller, through which ran the highway of intellectual development.

Basic in Puritan theology were the doctrines of original sin, human depravity and irresistible grace. Men not only inherit the Adamic guilt, they add to it by their own acts, produced by their innate desire to sin. Thus man's degradation is complete. All this man has brought upon himself, for he was created pure and holy, "a fit temple for the Holy Ghost to dwell in." Thus man's degraded condition is his own act, and for it he is completely and fully responsible. Nor has man any power within himself to cleanse his life, to gain the mastery over the evil within him; his only hope of deliverance is the grace of God. The Puritan doctrine of salvation or regeneration is premised upon the omnipotence ·of God and the impotence of man. Since man has no power of his own to cleanse himself, the act of cleansing, if performed at all, must be the work of God. The first step in salvation was called justification, or the act of pardoning. The justified man is now granted power to respond to God, a new life has been created within him, and thereby he has become a new man, a regenerated creature. How this was accomplished man does not know, for regeneration is a mystery. To make it the more difficult to understand there are some who are never certain as to whether or not they have been the recipients of God's grace.

This uncertainty of their real state caused the New Englanders to be continually casting up their accounts in the hope of gaining peace of mind; thus they became "experts in psychological dissection and connoisseurs of moods," evidence of which may be clearly seen in the personal diaries of the time. Indeed, worry over one's condition was evidence that one was on the way to salvation; when one ceased to be troubled over his state that was a sign of God's indifference toward him.

". . . in the Puritan age (men) were taught to follow by intense introspection the working of the law of predestination within their own souls." Theoretically all they could do was to watch, for they possessed no power themselves to further the process of regeneration. They were but witnesses of the drama going on within their own breasts. They therefore watched it with absorbing attention. "They looked into their own most secret thoughts for signs that the grace of God was at its work of regeneration. . . ." [27]

So long as sin vexed him, he might know that God was with him. All he had to do was to continue to be vexed, and he was sure to triumph, because all existence is the conflict of Christ against Satan, the foreordained outcome of which is the triumph of the elect.[28]

It was in the application of theology to the practical task in which he was engaged that the New England Puritan made his unique contribution, for his theology was not original with him. The New Englander was primarily a doer of the Word—the end of his theology was action. His complete confidence in the rightness and justice of God enabled him to face without flinching the tragedy and defeat so often attendant upon colonization, for he never doubted the eventual outcome. The New Englanders remembered their "cosmic optimism in the midst of anguish; they were too busy waging war against sin, too intoxicated with the exultation of the conflict to find occasional reversals, however costly, any cause for deep discouragement." The individual Puritan may have been at times uncertain as to whether or not he was among God's elect, but he never lost the basic certainty that "no adversity could be so immense as to cause complete despair" for the whole body of them. "Whatever their sufferings or however painful their ordeals, the Puritan could take heart through the darkest moments in the confidence that all things are ordered after the best manner, that serene and inviolate above the clouds of man's distress shines the sun of glorious harmony." [29]

Contrary to popular opinion the Puritan was unascetic. He believed that God had created the universe good, and that in spite of man's fall, the universe was still good and meant for man's use and enjoyment. The good things of the earth, however, should be used with moderation, for there was always danger of excess on the part of the user. Their emphasis was upon utility, not on

---

[27] William Haller, *The Rise of Puritanism: or The Way to the New Jerusalem as set forth in Pulpit and Press*, 1570–1643, New York: 1938, pp. 90–91.

[28] *Ibid*, pp. 153–154.

[29] For this discussion of Puritan theology I am particularly indebted to Perry Miller's, *The New England Mind*. This work is a solid contribution to our understanding of seventeenth-century New England Puritanism. See particularly Chapters II and III.

enjoyment, and enjoyment always must be a by-product, not an end in itself; that the godly must love the world with "weaned affections" was a favorite expression of the Puritan clergy. Man's natural desires and passions are not wrong in themselves, but only his enslavement to them. "You might meddle with all things in the world," said John Preston, under whom many a New England minister had studied at Cambridge, "and not be defiled by them, if you had pure affections, but when you have an inordinate lust after anything, then it defiles your spirit."

Professor Morison has made out a good case for the fact that the New England Puritans were not Predestinarian Calvinists; they quoted William Ames and William Perkins and the Church Fathers more than Calvin; the Puritan sermons assumed that salvation lay within the reach of all, by virtue of the Covenant of Grace and the efforts of the churches. Morison flatly denies that fatalism dominated the New England view of life. The Puritan believed that each individual had his own place in a divinely ordered universe, and that God had a personal concern for him and his work, it made no difference how humble he or it might be. True, he accepted without question the doctrine of election, but as long as life lasted there was always hope that he might be one of the Father's chosen.[30]

Such studies as those of Max Weber and Troeltsch have been at pains to show that Calvinistic spiritual teaching had a distinct bearing upon the emergence of the middle class to economic importance, and upon the rise of capitalism. If Puritanic Calvinism and Capitalism jibed at many points; if New England piety and business success went hand in hand, certainly it was not due to any deliberate plotting on the part of Puritanism. The Puritan doctrine of "calling," that a person is as divinely called to be a Christian merchant or a Christian sea captain as is one entering the ministry, naturally lent itself to business success. And the very qualities which made for the Christian life, as honesty, sobriety, moderation, faithfulness, made also for economic success. Colonial New England prospered, in spite of its stony soil and inhospitable

---

[30] Samuel Eliot Morison, *The Puritan Pronaos*, New York: 1936, pp. 10–11.

climate, largely because its Puritan ethics and way of life produced a type of men and women who had a holy concern for the well-being of the family, of the Church and of the Commonwealth, as well as for business.

VI

The Changing Religious Scene

It was inevitable that there should arise in Massachusetts Bay attempts to broaden the franchise, since the ranks of those excluded contained many persons of wealth, character and influence. In 1643, of the 15,000 people in the Bay colony only 1708 were citizens. It is true that in Plymouth, where Church membership was not a requirement for citizenship, the situation was even worse, for there of the 3000 inhabitants but 230 were citizens. The most determined attempt of the disfranchised to gain larger rights came in the midst of the Civil Wars in England. Though sympathetic with the Parliamentary party, the New England leaders were determined to remain neutral, since they were not in full agreement with either of the two groups—the Presbyterians and the Independents—which constituted that party. With the Presbyterians they disagreed on what constituted a true Church, and also on the question of the authority of assemblies over the congregation; they differed with the Independents because they included Brownists, Baptists and Seekers as well as Congregationalists, and therefore were tolerant of variant views. From their standpoint, whichever side won Massachusetts would be the loser, unless they were able to maintain themselves as a free state. And this became the policy of the Bay leaders.

Such was the general situation when there was presented to the Massachusetts General Court a Remonstrance (May 6, 1646) signed by several men of influence, of whom Dr. Robert Child, Samuel Maverick and David Yale, the latter the father of the founder of Yale College, were the most prominent. Dr. Child was perhaps the best-educated man among the early colonists, having graduated from one of the Cambridge colleges and also having a Doctor of Medicine degree from the University of Padua. He was a young man of fortune, and had made several investments in colonial enterprises; he was also a sincere Puritan and a Presbyterian. Maverick was an Anglican, but had been admitted to citizenship before the Church-member qualification had been imposed. In their Remonstrance they asked "that civil liberty and freedom be forthwith granted to all truly English" without any religious qualification. They also asked that all members of the Church of England, which was at that time Presbyterian, be admitted to communion in the Bay colony churches—to us perfectly reasonable and just requests. The Remonstrance closed, however, with the threat that if their requests were not granted forthwith they would appeal to both houses of Parliament. Here was a threat to the colony's independence in the control of its own affairs. The Bay colony leaders were at once fully aroused to the danger of having their whole political and religious structure brought down in ruins and they immediately bestirred themselves to ward off the threatened disaster. A search of Dr. Child's belongings revealed another petition, intended for Parliament, asking that Presbyterianism be permitted in Massachusetts; that a Governor-general be appointed by the crown for New England so that English laws and liberties might be guaranteed, and that the Massachusetts government be investigated. Here was sedition and treason; a violation of a recent law of the General Court that any one advocating change in Church polity or government was to be subject to the death penalty. Immediately Child and the other Remonstrants were arrested and imprisoned. All were later assessed large fines and Child soon afterwards departed American shores forever.

This was the background out of which came two of New England's most important historic documents—the *Book of the General Laws and Libertyes* (1648), and the *Cambridge Platform,* completed the same year. The first is a landmark in the political development of New England, the latter the first ecclesiastical constitution for American Congregationalism. The excitement caused by the Remonstrants had compelled a change in the political set-up of the colony, and provision was soon made for permission of non-freemen to vote in town-meetings. The attempt to set up Presbyterianism in the churches at Newbury and Hingham, which had produced the Remonstrance, was the determining factor in causing the ministers and magistrates to take steps to secure a united ecclesiastical constitution, making it impossible for individual churches to depart thereafter from "the New England Way." [31]

The Cambridge Synod was called by the General Court, though not without opposition from the deputies; as a result the call took the form of an invitation rather than a command. The Synod was supported by twenty-eight of the twenty-nine churches of Massachusetts—the Boston Church not being unanimous in its support—the two New Hampshire churches, together with the good will and a few representatives from the twenty-two churches of Plymouth, Connecticut and New Haven. At its first session (September 1646) Rev. John Cotton of Boston, Rev. Richard Mather of Dorchester and Rev. Ralph Partridge of Duxbury in the Plymouth colony, were asked to prepare a "model of church government" to be presented to the Synod at its next session in June 1647. An epidemic, which included among its victims Thomas Hooker and the wife of Governor Bradford, caused speedy adjournment. The final session opened August 15, 1648, and in two weeks it had completed its work. The plan of Church government submitted by Richard Mather formed the basis of that which was finally adopted. Meanwhile copies of the Westminster Confession, completed by the Westminster Assembly in 1643, had reached Massachusetts. On examination the Synod found themselves in complete agreement with the Confession and its adoption and inclusion in the Cambridge Platform doubtless gave the Synod deep satisfaction, since by so doing they silenced the charges of doctrinal unsoundness with which they had been charged by some of their English brethren. Thus there was established complete doctrinal accord with the Puritan party in England, whether

---

[31] Williston Walker's *Creeds and Platforms of Congregationalism* is indispensable for an understanding of the background out of which came the *Cambridge Platform*. See also S. E. Morison's *Builders of the Bay Colony*, Chapter VIII. His sketch of Robert Child is based on Kittredge.

Presbyterian or Independent, thereby removing a good share of the danger of English intervention.

The polity adopted in the Platform is Barrowist, the polity which had been in general practice in New England since the beginning. It was a "Congregationalized-Presbyterianism or a Presbyterianized-Congregationalism" as Dexter puts it.[32] Thus based on the polities of both wings of the Puritan party in England, it was not likely to arouse the jealousy of either faction. At the same time the *Platform* set a standard for the New England churches by which they might be regulated and innovation resisted. It was not until 1651 that the *Platform* received the approval of the General Court, and then it was not unanimous. But from then onward it remained the recognized "pattern of ecclesiastical practice in Massachusetts" for thirty years, and continued in a modified form until the end of the eighteenth century (1780).

By the middle of the century (1650) a goodly share of the first generation New England Puritans had passed away, and with their passing a new problem presented itself—namely, how could the Church, made up of regenerated members only, be maintained? The *Cambridge Platform* had incorporated the definition of the Church, as made up of proved saints who "walk in blameless obedience to the word" and "the children of such, who are also holy." The children of the "saints" were accounted Church members, because they shared the covenant with their parents, and were entitled to baptism because they were already Church members. The question of maintaining a regenerated Church arose when some of these children of the "saints" who had received baptism grew to maturity and it was found that they could not claim a religious experience which would entitle them to be called "converted." Were they now to be admitted to the Lord's Supper? The question became even more complex with the rise of the third generation; the children of the unconverted second generation. Should they receive baptism as had their parents and should they also be considered Church members on reaching maturity?

---

[32] Henry M. Dexter, *Congregationalism of the Last Three Hundred Years as Seen in Its Literature,* Boston: 1880, p. 463. See *Ante,* p. 20.

If so the whole idea of a true Church, composed only of a body of proved saints, would be impossible to maintain. If Church membership was to become a matter of birthright, what reason was there in limiting it to one generation only? Such were the knotty questions which now confronted the New England Congregationalists.

To these questions there were three possible solutions. The first was to admit the children of Church members who were of blameless life, regardless of whether they had experienced conversion or not, to full communion in the Churches. This of course meant the complete abandonment of the principle of a regenerate Church to which their fathers had so devotedly held. A second solution was to deny them all Church privileges; to shut the doors of the Church against them. This would mean that Church membership would be limited to a mere handful in every community, which would probably grow less and less as time went on. It would mean also that those denied Church membership could not be made amenable to Church discipline. Was not this practically giving them up to heathenism? Or perhaps even worse, would not this make them the easy prey of the Baptists since one of their cardinal principles was the limitation of baptism to adult believers? A third was to adopt some half-way measure.

The solution finally adopted has been nicknamed by its critics the Half-Way Covenant, a compromise reached by the Ministerial Convention of 1657 and later confirmed by the Synod of 1662. It was there agreed that the unregenerate members of the Church were entitled to transmit Church membership and baptism to their children, but as unregenerate members they could not be partakers of the Lord's Supper, nor could they have a part in Church elections. They were to be considered members of the Church, but not in full communion. Such was the plan by which the Puritans' Church attempted to keep within the sphere of its influence a large and growing class of people, who otherwise would have been lost to it. This half-way Church membership was not to be automatically secured, for it was required that those receiving it must give a public profession of willingness to be guided by Christian principles and to promise to bring up their children in the fear of the Lord. The Half-Way Covenant has generally been condemned by Congregational historians. In the long run it worked great injury to the Church, since it failed to hold the half-way members to any real attachment to the Church, and instead of settling the issue it inaugurated a controversy within New England Congregationalism which was to continue in one form or another until well along in the nineteenth century.

Controversy over the Half-Way Covenant divided the churches at Stratford and Windsor, Connecticut. It also led to the founding of Newark, New Jersey, by a body of settlers from Branford, Connecticut, who desired to be free from the Half-Way Covenant innovations. John Davenport, at seventy years of age, left his New Haven congregation to accept a call to First Church, Boston, where a majority of the members shared his opposition to the Covenant, which led to the withdrawal of a part of its membership who favored it to form the "Old South" church. These are examples of the havoc caused throughout New England, following the adoption of the Covenant. But though strongly and often bitterly opposed, the Half-Way Covenant was favored by the great majority of churches throughout New England.

The lowering of the bars to Church membership having been inaugurated by the wide acceptance of the Half-Way Church membership, it was not long until they were still further lowered. In many places Church membership was granted on a mere promise to lead a good life. Some churches made it the practice to admit to baptism any who were living a respectable life, and to baptize the children of birthright members without requiring any covenant promise. In other words, Church membership became so easy to obtain that its deeper significance was lost. And soon also the question was being asked, if people of this sort were good enough to receive one Sacrament (baptism), why ought they not be permitted to receive the other Sacrament (the Lord's Supper) as well? This position has been called "Stoddardeanism," since Solomon Stoddard, the respected minister at Northampton, was its most influential exponent. His position was that unconverted Church members should be permitted to receive the Lord's Supper since by so doing they might thereby obtain a conversion experience. This view came to be held widely throughout western Massachusetts. One of the consequences of the acceptance of this view was the increased stress placed upon the external means of salvation in New England preaching, termed Arminian tendencies by those who discounted the use of such human means.

A *decay in religion,* as Thomas Prince called it, began to appear after 1660, which "increased to 1670" and "grew very visible and threatening, and was generally complained of and bewailed bitterly by the Pious." [33] The number of Church members in full communion was rapidly declining, most people being satisfied with the half-way relationship. Coupled with these clear indications of spiritual decay was a whole series of material disasters. King Philip's War (June 20, 1673 to August 12, 1676) took its terrible toll of human life in the destruction of ten or more towns in Plymouth and Massachusetts. Hardly had the war ended when a fire (November 27, 1676) destroyed North Church in Boston and fourscore adjoining houses, to be followed three years later (August 7-8, 1679) by an even worse conflagration which "half ruined the whole colony, as well as the town." Pestilence in the form of smallpox also stalked through the colony. As if all this were not enough the Stuart colonial policy was a constant threat to their liberties, accompanied by the forcing of Anglicanism upon them. Was not all this a clear sign of God's judgment upon them, and was not the time ripe for a "returning unto God"? [34]

The calling of the Synod of 1679 was the natural result of the growing agitation for reform. The purpose of the Synod, as indicated in the call by the General Court, was to find out "What are the evils that have provoked the Lord to bring his judgements on New England?" and to determine "What is to be done that so these evills may be reformed?" The "evills" as listed by the Synod were, the "Pride that doth abound;" neglect of Church fellowship; "imprecation in ordinary discourse;" the falling off of family religion; "sinful heats and passions;" irreverent behavior in the solemn worship of God; "Intemperance, especially that

---

[33] Thomas Prince, *Christian History,* Boston: 1743, I, p. 94.
[34] Increase Mather, *Returning Unto God . . . A Sermon,* Boston: 1680.

which resulted from health drinking;" want of truth and promise breaking; "Inordinate affection to the world;" covetousness; "lack of public spirit," and finally the all-inclusive one, "Sin against the Gospel." The Synod's recommendations as to how to overcome these evils consisted of admonitions to make the churches more effective instruments in the life of the people, stressing particularly a solemn renewal of the Covenant and the "passage and enforcement of wholesome laws in the Commonwealth." But of more lasting importance than the listing of remedies for New England's spiritual distempers, which after all were a palliative rather than a cure, were the steps taken by the Synod to secure a New England Confession of Faith. This was done through the appointment of a committee, consisting of some of the most important of the second generation leaders, who were to report at a second session on May 12, 1680. Accordingly, on the reconvening of the Synod, the committee recommended the adoption of the Savoy Confession made by the English Congregationalists at the Savoy Palace in London in 1658. The adoption of the Savoy creed is a clear indication that New England Congregationalists had developed no doctrinal peculiarities of their own; quite in contrast, however, to what had happened in the matter of Church government.

VII

ATTEMPTS TO CURB CHANGE

THE PRINCIPAL developments in New England Congregationalism in the latter years of the seventeenth and the early years of the eighteenth centuries may be gathered conveniently about the name of Increase Mather, characterized by Kenneth B. Murdock as "the foremost American Puritan." [35] The youngest son of Richard Mather—whose leading part in the formation of the *Cambridge Platform* has been noticed—Increase was educated at

---

[35] Kenneth Ballard Murdock, *Increase Mather, the Foremost American Puritan,* Cambridge: 1925. See also Murdock's two articles, "Cotton Mather." and "Increase Mather," in the *Dictionary of American Biography.*

Harvard College (A.B. 1656) and at Trinity College, Dublin (M.A. 1658). He became the teacher of Second Church, Boston, in 1664, which post he retained to the end of his life. In addition to his Boston pastorate he became the Rector of Harvard College in 1685, where he encouraged the study of science; indeed, he was undoubtedly the most scientifically minded New England minister of his generation. With the loss of the Charter of Massachusetts in 1684, Increase Mather was sent to England to intercede with King James in behalf of the Congregational churches of the colony. He was still in England when the Revolution of 1688 overthrew James and he welcomed the coming to the throne of William and Mary, with whom he immediately got in contact in the interest of Massachusetts. In 1690 he was appointed one of four agents by the colonial government to secure the return of the old charter. He displayed great skill in handling the delicate situation, and, although the old charter was not restored, they were successful in securing one which guaranteed many of their old liberties, though the elective Governor and the Church-membership requirement for the suffrage were abolished. Mather's importance in the negotiations is indicated by the fact that King William accorded him the privilege of nominating the first Governor under the new charter and all other appointive officials.

Returning to Boston in the midst of the Salem witch-hunting craze, Increase Mather opposed the judges' methods in permitting "spectral evidence" against the prisoners to stand, and the publication of his *Cases of Conscience Concerning Evil Spirits* (October 1692) is credited with ending executions for witchcraft in Massachusetts. Though his famous son, Cotton Mather, defended the verdicts in some of the cases, he too disapproved of the use of "spectral evidence," and if his and his father's advice had been followed the story of Salem Witchcraft would have been less gruesome. But in the popular mind the two Mathers were mainly responsible for the terrible injustices permitted at Salem, an accusation which recent careful investigators have largely disproved.

After his return from England Increase Mather's popularity and prestige declined, partly due to his support of the new charter and the government inaugurated under it, but also because he and his son became the principal champions of a movement to head off a growing liberalism which was emerging under the leadership of the Harvard tutors, William Brattle and John Leverett, and which had made headway during his long absence. This growing revolt against the old conservatism found expression in the formation of a fourth church in Boston, the Brattle Street, in which innovations, bitterly opposed by the conservatives under Mather leadership, were introduced. In the first place the services were changed by the introduction of the Lord's Prayer, which the Puritans had eliminated as a consequence of their opposition to all fixed forms, and "dumb reading" of the Scriptures, or reading without comment, which was considered a Prayer Book practice. More important than these changes in the services was their advocacy of doing away with the public relation of a religious experience as a qualification for full communion and their insistence that baptism should be administered to all children, presented by any professing Christian who would sponsor for their religious training. Finally they held that all contributors to the support of the minister should have a voice in his selection, whether members of the Church or not.

The mere advocacy of these changes was bad enough; changes completely destroying every vestige of the ecclesiastical structure for which the Puritans had sacrificed so much, but to have them put into practice within the sacred precincts of Boston, was, to the Mathers and their followers, a clarion call to action. To cap the climax, the organizers of the Brattle Street Church called Benjamin Coleman, a graduate of Harvard and an avowed liberal, then in England, to be their minister. On November 1, 1699, Coleman, having received ordination at the hands of the London Presbytery, appeared in Boston to assume his duties. Thus everything for which New England Congregationalism had stood had been violated in the Brattle Street Church. To add insult to injury the innovators asked that their church be recognized by the other Boston churches, and what is more, they succeeded in compelling such recognition, though with poor grace on the part of the Mathers. The above happenings make clear the purpose of the *Massachusetts Proposals* adopted by the representatives of the

Ministerial Associations of Massachusetts on September 13, 1705.

The formation of permanent Ministers' Associations in New England Congregationalism was the result of English example. In the early years of the colony there had been ministers' meetings, but they had been gradually discontinued and by the end of the third quarter of the century had entirely disappeared. Their revival was due to the coming of Rev. Charles Morton from England to the pastorate of the Charlestown Church in 1686. Through his endeavors an Association of the ministers in the vicinity of Boston was formed in October 1690, to be followed by others of similar nature and, by the opening of the eighteenth century, there were at least five Associations in Massachusetts. During his stay in England Increase Mather had exercised no little influence in the formation of the Congregational and Presbyterian Union of London (1691) and in the drawing up of the *Heads of Agreement.* Though formulated by English Puritans for English use, their influence there was of short duration for the Union soon fell apart, but in New England the *Heads of Agreement* gained great influence, largely through the advocacy of the Mathers. Here was a model which might be utilized to check and control the dangerous trends in American Congregationalism.

The net result was their advocacy of the *Massachusetts Proposals* (September 13, 1705), a plan to create a stricter Church government for Massachusetts and to provide new ecclesiastical controls to keep the Church and ministry in the narrow path of orthodoxy as conceived by the Mathers and their followers. The Proposals, divided into two parts, provided, first, that all ministers form themselves into Associations, whose business was to deal with all "questions and cases of importance;" to pass on all candidates for the ministry; to recommend candidates to all churches seeking ministers; and to carry on correspondence with other Associations. The second part provided for the forming of standing committees or councils in each Association to act as a continuing, supervising authority over the churches, their acts to be "reckoned as concluded and decisive;" among its powers being the right to expel churches which fail "to be healed" by its action. But to secure their adoption by the five Massachusetts Associations was one thing; to gain their acceptance by all the Massachusetts churches was quite another. The first proposal providing for Ministerial Associations was willingly accepted, the second, providing for standing councils with final authority was a dead letter from the start. In the first place the Proposals failed to receive the support of the Massachusetts government, for the royal Governor, Joseph Dudley, though native born, was no friend of the Mather party and strict Congregationalism, nor was the Governor's Council, whose appointment he controlled. They were opposed also by "some very considerable Persons, among the *Ministers,* as well as the *Brethren,* who thought the *Liberties* of *particular Churches* to be in danger of being too much *limited* and *infringed* in them," to use Cotton Mather's phrase. Chief among their opponents was Rev. John Wise of Ipswich, whose two little books, *The Churches Quarrel Espoused* (1710), and *Vindication of the Government of New England Churches* (1717), were powerful expositions of the democratic principles which he thought were embodied in the *Cambridge Platform.* In the years immediately preceding the outbreak of the War for Independence John Wise's arguments were to be republished as a part of the Revolutionary propaganda.

The founding of Yale College and the adoption of the *Saybrook Platform* by Connecticut have a close relationship, in that both were brought about by the conservative element among the Connecticut ministers, with the aid and comfort furnished by the Mather party in Massachusetts. The ousting of the Mather influence from Harvard in 1701 coincides exactly with the founding of Yale. It was the growing liberalism at Harvard, combined with certain practical factors, which led the leading Connecticut ministers, urged by the conservative element around Boston, to consider the establishment of a new college.[36]

The steps leading to the calling of the Saybrook Synod are not entirely clear, but on May 24, 1708, the Connecticut Legislature passed a measure calling upon the churches to send two delegates each to meet at Saybrook at the time of the next Commencement,

---

[36] See letters from Increase Mather, Judge Samuel Sewell and others relating to the founding of Yale College in Theodore D. Woolsey, *An Historical Discourse . . . Before the Graduates of Yale College,* etc., New Haven: 1850, Appendix IV, pp. 82–99.

September 9, 1708—Yale College was then located at Saybrook—
there to draw up an ecclesiastical discipline to be submitted to the
legislature at its next session the following October. The delibera-
tions of the Synod—we know nothing of the discussion—led to
the adoption of the *Savoy Confession* as the creed of the Connecticut churches, the acceptance of the English Congregational-Presbyterian *Heads of Agreement,* and in addition *Fifteen Articles
for the Administration of Church Discipline.*

The *Fifteen Articles* bear a close resemblance to the *Massachusetts Proposals.* They provided that the churches within each
county were to be formed into a *Consociation,* which was to have
disciplinary oversight over them, and from whose decision there
was to be no appeal. The ministers in each county, also, were to
be formed into ministerial Associations which were to exercise
oversight over candidates for the ministry as well as "bereaved
churches" within their bounds. Finally it was recommended that a
General Association, made up of delegates from each local Association, be formed to meet annually, but its functions and duties
were not stated. In October 1708 the *Saybrook Platform* received
the approval of the Connecticut Legislature, with the provision,
however, that any churches allowed by the laws of Connecticut
"who soberly differ or dissent from the united churches hereby
established" shall not be hindered "from exercising worship and
discipline in their own way, according to their conscience." At
the previous session of the legislature (May 1708) a toleration act
had been passed, based on the English enactment of 1689, granting
freedom of worship to dissenters on the same terms as in England, "but requiring the payment of taxes for the support of the
Congregational establishment."

Within a relatively short time after its formulation the *Saybrook* system came to be accepted generally throughout Connecticut. And as time went on the *Consociations* functioned more and
more like Presbyteries, so that by the end of the colonial period
Connecticut Congregationalism had developed a stronger feeling
of kinship for the Presbyterianism of the Middle Colonies than
for the purer Congregationalism of Massachusetts. An extreme
expression of this feeling for Presbyterianism is found in a decla-

ration of the Hartford, North, Association passed in 1799, in which it is stated that

> the constitution of the churches of Connecticut . . . adopted at the earliest period of the settlement of this state, is not Congregational, but contains the essentials of the Church of Scotland or of the Presbyterian Church in America . . . though sometimes indeed the associated churches of Connecticut are loosely and vaguely, though improperly, termed Congregational.

Thus the paths of development of Massachusetts and Connecticut Congregationalism began to diverge, with far-reaching consequences for the future both to American Congregationalism and to American Presbyterianism.[37]

VIII

THE LIGHTER SIDE

LIFE IN colonial New England was far from being the drab affair generally pictured, for even the sternest among the Puritan fathers believed there was a place for "seasonable merriment." It is true they objected to the celebration of Christmas, because of the pagan practices which had become associated with it, but they established Thanksgiving Day, which took its place, as well as other holidays on which there was feasting and merriment. We have heard a great deal of the "Blue Laws" which were supposed to disgrace the statute books of all the New England colonies, but particular scorn has been reserved for those of Connecticut. In the popular mind they constituted a long list of petty restrictions on harmless pleasures, such as prohibitions against secular music, the kissing of babies on the Sabbath day or fast days, interspersed with extreme penalties for relatively minor offences. The whole question of the supposed legal cruelty may be dismissed with the following quotation from Mark Twain's *The Prince and the Pauper* (1882), Appendix:

---

[37] Documents relating to the Saybrook Synod and the *Saybrook Platform* may be found in Walker, *op. cit.*, pp. 495–514. See also Leonard Bacon (ed.), *Contributions to the Ecclesiastical History of Connecticut*, New Haven: 1861.

One hears much about the "hideous Blue Laws of Connecticut," and is accustomed to shudder piously when they are mentioned. There are people in America (and even in England) who imagine that they were a very monument of malignity, pitilessness, and inhumanity; whereas in reality they were about the first sweeping departure from Judicial Atrocity which the "civilized" world had seen. This humane and kindly Blue Law Code, of two hundred and forty years ago, stands all by itself with ages of bloody laws on the further side of it, and a century and three-quarters of bloody English law on this side of it.

The myth that Puritan New England outlawed all music except Psalm singing in the churches has been overwhelmingly refuted in a recent book by Percy A. Scholes, entitled *The Puritan and Music*. In this book the famous Diary of Judge Samuel Sewell has done yeoman's service in refuting this myth. The cutting down of the May Pole at Merry Mount has served as a stock illustration of the supposed Puritan intolerance of dancing and music. It is true that Governor Bradford in his account of the affair mentions the music and dancing, but he also mentions their "quaffing and drinking both wine and strong waters in great excess" as well as their "dancing and frisking" with the "Indian women" of easy morals and other "worse practices." Present-day Merry Mounts are just as objectionable to decent people as they were then and for the same reasons, and it is not because of the dancing and music.[38]

The first book to be printed in the American colonies was the Bay Psalm Book, printed in the house of President Henry Dunster of Harvard College in 1640. Its authors were Richard Mather,

---

[38] Percy A. Scholes, *The Puritan and Music in England and New England: a Contribution to the Cultural History of Two Nations*, London: 1934. In Chapter II, "The Blue Laws of Connecticut," the author discusses the origin of the misconception concerning them. This he traces to the Rev. Samuel Peters' *A General History of Connecticut by a Gentleman of the Province*, published in 1781. This work, called by Benjamin Trumbull "The Lying History," was a piece of Tory propaganda by an Anglican clergyman who had been forced to leave Connecticut because of his loyalist activities. For sections on music in New England, see pp. 33–57 ff.

Perry Miller and Thomas H. Johnson, *The Puritans*, New York: 1938, is a source book. Chapter IV deals with "Manners, Customs, and Behavior." See especially Increase Mather on "Dancing" (p. 411); and Cotton Mather on "The Accomplished Singer" (p. 451).

Thomas Welde and John Eliot. To the end of the colonial period it remained in use, seventy editions appearing in America, as well as numerous editions in England and Scotland. Toward the end of the seventeenth century thirteen tunes were added, the first attempt at printing music in America. With no instruments in the churches to set the tune, that duty was performed by a precentor, with the use of a tuning fork. Judge Samuel Sewell sometimes acted in this capacity, frequently with rather ludicrous results as the following quotations from his Diary indicate:

I try'd to set Low-Dutch Tune and fail'd. Try'd again and fell into the tune of 119th Psalm. (5 July, 1713)
In the morning I set York Tune, and in the 2d going over the Gallery carried it irristibly to St. David's, which discouraged me very much. I spoke earnestly to Mr. White to set it in the Afternoon, but he declined it. (2 Feb. 1718)

The famous *Tate and Brady Song Book* was evidently beginning to displace the *Bay Psalm Book* in the second decade of the eighteenth century as is indicated in the following entry:

At night Dr. Mather preaches in the School House to the young Musicians, from Rev. 14.3—No man can learn that Song—House was full, and the singing extraordinarily Excellent, such as has hardly been heard before in Boston. Sung four tunes out of Tate and Brady. (16 March 1720)

Another popular misconception, based on tradition, is that the New England Puritan clergy [39] was so immersed in hair-splitting theological controversy that the pulpit ministrations of the ministers consisted of little else than three-hour expositions of the fine points of doctrine. In the first place the Puritan sermon was rarely over an hour in length, and in the second place it is certain that much of the New England preaching was of a practical nature and was understood by the people who heard it. Of John Cotton's preaching it was said: "His sermons were simple, plain, direct, couched in language suited to the capacity of the humblest of his

---

[39] Samuel Eliot Morison in the first chapter of his *Puritan Pronaos,* pp. 3–24 has delightfully "debunked" the Puritan "debunkers."

hearers. His delivery was dignified, never florid, or oratorical, always forceful and emphasized by occasional gestures with his right hand." A random turning of the pages of the sermons of Richard Mather will show the same quality, with emphasis upon their clarity. Of Thomas Hooker's preaching Cotton Mather states:

> Although he had a notable Hand at the Discussing and Adjusting of Controversal Points, yet he would hardly ever handle any *Polemical Divinity* in the Pulpit, but the most practical religion.

The literary activity of the New England Puritan clergy is little short of astounding. The Increase and Cotton Mather bibliographies of their published works alone fill five volumes. The task of reading this vast literary output is so overwhelming that few if any historians have done more than merely scratch the surface.[40] To assume that one is able to give the essence of an era, and especially of the Puritan era in American history, without acquaintance with the sources is a most fallacious and presumptuous assumption. And here, perhaps, is one of the reasons for the anti-Puritan vogue which has dominated the last generation of American historians. At long last, however, there has arisen a group of young American scholars, working mostly in the field of American literature, who have set themselves to the task of getting to the bottom of American Puritanism by a thorough examination of their literary output, and already their labors have born abundant fruit.

New England was founded as an experiment in Christian living. It was an experiment in applying Christianity as they saw it to every interest and concern of daily life. Today we think of that experiment as a tragic failure; and no doubt it deserved to fail. But it failed in just the same way and for the same reason that the Christian Church has been a failure from the start; that public education has always failed; and that every other movement based on high idealism has failed. They have all failed in that none of them have reached the heights which they set them-

---

[40] Thomas James Holmes, *Increase Mather, a bibliography of his works*, 2 vols. Cleveland: 1931; *Cotton Mather, a bibliography of his works*, 3 vols. Cambridge: 1940.

selves to scale. In another sense all of these idealistic movements have grandly succeeded. For the world has vastly profited from all of these tragic failures, and will continue to profit from them, even as they continue to fail.

IV

The Baptist and Quaker Elements

THE BAPTISTS AND THE QUAKERS are rooted in the same soil; both had their rise in a period in English history characterized by economic, political and religious unrest. The land was full of people who had slipped their old religious moorings and were adrift. The typical course of development of the English religious radicals of the latter sixteenth and early seventeenth centuries "took them first out of the larger and more stable religious bodies, like the Episcopalians and Presbyterians, into Independency, then into some Baptist congregation, and ultimately beyond the limits of any organized group." Some became Quakers, others identified themselves as Levellers, still others repudiated all ecclesiastical organization whatever and became Seekers. Many early Quakers, as their records show, passed through several such stages before reaching the Quaker fold. Likewise the early Baptists found numerous adherents from among those who had already turned their backs upon their old religious affiliations.[1]

THE BAPTISTS

I

RISE OF THE ENGLISH BAPTISTS

THE FATHER of the English Baptists, John Smith, furnishes a good example of such religious wanderings. As a student at Cambridge he came under the influence of Puritan teaching, and soon after

---

[1] George H. Sabine (ed.), *The Works of Gerrard Winstanley, with an Appendix of Documents Relating to the Digger Movement*, Ithaca: N. Y., 1941. Introduction.

For an understanding of the background of English religious radicalism, see William Haller, *The Rise of Puritanism; or The Way to the New Jerusalem as set forth in Pulpit and Press, 1570–1643*, New York: 1938.

graduation adopted Brownish or Separatist views and became the pastor of a Separatist congregation at Gainsborough. Removing to Amsterdam (1606) where he ministered to an Independent Congregation, he became convinced that infant baptism lacked Scriptural authority, which led him to reject the validity of his own baptism. He then persuaded the congregation over which he presided to accept this view, which accordingly disbanded and a new communion was formed. There being none qualified to administer true baptism, Smith proceeded to baptize himself by affusion. He then baptized Thomas Helwys and they two administered baptism to the remainder of the congregation. Later he came to believe that the Mennonites of Amsterdam possessed true baptism, which led him to reject his self-administered baptism and seek baptism and membership in the Mennonite Church, carrying some of his congregation with him. The congregation from which Smith and his followers withdrew continued under the ministry of Thomas Helwys. In 1612 Helwys and most of his congregation, having reached the conclusion that it was wrong to run away from persecution, returned to England. There the propagation of Baptist views prospered and by 1644 there are records of some forty-seven Baptist churches with some 20,000 members in England.[2]

Smith's justification of his frequent changes in religion would doubtless have found support from most of his contemporaries who were seeking the true faith, for, said he:

To change a false religion is commendable and to retain a false religion is damnable. For a man of a Turk to become a Jew, of a Jew to become a Papist, of a Papist to become a Protestant, are all commendable changes though they all of them befall one and the same person in one year; nay, if it were in one month: so that not to change religion is evil simply; and therefore, that we should fall from the Profession of Puritanism to Brownism, and from Brownism to true Christian baptism, is not simply evil or reprovable in itself, except it be proved that we have fallen from true religion; if we, therefore, being

---

[2] Walter H. Burgess, *John Smith the Se-Baptist. Thomas Helwys and the First Baptist Church in England*, etc. London: 1911. See also *The Works of John Smyth*, W. T. Whitley, (ed.), 2 vols., Cambridge: 1915.

formerly deceived in the way of pedobaptistry, now do embrace the truth in the true Christian apostolic baptism, then let no man impute this as a fault unto us.

Influenced by the Dutch Mennonites these first Baptist congregations took a decided position on liberty of conscience. Among their articles of faith, prepared about 1611, Article 84 states:

the magistrate is not by virtue of his office to meddle with religion or matters of conscience, to force or compel men to this or that form of religion or doctrine, but to leave Christian religion free to every man's conscience, and to handle only civil transgressions (Rom. VIII), injuries and wrongs of man against man, adultery, theft, etc., for Christ only is the king and lawgiver of the church and conscience (James IV.12).

Probably due also to Mennonite influence was their doctrine of the general atonement, that Christ died for all and not for the elect only, and for that reason they became known as "General" Baptists. Congregations of "Particular" or Calvinistic Baptists date from a little later period, their first congregation being formed in London in 1633, and by 1644 there are records of seven "Particular" Baptist churches in England. During the Civil Wars Baptists increased rapidly in numbers and influence, many of them achieving prominence as officers and soldiers in Cromwell's army.

II

ROGER WILLIAMS AND THE BEGINNINGS OF RHODE ISLAND

THE SAME type of religious ferment which had produced the first Baptist congregations in England and Holland was responsible for the beginnings of Baptist congregations in the colonies. Roger Williams was the John Smith of America and like the father of the English Baptists passed through several stages of religious change, from Anglicanism to Puritanism, from Puritanism to Separatism, from Separatism to the Baptist position, and ended his life as a Seeker.

The group of settlements which sprang up about Narragansett Bay as a consequence of Massachusetts' intolerance was a veritable

Cave of Adullam where those who were "in distress" and those that were "discontented gathered themselves." People in trouble in the Bay Colony frequently turned to Roger Williams, as did the Hutchinson party in March 1637. That same autumn a group from Charlestown and Boston, under the leadership of Rev. William Hubbard, asked Williams' assistance in finding a location near Providence. In February 1638 came John Coggeshall and William Aspinwall, with their companies, and a little later John Clarke and William Coddington came to confer with him about a suitable place for a settlement. Not wishing to intrude on territory claimed by other colonies, Williams accompanied Coddington and Clarke to Plymouth to make sure the place determined upon should be "free." As a consequence they were advised to settle on Aquidneck Island, which Williams secured for them from the Indians.[3] Portsmouth was immediately settled and the next spring Coddington and Clarke led a company to found Newport. In 1640 Samuel Gorton, a mystic and an extreme individualist appeared in Providence, after having been expelled from Plymouth and Portsmouth, and with him came turmoil and factional strife. The settlement was divided into contending political groups, while all the advanced religious opinions of the time were to be found in the colony.[4] But eventually Roger Williams harnessed "every wind of doctrine, whether religious or political" and out of these diverse elements forged a "written constitution, granting religious liberty," freedom of the press and speech, and incorporating the principles of the separation of Church and State. In an address to the English authorities in 1659 Rhode Island is thus described:

---

[3] As a result of Williams' good offices peace had been made between the Indians and the English in the Pequot War, a favor which the Indians did not forget. Williams states that he obtained Aquidneck "by love and favor" rather than by purchase. John Callender, *An Historical Discourse on the Civil and Religious Affairs of the Colony of Rhode Island,* Boston: 1739, p. 31.

[4] "It is no ways unlikely," says John Callender (*op. cit.,* p. 51), "some odd and whimsical opinions may have been broached. The liberty enjoyed here, would tempt Persons distressed for their Opinions in the neighbouring Governments to retire to this Colony as an Asylum."

For Gorton's activities and religious views see *ibid.,* pp. 35–38. Andrews (Vol. II, 13–16) gives a more favorable account of Gorton.

We being an outcast people, formerly from our Mother-Nation, in the Bishop's days, and since from the rest of the *New English* over zealous Colonies. Our whole Frame, being much like the Present Frame, and Constitution of our dearest Mother *England,* bearing with the several Judgements and Consciences of each other, in all the towns of the colony; which our neighbour colonies do not; and which is the only Cause, of their great Offence against us.[5]

The four separate communities, Providence, Portsmouth, Newport and Gorton's settlement, later called Warwick, were soon forced to unite to resist the attempts of the Puritan colonies to extend their authority over them. The formation of the New England Confederation in 1643, as a protection against the Indians, which had left out Rhode Island, was the determining factor which led Roger Williams to go to England to secure a patent, for up to that time none of the Rhode Island settlements had legal status. Forbidden to sail from Boston, Williams journeyed to New Amsterdam from whence he took ship for England in March 1643. Arriving in England he immediately got in touch with his former friends, many of whom were among the leading officials in the government, such as Sir William Masham, Oliver Cromwell, the Earl of Warwick, and especially Sir Henry Vane, at whose house he was entertained. Fortunately the Committee on Foreign Plantations was dominated by his friends, and as a result Williams' request for a patent was soon forthcoming. Thus legal status was given to the Narragansett settlements, checkmating the schemes of Massachusetts and also the attempts of William Coddington to secure a separate patent for Aquidneck Island.

While the securing of the patent was the principal purpose of Williams' visit to England, the publication there of his *Bloudy Tenent of Persecution for cause of conscience discussed* (1644) must be considered an event of greater significance. While in England there came into Williams' hands a copy of a treatise of John Cotton's, answering the arguments advanced by a prisoner in Newgate against persecution for conscience. Though busily

---

[5] John Callender, *op. cit.,* p. 31.

engaged in the affairs of the Rhode Island patent, Williams undertook to refute the sophistries of his old Boston antagonist, and the result was the *Bloudy Tenant*. To this Cotton replied in his *Bloudy Tenent washed and made white in the Bloud of the Lamb* (1647), which Williams, in turn, answered in the *Bloudy Tenent yet more Bloudy* (1652). The *Bloudy Tenent* at once became the text book of all the more radical religious and political groups in England, which were united about the doctrines of full liberty of conscience, the separation of Church and State, and the right of the people to choose their own rulers, and played an important part in bringing the Independents to power in 1648. Both the *Bloudy Tenent* and the *Bloudy Tenent yet more Bloudy* are treatises on government as well as religion, and together they may be considered as setting forth a program which Roger Williams and those associated with him hoped might be fully carried out in the colony of Rhode Island. And in this hope they were not to be disappointed.

The conception of the Church as a part of the State Williams totally rejected, on the ground that they were essentially different. The State's function, whether among Christians or pagans, is to exercise temporal control. The source of civil power is not religious, but natural and flows from society. He denied the supernatural origin of civil government, thus flatly contradicting the whole Massachusetts contention regarding the divine character of their magistracy. Even in States where other religions than Christianity are practiced, as in Jewish, Turkish or anti-Christian lands, there "may be peaceable and quiet subjects, loving and helpful neighbors, fair and just dealers, true and loyal to the civil government." Since the source of the civil authority is not religious, religion possesses no power to interfere in the State. Therefore every person, irrespective of his religion, whether Christian or pagan, Turkish or Jewish, possesses full rights and privileges as a citizen; for to deprive a man of "any civil rights or privilege, due to him as a man, a subject, a citizen, is to take from Caesar that which is Caesar's." Though this ideal is embodied in the Constitution of the United States, yet, as Professor Mecklin suggests, it is doubtful whether we as a people have as yet attained the advanced position taken by Williams three hundred years ago.[6]

When religion attempts to interfere in the affairs of the civil State, as in Massachusetts, it weakens and undermines the State's legitimate power—the State becomes the tool of the Church and does not function in its own right. Persecution by the State because of religion, in the attempt to secure religious uniformity, confuses the "civil and the religious, denies the principles of Christianity and civility." To Williams such a State as Massachusetts, sanctioning and practicing persecution of "conscience and ways of worship," was not a State at all, but a "political monstrosity."

As the State is supreme in temporal affairs, so religion is supreme in spiritual. Williams contended that the Church in its external form was like other civil corporations, such as the East India Company, all of which were to be protected by the State in performing their legitimate functions. Williams had no appreciation of the accumulated religious experience coming down through the centuries through the historic Church; a weakness, as Mecklin suggests, inherent in dissent. Rather, Williams stressed the inner experience, and to him the true Church was an invisible entity made up of the regenerate—an inward experience without physical form. The visible Church, therefore, to Williams was of slight importance, in fact, even less important than trade organizations, since the dissolution of the latter would tend to disturb and endanger the welfare of society.

Out of this view of the complete separation of the Church from the State comes naturally freedom of conscience and worship. But to Williams, freedom was not a right to do as one pleased, "but a privilege acquired by him who was one of a social group, in which the individual had duties as well as rights." Writing to the town of Providence in January 1654, in an attempt to curb

---

[6] Both the *Bloudy Tenent of Persecution* and the *Bloudy Tenent yet more Bloudy,* are found in the *Publications of the Narragansett Club,* Vols. III and IV. John M. Mecklin's *The Story of American Dissent,* New York: 1934, Chapter v, is an enlightening study of Roger Williams' thought. See also his comment on Ernst, *Roger Williams,* pp. 87–88.

Charles M. Andrews, *The Colonial Period of American History,* New Haven: 1934, Vol. II, pp. 18–21, has a brief but clear analysis of Williams' thought. An edition of the *Bloudy Tenent* is also found in the publications of the Hanserd Knollys Society, E. B. Underhill, Ed., London: 1848.

certain radical individualists who were refusing to cooperate in the government of the colony, Williams drew "a sharp line between liberty and license," using the illustration of a ship at sea, a figure of which he was fond:

There goes many a ship at sea with many hundred souls in one ship, whose weal and woe is common and is a true picture of a commonwealth, or human combination of society. It hath fallen out some times that both Papists and Protestants, Jews and Turks may be embarked in one ship; upon which supposal I affirm, that all the liberty of conscience that ever I pleaded for, turns upon these two hinges—that none of the Papists, Protestants, Jews or Turks be forced to come to the ship's prayers or worship nor compelled from their own particular prayers or worship, if they have any. I further add that I never denied, that notwithstanding this liberty, the commander of this ship ought to command the ship's course, yea, and also command that justice, peace and sobriety, be kept and practiced, both among the seamen and all the passengers. If any of the seamen refuse to perform their services, or passengers to pay their freight; if any refuse to help in person or purse toward the common charges or defense; if any refuse to obey the common laws and orders of the ship concerning their common peace or preservation; if any shall mutiny and rise up against their commanders and officers; if any should preach that there ought to be no commander or officers, no laws, nor orders, nor corrections, nor punishments;—I say, I never denied but in such cases, whatever is pretended, the commander, or commanders may judge, resist, compel and punish such transgressors, according to their deserts and merits.[7]

III

The First Baptist Churches in America

THE SLIGHT importance which Williams attached to the visible Church, as well as the rank individualism which prevailed in

---

[7] *Letters of Roger Williams,* in the *Publications of the Narragansett Club,* Vol. VI, p. 278. See James Ernst, *The Political Thought of Roger Williams,* Seattle: University of Washington Press, 1929. The best as well as the most recent survey of Williams' political thought is that by W. K. Jordan, *The Development of Religious Toleration in England,* Vol. III, *From the Convention of the Long Parliament to the Restoration, 1640–1660; The Revolutionary Experiments and Dominant Religious Thought,* Cambridge: 1938, pp. 472–506. "Williams, in his voluminous denunciations of the iniquity of persecution, clung doggedly to a few principles upon which religious liberty has come to rest." *Ibid.,* 505.

early Providence, helps to account for the slow progress made in organizing a church in this oldest of the Rhode Island settlements. Religious services seem to have been held from the start, usually in Williams' house, where Williams himself frequently preached. But it was not until March 1639 that a church was formed, and then among the nearly sixty residents in the settlement only twelve were united into a church fellowship. Baptists have called this the first Baptist Church in America. All of the original members were rebaptized, the story being that Ezekiel Holliman rebaptized Roger Williams, and then Williams baptized Holliman and the ten others.[8] It is now, however, well established that their rebaptism was not by immersion, and it is doubtful also whether Williams had any part in the formation of the Providence Church. It was at about this time that Williams repudiated all visible Churches, holding that there was no true Church left in the world, therefore there was nothing to do but await the reestablishment of the true Church by some divine intervention.

As might be expected, the Providence Church went through a whole series of internal convulsions. Some of the leading members

---

[8] In a note in Callender's *An Historical Discourse,* published in 1738, is the statement that there are reasons to suspect that "Mr. Williams did not form a church of the Anabaptists and that he never join'd with the Baptist church there. Only, that he allowed them to be nearest the Scripture rule, and true primitive Practice as to the mode and subject of *Baptism.*" The oldest inhabitants in the colony, who knew Williams, "never heard that Mr. Williams formed the Baptist church there . . ." Hugh Peters wrote on July 1, 1639, that Roger Williams and wife had not been baptized (Ernst, *op. cit.,* p. 209).

In a letter to John Winthrop in 1649, Williams states: "At Seekonk a great many have lately concurred with Mr. John Clarke and our Providence men about the point of a new baptism, and manner of dipping; and Mr. John Clarke hath been there lately (and Mr. Lucar) and both dipped them. I believe their practice comes nearer the first practice of our great Founder Jesus Christ than other practices of religion do, and yet I have not satisfaction neither in the authority by which it is done, nor in the manner." This implies that "dipping" is a new mode of baptism but recently adopted in Rhode Island (*Letters of Roger Williams*).

See also R. E. E. Harkness, "Principles of the Early Baptists of England and America," *Crozer Quarterly,* V (1928), pp. 440–460.

John Callender was a graduate of Harvard College, and was called to the pastorate of the Newport Church in 1730 when but twenty-one years of age. The *Discourse* was preached on the occasion of the one-hundredth anniversary of the settlement of Aquidneck.

Morgan Edwards in *Materials for a History of the Baptists in Rhode Island* (*Collections of the Rhode Island Historical Society,* Vol. VI, Providence: 1867, pp. 302–303), contends that Williams was among those rebaptized.

held Arminian views, others were strict Calvinists, as was Roger Williams. The principal cause of controversy, however, was the question as to whether the laying on of hands after baptism as a symbol of receiving the Holy Ghost was commanded in Scripture.[9] The Arminians generally held to this view, and became known as "Six Principle Baptists," while their Arminian views gave them also the name "General Baptists." This controversy caused division in 1652, and because the Six Principle Baptists had the better leadership their Church survived, while the Calvinistic wing soon disappeared. Church life in Providence, however, seems to have been so feeble that it was not until 1700 that the first church building was erected.[10]

The Newport Church, though founded later than the church at Providence, has a better claim to priority as the first Baptist Church in America. Here, as in Providence, there was religious confusion. William Coddington, John Coggeshall and Nicholas Easton entertained extreme antinomian views, very near those held by the Quakers. Later all three became Quakers. Opposing them was a group led by John Clarke, under whose leadership a Baptist church was established. Religious services were held probably as early as 1641, but it was not until 1644 that a Baptist Church was fully organized. The church seems to have prospered from the start, as Newport became more attractive to those holding antipedobaptist views than Providence. The records tell of the early building of a meeting house at common expense. As in Providence, six principle views caused controversy and in 1656 a new church was formed on that basis, and in 1671 a Seventh Day Baptist Church was organized.

John Clarke, "the most important American Baptist of the century in which he lived," arrived in Boston in November 1637, just after Anne Hutchinson's conviction. He at once identified

---

[9] The controversy is thus described by John Callender (*op. cit.*, p. 61): "About the year 1653 or 54 there was a Division in the *Baptist Church* at *Providence about the Rite of laying on of Hands,* which some pleaded for as essentially necessary to Church Communion, and the others would leave indifferent. Hereupon they walked in two Churches, one under Mr. C. Browne, Mr. Wickenden, etc., the other under Mr. *Thomas Olwy,* but *laying on of Hands* at length generally obtained."

[10] Chad Brown, the most important early leader in Providence Church, was the ancestor of the Brown Brothers who gave their name to Rhode Island College.

himself with the defeated supporters of the "Covenant of Grace," and was immediately recognized as a leader. After a winter spent with the Wheelwright colony at Exeter, in what is now New Hampshire, he and Coddington went to Providence where, as it has been noticed, he was kindly received by Williams, who helped them secure Aquidneck Island as a location for a colony. In 1639 he, Coddington, and eleven others established Newport at the south end of the island.

Clarke was a well-educated physician and a preacher, though where he came by both professions is unknown. His influence at Newport equaled that of Coddington, and, of the two, Clarke was undoubtedly the abler. In 1651 he accompanied Williams to England to protect the interests of the colony against Coddington's scheme to make Aquidneck independent, with himself as Governor for life. Williams, having succeeded in defeating Coddington's claims to an independent patent, soon returned, but Clarke remained nearly twelve years and, in 1663, secured the charter for Rhode Island. Returning to the colony in 1664 he was chosen Deputy Governor three times. He also resumed his ministry at the Newport Church, which he continued to his death. Though his writings are less important than are those of Roger Williams, his views on liberty of conscience are equally forthright. In his petition to Charles II (1662) for the Rhode Island charter is this statement: "A most flourishing Civill State may stand, yea, and best be maintained . . . with full liberty in religious concernments." [11]

John Clarke's name is perhaps best known in connection with the whipping of Obediah Holmes by the Massachusetts authorities, and by the little book he published in England in 1652 entitled *Ill Newes from New England*,[12] in which is described the intolerance and cruelty practiced by the Massachusetts authorities upon the Baptists.

All those infected by the Baptist virus in New England did not find their way to Rhode Island. The Salem Church furnished sev-

---

[11] For Clarke's achievements in England, see Andrews, *op. cit.*, Vol. II, pp. 40–48.

[12] The full title of John Clarke's book is: *Ill Newes from New England: or A Narrative of New England Persecution, Wherein is declared, That while Old England is becoming New, New England is becoming Old*, London: 1652.

eral notable cases. One was that of Lady Deborah Moody, characterized by Winthrop as "a wise and anciently religious woman, who being taken with the error of denying baptism of infants was dealt with (1642) by the elders and admonished by the Salem Church." After her expulsion from the church she departed for New Netherland with a large number of Lynn settlers "infected with Anabaptism." There she established a settlement at Gravesend, Long Island, and later had a part in forming a Baptist Church. Another Baptist heretic was William Witter, a resident of Lynn, who was arraigned before the Salem Court (February 1644) for calling the baptism of infants "a badge of the whore." The next year he was before the court again charged with saying "that they who stayed while a child is baptized do worship the devil." Cases of persons refusing to present their newborn infants for baptism became increasingly common, and in November 1644 the Massachusetts Court enacted a law making it a crime punishable with banishment for any to deny the validity of infant baptism, or for holding any of the other views peculiar to the Anabaptists.[13]

IV

PERSECUTION

PLYMOUTH colony seems to have been a veritable hotbed of incipient Baptists, and although charges were brought against numerous individuals none were actually punished. Obediah Holmes was one of the principal disturbers of the orthodox peace in Massachusetts. He was the leader of a group of Baptist converts at Seekonk who were carrying on their worship in private houses. Threats of arrest and punishment led them to remove to Newport, where they swelled the membership of Clarke's church.

Persecution of Baptists in Massachusetts reached a climax in

---

[13] Baptist historians have denied that the early American Baptists entertained Anabaptist views. The term "Anabaptist" was used loosely by the Massachusetts authorities to designate any one who opposed the Massachusetts system, in much the same way that the term "Communist" is used today to apply to all who advocate any change in the economic system. A. H. Newman, *A History of the Baptist Churches in the United States,* New York: 1894. Chapter IV.

1651, when John Clarke, John Crandall and Obediah Holmes journeyed to Lynn, at the request of the aged William Witter, to administer baptism and the Lord's Supper to a group of his neighbors who had adopted Baptist views. While in the midst of their worship in Witter's house on the Sabbath, two constables arrived with a warrant to arrest "certain erronious persons being strangers." The constables insisted on taking the prisoners to the church, in spite of Clarke's warning that if they were forced to attend the meeting they would "be constrained to declare that they could not hold communion with them." To this the constable replied, "That is nothing to me, I have not power to compel you to speak or to be silent." The prisoners sat with their hats on until they were forcibly removed by the constable and when the "praying, singing and Preaching" were ended Clarke arose to explain wherein the Baptists differed from the Standing order. His attempt, however, was soon silenced by the minister. The next day they were taken to Boston and placed in prison. A few days later they were taken to the court and, as Clarke states, "without producing either accuser, witness, jury, law of God, or man," they were sentenced. In the course of the trial the Governor called them Anabaptists, when Clarke exclaimed, "I disown the name, I am neither an Anabaptist, nor a Pedobaptist, nor a Catabaptist." He admitted, however, that he had baptized many, but had never rebaptized any. At this the Governor exclaimed, "You deny the former baptism and make all our worship a nullity," all of which Clarke admitted. The exchanges between Clarke and the Governor ended with this warning from Clarke: "If the testimony which I hold forth be true, and according to the mind of God, which I undoubtedly affirm it is, then it concerns you to look to your standing."

When it came Crandall's and Holmes' turn to be examined they were equally outspoken, which only made Governor Endicott the more vindictive. Heavy sentences were then imposed; Clarke was fined £20, to be paid before the next meeting of the Court or be well whipped; Holmes was assessed a fine of £30 or be well whipped; Crandall's fine was £5 or a whipping. When Clarke remonstrated against the severity of the sentences the Governor exclaimed, "You have denied 'Infants Baptism,' and deserve death," and added further that "he would not have such trash brought into their jurisdiction." He accused them of going up and down insinuating their teaching into those that were weak, but, he exclaimed, "you cannot maintain it before our ministers, you may try, and discourse with them." This Clarke interpreted as a challenge to a public debate, and on his release attempted to arrange for such a public meeting, but the Governor denied that he had any such intention. The fines of Clarke and Crandall were paid by friends unknown to them, but Holmes refused to allow it in his case, and he was publicly whipped with a three-corded whip. When the cruel punishment was ended Holmes said to the Magistrates, "you have struck me as with roses." [14] And just as the blood of the early Christian martyrs was the seed of the Church, so the blood of Obediah Holmes served to fertilize New England soil for the raising up of other Baptists, for, he said, "before my return [to Newport] some submitted to the Lord, and were baptized, and others were put upon the way of enquiry."

Soon after the appearance of Clarke's *Ill Newes from New England* (1652), Sir Richard Saltonstall, one of the first Magistrates of Massachusetts, who had since returned to England, wrote to John Cotton and John Wilson the following rebuke:

It doth not a little grieve my spirit to hear what sad things are reported daily of your tyranny and persecution in New England, as that you fine, whip and imprison men for their consciences. First you compel such to come into your assemblies as you know will not join you in your worship, and when they show their dislike thereof or witness against it, then you stir up your magistrates to punish them for such (as you conceive) their public affronts. . . . We . . . hoped that the Lord would have given you so much light and love there, that you might have been eyes to God's people here, and not to practice those courses in a wilderness, which you went so far to prevent. These rigged

---

[14] Holmes wrote an account of his arrest, trial and whipping, in a letter to the Baptists of London, which Clarke printed in his *Ill Newes from New England*, pp. 7–23. See also Isaac Backus, *A History of New England with Particular Reference to the Denomination of Christians called Baptists*, 3 Vols., Boston: 1777–1796, Chapter IV, "An Account of Mr. Clarke and Mr. Holmes and other sufferings at Boston," largely based on Clarke's account.

ways have laid you low in the hearts of the saints. I do assure you I have heard them pray in the publick assemblies that the Lord would give you meek and humble spirits, not to strive so much for uniformity, as to keep the unity of the spirit in the bond of Peace.

John Cotton, in his reply, repudiated any responsibility in the affair, though he proceeded to justify all that was done, and ended his letter with,

You know not if you think we came into this wilderness to practice those courses here which we fled from in England. We believe there is a vast difference between men's inventions and God's institutions; we fled from Men's inventions . . . we compel none to men's inventions

since, of course, New England's institutions are of God's making. "Nevertheless," he continues,

I tell you the truth, we have tolerated in our church some anabaptists, some antinomians and some seekers, and do so still at this day. We are far from arrogating infallibility of judgement to ourselves or affecting uniformity; uniformity God never requireth, infallibility he never granted us.

Which seems to indicate that the "unmitred pope of a pope hating people" was beginning to have some faint misgivings.

The whipping of Obediah Holmes and the heavy fines imposed upon Clarke and Crandall, may well have been one of the influences which caused Henry Dunster, the highly respected President of Harvard College, to come out in the open against infant baptism. But whatever the cause, in the words of Cotton Mather, this is what happened:

That good man who was the President of the College was unaccountably fallen into the briars of Antipedobaptism, and being briar'd in the scruples of that persuasion, he not only forebare to present an infant of his own unto the baptism of our Lord, but also thought himself under some obligation to bear his testimony in some sermons against the administration of baptism to any whatsoever.

But if Dunster had been willing to keep his views on infant baptism to himself, as doubtless many others were doing at that time, he could have remained at Harvard College to the end of his days. For this is exactly what the General Court and the Overseers of the college desired him to do, as the College had prospered under his administration, and he was universally liked. Accordingly the Overseers refused to accept his first resignation. But to Henry Dunster the evils of Pedobaptism were so real that nothing could persuade him to hide his new-found light under a bushel. Within a month after the refusal of his resignation (July 30, 1654), Dunster brought the whole matter to a climax by interrupting the baptism of infants in the Cambridge Church, to protest against it as not in accordance with the institution as established by Christ, and under six heads proceeded to answer the arguments in its favor which had just been advanced by the minister in his sermon. There was no question, now, in the minds of the authorities as to what must be done, and they proceeded at once to do it. Dunster's resignation was demanded, and at the April (1655) meeting of the General Court he was tried and convicted of disturbing public worship and sentenced to be publicly admonished.[15] It is an interesting fact that his successor to the Harvard presidency was Charles Chauncy, who had but a short time before raised a considerable rumpus at Scituate because of his defense of immersion of infants; and it is also significant that Dunster should be called to succeed him at Scituate, another indication of the greater liberality prevailing in the Plymouth colony.

Outside Rhode Island, the Baptist cause made small progress in New England until toward the end of the century. A group of Welsh Baptists, with their minister John Myles, fleeing from persecution which followed the enactment of the Act of Uniformity of 1662, found refuge in the Plymouth colony at Rehobath, where a church was formed. On the complaint of the Congregational minister of the town, Myles and some of his leading members were arraigned before the Court (July 1667) for setting up a public meeting without knowledge or permission. On this charge they were convicted and fined, but the Court advised that if they removed their meeting to some place where they would not

---

[15] A detailed account of the Dunster affair will be found in Newman, *op. cit.,* Chapter v, "President Dunster and the Baptists."

prejudice any other (Congregational) church and gave reasonable satisfaction as to their principles, the government might give its approval. Accordingly, not long afterwards, a large tract of land was set aside for them on the Rhode Island border where they set up their church, naming the place Swansea after their old Welsh home.

About the same time (1665) a Baptist Church was being formed in Boston, under the leadership of Thomas Gould and several others who had been excommunicated from the State Church. But in contrast to the peaceful development of the Swansea Baptists, the Boston Baptists were compelled to travel the thorny road of persecution for twenty-five years. The first charge against them was that they admitted to membership excommunicated persons from the Churches of the Standing Order. This led to the disfranchisement of all Baptists who were freemen. The next year (1666) Gould and several others were fined by the County Court of Cambridge and required to give bond to appear before the General Court. On their refusal they were thrown into prison where they remained for nearly a year. And so it went on, year after year, until even some of the Massachusetts officials began to oppose such measures, and increasing protests from English Congregationalists and Baptists and finally from the King himself, brought it to an end.

The following extract from a letter written by Robert Mascall, an English Congregationalist (March 25, 1669), is typical of the type of protests coming out of England:

Oh, how it grieves and affects us that New England should persecute! will you not give what you take? . . . must we force our interpretation upon others, Pope-like? . . . And what principles is persecution grounded upon? Domination and infallibility. This we teach is truth. But are we infallible, and have we the government? God made none, no not the Apostles who could not err, to be lords over faith; therefore what monstrous pride is this? . . . Oh, wicked and monstrous principle! . . . And what! is that horrid principle crept into precious New England, who have felt what persecution is . . .? Have not those (Baptists) run equal hazards with you for the enjoyment of their liberties; and how do you cast a reproach upon us, that are Congregational in England, and furnish our adversaries with weapons upon us? We blush and are filled with shame and confusion of face, when we hear of these things.

The letter closes with:

Dear Brother, we here do love and honor them [Baptists], hold familiarity with them, and take sweet council together; they lie in the bosom of Christ and therefore ought to lie in our bosoms. In a word, we freely admit into our churches; few of our churches but many of our members are Anabaptists; I mean Baptized again. . . . Anabaptists are neither spirited nor principled to injure nor hurt your government nor your liberties. . . .[16]

An expression of amazement from a group of Baptist ministers in England, that Protestants should persecute Protestants in New England, brought a reply (1681) from Samuel Willard, the learned minister of the South Church in Boston, to which Increase Mather contributed the preface. Mather admits that Protestants ought not to persecute Protestants, but insists that it cannot be denied "that Protestants may punish Protestants," and asks the English Baptist brethren to bear in mind the differences in the situations in New England and England, stating that, "that which is needful to ballast a great ship [England], will sink a small boat [New England]." In Willard's argument is this choice bit:

They [Baptists] say baptized persons are true matter of a visible church, and they say those that were only sprinkled in their infancy were never baptized; and will not this undermine the foundation of all the churches in the world but theirs? and what more pernicious! . . . Experience tells us that such a rough thing as a New England Anabaptist is not to be handled over tenderly.

---

[16] Isaac Backus, *op. cit.,* Vol. I, pp. 390–395. Another letter bearing the same date was sent to the Massachusetts Governor, signed by the most prominent Congregational ministers in London, ending with, "Only we make it our hearty request to you that you would trust God with his truths and ways so far, as to suspend all rigorous proceedings in corporal restraints or punishments, on persons that differ from you, and practice the principles of their dissent without danger, or disturbance to the civil peace of the place." *Ibid.,* p. 397.

The senseless persecution of Baptists in Massachusetts came to an end with the close of the seventeenth century. The new Charter of 1691 granted "liberty of conscience to all Christians, except Papists," but the taxation of dissenters for the support of the ministry of the Standing Order went on until 1728. In that year an act was passed exempting Anabaptists and Quakers "from being taxed for and toward the support of ministers," but in order to secure exemption Baptists were required to obtain certificates signed by two principal members of that persuasion, "which were to be presented to the town officials."

In Connecticut also, Baptists had gained the right, not only to worship in their own meeting houses (1708), but, in 1729, to secure exemption from contributing to the support of the Established ministry, or from paying any tax levied for the building of meeting houses.[17]

The ending of the war against Baptists in Massachusetts was symbolized in 1718 by an invitation to Increase and Cotton Mather to take part in the ordination and installation of Elisha Callender as the minister of the Baptist Church in Boston. Cotton Mather's ordination sermon, entitled "Good Men United," was a plea for unity as far as conscience will allow and for toleration when agreements cannot be achieved.

Baptist historians have credited the participation of the Mathers in Elisha Callender's ordination as the immediate cause of the bringing to Harvard College of the Thomas Hollis benefactions, the largest received during the entire colonial period. Thomas Hollis, a wealthy English Baptist merchant of liberal views, having learned of the Mathers' good will shown to the Boston Baptists, was led, the year following, to begin his benefactions to Harvard, in the hope that the two denominations might be led to a closer cooperation. This might well have been the determining factor, although Hollis' interest in Harvard College dates from 1690, when he became a trustee of the estate of an uncle who had made Harvard College the object of a bequest. He also had met Increase Mather, during the latter's stay in England, and soon

---

[17] *Colonial Records of Connecticut,* Vol. V, p. 50; VII, pp. 237–257.

after had made Harvard the recipient of a legacy in his own will. It is significant, however, that his gifts began in 1719, after he had assured himself that the "views" of the corporation were "catholic and liberal." And the participation of the Mathers in a Baptist ordination might well have clinched the matter in his mind, that Harvard College was "more catholic and free in its religious sentiments than any other institution existing at that period." He knew full well how Baptists had been feared and despised in Massachusetts, but he did not let that deter him. Nor were the professorships he endowed—Theology and Mathematics —or the scholarships he established, hedged about with petty conditions or dogmatic safeguards. The only requirements laid down were that Baptists should not be disqualified from holding either the scholarships or the professorships, and the only subscription for the professorships was to be a "belief that the Scripture of the Old and New Testaments are the only perfect rule of faith and manners." [18] It was a fortunate circumstance for Harvard that the first in her long life of generous donors was a liberal-minded Baptist, who held firmly to the first and greatest of the Baptist principles—freedom of conscience.

Even after persecution ceased the Baptists made little progress in New England until the Great Awakening created a new religious situation, and gave new opportunity for Baptist expansion. A Baptist society was formed at Kittery, in the province of Maine, in 1682, made up of English Baptist immigrants, under the leadership of William Scriven, who received ordination at the hands of the Baptist Church in Boston. But it was so harried by fines and imprisonments that Scriven removed to South Carolina, taking some of the Kittery members with him. By 1735 only four Baptist churches had been formed in Connecticut, the first being that at Groton which was constituted in 1705. In 1740 there were in all New England but twenty-two Baptist churches, and of these eleven were in Rhode Island.

---

[18] David Benedict, *A General History of the Baptist Denomination in America*, 2 Vols., Boston: 1813. Vol. I, pp. 401–442. Newman, *op. cit.*, pp. 196–197. An extended account of Thomas Hollis and his benefactions to Harvard College may be found in Josiah Quincy, *The History of Harvard University*, 2 Vols., Cambridge: 1840. Vol. I, Chapter xii.

V

BAPTISTS IN THE MIDDLE COLONIES

BAPTIST BEGINNINGS in the Middle Colonies came just as persecution was ending in New England. In the Quaker colonies where freedom of conscience prevailed, the Baptists flourished from the beginning, and Philadelphia soon became the principal Baptist center in the colonies. The first Pennsylvania Baptists were immigrants from Wales, and "the first church in the Province of any note and permanency," to use the words of Morgan Edwards, was that at Pennepek, organized about the year 1686. It drew its membership from numerous scattered communities, some as far away as Burlington, New Jersey, Chester and Philadelphia. As these communities organized churches of their own, the Pennepek Church became the mother of many daughters. The Welsh Tract Church (1701), as the name implies, was also made up of Welsh immigrants, who had formed themselves into a church before leaving Wales. The Church remained so dominantly Welsh that until 1732 the records were kept in the Welsh language. Another Welsh Church was formed northwest of Philadelphia in 1711, known as the Great Valley Church, as was also the Montgomery Church formed in 1719. The church in Philadelphia was the eighth Baptist Church organized in Pennsylvania and dates from 1698. It was made up of a group of English Baptists.

The Pennsylvania Baptists, as did the Anglicans, profited from the Keithian controversy among the Quakers. With Keith's defection to the Episcopalians his followers were soon scattered. Some followed Keith into the Anglican fold, some returned to the Penn Quakers, and not a few found their way into the Baptist fellowship. "These," to use Morgan Edwards' words, "by resigning themselves to the guidance of Scripture began to find water in the commission; bread and wine in the command," [19] with the result that from no baptism at all, they now accepted immersion and the

---

[19] Morgan Edwards, *Materials Towards a History of the Baptists in Pennsylvania, both British and German,* etc., Philadelphia: 1770. Edwards was the Baptist minister in Philadelphia from 1761 to 1771.

Lord's Supper as well as foot washing and other primitive practices.

By the opening of the eighteenth century Philadelphia had become the strongest Baptist center in the colonies, and because there were several Baptist churches in the vicinity, the custom arose of holding "general meetings" made up of all Baptists who could attend. In 1707 the "meeting" had become a delegated body, five churches having sent representatives. This was the origin of the Philadelphia Association, which speedily developed into an agency of commanding significance among American Baptists. Up to this time the American Baptists had been chiefly Arminian in their doctrinal position, but the growing importance of the Philadelphia group of churches, largely influenced by the Calvinist emphasis, gradually displaced the Arminianism of the earlier New England churches. In 1742 the London Confession was adopted by the Philadelphia Association, and through its expanding influence it set the theological pattern for the American Baptists throughout the remainder of the colonial period.

By the seventeen fifties three Baptist churches had been formed in Virginia, in spite of Anglican opposition; the oldest, Opekon in Berkeley county, dating from 1743, the Ketockton and Smith's Creek, organized in 1756. These early Virginia churches were all members of the Philadelphia Association. The Carolinas were fertile soil for the Baptists, principally because of the wide toleration established by the proprietors. Present-day Charleston was the seat of the oldest Baptist Church in either of the Carolinas, which was in existence in 1699 and may have been formed as early as 1683. In 1708 it had ninety members and was active enough to elicit the condemnation of the S. P. G. Missionary.[20] A second church on Port Royal Sound was formed about 1700 and seems also to have come from the activities of William Scriven, who was driven from Kittery, Maine. Baptists were among the first comers to North Carolina, though the first fully

---

[20] Robert B. Semple, *A History of the Rise and Progress of the Baptists in Virginia*, Richmond: 1810, is the fullest account of the earliest activities of Virginia Baptists. Two recent books, Leah Townsend, *South Carolina Baptists*, Florence, South Carolina: 1935, and George W. Paschal, *History of North Carolina Baptists*, Vol. I, 1663–1805, are both excellent studies.

organized Church was not formed until 1746 in what is now Camden county. Though the Baptists had gained a foothold in all the Southern Colonies by the middle of the century, their greatest expansion in the south did not begin until the latter third of that century, with the coming of the Separate or revivalistic Baptists. This, however, is a part of the story of the Great Colonial Awakenings.

THE QUAKERS

THE HIGH-WATER mark of Quaker missionary zeal coincides exactly with the most active period of England's colonization of America. Quite naturally Holland was the first country to which Quaker missionaries came, and by 1660 Amsterdam had become a missionary base for Quaker propaganda in Europe. Quaker missionary zeal, however, was not content to confine itself to nearby lands, but "The Word," which was as a fire and hammer in them, drove them to far distant regions, east as well as west. In 1657 a party of six Quakers, three men and three women, set out for Turkey and Jerusalem to convert the Sultan and to preach to the Jews. Among them was Mary Fisher, whom we are soon to meet again in Massachusetts. Through a series of interesting circumstances she actually was brought into the presence of the Sultan and delivered her Quaker soul before him. Two others, John Perrot and John Love, visited Rome, where the latter was examined before Pope Alexander VII and because of his bold denunciation of the papacy, was hanged. In 1661 four Quaker missionaries were moved to set out for China, carrying letters from George Fox to the King of Spain, the King of France, the Magistrates of Malta, the Turk, the Emperor of China, Prester John, and one addressed to "all the nations under the whole heavens." [21] These ill-considered expeditions, so costly in human life, as well as in money, must be classed as aberrations rather than legitimate missionary enterprises, but they well serve to illustrate the heroism and persistence of the early bearers of the Quaker gospel.

---

[21] Elizabeth Braithwaite Emmott, *A Short History of Quakerism* (Earlier Periods), London: 1923. Chapter xii, "The First Quaker Missionaries."

The first Quaker missionaries to the American colonies were imbued with the same fanatical, persistent zeal which led John Love to denounce the Pope to his face, and Daniel Baker to interrupt worship in a Catholic church in Gibraltar, by rending his outer garment and stamping upon his hat, as a symbol of disapproval of what he considered a mockery of true religion. It will help to explain the fiery exaltation of the early Quaker missionaries when it is recalled that they believed devoutly that they were being led by the direct word of the Lord in everything they said and did. They were merely human instruments in God's hands. Theirs was "a religion of first hand experience, based primarily not on historical happenings, but on inward events." Quaker writers are inclined to justify the extravagances, denunciations and the intolerance shown by these early Quaker propagandists on the ground that they were driven to them by cruel opposition. In many cases this was doubtless true, but in other instances a martyr complex was evidently present. At any rate the civil authorities whose duty it was to deal with them deserve some of our sympathy.

I

THE FIRST QUAKER MISSIONARIES TO AMERICA

QUAKERISM WAS FIRST planted in America, not by Quaker immigrants from Great Britain, but through missionary effort. Indeed, nearly ten years before the establishment of Pennsylvania as a Quaker refuge, Quaker meetings had been established along the coast of North America from New Hampshire on the north to South Carolina on the South. And it was missionary activity, not immigration, which made Quakerism one of the most widely distributed religious bodies in the colonies and which enabled them to exercise a far larger influence in the eighteenth century than they have had since.

As was the case with the Baptists, Massachusetts' intolerance helped prepare the American soil for the Quaker seed. Not only Anne Hutchinson's teachings, which in many respects were strikingly similar to Quaker doctrine, but several prominent actors in her drama, as William Coddington, John Coggeshall, Nicholas Easton and Mary Dyer, were to play leading roles in the planting of Quakerism in Rhode Island, and especially on the island of Aquidneck, "destined to be the shelter and safe nursery of Quakerism in the days of its early stress in the New World."

Quaker missionaries came to New England by way of the Barbadoes, already a rich and populous English colony, which by the latter half of the sixteen hundreds had become a veritable hive of Quakerism. The first to arrive in Boston were Mary Fisher and Ann Austin, the former a young unmarried woman of twenty-two, the latter an elderly woman, the mother of five children. New England had been well warned against the Quakers, through many anti-Quaker pamphlets, some of which had been written by ministers who had formerly resided in the colony. The "horrid opinions" and "diabolical doctrines" of the Quakers were described as endangering the safety of the established Church and even of the Commonwealth itself. Believing, as the New England Puritans did, that their own Church and government were divinely appointed and they themselves were God's chosen instruments in carrying out His will in State and Church, their persecution of the Quakers was but a natural consequence. They were, indeed, as Rufus Jones states, "two different spiritual empires" foredoomed to clash.[22]

II

THE MARTYRS

THE HISTORY OF colonial Quakerism may be divided conveniently into two periods, the period of martyrdom, 1656 to 1670, and the period of phenomenal growth and expansion, 1670 to 1740. The first period begins with the imprisonment of Mary Fisher and Ann Austin in the Boston jail in July 1656. Hardly had they departed, after five weeks of close confinement, before another

---

[22] Rufus M. Jones, *The Quakers in the American Colonies*, New York: 1910, is the best single volume on Colonial Quakerism.

ship bearing eight more Quaker "publishers" arrived (August 7, 1656). They too were clapped immediately into prison, and after eleven weeks were sent out of the colony on the same ship in which they had come, the ship's master being placed under bond to take them back to England. Meanwhile the Massachusetts General Court hurried to pass its first law against the Quakers. This law placed a fine of £100 upon any ship's captain bringing Quakers into the colony, and arrest, whipping and imprisonment for any Quaker finding his or her way into her borders. Even while the law was being proclaimed through the streets of Boston, the first convert to Quakerism was made in the person of a respected citizen, Nicholas Upshaw, whose vigorous protest against the law brought him a fine and banishment.

With Rhode Island as a base—that "little corner of the earth consecrated to freedom of belief and worship, where one could follow his inward light without fear of dungeon or gibbet"—successive Quaker "publishers," by ones and twos, and in larger groups, began their assault upon New England. Rhode Island soon had several successful Quaker meetings, for such leaders as William Coddington, Joshua Coggeshall, the son of John Coggeshall, Nicholas and John Easton, accepted the Quaker faith as soon as they heard it proclaimed. News of Quaker success in Rhode Island brought a protest from the Commissioners of the United Colonies in September 1657, in which they point out the danger of spreading the contagion of the Quaker pest into surrounding colonies, and urge that they be sent out of Rhode Island and their future returning prohibited. To this Benedict Arnold, the President of Rhode Island colony, replied.

And as to the dammage that may in likelyhood accrue to the neighbor collonys by theere being here entertained, we conceive it will not prove so dangerous as the course taken by you to send them away out of the country as they come among you.

The next General Assembly of Rhode Island in March 1657 sent a letter to Governor Endicott, to be imparted to the Commissioners of the United Colonies, calling attention to the fact that Rhode Island was founded on the principle of "freedom of different consciences," "which freedom," they state, "we still prize as the greatest hapines that men can posess in this world." Thus it was settled that the Quakers were to find safety in Rhode Island, where before many years they were to become the rulers of the colony.[23]

While Rhode Island was thus going on record as a Quaker haven, Massachusetts was girding up her loins to make bitter war upon them. In October 1657 a new anti-Quaker law was passed providing a fine of £100 for any one bringing a Quaker into the colony, while any person found entertaining or concealing a Quaker was to be fined 40 shillings for every hour, and any Quaker returning to the colony after having been banished, was, if a man, to have one ear cropped, for a second return the other ear, and for a third his tongue was to be bored with a hot iron. If a woman, whipping was the penalty for the first two offenses, but for a third, her tongue was to be bored. When none of these barbarous penalties proved effective in stopping the Quaker missionaries from proclaiming the gospel of the inner light, the death penalty was added (October 1658) for those who returned after banishment.

In 1658 fifteen Quaker missionaries were at work in New England, and were soon furnishing grist for Massachusetts' persecution mill. Among the first to suffer were William Brend and William Leddra. They were holding a meeting in the woods near Salem when they were seized and carried to Boston. After a trial, which was little more than a mockery, they were condemned to be beaten. Brend, an elderly man, received one hundred and seventeen blows on the bare back with a tarred rope, and was picked up, thought to be dying. In August 1658 John Rous, Christopher Holder and John Copeland were arrested in Dedham, and brought before Governor Endicott. After a "frivolous examination" each of them was sentenced to have an ear cropped. These are but random examples of numerous other cases of punishment meted out to Quakers apprehended in Massachusetts. Instead of cooling Quaker ardor, however, it only served to fan the fire. Finally, in September 1658 three Quakers were apprehended who had made themselves liable to the death penalty. William Robin-

---

[23] *Records of the Colony of Rhode Island*, I, pp. 374–380.

son, Marmaduke Stevenson, and Mary Dyer had deliberately returned to Boston after having been banished, well knowing the terrible consequences. They came, as they stated, "to bear testimony against the persecuting spirit." Brought to trial before the General Court in October they were condemned to be hanged, and October 27 was fixed as the execution day. Walking hand in hand, with Mary Dyer in the middle, they ascended the gallows and the two men sealed their faith with their lives, but at the last moment Mary Dyer was reprieved,[24] was placed on a horse and sent out of the colony. But, refusing to accept her life, she was back again in Boston in May 1660, deliberately, to give up her life in order to compel the repeal of "that wicked law against God's people." And this time there was no reprieve. Offered her life as she stood on the ladder to the gallows if she would but return home, she replied, "Nay, I cannot."

"As Mary Dyer's lifeless body hung from the gallows, and swung in the wind," one of the many spectators was heard to remark in jest, "She hangs there as a flag." As Rufus Jones remarks, this statement made in jest was literally true. Mary Dyer did hang as a flag, "a sign and symbol of deathless loyalty" to what she thought was the voice of God in her soul.

The next March 1661, the fourth Quaker martyr suffered death upon the gallows, when William Leddra, a citizen of the Barbadoes, was hanged. He had already suffered imprisonment and the winter before had been chained to a log in an unheated prison. Some of the charges brought against him were: sympathy for those who had been executed, refusal to remove his hat, and persistence in the use of "thee" and "thou." Or in other words, his crime, as in the case of all the others, was that of being a Quaker. While in prison before his execution he wrote,

all the imprisonments, and banishments on pain of death, and the loud threatenings of a halter did no more affright me, through the strength

---

[24] Mary Dyer's reprieve had been previously determined by the action of the Court, as a part of the sentence. It reads: ". . . that she shall be carried to the place of execution, there to stand upon the gallowes, with a rope about her necke, till the rest be executed, and then to retourne to the prison and remaine as aforesaid." *Massachusetts Records*, IV, Part I, p. 384, October 18, 1659.

and power of God, than if they had threatened to bind a spider's web to my finger.[25]

To John Norton, the chief defender of Massachusetts orthodoxy, was given the task, by the Court, of preparing the official argument against the Quaker tenets and practices. Accordingly in 1659 he fulfilled that duty in his *The Heart of New England rent at the Blasphemies of the Present Generation* (Cambridge, 1659). He contended that the Quakers had borrowed their basic ideas from the violent Anabaptists of Münster, and it came to be generally believed that the atrocities of Münster would be repeated in New England once the Quakers became numerous enough. One of his most telling arguments (Chapter III) was that the Quakers opposed civil order since they denied obedience "unto the order of magistracy," which, he states, is evidenced both by "their scripts & behaviour." He closes his defense with the solemn warning:

It concerneth N. E. always to remember that originally they are a Plantation Religious not a Plantation of Trade. The profession of the purity of doctrine, worship & discipline, is written upon her forehead. . . . All these (her temporal prosperity) notwithstanding, if she fall away from her profession, call her Ichabod, the Glory is departed. . . . God forbid, that after N. E. hath now shined twenty years and more, like a light on a hill, it should at last go out in the snuff of Marcellianism (an extreme democratic theory of church government).

In justifying the execution of Robinson and Stevenson the General Court used Norton's conclusions, stating that just as one

---

[25] In 1661 there was printed in London a detailed account of Quaker persecutions by George Bishop, a citizen of Bristol, England, and a devout Quaker, based upon letters and first-hand accounts of visiting Friends. It is entitled *New England Judged, Not by Man's, but the Spirit of the Lord: And the Summe sealed up of New England's Persecutions. Being a brief Relation of the Suffering* of *the* People called Quakers in those parts of America, from the beginning of the Fifth Month 1656 (the time of their first arrival at Boston from England) to the later end of the Tenth Month, 1660.

An earlier account, by an English Quaker, Humphrey Norton, written on shipboard, was printed in London in 1659, entitled *New England's Ensigne . . . This being an Account of the Sufferings sustained by us in New England . .* These are the chief sources.

Jones, *op. cit.*, Chapter IV, "The Martyrs," is an excellent summary.

The first general historian of the Quakers, William Sewel, gives a full account of the Quaker executions in his *The History of the Rise, Increase, and Progress of the Christian People called Quakers . . .* 3d edition, Philadelphia: 1728, pp. 218–230.

would protect his family by keeping out persons infected with the plague and other contagious diseases, if they should try to force their way into private dwellings, so it is the duty of the fathers of the Commonwealth to protect it from the moral contagion which comes directly from Quaker teaching.[26]

After this recital of the cruel persecution meted out to the Quakers at the hands of Puritan New England, the following malediction upon Boston, written by William Robinson and Marmaduke Stevenson while in prison awaiting execution, has a particular appropriateness,

Oh ye Hypocrits! how can you sing and keep such noise concerning Religion, when your hands are full of blood, and your hearts full of Iniquity? Wash you, make you clean, put away the evil of your doings, cease to do Evil, learn to do Good, cleanse your hands you sinners, and your hearts you Hypocrits, for your Prayers are abomination to me, Saith the Lord; my Spirit is weary with hearing, and my Soul is vexed day after day with your abominations. *Wo Wo* to thee thou Bloody Town of Boston and the rest that are Confederate with thee. . . .[27]

Strange as it may seem, relief was soon to come, through the direct intervention of Charles II. The English Quakers were now fully aroused over the terrible sufferings of their brethren in New England. The Quaker claim of the right to appeal to the English government for justice, made on several occasions, brought only scoffing remarks from the New England officials. This was all set forth in Bishop's *New England Judged,* which King Charles read. "Lo, these are my good subjects of New England," he remarked, as he read the passage to his courtiers, and added, "but I will put a stop to them." He had also received a petition signed by several Quakers who had been banished from New England, listing in detail the many instances of persecution that had taken place there. All this made a deep impression upon the King, and in spite of attempts of the Massachusetts authorities to persuade him of the necessity of suppressing the Quakers, the King acted and in a most dramatic manner.

---

[26] A good summary of opinions as to the danger arising from Quaker teachings is to be found in H. L. Osgood, *The American Colonies in the Seventeenth Century,* New York: 1930, Vol. I, pp. 275–277.

[27] This is found in the Appendix of *New England Judged,* pp. 177–194.

Edward Burroughs, a leading London Friend, in a personal interview with the King, said to him, "There is a vein of innocent blood opened in thy dominions which will run over all if it is not stopped." To this the King replied, "But I will stop that vein." Then said Burroughs, "Then stop it speedily." "As speedily as ye will, call the Secretary and I will do it presently," replied Charles. When the *mandamus* was prepared Burroughs was granted the privilege of selecting a special messenger to carry it to Massachusetts, and he selected Samuel Shattuck, the Salem Quaker who had been banished on pain of death. It was a bitter pill indeed for Governor Endicott to receive such a command; it was even a more bitter one to have that message at the hands of a hated Quaker. The King's message ordered that all Quakers condemned and imprisoned in Massachusetts were to be sent to England for trial. This was the thing which Massachusetts dreaded most of all, the interference of England in the internal affairs of the colony. Though this did not put an immediate stop to Quaker persecution, it did bring immediate modification of the laws against the Quakers, though there were still to be some harrowing experiences under the brutal "Cart and Whip Act." In the year Governor Endicott died, 1665, a law was passed permitting Quakers to go about their secular business without molestation.[28] The year 1677 marks the end of Quaker persecution in New England.

During the years when the first Quaker missionaries were entering New England, others were finding their way into the Dutch colony of New Amsterdam. Here, as in Rhode Island, they found the way prepared by exiles from New England, who had established a series of settlements along the north shore of Long Island. Many of these ex-New Englanders, as Lady Deborah Moody, were inclined toward Baptist and Seeker opinions, or had, at least, an open mind toward new religious views. Accordingly when the first Quaker missionaries appeared in 1657 they found many ready to be "convinced" and the formation of groups

---

[28] Joseph Besse, *A Collection of the Sufferings of the people called Quakers for the Testimony of a Good Conscience . . . 1650 to the . . . Act of Toleration . . . in the year 1689*, 2 vols., London: 1753. Vol. II, Chapter v, is devoted to New England.

for Quaker worship soon followed. Among the first converts was Lady Deborah Moody, and many of her neighbors followed her into the Quaker fold. Immediately Governor Stuyvesant, urged on by the Massachusetts authorities, attempted to check the movement and issued a proclamation imposing a fine of £50 on any one entertaining a Quaker, and confiscation of any ship bringing Quakers into the colony, while an old law against conventicles was revived. This action brought a remonstrance from the town of Flushing, signed by thirty-one residents, including the town clerk and the sheriff. The Governor responded by depriving the town of the right to hold town meetings, but instead of hindering the Quaker cause, it only hastened the forming of a Quaker meeting in the town.

The most famous case of Dutch persecution of the Long Island Quakers was that of John Browne, who was arrested and fined £25 for permitting the use of his house for a Quaker meeting, on the ground that he was violating the conventicle law. Browne refused to pay the fine; was imprisoned and finally transported to Amsterdam. Nothing could have better served the Quaker cause in New Amsterdam, for immediately on landing· he laid his case before the directors of the Dutch West India Company. The story of his treatment aroused the spirits of the liberty-loving Dutchmen to action, and a letter was at once forwarded to Governor Stuyvesant, which settled the matter once and for all. The entire letter is worth reproducing here, for it shows clearly some of the practical considerations upon which Dutch liberties were based.

Amsterdam, 16th April, 1663.
We finally did see, from your last letter that you had exiled and transported hither a certain Quaker named John Browne, and although it is our cordial desire that similar and other sectarians might not be found there, yet as the contrary seem to be the fact, we doubt very much if vigorous proceedings against them ought not to be discontinued, except you intend to check and destroy your population; which, however, in the youth of your existence ought rather to be encouraged by all possible means: Wherefore, it is our opinion, that some connivance would be useful; that the consciences of men, at least, ought ever to remain free and unshackled. Let everyone be unmolested, as

long as he is modest; as long as his conduct in a political sense is irreproachable; as long as he does not disturb others, or oppose the government. This maxim of moderation has always been the guide of the magistrates of this city, and the consequence has been that, from every land, people have flocked to this asylum. Tread then in their steps, and, we doubt not, you will be blessed.[29]

Soon after Browne's return to his home on Long Island he met Governor Stuyvesant on the street of Flushing. Though somewhat abashed the Governor greeted the returned exile by saying, "I am glad to see you safe home"; whereupon Browne replied, "I hope you never harm any more Friends." And he never did. By the opening of the eighteenth century at least seven Quaker meetings had been established in New York, four on Long Island, two on the mainland, and one on Shelter Island.

Both in New England and New York Quakerism won its first converts mainly from among those already in revolt against other forms of religion, but especially the established Churches; in the Southern Colonies, and especially in the Carolinas, Quakerism gained its main following from among the unchurched. And outside of a few instances of rough treatment in Maryland and Virginia, it met little persecution.[30]

The first planters of the Quaker seed to appear in Virginia were two Englishmen, Josiah Coale and Thomas Thurston, who landed in Virginia in 1657. That they were successful in winning converts is evidenced by the fact that in 1660 a law was passed entitled, "An Act for Suppressing Quakers." It provided that all Quakers in the colony should be arrested, imprisoned and sent out of the colony, and in case of their return they should be proceeded against as felons. It also provided a fine of £100 for any one entertaining Quakers, or for permitting Quaker assemblies in or near his house. In spite of a somewhat vigorous application of this law, the number of Quaker "convincements" increased, as the Quaker message was spread abroad by a continuous stream of new

---

[29] James Bowden, *The History of the Society of Friends in America,* 2 vols., London: 1850, is particularly valuable because of the reproduction of letters and other contemporary documents.

[30] Besse, *op. cit.,* Vol. II, Chapter x, "Maryland."

messengers. Maryland also proved good soil for Quaker propaganda. At first there was some trouble over Quaker opposition to the taking of oaths, and a few Quaker preachers were whipped out of the Province, but nowhere in the South was there anything like the opposition which Quakerism met in New England.

III

Spread of Quakerism

THE SECOND PERIOD in colonial Quakerism opens with the coming of a group of the most effective Quaker missionaries that ever left the shores of Britain for America. Among them were John Burnyeat, William Edmundson and George Fox, the founder himself. Burnyeat had already made his first visit to America in 1664, spending three years in visiting Quakers and in propagating the Quaker gospel, and was in America on his second visit at the time George Fox landed. William Edmundson, one of the most forceful among the early Quaker preachers, accompanied George Fox to America, and later made two additional visits in 1675–77 and in 1683. It was George Fox, however, who left the greatest impact upon early American Quakerism. Leaving England on June 6, 1671, with twelve Quaker companions, he landed in the Barbadoes on August 3. From thence he went to Jamaica, and after a three months' stay on that British island, arrived in Maryland March 3, 1672, and on the thirtieth of the same month he reached Rhode Island. After two months in that Quaker haven, he turned southward, visiting New Jersey and the Quaker communities on Long Island, and thence southward again, "through the woods toward Maryland." During the autumn of 1672 he itinerated through Virginia and the Carolinas, and from thence back to Maryland, from whence he sailed March 21, 1673, for Bristol.[31]

All that we can hope to do here is to sample, here and there, George Fox's own account of his American experiences. He

---

[31] *The Journal of George Fox,* edited from the MSS, by Norman Penney, 2 vols., Cambridge: 1911. For the American *Journal* see Vol. II, pp. 176–247.

arrived in Maryland just in time to take part in a great General Meeting which John Burnyeat had called, which was attended by "many people of considerable quality," including "five or six Justices of the Peace, the speaker of their Parliament or Assembly" as well as others of note. It is interesting to notice throughout his American itinerary with how much satisfaction Fox mentioned the interest of important people in the Quaker message. It was this meeting which set the mark of respectability on Maryland Quakerism. After this Fox and Burnyeat joined forces in many "large and heavenly" meetings on the eastern shore and elsewhere in that colony. The two months spent in Rhode Island naturally formed the climax of his American experiences, and from start to finish it was a constant round of meetings, most of them attracting literally multitudes from far and near. Nicholas Easton, the Quaker Governor, traveled with him extensively and also entertained him. With Fox also were the Quaker missionaries who had accompanied him to America, while others joined him from time to time. During his stay in Rhode Island Quakerism was planted for the first time on the western shore of Narragansett Bay. Fox reports that people came to hear him there from as far away as Connecticut. Before leaving Rhode Island he took occasion to send a letter to the Assembly of the colony, recommending remedial laws against drunkenness, fighting, and swearing, and suggested the building of a market house for a weekly market, an indication that his head was not always in the clouds. He ends his letter by urging the legislators to "look into all [their] your ancient liberties and privileges—your divine liberty, your national liberty, and all your outward liberties, which belong to your commons, your town, and your island colony."

It was during his Rhode Island sojourn that Fox and his helpers came into collision with Roger Williams, then an old man of three score and ten. The great meetings which Fox held in Newport and Providence and other places in the colony, and the news of the large numbers of converts to Quakerism, stirred Roger Williams to wrath and action, for among the many types of religious expression which Roger Williams did not like, Quakerism took first rank. Twice he had tried to speak in their meetings to point out Quaker errors, but both times he had been headed off, once "by the sudden praying of the governor's wife." He then tried a new method of attack. He drew up fourteen formal propositions, showing the errors of Quakerism, and sent them to George Fox, with a challenge to a public debate. For some reason they were not delivered to Fox, and Williams concluded that the Quaker founder feared to meet him. He says, "The old Fox thought it best to run for it, and leave the work to his Journeymen and chaplains." "G F hath pluckt in his Horns." It seems, however, that Fox was on his way out of the colony before the news of the challenge reached him. A debate, however, was finally arranged, and it was agreed that seven of the propositions were to be discussed at Newport and the remaining seven at Providence. There were three Quaker defenders, John Stubbs, John Burnyeat, and William Edmundson, against the doughty old Seeker. Immense crowds attended and, as generally happens, both sides claimed the victory, while the Quakers boasted many converts as a result. The comments of Williams on Edmundson, who did most of the talking for the Quakers, and the latter's estimate of Williams are amusing if not greatly to the credit of either. Of Edmundson, Williams remarked,

A stout portly man of great voice, who would often vapour and preach long, and when I patiently waited till the gust was over, and began to speak, he would stop my mouth with a very unhansome shout of a grevious interruption . . . a pragmatical and insulting soul. . . . A flash of wit, a face of brass, and a tongue set on fire from the hell of Lyes and Fury.

Of Williams, Edmundson states,

the bitter old man could make nothing out, but on the contrary they were turned back upon himself: he was baffled and the People saw his weakness, folloy and envy. . . . There were many prejudic'd Baptists would fain have helped the old priest against the Friends; but they durst not undertake the Charge against us for they saw it was weak and false.

The only good thing that can be said of this sorry spectacle is that both sides were practicing freedom of conscience and freedom of speech, in which both equally believed, and it furnished proof that Rhode Island was living up to the great principles upon which she was established.[32]

The most constructive work performed by Fox and his band of missionaries was in the Southern Colonies. Although he spent only eighteen days in North Carolina, it was sufficient to plant the Quaker seed in a number of localities. Edmundson had preceded Fox by several months and reported, "several were tendered with the sense and power of God, received the truth and abode in it." Fox was received "loveingly" by the Governor and his wife, and "having visited the north part of Carolina, and made a little entrance for the truth among the people there," he turned toward Virginia. The Quakers were the first to undertake missionary work in North Carolina.[33] Weeks states that by 1676 the Quakers were fully organized there, and in 1681 Fox wrote to Friends in South Carolina urging them to unite with those of North Carolina to form a yearly or half-yearly meeting. The region between the James River and the North Carolina border was the scene of Fox's activities in Virginia. In Maryland, however, he met the largest response. A great General Meeting for all Maryland was held on the Eastern Shore in October 1672. It lasted five days, and perhaps never before had so many people gathered in one place in Maryland. It was a "very heavenly meeting" and "Friends were sweetly refreshed," and "Justices and other persons of quality" were convinced. For weeks Fox and his companions almost lived in boats, and he was often "wet and weary from rowing."

Following the departure of George Fox and his companions, other visiting Friends from England and Ireland continued to

---

[32] Out of this melancholy battle came two equally melancholy books. The first by Roger Williams, entitled *George Fox Digg'd out of his Burrowes or an offer of a Disputation on fourteen proposals made this Summer 1672 (so called) unto G. Fox then present in Rhode Island in New England by R. W.*, Boston: 1676. Two years later this was answered by George Fox and John Burnyeat in *A New England Fire-Brand Quenched, Being Something in Answer unto a Lying, Slanderous Book, Entitled George Fox Digged out of his Burrowes, etc. Printed at Boston in the year 1676 of one Roger Williams . . . Where his proposals are turn'd upon his own Head, and there and here he was and is sufficiently confuted*, etc., London: 1678.

[33] Stephen B. Weeks, *The Religious Development of the Province of North Carolina*, Johns Hopkins University Studies, Tenth Series, V–VI, Baltimore: 1892.

come, traveling widely through the colonies. In fact one of the distinguishing characteristics of eighteenth-century Quaker history is that connected with the work of these voluntary missionaries. Among their number Thomas Chalkley was one of the most indefatigable and effective. He came from London to Philadelphia in 1701, and for forty years ranged up and down the country from Maine to South Carolina. The *Journal*[34] of his life and travels constitutes one of the most valuable sources for the social history of the time. Another Quaker "publisher" who had a large part in the eighteenth-century Quaker expansion in America was Thomas Story.[35] Converted to Quakerism in Carlisle in 1791, he soon became an active publisher of the Quaker gospel in England and Scotland. He came to America in 1698, where he was equally active in the cause of spreading the "truth." For a time, 1700 to 1705, he served William Penn and Pennsylvania as a member of the Provincial Council and Keeper of the Rolls. His voluminous *Journal* records experiences in many parts of the world, from America on the west to Turkey on the east.

This itinerant Quaker ministry was, of course, purely voluntary as well as self-supporting, and when the difficulty of travel and the expense involved is considered, it was a truly astonishing type of sacrificial work. Rufus Jones lists one hundred and eleven such Quaker ministers, from England and Ireland alone, who visited the Philadelphia Yearly Meeting from 1684 to 1763. Some of these spent years in the colonies, visiting Quaker communities from one end of the country to the other. They were entertained in the homes of the people, and through these personal relationships often performed their most effective service to the cause. There were also numerous American "Public Friends," performing the same kind of service. Of these John Woolman is perhaps the best known. The part played by these traveling Friends in keeping American Quakerism a unit in life and ideals, cannot be overestimated. But one of the unfortunate circumstances of this type

---

[34] *A Journal or Historical Account of the Life, Travels and Christian Experience of that ancient, faithful servant of Jesus Christ, Thomas Chalkley*, 2nd edition, London: 1751.

[35] *Journal of the Life of Thomas Story*, etc., London: 1747.

of ministry was that the local meetings came to depend so fully upon the visiting Friends that it tended to stifle the development of a local ministry.

IV

THE QUAKER COLONIES

THE AVERAGE intelligent American thinks of Quaker beginnings in America in terms of William Penn and Pennsylvania. The preceding pages have shown, however, to what extent Quakerism had been established in America before the great Quaker migration to Pennsylvania had begun. The Quakers would have been an important religious body in the American colonies even if Pennsylvania had never been established as a Quaker refuge or if William Penn had never come to America. The first Quaker colony, however, was not Pennsylvania, but rather it is New Jersey which has that distinction.

With the final transfer of New Netherland to the English in 1674, the Duke of York, who had been given the proprietaryship of both New York and New Jersey, released the lands across the Hudson to two of his friends, Sir George Carteret and John Lord Berkeley. Within a short time after this transfer Lord Berkeley, then an old man, sold his interest to two Quakers, John Fenwick, a farmer of Buckinghamshire and a former Cromwellian soldier, and Edward Byllynge, a London merchant. Just previous to the sale New Jersey had been divided into east and west sections, and it was Berkeley's share, West Jersey, which now came into Quaker hands. Business complications and disagreements with the testy Fenwick led Byllynge to sell his share, which was nine tenths of the whole, to four other Quakers, one of whom was William Penn. Carteret, also an old man, died in 1680. His estate proved badly involved and in the process of its settlement East Jersey was put up at auction and was bid in by a group of twelve men, most of whom were Quakers, for the sum of £3,400. Among the twelve were also William Penn and Edward Byllynge. This was the beginning of William Penn's interest in American colonization.[36]

---

[36] Andrews, *op. cit.*, II, Chapter VI.

Quaker control of New Jersey, however, was of short duration. In 1692 a new set of men, mostly members of the Church of England, gained control of West Jersey, and Quaker supremacy was at once overthrown. In East Jersey there was some Quaker influence, but as a whole the Proprietary period in New Jersey was one of confusion and came to an end in 1702, when New Jersey became a royal province. New Jersey's significance in American Quakerism lies in the fact that it gave to William Penn his first intimate contact with America and furnished the Quakers, under Penn's leadership, an opportunity to try an experiment in government. It also induced the first large Quaker immigration to America.

The "Concessions and agreements of the Proprietors, Freeholders, and Inhabitants of West Jersey, in America," of March 1677, undoubtedly in large part the work of William Penn, "gave to the spirit of liberty a wider range than had heretofore been the case in any record of Anglo-Saxon organic law." It provided for complete liberty of conscience, security from illegal arrest, trial by jury, control of taxation by representatives, elected by a secret ballot of the entire body of proprietors, freeholders, and inhabitants of the colony. Without this New Jersey experience William Penn doubtless would never have asked Charles II for the Pennsylvania grant. Quaker control of West Jersey started the Quaker immigration movement to America. Literature was prepared and distributed to induce Quaker immigration, which began in 1675 when the ship *Griffin* sailed from London with a large number of Quaker settlers. Two years later the *Kent* brought over two hundred and thirty additional Quaker emigrants who became the founders of the city of Burlington, New Jersey. Within eighteen months "fully eight hundred Quakers . . . settled in the new colony," and by the time William Penn had secured the Pennsylvania grant some fourteen hundred settlers had arrived. Many of them were people of influence and large means. Immediately Quaker meetings were set up. The Burlington Monthly Meeting dates from May 1678 and for a time was the greatest Quaker center in America.

East Jersey had attracted a considerable population during the

Dutch period.[37] Some had come from Long Island as a result of the intolerant policy of Governor Stuyvesant; others had departed from Massachusetts for the same reason. Baptists and Quakers were numerously represented among them, Middletown becoming a Baptist haven, while Piscataway was founded by New Hampshire Baptists in 1680. Reaction against the growing laxity of New England Congregationalism, as a result of the operations of the Half-Way Covenant, led to a considerable exodus from the New Haven colony into New Jersey, and Newark, Elizabethtown and Woodbridge became Congregational colonies. Monmouth County attracted a large number of Scotch Covenanters and a considerable sprinkling of Scotch Quakers. Among the latter was George Keith, a graduate of the University of Aberdeen, a surveyor and a mathematician, who had left the Presbyterian fold to become a Quaker. He arrived in 1684 with his wife and two daughters, and two years later was appointed Surveyor General of East Jersey. His later conversion to Anglicanism and his work for the S.P.G. in the colonies already has been noted in Chapter Two.

The beginnings of William Penn's great Proprietary colony of Pennsylvania have received more attention than those of any other colony with the exception of New England and Virginia. William Penn (b. 1644), the son of an English Vice-Admiral, Sir William Penn, was first exposed to Quaker ideas on his father's estate in Ireland when as a boy of twelve he heard Thomas Loe, a famous Irish Quaker preacher, who had been invited by his father to preach at his house. The seed there planted in young Penn's mind and heart sprouted when, as a student at Oxford, he, with a group of like-minded students, revolted against the ritualistic services conducted in the college chapel. This led to his expulsion. His father, hoping to cure him of Quaker notions, sent him to travel in Europe. When on his return (1666) he was sent to Ireland to settle a business matter for his father, he again heard Loe, and his complete conversion to Quakerism followed (1667).

Within the space of three years after his conversion William

[37] Thomas Jefferson Wertenbaker, *The Founding of American Civilization. The Middle Colonies,* New York: 1938. See particularly Chapter IV, "The Puritans in New Jersey."

Penn had become one of the most conspicuous Quakers in England. Because of his wealth, which he inherited on the death of his
father in 1670, and social position, he was looked upon by English
Churchmen as one of those dangerous fellows who made radicalism respectable. Penn also inherited from his father friendly
relations with the Court, and the Duke of York, later James II,
entertained a personal liking for him. When James ascended
the throne, Penn secured from him the release of more than
a thousand Quakers from prison. It was through his close and
intimate friendship with the Duke of York that William Penn
received the grant of the great province of Pennsylvania in
March 1681, to satisfy an indebtedness of £16,000 which the
English government had long owed his father.

With all his tremendous energy William Penn threw himself
into the organization and settlement of his great grant. A young
man of thirty-seven, he was now undertaking the greatest enterprise of his life. Sending a cousin, William Markham, to America
to make preparations for the first settlers, he took steps to spread
broadcast information regarding his colony. A descriptive booklet
was printed to be distributed throughout England, Scotland and
Wales, which was translated into German for distribution in
Southern Germany and into Dutch to interest prospective colonists
from Holland. Meanwhile Penn was drawing up his *Frame of
Government.* Though the charter placed numerous restrictions
upon the Proprietor, he was left full and unrestricted possession
of the land, and a wide territory within which to apply his ideas
of government. Though not as significant as his Concessions and
Agreements for West Jersey, Penn's Pennsylvania Laws "are a
witness to Penn's (his) purity of soul, and almost childlike faith
in the goodness of his fellowmen." It is a noble code of Quaker
principles applied to actual government, and "above all else they
lay stress on the liberty of worship, on toleration for all who
believed in God."

A tremendous flow of Quaker immigration immediately began.
Two boatloads came in 1681; but the next year saw twenty-three
vessels sail up the Delaware with something like two thousand
settlers. Most of them were undoubtedly Quakers, though others

were welcome, and they came from every part of the British Isles. In August of 1682 came William Penn. Throughout his stay of ten months he was constantly occupied. He directed the laying out of Philadelphia, as well as the building of a mansion house at Pennsbury. He inspected the interior of his province; visited New York, New Jersey and Long Island; discussed with Lord Baltimore the boundary between Pennsylvania and Maryland, later to be drawn by Mason and Dixon; preached constantly at Quaker Meetings, and negotiated with the Indians several agreements which outlasted his life. Believing that Indians were the children of God, and therefore his brothers, he determined that they should be treated with understanding and generosity. He made several treaties with them, which have been fused by tradition into the treaty made at Shackamaxon, where it was agreed that "the Indians and English must live in love as long as the sun gave light."

Called back to England just as his friend James II was ascending the throne, Penn was unable to return to Pennsylvania until 1699, and then only for a little more than a year. The outbreak of the War of the Spanish Succession in 1701 and the threat to all Proprietary colonies, caused his return to England, never again to set foot upon his great American province. During his long absences from Pennsylvania a series of incompetent and unworthy deputy governors and a grossly dishonest business agent testify to Penn's inability to judge character. His latter years were full of disappointment and sorrow. For a time he was imprisoned for debt as a result of involvement for which his Pennsylvania agent was responsible. His eldest son, William Jr., was a rake and a libertine and became a constant grief to his father. A stroke of paralysis destroyed his memory in 1712, but even before that his life's work was done. His crowning achievement and the principal reason for the permanent place he occupies in history is the founding of a State where liberty of conscience was guaranteed.[38]

In none of the colonies at the end of the colonial period was

---

[38] Among the best recent biographies of William Penn are M. R. Brailsford, *The Making of William Penn*, London: 1930; B. Dobree, *William Penn, Quaker and Pioneer*, Boston: 1932; C. E. Vulliamy, *William Penn*, London: 1933. S. M. Janney, *The Life of William Penn*, Philadelphia: 1852, is the best of the older lives.

there so great a variety of religious groups as was to be found in Pennsylvania—proof conclusive of the fact that there freedom of worship and conscience had been practiced. In 1776 there were in Pennsylvania 403 different congregations. Of these 106 were German Reformed; 68 were Presbyterian, 63 Lutheran, 61 Quaker; 33 Episcopalian; 27 Baptist; 14 Moravian; 13 Mennonite; 13 Dunker or German Baptist Brethren; 9 Catholic and 1 Dutch Reformed.[39]

V

QUAKER ORGANIZATION

To DISPENSE completely with a professional ministry, and "to assume that all men were potentially near enough God to be their own priests" was a bold venture in the seventeenth century. It is true that Luther's doctrine of the universal priesthood of all believers seems to uphold Quaker practice, but like Luther's theory of Church-State relationship, it remained to him little more than a theory. The principal difference between the Quakers and Luther in respect to the universal priesthood was that they put into actual practice what he had advanced only as a doctrine. In fact, one of the basic differences between the right and left wings of the Reformation lies here; the former often held in theory what the latter practiced.

The central institution of Quakerism was the meeting for worship. The large living rooms of well-to-do members served as their first meeting places in America. Here they gathered on each First Day, sitting in silence until the great God of the Universe "prepared a mouthpiece for his Word." When finally the speaking came it was "rhythmical and rapturous, loaded with emotion," interwoven with Scripture texts and phrases, often ending with a simple relation of a personal experience. If a traveling Friend were present, it was believed implicitly that he had been sent by Divine leading. When some one felt the call to pray, he knelt, while all the worshippers stood, removing their hats until the

---

[39] Lillian M. Barr, "Status of the Churches in Pennsylvania in 1776" (unpublished Master's thesis, University of Chicago, 1920).

prayer was ended. Worship for the Quakers was, for each one, the experiencing of the presence of God. They did not come primarily to be instructed, but to achieve the feeling of oneness with the mighty God.

When George Fox came to America, outside the meetings for worship Quaker organization had hardly begun. Meetings for business had been held only occasionally, generally at the call of some visiting Friend. Fox changed all this, and by the time of his departure Quaker organization and discipline had been established on a definite basis. Quaker organization as finally perfected consisted of First Day Meetings, which were purely for worship; Monthly Meetings, which were business meetings of a local congregation; Quarterly Meetings, which combined worship and business of a group of congregations, and the Yearly Meeting. It was the Monthly Meeting which exercised power over the individual members, received new members and disowned those who had departed from the "truth." Its officers were the Elders and the Overseers; the former looked after the spiritual concerns of the Meeting, the latter after the business matters. The Quarterly Meeting, made up of a group of Monthly Meetings, exercised supervision and received appeals from the Monthly Meetings or from individual members. The Yearly Meeting was made up of all the Monthly Meetings within its bounds and was the unit of Quaker authority. Its officers were a Clerk and Assistants. It had no President, for the Clerk was the presiding officer as well as the secretary. Even to the present day, no formal vote is ever taken. After discussion on any matter has come to a close the Secretary draws up what he thinks to be the general judgment. If approved it is recorded as the decision of the Meeting, but if any object, further discussion is carried on until all have come to the same mind. Because of this method Quaker action was generally conservative. In all meetings the women were on an equality with men, though at times men and women met separately, and what was done in one Meeting was sent to the other for approval.[40]

---

[40] Rufus M. Jones, *Faith and Practice of Quakers,* London, n. d., Chap. IV. "The Structure and Method of the Society of Friends."

By the beginning of the eighteenth century the colonies were covered with a network of Quaker Meetings from Maine to South Carolina, and for the next fifty years Quakerism was an expanding movement. There were six Yearly Meetings before the end of the seventeenth century, as follows: the Rhode Island, later the New England, was the oldest and dates from 1661; the Baltimore Yearly Meeting was formed in 1672; the Virginia in 1673; the Burlington, later the Philadelphia, was organized in 1681; the New York in 1696; and the North Carolina in 1698. Each Yearly Meeting was an independent unit, though advice of the other Yearly Meetings was often sought, while the London Yearly Meeting came to be considered in a rather indefinite way as a court of last appeal. The principal connecting link between the Yearly Meetings were the Traveling Friends, whose significance in colonial Quakerism has been considered already.

Quakerism was not an ascetic system. Like other puritans they glorified labor; nor did they believe that God intended men to be poor and uncomfortable. They therefore did not withdraw from the world, though there was great insistence that Quakers must not marry outside the fold. The records of the colonial Monthly Meetings abound in "dealings" with members who had transgressed in this respect. The Quakers were strict also in their prohibitions of the common vices, and in this respect they were ahead of their time. Quakers soon gained the general reputation for integrity in business dealings, with the result that they early began to reap an enviable temporal reward, and they became, generally, a prosperous class. But with economic prosperity and the comfort and ease which accompanied it, the old spirit of daring and adventure which had characterized the first generation gave place to one of caution and compromise. Many, especially those who held public office, and they were numerous, while giving a formal adherence to the Society of Friends, did so because of hereditary attachment rather than from conviction. This tendency was accelerated by the precedent established by the London Yearly Meeting in 1737 in establishing birthright membership. This permitted the wife and children "to be deemed members of the Monthly Meeting of which the husband or father is a mem-

ber, not only during his life, but after his decease." Thus what
had happened in New England Congregationalism, after the
adoption of the Half-Way Covenant, now took place in Quakerism; from a Church made up of converted believers, they became
a society based upon heredity. And even more than in Congregationalism Quakerism tended to become more and more a
social caste.

V

Roman Catholic Contributions

THE BEGINNINGS of English colonization of America and the outlawing of Roman Catholicism in England were contemporaneous events. The English Reformation and the religious settlement of Queen Elizabeth's reign had swept Roman Catholics out of practically every influential place in the kingdom, while the increasingly severe anti-Catholic laws made it legally impossible to carry on Catholic worship. The vast majority of the people were members of the Established Church, or were leaning toward the more radical Protestant bodies, leaving those who still adhered to the old faith in a very small minority. Generally speaking, this Catholic minority was made up of the landed gentry among whom the lure of trade and commercial profit, which was so powerful an influence in attracting merchants and capitalists to the New World, was almost completely lacking. The Catholic minority were naturally economic and political conservatives, and therefore little moved by the many schemes of that time to build a new social or political order. Rather they longed for the restoration of the good old times and the good old ways. These were the basic reasons why English Catholics played a minor rôle in the colonization of America.[1]

---

[1] A partial list of the great Catholic families in England is obtained from the signatures of the *Protest of the Catholic Peers* in the controversy between the Bishop of Chalcedon and the lay Catholics of England. The list includes: John Talbot, Earl of Shrewsbury; Henry Somersett, Earl of Worcester; Thomas Darcy, Earl Rivers; James Touchet, Earl of Castlehaven and Baron Audley; William Howard, Lord Naworth; Thomas Somersett, Viscount Cashell; Edward Somersett, Baron Herbert; Henry Nevell, Baron Abergavenny; Thomas Windsor, Baron Bradenham; William Petre, Baron Writle; Thomas Brudenell, Baron Stourton; George Calvert, Baron Baltimore. Five other Catholic peers acceded to the protest without signing; two others were partially in favor but did not sign; three were noncommittal. Also the *Protest* contained the signatures of some three hundred Catholic knights, esquires and other gentry. (Thomas A. Hughes, *The History of the Society of Jesus in North America*, New York: 1917, I, pp. 224–228.)

I

THE LORDS BALTIMORE AND THE FOUNDING OF MARYLAND.[2]

THE ONLY successful attempt of a Catholic to establish a colony in Anglo-America was that undertaken by George Calvert, the first Lord Baltimore, who but a short time before had professed conversion to the Catholic faith. Previous to his conversion he had been a Member of Parliament and had served in several minor positions in the government, the first being that of private secretary to Sir Robert Cecil, upon whose friendship his political fortunes were largely based. Later he became a clerk of the Privy Council, served on an Irish Commission, was raised to knighthood, became principal Secretary of State, and *ex-officio* member of the Privy Council. From several contemporary accounts we learn that he was a man of moderate abilities, but a prudent and tactful official. He seems to have been universally respected for his integrity and for the high moral standards which he maintained.

Just what were the influences which led George Calvert to become a Roman Catholic are not clear. It has been suggested that his experiences in Ireland as a member of one of the Irish Commissions, attempting to force a hated religion upon the Irish people, caused a revulsion of feeling against attempts to compel religious uniformity. It was not unlikely that he was familiar with Sir Thomas More's *Utopia,* in which religious freedom was advocated. At any rate, after his conversion Father Henry More, the great-grandson of the author of *Utopia* and the Provincial of the English Jesuits, became his friend and spiritual counselor. His announced conversion to Catholicism made necessary his withdrawal from his government posts, although he was retained as a Privy Councilor, and as a mark of the King's favor was created first Baron of Baltimore in the Kingdom of Ireland.

George Calvert had long been interested in colonization, evi-

---

[2] B. C. Steiner, "The First Lord Baltimore and his Colonial Projects" (Annual Report, American Historical Association, 1905), furnishes a long list of authorities. Charles M. Andrews, *The Colonial Period of American History,* New Haven: 1934, II, pp. 275–281. For a Jesuit account of Lord Baltimore and his conversion see Hughes, *op. cit.*

denced by his membership in both the Virginia and New England Companies. In attempting to found colonies in Newfoundland and Virginia he had twice journeyed to America. Both attempts had failed. The King had sought to dissuade him from further colonizing projects, but he was not to be turned aside. "He was under the impelling influence of motives and obligations that were more imperative than those of a mere colonizer," for it evidently had been laid upon his conscience as a sacred duty to find a refuge for his Roman Catholic brethren, an obligation which Andrews tells us had long been felt by the Arundel group. Lord Baltimore's importunity finally was rewarded by a patent for the Province of Maryland, but before the charter had passed the' seal, he died at the early age of fifty-two, leaving to his son Cecelius his plans, his obligations and his hopes.

Except in religious matters Lord Baltimore was not ahead of his time, and in this respect he was tolerant and sympathetic rather than liberal. His religious attitudes were not the result of any profound theorizing, but of his sincere benevolence. These traits his son Cecelius seems to have inherited along with the colonizing schemes to which his father had given the last years of his life. Cecelius had married Lady Anne Arundel, the daughter of the Earl of Arundel, and thus was tied to one of the most influential Catholic families of the time.

In several respects the Maryland charter was a remarkable document. In the first place it gave to the Proprietor complete control over the government as well as absolute ownership of the land, subject only to the yearly payment of two Indian arrows at the castle of Windsor. Baltimore, in other words, was an absolute lord, holding his lands and exercising his authority as had the mediaeval bishop of Durham, where, as the old maxim stated, "What the king was without, the bishop was within." As far as the charter could make it, the proprietaryship of Maryland "was as free from royal intervention and control as ever had been" the old palatinate counties on the Scottish and Welsh borders. The Maryland charter was also remarkable in that it set the model for a whole series of later grants which were to be made in America.

The second Lord Baltimore had the assistance of many Catho-

lic gentlemen in bearing the great expense of planting his colony.
It was not easy to secure colonists. Few Catholics could be induced
to go, one of the immediate reasons being that all who went were
required to take an oath denying papal authority in England. It is
known that of the two hundred and more who sailed on the *Ark*
and the *Dove,* November 22, 1633, only one hundred and twenty-
eight took the oath. It has been supposed that most of the Catholics, including the two Jesuits, Fathers White and Atham, and two
lay brothers, came on board later at the Isle of Wight to avoid
the oath. Probably all of the sixteen gentlemen-adventurers with
their wives and families were Catholics, while of the two hundred
or so laborers and servants most were Protestants. There is no
doubt that Lord Baltimore was fully aware, from the very
start, that his colony could not be planted successfully if he were
to depend solely upon his co-religionists. The instructions which
he gave to the Governor and commissioners previous to the sailing of the first expedition show clearly how much he felt the
success of his enterprise depended upon his ability to induce
Protestants to settle in his Province. "No scandall nor offence"
was "to be given any of the Protestants," and they were to "cause
all acts of Romane Catholique Religion to be done as privately
as may be," and all Roman Catholics were "to be silent upon all
occasions of discourse concerning matters of Religion." Protestants
were to be treated "with as much mildness and favor as Justice
will permit." On arrival they were to dispatch a messenger, "conformable to the Church of England," to Jamestown to announce
their arrival, and they were to assure the Virginia authorities of
their desire to "hold a good correspondency with him [the Gov-
ernor] and the Plantation of Virginia." [3]

In the year 1675, Charles, the second Lord Proprietor, gave the
following account of how his father, more than forty years before,
had made the promise of toleration to the first Maryland colonists:

At the first planting of this Province by my ffather Albeit he had an
Absolute Liberty given him and his heires to carry thither any Persons
out of the Dominions that belonged to the Crowne of England who

---

[3] *Calvert Papers,* I, Maryland Historical Society Publication, 28, Baltimore: 1889.

should be Wylling to goe thither yett when he came to make use of
this Liberty He found very few who were inclyned to goe and seat
themselves in those parts But such as for some Reason or other could
not lyve with ease in other places And of these a great part were such
as could not conforme in all particulars to the several Lawes of England relateing to Religion Many there were of this sort of People who
declared their Wyllingness to goe and Plant themselves in this Province
so as they might have a Generall Toleraccōn settled there by a Lawe
by which all sorts who professed Christianity in Generall might be at
Liberty to Worship God in such Manner as was most agreeable with
their respective Judgm^ts and Consciences without being subject to any
penaltyes whatsoever for their so doeing provyded the civill peace were
perserved And that for the secureing the Civill peace and preventing all
heats [and] Feuds which were generally observed to happen amongst
such as differ in oppynions upon Occasion of Reproachfull Nicknames
and Reflecting upon each Other's Oppynions It might by the same Lawe
be made Penall to give any Offence in that kynde these were the condicōns proposed by such as were willing to goe and be the first planters
of this Provynce and without the complying with these condicōns in
all probability This Province had never been planted.[4]

II

LORD BALTIMORE'S CONTROVERSY WITH THE JESUITS

THUS MARYLAND was established on the basis of full religious
toleration, and the Proprietor was determined that it should
remain on that basis. This is shown by his bitter controversy with
the Jesuits. It was not long until he discovered a movement on
foot among the Jesuit priests to make themselves independent of
the Proprietor's authority. The information came to him that the
Jesuits claimed the right to accept for their Society gifts of land
directly from the Indians. They asserted that in a new and unset-
tled country the canon law prevailed without assent or adoption
by prince or people, and that under this law they were entitled to
exemptions from lay jurisdiction. Under such exemptions they
would have the right to receive gifts of land from their Indian

---

[4] *Maryland Archives: Proceedings of the Council*, V, pp. 267–268.

converts without regard to the rights in the land which the Proprietor had received from the royal charter.

The Proprietor looked upon the Jesuit claim as imperiling his whole enterprise and he immediately dispatched his secretary, John Lewger, to head off this threat. Like the Baltimores, Lewger was a Catholic convert, though that did not hinder his stanch defense of his employer's interests. To make the situation still more serious, the Jesuits had gathered around them a party of laymen, among them one of the largest planters and the military leader of the Province, Thomas Cornwallis. The latter wrote the Proprietor on behalf of the Jesuit claim [5] urging him to do nothing that would be "prejuditiall toe the Immunettyes and Priveledges of that Church wch is the only true guide toe all Eternall Happiness," and declared,

I will rather Sacrifice myself and all I have in the defence of Gods Honor and his Churches right, than willingly Consent toe anything that may not stand with the Good Contiens of a real Catholick.[6]

The Proprietor also was informed that the priests were ready to shed their blood in defense of the faith and the liberty of the Church.

The extent to which Lord Baltimore was wrought up over the situation is fully revealed in the following quotation from a letter to his brother Leonard, the Governor, dated November 23, 1642.

I am (upon very good reason) satisfied in my judgm^t that they doe designe my destruction and I have too good cause to suspect, that if they cannot make or maintaine a partie by degrees among the English, to bring their ends about they will endeavour to doe it by the Indians within a very short time by arming them etc. against all those that shall oppose them and all under the pretence of God's hon^r and the propagacon of the Christian faith, wch shall bee the maske and vizard to hide their other designes w^thall. If all things that Clergie men should doe upon these p^rtences should bee accounted just and to proceed from God, Laymen were the basest slaves and most wretched creatures upon the earth. And if the greatest saint upon earth should intrude

---

[5] *Calvert Papers* (April 16, 1638), pp. 169–181.
[6] *Ibid.*, p. 172.

himselfe into my howse against my will and despite of mee wth intention to save the soules of all my family, but wthall give just cause to
suspect that hee likewise designes my temporall destruction, or that
being already in my howse doth actually practice it, although wthall
hee doe perhaps manie spirituall goods, yet certainlie I may and ought
to p^rserve myselfe by the expulsion of such an enemy and by provide-
ing others to performe the spirituall good hee did, who shall not have
any intention of mischiefe toward mee, for the law of nature teacheth
this, that it is lawfull for evrie man in his own just defence, *vim vi
repellere* those that wilbee impudent must be as impudently dealt
wthall.[7]

Through Lewger's activity the Proprietor won a complete victory over the Jesuits.[8] Acts were soon passed by the Maryland
Assembly taking away Catholic jurisdiction over marriages and
wills, while Lord Baltimore obtained from Father More, the
Jesuit Provincial in England, a renunciation by the Society of
Jesus of any and all claims of exemptions from the law of the
Province. A release was also executed for all lands acquired by
them from the Indians. Further they agreed to recognize that
grants in the future were to be obtained only through the Proprietor's sanction, and that henceforth no Jesuit priest should be
admitted to Maryland except by the Proprietor's license. The Proprietor made application to the *Propaganda Fide* at Rome to
establish a mission in Maryland and in 1642 two secular priests
arrived. A reconciliation between the Lord Proprietor and the
Jesuits was soon secured, however, and the Jesuit mission was
reestablished. Catholic authorities are extremely critical of both
Lord Baltimore and his agent John Lewger, and take the ground
that though sincere Catholics they were too unfamiliar with the
canons of the Church to act dispassionately.

The attitude of the General of the Jesuit Order at Rome toward
the Maryland controversy is revealing. In a letter to Father More
dated in October 1643 he states: "I should be sorry, if differences
about temporal things placed a hindrance in the way of conver-

---

[7] *Calvert Papers,* I, pp. 217–218.

[8] John Gilmary Shea, *History of the Catholic Church in the United States (Colonial
Days),* 1521–1763, New York: 1886, I, pp. 50–52. Lewger later became a priest.

sion of souls; or on account of perishable goods we should be hampered in bringing the natives to goods eternal." He asks that the "Right Honourable Baron" be assured "that we shall not be a source of detriment to his temporal dominion," but on the contrary they (we) would "be always ready to enlarge and promote the interests of his proprietary rights." Accordingly he instructs Father More to issue an order that the Maryland Jesuits do not accept "any landed property offered them whether by the faithful or by infidels, without the consent of the same Right Honourable Baron." In his December letter he states:

I shall be sorry indeed to see the first fruits, which are so beautifully developing in the Lord, nipped in their growth by the frost of cupidity.

From this last statement it would seem that the General of the Order shared, at least to some degree, the Proprietor's opinion of the Maryland Jesuits. The bitter struggle between the Proprietor and the Jesuits has left its permanent mark upon Maryland law, for to this day land cannot be acquired in Maryland for any religious purpose except by an act of the legislature nor can a priest or clergyman sit in the General Assembly.[9]

Lord Baltimore's conflict with the Jesuits furnishes indubitable evidence of his sincerity in his attempt to establish in Maryland real religious freedom. From the Jesuit point of view, the Proprietor's action was, to put it mildly, very unjust. Since he had asked them to come to serve the colonists and carry on missionary work among the Indians, they assumed that they would be provided for by the Proprietor. In this expectation they were doomed to disappointment, for although in the words of the historian of the American Jesuits, the Proprietor had ten millions of acres "clamouring to be given away," and in the face of the fact that the cooperation of the priests was good advertisement, and undoubtedly was one of the factors in inducing "pious Catholics" to come to Maryland, yet he refused to give "aid in extending the kingdom of Christ." Interpreted, however, from the standpoint of Lord Baltimore his action was fully justified on the ground that

[9] Bradley Johnson, *The Foundations of Maryland and the Origin of the Act concerning Religions*, Maryland Fund Publications, No. 18, pp. 60–61. The whole story of the controversy from the Jesuit angle may be found in Hughes, *op. cit.*, Chapters v and vi.

religious freedom in Maryland would have been impossible if what the Jesuits demanded had been granted, for that would have meant the practical establishment of Roman Catholicism. The Proprietor interpreted the separation of Church and State as meaning that the government was not to interfere with spiritual matters, but, on the other hand, he aimed at bringing under civil jurisdiction all temporal holdings of ecclesiastics, whether individual or corporate. And as is now fully recognized this was fundamentally necessary in the establishment of any real religious freedom. "The Jesuits based their contention for clerical privileges upon the usual practices in Catholic countries." They failed to realize that to make Maryland a Catholic State would be fatal to Lord Baltimore's interest and for that reason, if for no other, he was determined to place all religious groups on an equal footing.[10]

III

EARLY CATHOLIC ACTIVITY IN MARYLAND

GENERALLY SPEAKING, the land in Maryland was held in large estates, there being sixty manors erected during the seventeenth century besides the several six thousand acre tracts which had been set aside for the Proprietor and his relatives. The manors were from one thousand to three thousand acres and their owners had all the rights and privileges belonging to a lord of the manor in England, subject of course to the quitrent due the Proprietor of the Province. This system of large estates created distinct social classes. The manor holders and the plantation owners constituted the upper class, the tenants and the servants the lower classes. Roman Catholicism was the prevailing religion among the upper class, and on many of the large estates chapels and priests were maintained and regular services of the Catholic Church conducted. The landed class, the great majority of whom were Catholics, were all freemen and were in control of the government.

The Maryland Jesuits were under the necessity of supporting themselves, and they took up land on the same conditions as did

---

[10] Matthew Page Andrews, *The Founding of Maryland*, New York: 1933. See especially Chapter x, "Freedom of Conscience."

the other colonists and subject to the same quitrent to the Proprietor. By this process Jesuit land-holdings came to be of considerable proportions. Saint Mary's was the center of early Jesuit activity, but from the beginning the priests were interested in taking Christianity to the neighboring Indians. The Patuxents and Piscataways were mild tribes exposed to the inroads of the fierce Susquehannas, and, as was generally true of the weaker tribes, were fairly hospitable toward Christian teaching. Father White for a time was a resident among the Patuxents, and reported many conversions among them. Later he went to reside among the Piscataways, where he was successful in converting one of the chiefs, Chilomacon, who was baptized in the presence of the officials of the colony. Maryland was spared the dreadful Indian wars so common in the New England colonies. In 1651 Lord Baltimore set aside ten thousand acres on the Wicomico River as an Indian reservation for the remnants of the Maryland tribes and here Catholic work was carried on among them. Here the Indians developed a settled life and after a few generations, through intermarriage with the whites and because of their susceptibility to the diseases brought by the Europeans, they gradually disappeared.

In 1669 the Proprietor complained that there were but two priests in Maryland to minister to the two thousand Catholics in the colony. This complaint was reported to the *Congregation de Propaganda Fide* at Rome, with the result that two Franciscans were sent out in 1673. Four years later three additional Franciscans arrived as well as three additional Jesuits. This increased staff of laborers led to the founding of the first Catholic school for the education of the sons of the planters and also to the expansion of Catholic work northward, as Catholic settlers gradually filtered into the adjoining colonies.

IV

PROTESTANTS AND CATHOLICS IN MARYLAND

MARYLAND HOLDS a unique place in the history of American colonization in that here alone the attempt was made to have Catholics and Protestants live side by side on terms of equality. Conditions in England were particularly unfavorable to such an experiment and the wonder is that it succeeded as well as it did. From 1640 to 1649 the Puritans and the royalists were contending for power, and from 1649 to 1660 England was ruled by a Puritan minority bitterly hostile to everything Lord Baltimore stood for—prerogative and Roman Catholicism. From the beginning Virginia was opposed to Lord Baltimore's grant, while William Claiborne, a rabid Catholic hater and the Secretary of the Virginia colony, was his arch enemy. A short time before, Claiborne had taken possession of Kent Island located well within the Maryland boundaries and he refused to recognize Baltimore's Proprietaryship. With the outbreak of the civil war in England the Protestant element in the Maryland population combined with Claiborne to oppose the Catholic government in Maryland and charges against the Proprietary government were presented to Parliament. The committee of Lords and Commons for foreign plantations decided that the Proprietor had forfeited his rights and recommended that the Maryland charter be declared null and void. To meet this attack Lord Baltimore appointed a Protestant Governor (1648), William Stone, and he in turn invited some four or five hundred Puritans who had been living in Virginia on the James River since 1629 to take up their residence in Maryland, promising them political and religious freedom. They settled near the present city of Annapolis and within a few years became a most prosperous and assertive community and were soon constituting an important element in the opposition to the Proprietor.

It was during this period of uncertainty both in England and in Maryland that the famous Maryland Act concerning Religion was passed. Its purpose was to meet the accusation that Maryland was a hotbed of popery, to protect the interest of the Proprietor, and to preserve the wide toleration which had been practiced in Maryland from the beginning. It has been suggested by Professor Andrews that the act was drafted by Cecelius "as a kind of ratification of the original purpose of his father and himself and for the protection of the Roman Catholic Church in the province," since the Protestants in the colony were rapidly increasing and the Catholics steadily declining.

As a matter of fact the act was less liberal than the toleration which had been in operation from the beginning, in that it limited freedom of religion to trinitarians. Persons denying that Jesus was the Son of God, or the Holy Trinity or the Unity of the Godhead, or who used reproachful language concerning the Holy Trinity were subject to the death penalty. It forbade the disparaging of groups or individuals by the calling of such names as "Heretick, Schismatic, Idolator, Puritan, Independent, Presbyterian, Popish Priest, Jesuite, Jesuited papist, Lutheran Calvinist, Anabaptist, Brownist, Antinomian, Barrowist, Roundhead, Separatist," or the use "of any other name or term in a reproachful menner relating to matters of religion." The purpose of the act was to provide "for the more quiett and peacable government of this Province and the better to preserve mutuall Love and amity among the Inhabitants thereof." Aside from the anti-trinitarians "no person or persons whatsoever within this Province . . . professing to believe in Jesus Christ shall from henceforth be any ways troubled, molested or discountenanced for or in respect of his or her religion, nor in the free exercise thereof in this Province or the Islands thereunto belonging nor any way compelled to the belief or exercise of any other Religion against his or her consent." The anti-trinitarian clause was not a part of the original text sent by Lord Baltimore from England, but was added by the Puritan-Protestant party in the Maryland Assembly, so as to jibe with the policy of the Long Parliament in punishing heresies and blasphemies.[11] This clause placed a definite limitation on Maryland toleration and gave a ground for religious persecutions which formerly had been absent.

The coming of the Puritan party to power in England gave encouragement to the increasing Puritan element in Maryland and soon resulted in their taking over the control of the Province (1654–58). One of the first enactments of the Puritan majority in the Maryland Assembly was an act disfranchising Roman Catholics (1654). The Protestant Governor Stone in his attempt

---

[11] Andrews, II, pp. 310–311.

to uphold the Proprietor's rights resorted to arms, and a petty civil war ensued in which Claiborne and the Puritans won a complete victory and savage vengeance was meted out upon Catholics. Four were hanged, others were fined and their property confiscated. The Jesuit priests fled to Virginia and their houses were plundered. However, brighter days were ahead for the Proprietor and the Catholics. With the coming of Charles II to the throne Lord Baltimore's prerogatives were once more fully recognized and the Puritan opposition was reduced to a minimum. Likewise the liberal religious policy was restored and Maryland became the home of an increasing number of religious groups. Catholics remained socially and politically prominent, but on the whole Catholics and Protestants lived together in an atmosphere of amity and tolerance.

The twenty-four years from 1664 to 1688 were particularly favorable for the American Catholics. This was due primarily to the influence of the Duke of York, who in 1685 ascended the throne of England as James II. In 1669 he had publicly announced his conversion to Roman Catholicism, and from that time on, both in England and America, he left no stone unturned in promoting the interests of Catholicism. As the Proprietor of New York and New Jersey he promulgated the Duke's Laws (1665) in the interests of his co-religionists. He gave important colonial offices to Catholics, among them being Anthony Brockholls, second in authority under Governor Andros, and Thomas Dongan, an Irish Catholic whom he appointed Governor of New York in 1682. Dongan was accompanied to his post by a Jesuit priest, Father Harvey. Under Dongan's rule the first legislative assembly of New York (October 17, 1683) enacted a measure providing

that no person or persons which profess faith in God by Jesus Christ shall at any time be anyways molested, punished, disquited or called in question for any difference of opinions, or matter of religious concernment, who do not actually disturb the civil peace of the province.

It was during these years also that William Penn and his Quaker associates were beginning their great experiments in colonial government which guaranteed that persons, shall in no way be molested or prejudiced for their religious persuasions, or practice in matters of faith and worship, nor shall they be compelled at any time to frequent or maintain any religious worship, place or ministry whatever.

King James' pro-Catholic policy also enabled England to receive her first Catholic bishop since Queen Elizabeth's time, when in 1685 Dr. John Leyburn was made Vicar-Apostolic of all England and England was divided into four ecclesiastical districts, the London, the Western, the Midland and the Northern. The Catholics in America were placed under the supervision of the London district and this arrangement was continued until the end of the colonial period.

As the seventeenth century neared its close it appeared that Catholicism, both in England and America, was particularly favorably situated for a rapid advance. A Catholic King was on the throne; Catholic officials were occupying influential positions in several of the colonies; episcopal supervision from England had been established; while the wide religious toleration promised by the Quaker colonies, in process of formation, gave promise of Catholic expansion in that direction. It is not strange that Catholic historians speak in kindly terms of James II. His willingness to sacrifice everything for the advancement of the Catholic Church would naturally win him their praise. But this very fact was one of the principal reasons for his downfall, and with his overthrow the bright hopes for Catholicism in America came to a speedy end.

American Catholics are immensely proud of the religious toleration which prevailed in colonial Maryland. The consciousness of that proud chapter in their history has placed the American Catholics emotionally on the side of religious freedom. Historically it definitely places them on record. But it is well to point out that the Maryland policy was in no sense a Catholic Church policy. Rather it was carried forward in spite of the Church. If the early Maryland Jesuits had had their way in their contest with Lord Baltimore in their attempt to secure special treatment at his hands, which they conscientiously thought was their right to receive, the continuation of the Proprietor's toleration policy would there and then have been rendered impossible, and doubtless would have led to the immediate annulment of Lord Baltimore's Proprietary rights.

In considering religious toleration in the colonies, or anywhere else, a distinction must be made between the policies of individuals and the policies of ecclesiastical bodies. The Roman Catholic Church has never endorsed the broad principle of religious freedom; in fact the Catholic Church is committed by principle to intolerance.[12] Therefore the statement by Shea that the broad principle of religious freedom was recognized in the colonies "wherever Catholics had any influence" is, to put it mildly, misleading. It must be understood that wherever there were Catholics in the American colonies they were thinking in terms of their own "religious freedom" and were not necessarily concerned with "the broad principle" except where their own religious privileges were tied up with those of others. It has been pointed out that minorities were always in favor of toleration, whatever their real principles might be. The above statement, however, is not meant to detract from the honor which is rightfully due to the liberal-spirited Lord Baltimore, nor is it intended in any way to excuse the intolerance of the Maryland Protestants who were primarily responsible for nullifying all his efforts to organize his government on the broad basis of toleration and justice to all.

V

COLONIAL CATHOLICISM AFTER 1700

THE PASSAGE of the Toleration Act of 1689 gave no relief to Catholics either in England or America. Papists and those who did not believe in the Trinity were expressly excluded from its benefits. John Locke's argument was generally accepted, that Roman Catholics, not believing in toleration themselves, should not come

---

[12] For a clear statement of the Catholic position on religious toleration see John A. Ryan and Moorhouse F. X. Millar, *The State and the Church*, New York: 1936, pp. 34–39. The Catholics holds that "error has not the same right as truth" and since they alone have the truth, they have rights which other religious bodies do not inherently possess.

under any toleration agreement; that their tenets were incompatible with civil allegiance, since their first allegiance was to the Pope. So the long list of anti-Catholic laws on the statute books of England remained, and although these laws did not apply to the American colonies, the spirit that produced them was transplanted with the colonists, and it was not long until similar laws had been placed on the statute books of every one of the thirteen colonies. And there they remained until the close of the colonial period, even though many of their provisions had come to be enforced no longer. Only Quakers and Baptists refused to believe that Catholics were dangerous to civil government. But even in the colonies controlled by Baptists and Quakers, as Rhode Island and Pennsylvania, Catholics were disfranchised and made ineligible to hold offices of trust. Nor was there any place for Catholics in colonial education outside the Quaker and Baptist colonies, for only two of the colonial colleges admitted Roman Catholics—the College of Philadelphia and the College of Rhode Island—while Catholic schools were absolutely outlawed. The period from the beginning of the eighteenth century to the opening of the War for Independence was indeed a gloomy one for American Catholics.[13]

The establishment of the Church of England in Maryland in 1702 was soon followed by the removal of the seat of government from St. Mary's, the old Catholic center, to Annapolis, the most active Protestant center in the Province. Two years later (1704) an act was passed by the Maryland Assembly making it a crime for any Catholic priest to baptize any child except those of Catholic parentage, or to say mass in the Province. Catholic parents sending their children abroad to be educated in the Catholic faith were liable to a fine of £100. This law so aroused the indignation of Protestants as well as Catholics that it was suspended and a few years later annulled. Eventually Catholic Church offices were permitted to be carried on privately. As a consequence of this provision the houses of the priests were adapted to worship, there being a large chapel-room provided in each of them, where the people of the vicinity might gather for

---

[13] Sister Mary Augustina (Ray), *American Opinion of Roman Catholicism in the Eighteenth Century*, New York: 1936, tells the whole sad story in great detail.

worship. The Jesuit missionaries continued to be self-supporting, the people contributing nothing for the services they performed, nor, as Bishop Carroll states, "did they require any so long as the produce of their lands was sufficient to answer their demands."

During the "Penal period," as O'Gorman, in his *History of the Roman Catholic Church in the United States,* characterizes these years, Catholicism made more progress in Pennsylvania than in any of the other colonies. As Maryland became less and less desirable for Catholic residence, an increasing flow of Catholic people began to move across the border into Pennsylvania. Here they were free to build their churches and chapels, educate their children in the Catholic faith, and carry on their public worship without molestation. The large German immigration into Pennsylvania after 1700 contained a considerable number of German Catholics and in 1741 two German Jesuits from Maryland came to Philadelphia and laid the foundations of several Catholic congregations. Schools were also begun for German Catholics, the most noted being that at Goshenhoppen. Much of this work among the German Catholics in Pennsylvania centers about the name of Father Theodore Schneider who gave twenty-three years of devoted service to the German Catholics of that Province.

The cruel removal (1755) of some 6000 Acadians from present-day Nova Scotia, and the scattering of them among the thirteen colonies from Massachusetts to South Carolina and Georgia has received well-deserved condemnation among historians of all religious complexions. It can be said, however, that the deportation was determined upon by the Governor of Nova Scotia and his council without the knowledge or consent of the British home government. The reason for it was the refusal of the Acadians to take the oath of allegiance to the British government, although they had been allowed the full enjoyment of their religious rights, and French priests, subject to the French authority at Quebec, had been permitted to live among them. The Acadians were willing to pledge their neutrality in the war which was about to break out between France and England, but that was as far as they were willing to go. This forced emigration of the Acadians was solidly Catholic, but few of them remained in the English colonies. Some found their way to the French West Indies; others to Louisiana, while still others made their painful way back to their old homes. Some remained in South Carolina; a larger number found homes and employment in Maryland; others became permanent residents of Philadelphia, but the effect of their coming upon colonial Catholicism was negligible.[14]

In the year 1756 Father George Hunter, the Superior of the Maryland mission, in his report for that year estimated that there were about 10,000 adult Catholic communicants in Maryland and Pennsylvania, with some 7000 in the former and 3000 in the latter. There were twelve mission stations with eighteen priests in attendance. In Maryland the Catholic laity, with no obligation to support the clergy or maintain churches and chapels, were inert and were fast "losing the energy of faith that shows itself in self-sacrifice." The Pennsylvania Catholics, on the other hand, though poor and fewer in number, contributed toward the erection of churches and to the support of the priests. A report of the financial condition of the Catholic missions for the year 1765 shows that they possessed 13,220 acres of land which that year had produced £761. This would indicate that in spite of the fact that the Catholics had been under a cruel ban as far as their spiritual activities were concerned, financially they had little of which to complain.[15]

The brave work of the Catholic missionaries in those sections of what is now the United States which formerly made up a part of the Spanish and French colonial empires is an entirely different story.

---

[14] Catholic accounts of the Acadian deportation are, of course, bitterly critical. See Shea, *op. cit.*, I, Chapter IV. For a well-reasoned treatment see George M. Wrong, *The Rise and Fall of New France,* New York: 1928, Vol. II, pp. 761–783. The Catholic priest Father Le Loutre must bear a good share of the responsibility for the impasse which brought about the deportation of the Acadians. Wrong characterizes Le Loutre as an example of "the priest in politics, who brings to secular affairs the burning conviction that his enemies are the enemies of God" (*Ibid.*, p. 765).

[15] The Catholic holdings were as follows: St. Inigoes, with a plantation of 2000 acres, 90 pounds revenue; St. Xavier's, 1500 acres, 88 pounds revenue; St. Ignatius, Port Tobacco, 4400 acres, 188 pounds revenue; St. Francis Borgia, White Marsh, 3500 acres, 180 pounds revenue; St. Josephs, Deer Creek, 127 acres, 24 pounds revenue; St. Mary's, Tuckahoe, 200 acres, 18 pounds revenue; Bohemia, 1500 acres, 108 pounds revenue; Goshenhoppen, 500 acres, 45 pounds revenue; Conewago, 120 acres, 20 pounds revenue. Besides there was 100 pounds received annually from London. T. O'Gorman, *History of the Roman Catholic Church in the United States,* New York: 1895, p. 246.

VI

Trade and Religion in New Netherland

I T TOOK a struggle of almost sixty years (1523–81) before the people of Holland gained their political and religious freedom. But out of that holocaust came at last a new, vigorous Protestant nation, which in the seventeenth century was to become not only one of the world's greatest commercial and colonizing powers but also the first European State to be founded upon the principle of religious toleration. All of these facts— Dutch commerce, Dutch colonization and Dutch religious toleration—have great significance in the history of colonial America.

I

RELIGIOUS TOLERATION IN HOLLAND

To TRACE the rise of religious toleration in Holland it will be necessary to follow the course of Dutch political and religious development during the sixteenth century. All shades of religious opinion which arose out of the Reformation found adherents in Holland. Calvinism won the most converts, but the views of Luther and Zwingli also found a wide acceptance, and in the great commercial cities such as Amsterdam and Leyden Anabaptism took a firm hold. Even before the Reformation, heresy had been widespread in the Low Countries and there had developed an attitude of acquiescence toward it that was not to be found in any other European country. Even those who remained Catholics were not of the bigoted type, for it seemed to be generally accepted among the people that religious toleration was essential to the prosperity of the country, for trade was her very life and her great cities, Antwerp and Amsterdam, were the trade centers of Europe.[1]

The movement to suppress the religious independence of the Low Countries and compel conformity to Roman Catholicism did not originate with the Catholic element in the population. Unfortunately for the peaceful political and religious development of the Dutch people, the Netherlands were a part of the patrimony of the Emperor Charles V and of his son Philip II of Spain, the latter the most bitter enemy of Protestantism in the age of the Reformation. Left to themselves the Dutch people doubtless would have reached an early religious equilibrium, but because of Spanish interference they were compelled to pass through a period of persecution such as no other European people endured. In this long struggle religion became a unifying element which enabled the people of Holland to resist successfully Spanish domination.

It is significant that Dutch Catholic noblemen were opposed to the enforcement of the "Placards," as the anti-Protestant edicts were called. William of Orange, himself a Catholic, who soon became the recognized leader of the Dutch people in the bitter struggle against the Spaniards, took the lead in drawing up a petition to Philip II, urging that the "Placards" be suspended, pointing out the necessity of recognizing the presence of Protestantism in the country, adding:

> I am a Catholic, and will not deviate from religion, but I cannot approve the custom of Kings to confine men's creeds and religion within arbitrary limits.

It is impossible to exaggerate the horrors of the Duke of Alva's administration of the Netherlands. In that story, as Motley suggests, tyranny "paints her own portrait," and beholding it "will not make us love popular liberty the less." It is beyond human comprehension how such crimes could be perpetrated in the sacred name of the Almighty. But it would seem necessary that many generations must wade through blood "in order to acquire

---

[1] P. J. Blok, *History of the People of the Netherlands,* 1892. English translation by O. A. Bierstadt and Ruth Putnam, New York and London: 1898–1912. Part III, The War of Independence, 1568–1621.

for their descendants the blessings of civil and religious freedom."
It would seem necessary that "an Alva should ravish a peaceful
nation with sword and flame, that desolation should be spread
over a happy land, in order that the pure and heroic character of a
William of Orange should stand forth . . . like an antique statue
of spotless marble against a stormy sky." [2] Even after Catholic
intolerance had caused William of Orange to renounce his Catholic
faith and he had become an avowed adherent of the Reformed
religion, he did not change his attitude toward toleration. In 1572
he instructed his lieutenants "to restore fugitives and the banished
for conscience' sake, and to see that the Word of God is preached,
without, however, suffering any hindrance to the Roman Catholic
Church in the exercise of its religion."

It was due chiefly to William of Orange that religious toleration
became the established policy of the Dutch nation. Though of a
Lutheran family he was raised a Catholic, which was the condition
imposed by Charles V before he would consent to his succeeding
to the title of Prince of Orange. In his early years religion sat
lightly upon him, but he always had a constitutional aversion to
persecution. He was a liberal Catholic until about the year 1559,
when he announced himself ready to return to the faith of his
childhood, and in 1573 publicly declared himself a Calvinist. The
ruling passion of his life was his hatred of oppression in every
form, and of all the leaders of an intolerant age he alone rose
above the passions of the time. His liberal spirit may be accounted
for in part by his lack of interest in theology. Theological controversy seemed to him to be based upon petty differences; "what
he wished was that each person should have what seemed the one
thing needful." "No statesman," says Miss Putnam, "ever had a
clearer vision of individual rights and of national unity than had
William of Nassau." [3]

The year 1579 marks the beginning of an independent Dutch
nation, when representatives of the five northern provinces met

---

[2] J. T. Motley, *The Rise of the Dutch Republic: A History*, 3 vols., New York: 1870,
Vol. II, pp. 424–25.

[3] Ruth Putnam, *William the Silent, Prince of Orange*, 2 vols., New York: 1895, Vol.
II, pp. 420–31.

at Utrecht and formed a league to maintain themselves against all foreign princes. Two years later (1581) they solemnly renounced allegiance to the King of Spain and constituted themselves an independent republic. In the Union of Utrecht, toleration was established as one of the fundamental laws of the new nation (Article 13). Each province was left free to regulate its own religion, provided, however, that every individual was to be free to exercise his own religion. This policy of toleration led to a large influx of Protestant refugees from the Spanish Netherlands as well as from other countries where Protestants were persecuted, and by 1609 the Dutch Netherlands had a population equal to that of England proper. Amsterdam nearly doubled its population between 1588 and 1609. From the beginning, Holland's economic policy was as liberal and wise as was her religious policy. As a result, the whole country was a hive of industry and trade. "Nowhere in the world was there so large a production in proportion to the numbers of the people." With practically no natural resources, "Holland with freedom of thought, of commerce, of speech, of action, placed itself by intellectual power alone, in the front rank of civilization." [4]

Toleration was the chief glory of the United Netherlands, and their Protestantism, intensified by long years of persecution, gave to the young nation strength, vigor, and enterprise. The intense bitterness of the long struggle against Spanish Catholicism made Dutch Protestantism the more militant and pronounced. The assassination of their beloved Prince intensified and deepened their religious and political hatreds of everything Spanish and Catholic. And once the tide of battle had turned in their favor the Dutch people were eager to launch out in every direction. The very fact that trade expansion and colonization would bring them into further conflict with Spain, and with Portugal also, only added zest to these enterprises.

The seventeenth century was the golden age of the Dutch Netherlands. It was during this century that their trade circled the globe. Numerous Dutch trading companies were formed and

---

[4] J. T. Motley, *History of the United Netherlands from the Death of William the Silent to the Twelve Years Truce,* 4 vols., London: 1869, Vol. IV, Chapter LIII.

trading colonies were established in Africa, in India, and the islands of the East Indies; America was exploited and colonized. Three thousand Dutch ships and 150,000 men were employed in the fishing industry alone. In 1603 Holland possessed twenty thousand ships and all were employed. Amsterdam became the warehouse of Europe and the financial center of the world. Her universities and scholars were the equal of the best in Europe. Dutch art and Dutch theology set the standards for Protestant Europe, while Hugo Grotius was writing those treatises which laid the foundation for the freedom of the seas and international law.[5]

II

ORIGINS OF THE DUTCH CHURCH

It HAS already been noted that all forms of Protestantism found adherents in the Low Countries. But it was Church polity and not theology that determined which of the Reformation patterns was to be followed in Holland. To have followed the Lutheran or Zwinglian patterns a favorably disposed government would have been necessary, and this, of course, was out of the question in the Holland of the first half of the sixteenth century. Accordingly, as Protestant congregations were formed here and there throughout the several provinces they organized on the principle of entire independence of all relationship to the State. This was the form of polity adopted in the early Christian centuries while the Church was still under the ban of the Roman Empire.[6] In the year 1569 at a meeting of the representatives of the Dutch Churches it was resolved formally to adopt the Presbyterian system. The Church was to be ruled by *Consistories, Classes* and *Synods*. The *Consistory* as developed in the Dutch Reformed Church has certain distinctive features, differing from other Presbyterian bodies. Instead of each church building having its own church organization and minister, all the members of the Church in a city were regarded

---

[5] J. Ellis Barker, *The Rise and Decline of the Netherlands*, London: 1906, pp. 121–45.
[6] T. M. Lindsay, *The Church and the Ministry of the Early Centuries*, London: 1903, pp. 204 ff.

as one congregation. If there were several church buildings and several ministers, they preached in turn in all the places of worship, while the people were not attached as members to any one church building. Thus there came to be but one *Consistory* for a whole city.

Another distinctive feature of the Dutch Church was that each province controlled its own ecclesiastical affairs, and there could be no meeting of a national Synod unless each of the provinces gave approval. The General or National Synod was to meet triennially, while the Provincial Synods were to be constituted of representatives from the Classes, or Presbyteries. By 1581 the Reformed Church of Holland was fully organized and became the State Church.

The Reformed Church of Holland had hardly gotten under way as an independent ecclesiastical body before a great theological controversy began which nearly eventuated in civil war. With the injection of political issues into the already bitter theological strife, the unity of Holland was for a time destroyed and the people were divided into warring camps. A sorry spectacle, indeed, in the new nation which had so recently adopted toleration as a fundamental principle! The controversy arose over the teaching of Jacob Arminius, a Reformed minister who had become one of the professors of theology in the University of Leyden in 1603. He disputed some of the cardinal doctrines of Calvinism, rejecting unconditional election, and advocating an unlimited atonement. His opponents were led by Franz Gomarius, also a professor of theology at Leyden, and a disciple of Calvin. Carried on at first between Arminius and Gomarius, the controversy soon became an issue among the students, was then introduced into the pulpits, and from there it "was bandied about in the mouths of the ignorant, and became watchwords of vulgar clamour and popular cabal." In the year 1618 a vast conflict between Catholicism and Protestantism began in Europe, but the tempest raging on all sides was lost on the Dutch "in the din of conflict among the respective supporters of conditional and unconditional damnation within the pale of the Reformed Church." [7]

Maurice, Prince of Orange, identified himself with the orthodox

---

[7] J. T. Motley, *The Life and Death of John of Barneveldt*, 3 vols., New York: 1900.

party, which had the larger popular following. By overriding the
constitutional rights of the provinces, and by arresting the chief
political leaders of the Arminian party, known as the *Remonstrants,* the threatened civil war was avoided. Politically it was
a controversy between national and provincial authority, the
Remonstrants standing for provincial power while Prince Maurice
contended for strong central authority. Theologically the *Remonstrants* stood for toleration, while the orthodox party of Gomerius
stood for repression and persecution.[8]

For some reason the followers of Calvin have been more prone
to persecute their fellow Protestants who differ from them than
have their opponents. Perhaps this is due to the complete assurance they possess that they are in the right, and that those who
differ from them are not only in the wrong, but are traitors, and
in the interest of public safety therefore must be punished. It was
this spirit which gave rise to the great Council of Dort which
convened under the leadership of Prince Maurice November 13,
1618, and continued its sessions until May 1619. Its purpose was
to put an end to the theological controversies which had been
raging for fifteen years. This was accomplished by force and not
by conference. The Arminian party, instead of being represented
by a fair proportion of delegates, was permitted to have but thirteen ministers present, and they were summoned, not as members of the Synod, but as culprits on trial. The result, of course,
was the complete condemnation of their views, and their rude
dismissal as unworthy to hold conference with the venerable
Synod. The doctrines of Calvinism in their most extreme form
were now proclaimed by the Synod to be orthodox, a Calvinism
more Calvinistic than Calvin. They asserted that

God had pre-ordained, by an eternal and immutable decree, before the
creation of the world, upon whom he will bestow the free gift of his
grace; that the atonement of Christ, though sufficient for all the world,
is efficacious only for the elect; that conversion is not effected by any

---

[8] Historians have taken different viewpoints in their accounts of the Arminian controversy. J. Ellis Barker, *op. cit.,* Chapter ix, condemns the Arminian leaders as unscrupulous politicians. J. T. Motley, *The Life and Death of John of Barneveldt,* ably defends
Barneveldt and Hugo Grotius as does C. M. Davies, *The History of Holland and the
Dutch Nation,* 3 vols., London: 1851, Vol. III, Chapter v.

effort of man, but by the free grace of God given to those only whom he has chosen from all eternity; and that it is impossible for the elect to fall away from this grace.

Thus came to an end the Synod of Dort, having adopted a Creed and a Catechism for the Church of the Netherlands to which all candidates for the ministry as well as schoolmasters were required to subscribe. Loyal members of the Dutch Church, through the years, have looked upon the Synod of Dort as an assembly of learned and pious divines, whose decrees were inferior in purity and excellence only to the Scripture itself; others have considered it as a meeting of fanatics bent upon bringing discomfiture, condemnation, humiliation, and finally exile upon their enemies. Perhaps the truth lies somewhere between these two extremes. Fortunately, this orgy of intolerance was short-lived. Within six years, or upon the death of Prince Maurice (1625), the *Remonstrants* were permitted to return and full toleration was granted them. It has been suggested that if they had been a separate sect they doubtless would have received toleration from the start.

III

The Dutch Church in New Netherland

The transplanting of the Reformed Dutch Church to the New World was accomplished through the medium of the Dutch West India Company—trade and religion going hand in hand. As early as 1607 the Dutch merchants engaged in trading and freebooting in the New World had received a charter from the States General. Out of this interest grew the voyage of Henry Hudson (1609) and his discovery of the river which bears his name, and eventually the Dutch West India Company, incorporated June 3, 1621.

The great protagonist of the development of Dutch interest in the New World was Willem Usselinx,[9] a devout Calvinist, who

---

[9] J. F. Jameson, *Willem Usselinx, Founder of the Dutch and Swedish West India Companies* (Papers of the American Historical Association, Vol. II, No. 3), New York: 1887.

devoted the best years of his life to this enterprise. His object was to increase the wealth and power of the Dutch nation and to undermine the power of Spain, for his ruling passion was his hatred of Spain and Catholicism. In 1600 he began to advance the American project in a series of extremely able pamphlets and books, as well as by personal interviews, and by 1606 he had won the approval of the States of Holland. He was no ordinary pamphleteer, for no man of his time had a fuller understanding of seventeenth-century economics. He thought in terms of a colonial empire, not in terms of advantage to a few individual merchants. At first the Dutch West India Company centered its chief interest in the Spanish West Indies and South America. It established a colony in Guiana and captured and held for a time the Brazilian cities of Bahia and Pernambuco. By 1626 also Dutch trading posts had been established at Fort Orange on the present site of Albany; at Fort Nassau, on the Delaware, opposite present-day Philadelphia; at the mouth of the Connecticut, and on Manhattan Island.

The development of the fur trade was the Company's chief interest and there was little concern in making the colony attractive to colonists. The charter contained no mention of religion, though in Willem Usselinx's proposed charter religion was given a prominent place among the declared objects of the company. Provision was made for a council of theologians which should provide godly ministers and teachers both for the colonists and the Indians. But the company as organized was more interested in beaver skins than in the souls of colonists and Indians. With the exception [10] of Protestant refugees from Catholic Belgium, and the Huguenots who early began to come to New Amsterdam, the colonists in New Netherland did not come to America because of religious persecution. For the first three years there seems to have been no effort to introduce religion into the colony, but with the coming out of Peter Minuit as Director in May 1626, organized religion made its appearance. A native of Wesel on the Rhine, Minuit had been a ruling elder in a French Reformed Church, and was actively interested in religion. With him came

---

[10] The seal of New Netherlands was a shield bearing a beaver, surmounted by a Count's coronet and encircled by the words *Sigillum Nova Belgii.*

two Comforters of the Sick (*Krankenbesoeckers*), recognized officials in the Dutch Church, who assisted ministers of large parishes, and were sometimes sent to destitute places. A contemporary account of New Netherlands in 1626 contains the following description:

The counting house there is kept in a stone-building, thatched with reed; the other houses are of the bark of trees. Each has his own house. The Director and *Koopman* live together; there are thirty ordinary houses on the east side of the river which runs north and south. The Honble Pieter Minuit is Director there at present; Jan Lempo Schout [Sheriff]; Sebastian Janez Crol and Jan Huych Comforters of the Sick, who whilst awaiting a clergyman, read to the Commonality there on Sundays, from texts of Scripture with the comment. Francois Nealemaccker is busy building a horse-mill, over which shall be constructed a spacious room sufficient to accommodate a large congregation, and then a tower to be erected where the bells brought from Porto Rico will be hung.

The historian also records (1626) the arrival at Amsterdam of the ship *The Arms* of Amsterdam with a cargo of "7246 Beavers, 675 Otter skins; 48 Minx, 36 wild cat and various other sorts; several pieces of oak timber and hickory." [11] Here we have epitomized in this contemporary statement the main purposes of the Dutch West India Company: the fur trade, and the combating of Spain—the bells from Porto Rico were a part of the plunder of a Dutch raid—while religion is only an incidental matter to be accommodated above the horse mill.

Between the years 1626 and 1628 feverish excitement prevailed in New Amsterdam, for it was at this time that the Dutch gained some of their most brilliant victories over the Spaniards, and rich spoils began to pour into the coffers of the West India Company. The luckiest stroke of them all was the capture of the Spanish Silver Fleet near Cuba with a hundred and forty thousand pounds of pure silver on board, which enabled the Company to declare a 500 per cent dividend. It was at this very time that Reverend Jonas Michaelius came out to New Amsterdam, the first Dutch

[11] *Wassenaers Historie van Europe*, Amsterdam, 1621–1632, from *Documentary History of New York*, Albany: 1850, Vol. III, pp. 42–43.

minister of the Gospel to set foot on American soil. Until the discovery of an elaborate letter of Michaelius' in 1858, his coming had been entirely forgotten. But it is not strange that this was true, for such an event had little chance of being remembered in the excitement of the events of those years. It is from this letter that we learn of the formation of the first Dutch Church in America, and the simple facts are soon told.[12]

Domine Michaelius owed his appointment to New Amsterdam to the West India Company, which promised him a farm, and seeds and plants to stock it. He had been recommended by the Classis of Enkhuysen, though he was the only minister to come to America from that Classis, for the ecclesiastical control of the Dutch colonies soon was transferred to the Classis of Amsterdam. With his wife and three children Michaelius landed in New Amsterdam April 7, 1628. The voyage had been long and stormy, the ship small and uncomfortable, the food scanty, and to make things worse the drunken captain was as "unmannerly as a big buffalo." At this time Michaelius was forty-four years of age, had been educated at the University of Leyden, had served pastorates in Holland, and had been naval chaplain on the coasts of Africa and Brazil. Thus by age and experience he was well fitted to be the pioneer minister in that far-away infant Dutch colony. The colonists, whom he found "rather rough and unrestrained," welcomed his coming, and he proceeded at once to form a church, appointing the Director Peter Minuit and the storekeeper Jan Huygen, the Director's brother-in-law, elders, and Bastien Crol, deacon, the latter in charge of trade at Fort Orange. Thus was begun the first Dutch Church in America, which was also the first church of any sort organized in the middle colonies. As the Collegiate Reformed Dutch Church of the City of New York, it continues to this day.

It was a mixed congregation of Walloons, French and Dutch,

---

[12] Edward Tanjore Corwin, *A Manual of the Reformed Church in America, 1628–1902*, Fourth Edition, New York: 1902. The letter of Reverend Jonas Michaelius has been reproduced in Dutch with an English translation in *Ecclesiastical Records of the State of New York*, Albany: 1901, Vol. I, pp. 48–68. Dr. A. Eekhof, *Jonas Michaelius, Founder of the Church in New Netherland*, etc., Leyden: 1926, gathers together all the documents relating to Michaelius, which includes a second Michaelius letter dated August 4, 1628, discovered in 1902.

to which Domine Michaelius ministered. At the first administration of the Lord's Supper there were some fifty communicants, and it gave "great joy and comfort to many." Some had forgotten to bring their church certificates, others had lost them, "not thinking that a church would be formed" in that far-away region. From that time forward the Holy Supper was administered every four months, while services were conducted in the Dutch language every Sunday. The French and the French-speaking Walloons were numerous enough to warrant his preaching to them at special times and administering the sacrament in the French language.

Nor was the religious welfare of the colonists the only concern of Domine Michaelius, for in his letter of August 8, 1628, he devotes considerable space to the religious needs of the Indians. Although he found the natives "entirely savage and wild, strangers to all decency, . . . uncivil and stupid as garden poles, proficient in all wickedness and godlessness," yet he was of the opinion that some means ought to be found "to make a salutary breach" for their salvation. He suggests that attention be centered upon the instruction of the Indian children, and that they be placed "under some experienced and godly schoolmaster" where they may not only learn to speak, read, and write the Dutch language, but also some of the fundamentals of the Christian religion.

In 1632 Michaelius was back in Holland, as was also Director Peter Minuit, against whom Michaelius made serious charges before the directors of the West India Company. The following year (1633) a new Director, Wouter Van Twiller, and a new minister, Everardus Bogardus, came out to New Amsterdam in the same ship. The first schoolmaster, Adam Roelandsen, also came out at the same time. Of Bogardus' ministry in New Amsterdam we know little, but we know much more of his quarrels with the Directors, Van Twiller and Willem Kieft, both of whom he denounced from his pulpit, calling the former a "child of the devil and an insensate villain, whose buck goats are better than he." In 1638 Bogardus married a rich widow, Annetje Jansen, the owner of a farm of sixty-two acres on Manhattan Island which became known as The Domine's "Bouweria." In the reign of Queen Anne it was given to Trinity Church, New York, and is the source of its great wealth. The very year Bogardus arrived a frame church was built and also a dwelling with stable adjoining for the use of the minister. In 1642 a second church was erected in the Fort, to replace the frame building which had been permitted to fall into a state of dilapidation and had become little better than a "mean barn."

The dilapidated church was symbolic of the condition of religion in the colony at this time, for the minister as well as the schoolmaster seemed to be occupied more with quarrels with the Director and with their own temporal interests than with the spiritual and intellectual welfare of the people. Captain David De Vries, an influential merchant and colonizer, was responsible for the decision of Director Kieft to erect a new church. One day dining with the Director, he stated that, "It was a shame that the English should see, when they passed, nothing but a mean barn in which public worship was performed. The first thing they did in New England," he stated, after they had built their houses, was "to build a fine church." "We ought to do the same," he continued, especially since good materials are so abundant, "fine oak wood, fine building stone, good lime made from oyster shells, which was better than the lime in Holland." The result was the erection of a stone church, the funds for which were secured from the public chest and by a subscription taken at the wedding party of the minister's step-daughter, when the guests were mellow with the host's good cheer.[13]

The Directors of the West India Company soon realized that their New Netherland colony was not attracting real colonists,

---

[13] Among the abundant materials on early New Netherland the following are the most important. *History of the State of New York* (A. C. Flick, State Historian, Editor), New York: 1933, Vols. I–III; *Ecclesiastical Records of the State of New York* (Hugh Hastings, State Historian), Albany: 1901. Vol. I; E. B. O'Callaghan, *History of New Netherland; or New York Under the Dutch*, 2 vols. New York: 1848; J. F. Jameson (Editor), *Narratives of New Netherland, 1609–1664*, New York: 1909; A. J. F. Van Laer (Editor), *Documents Relating to New Netherland, 1624–1626*, San Marion, California: 1924; *Documentary History of the State of New York* (E. B. O'Callaghan, Editor), Albany: 1850, Vol. III; Hendrik W. Van Loon, *Life and Times of Peter Stuyvesant*, New York: 1928; Frederick J. Swierlein, *Religion in New Netherland*, Rochester, New York: 1910; J. R. Broadhead, *History of the State of New York*, Vol. I, New York: 1853; Articles on Jonas Michaelius, Everardus Bogardus, Willem Kieft, etc. in *Dictionary of American Biography;* J. H. Innes, *New Amsterdam and Its People*, New York: 1902; S. G. Nissenson, *The Patroon's Domain*, New York: 1937.

and in 1629 what was known as the Patroonships were inaugurated in the attempt to remedy this situation. This was a scheme whereby any member of the Company might secure a great estate to be held as a perpetual inheritance provided he bring over fifty colonists within four years. He was to have the right of transporting his colonists in the Company's ships at fixed charges, while all agricultural implements and cattle were to be carried free. The Patroon was also to have extensive political and commercial privileges. Among the Patroon's obligations was that of providing for the support of a minister and a schoolmaster. By 1630 five Patroonships had been granted, though of the five only one, that of Kiliaen Van Rensselaer at Fort Orange (Albany) was successful. For the first decade Van Rensselaer evaded the employment of a minister by directing that one of his feudal functionaries should read the Scriptures every Sunday to the assembled tenants. Finally in 1642 Reverend Johannes Megapolensis was employed, and arrived in August of that year with his wife and four children. On August 17 he preached his first sermon in the Patroon's storehouse. Megapolensis was a convert from Catholicism and had served two parishes in Holland before coming to America. The Patroon of Rensselaerwyck made a wise choice in Megapolensis, for he served faithfully the six-year term for which he had contracted, and organized the second Dutch Church in America.

We may surmise from several known facts that the six years at Rensselaerwyck were not happy ones for Megapolensis, for he was unwilling to remain longer, even though the Patroon had been well pleased with his services. In the first place Rensselaerwyck was located in a wilderness, a long way from the rest of the world, but the chief reason for his desire to return to Holland was the fact that the colonists were greedy and selfish, addicted to drink and were unrestrained in their relations with the Indian women. The Patroon could force them to attend church by imposing heavy fines, but he could not prevent them from sleeping through the services or from spending the remainder of the Sabbath in playing cards and in carousing. In other words, the debauchery and godlessness of the tenants were too much for the good domine. Nor were the conditions at New Amsterdam much better. There the congregation in 1647 numbered about one hundred and seventy, but most of them were "very ignorant in regard to true religion and very much given to drink," for every fifth house in the town was a taphouse. In spite of his desire to return to Holland, when Megapolensis' term was over at Albany, the Director and Council persuaded him to remain as the minister at New Amsterdam. Thus he placed "the saving of human souls above his own important business" and remained in New Amsterdam until his death in 1670.

Religious conditions in New Netherland were in a sad state generally when the new Director General, Petrus Stuyvesant, arrived on May 11, 1647. A son of a Dutch Reformed minister and son-in-law of another, Stuyvesant's first act on his arrival was the promulgation of an ordinance restricting the sale of liquor and providing for a stricter observance of the Sabbath. No liquor was to be sold after nine o'clock to any one, and tippling was prohibited during divine service. The next year (1648) he decreed that there should be preaching in the afternoon as well as in the morning each Sabbath, and all persons were required to attend. It was Director Stuyvesant who had persuaded Megapolensis to become the minister at New Amsterdam, and the two worked together in great harmony. In 1652 Reverend Samuel Drisius was sent out by the Company as a colleague for Domine Megapolensis, and as he was able to preach both in French and Dutch he was particularly useful in preaching in the new settlements forming on Long Island. In the new Long Island villages, Midwout (Flatbush), Amersfoort (Flatlands), and Breuckelen (Brooklyn) all founded in 1654 and 1655, churches were organized and at first all were served by Reverend Johannes T. Polhemus, who came to New Netherland from Brazil. Other churches were formed at New Amstel (Newcastle), 1657, Harlem (1660), and Bergen, New Jersey (1662). By 1664 there had been eleven churches organized in New Netherland with two out-stations, and thirteen ministers had labored in the colony and six were in service at the time the English took possession.[14]

---

[14] For a brief but excellent account of the religious situation during the Dutch period, see A. Everett Peterson, *The Cultural Heritage from the Dutch in the History of New York* (A. C. Flick, Ed.), Vol. I, *op. cit.*, pp. 3–32.

In the charter of *Freedoms and Exemptions* issued by the Company in 1640 it was stated that "No other religion shall be publicly admitted in New Netherland, except the Reformed . . . and for this purpose the Company shall provide and maintain good and suitable preachers, schoolmasters, and Comforters of the Sick." [15] The Director of the Colony was in direct control of the colonial Church, and all matters relating to the erection of churches and schools and their support had to be confirmed by the Director General and his Council, except in the case of Patroonships. The Company contributed toward the salaries of ministers, though in most cases the attempt was made to persuade the congregation to contribute a part of their support. The school was considered a religious institution and the schoolmasters as well as the ministers had to receive the recommendation of the Classis of Amsterdam. [16]

As Professor Corwin states, "the story of the relation of the Dutch Reformed Church in New Netherlands to other religious bodies, is one of the darker pages of her history." The general reputation of the Dutch for religious tolerance throughout Europe was responsible for making the Netherlands a refuge for people persecuted for conscience in other lands. New Netherland inherited that tradition. As a result there was soon a large influx of people representing many religious complexions. The large emigration of New Englanders to Long Island and northern New Jersey has already been noted. The New Englanders, however, did not differ in fundamentals from the Reformed, so that their congregations were granted freedom of worship. But in the case of the Quakers, the Lutherans, and the Jews, it was a different story. Director Stuyvesant's persecution of the Quakers has already been noted.

Lutherans had been in the colony from the beginning and at first had worshipped with the Reformed people. As they became more numerous there was a movement to establish their own worship. This led to a prohibition of conventicles under heavy

---

[15] *Ecclesiastical Records of the State of New York,* Vol. I, p. 152.

[16] These matters are fully treated in F. J. Swierlein, *Religion in New Netherland, 1623–1664,* Rochester: 1910, Chapters II and III.

penalties, though the Director was careful to state that he had no desire to interfere with the liberty of conscience, and that the decree did not interfere with "the reading of God's Holy Word, family prayers and worship, each in his own home." When a Lutheran minister, John Ernst Goedwater, arrived in the colony, vigorous protests were made by Domines Megapolensis and Drisius, who pointed out to the Director and the Burgomasters that not only would there be serious injury to the cause of religion in the colony as the result of the introduction of Lutheranism, but that it would also lead to political confusion. The result was that Goedwater was ordered to return to Holland on the ship *Waag* which was ready to sail. But it was one thing to order his going, and another to get rid of him, for Goedwater refused to leave and for a time concealed himself in the house of a Lutheran farmer. When sickness, however, made his return to New Amsterdam necessary, he was placed under arrest and in the spring of 1658 was sent to Holland.[17]

Jews had appeared in New Netherland almost from its beginning. The first of them had come from Holland where they had been granted citizenship and the right to hold property as well as a considerable degree of religious freedom. The Jewish question in New Amsterdam became acute when the Portuguese Jews who had found refuge in the Dutch colonies in Brazil began to arrive following the Portuguese recapture of Bahia and Pernambuco. Director Stuyvesant and the Reformed ministers did their utmost to keep them out. Stuyvesant petitioned the Directors of the Company to that end, while Megapolensis urged the Classis of Amsterdam to use its influence to have "these godless rascals, who are no benefit to the country, but look at everything for their own profit," removed. The Directors of the Company in Amsterdam, however, refused to fall in line with the anti-Semitic policy of Stuyvesant and Megapolensis and the Jews were permitted to reside and to trade in the colony. They were not, however, per-

---

[17] The statement in H. W. Van Loon, *Life and Times of Peter Stuyvesant*, p. 226, that Stuyvesant "had little time to give to the suppression of the Lutheran form of worship and in the end the Lutherans got a meeting place of their own and even imported a minister from Germany and no one said a word" . . . is a good example of careless popularization.

mitted to exercise their religion publicly, but only in their own homes.[18]

The Dutch West India Company was no benevolent or missionary enterprise, and what little interest was taken in the Christianization of the Indians did not emanate from its officials in Holland. The Classis of Amsterdam, however, did show some interest in the matter and exhorted Everardus Bogardus and his Consistory to engage in this work, though they note that the Dutch colonists seemingly are "more likely to turn heathen than to turn others to the Christian faith." Domine Megapolensis during his six years at Rensselaerwyck became actively interested in the Indians. He studied their language and wrote a treatise on the Mohawks which was later published in Holland. It was not unusual for Indians to attend his services, and they came with their long tobacco pipes in their mouths. In his treatise on the Mohawks Megapolensis stated that "Dutchmen run . . . very much" after the Indian women, who are "exceedingly addicted to whoring." The Dutch also set a poor example to the Indians in their own intemperate use of liquor and in the active and profitable liquor trade which they carried on with the Indians. It was not uncommon for Indian children to be taken into Dutch families as servants, "but as soon as they grow up and associate again with the Indians, they forget their religious impressions and adopt Indian customs." [19] The prize Indian convert was a chief who had professed conversion and after instruction was given a Bible with the hope that "he might be the instrument of accomplishing considerable good among the Indians." He was, however, too much like the Dutch in that he was inclined to drunkenness, and the Domines were compelled to say that he was no better than other Indians. Nor do they "expect much fruit of religion among these barbarous nations, until they are brought under the government of Europeans." Toward the end of the period of Dutch control of New Netherland Domine Polhemus wrote to the Classis that "there is no communication among us . . . nor plans for propa-

---

[18] Swierlein, *op. cit.*, Chapter VIII, "Persecution of the Jews," pp. 247–65.

[19] *Ecclesiastical Records of the State of New York*, Vol. I, pp. 326–27; Jameson, *Narratives of New Netherland*, p. 178; Swierlein, *op. cit.*, pp. 266–76.

gating the Gospel among the savages. . . ." The following quotation from the "Representation of New Netherland" (1650) is an indication that the better element among the Dutch colonists were conscience-stricken at their neglect of the Indians:

> Great is our disgrace now, and happy should we have been . . . had we striven to impart the Eternal Good to the Indians, as much as was in our power, in return for what they divided with us. It is to be feared that at the Last Day they will stand up against us for this injury.[20]

IV

NEW SWEDEN AND THE LUTHERAN CHURCH

WILLEM USSELINX was the chief promoter in the establishment of New Sweden. After his departure from the Netherlands, he had been employed by Gustavus Adolphus to assist in the establishment of a Swedish trading company. Peter Minuit, the first Governor of New Amsterdam, also had been engaged in furthering the enterprise, and it was under his leadership that the first colony arrived on the Delaware River in the early part of 1638. Land was purchased from the Indians and a fort was erected and called Fort Christina in honor of the Queen of Sweden. Although the Dutch West India Company protested this invasion of their American territory, the Swedes were permitted to remain, since the Dutch and Swedes were allies in the great Thirty Years' War then going on in Europe. A few years after the close of the war the Dutch sent an expedition of seven ships to force the surrender of Fort Christina, and the Swedish settlement became a part of New Netherland.

Among the instructions given the second Governor of New Sweden, John Printz, was the admonition that he was to:

> Labor and watch that he render in all things to Almighty God the true worship which is his due, the glory, the praise, and the homage which belong to him, and to take good measures that the divine serv-

---

[20] Jameson, *Narratives of New Netherland*, p. 319.

ice is performed according to the true confession of Augsburg, the Council of Upsala, and the ceremonies of the Swedish church, having care that all men, and especially the youth, be well instructed in all parts of Christianity, and that a good ecclesiastical discipline be observed and maintained.

The first Lutheran minister to come out to New Sweden was Reorus Torkillus, who arrived in 1639. He conducted worship in the block house at Fort Christina until his untimely death in 1643. With Governor Printz came the second minister, John Companius, who built the first Lutheran church in America at Fort Gottenburg, located at Tinnicum Island nine miles below present-day Philadelphia. In 1647 two additional ministers arrived to care for the increasing number of Swedish colonists. In the fall of 1653 three hundred and fifty new colonists arrived, accompanied by two clergymen. With them also came John Claesen Rising, who was commissioned temporary Governor, as Governor Printz had returned to Sweden. Rising's action in seizing the Dutch Fort Casimir on the Delaware led the Directors of the Dutch West India Company to order Governor Stuyvesant to invade New Sweden and demand its submission. This he accomplished in August 1656. With this expedition went Domine Megapolensis. At the time of the Dutch seizure of New Sweden there were three Swedish ministers on the Delaware, and it was the intention of the Dutch to expel them all. But as the negotiations were in progress news came of an Indian uprising at New Amsterdam, which made Stuyvesant's speedy return necessary. It was doubtless this exigency which made him consent to the stipulation that "those who will then remain here and earn their living in the country, shall enjoy the freedom of the Augsburg Confession, and one person to instruct them." [21]

The Reverend Lars Carlson Lock (Lokenius) was the Swedish minister selected to remain, and, if the Dutch Domines are to be believed, it was a poor selection. They describe him as

a man of impious and scandalous habits, a wild drunken, unmannerly clown, more inclined to look into the wine can than into the Bible.

---

[21] A letter from the New Amsterdam ministers Megapolensis and Drisius dated August 5, 1657, to the Classis of Amsterdam gives a full account of the negotiations with the Swedes (*Ecclesiastical Records of the State of New York*, Vol. I, pp. 393–99).

He would prefer drinking two hours to preaching one . . . during last spring this preacher was tippling with a smith, and while yet over their brandy they came to fisticuffs, and beat each others heads black and blue; yea, that the smith tore all the clothing from the preacher's body, so that this godly minister escaped in primitive naked-ness, and although so poorly clothed, yet sought quarrels with others. Sed hoc parergiccos.[22]

Although this was an unfortunate start for the Swedish Luther-ans under Dutch rule, the churches which had been formed per-sisted. This whole situation was changed for the better when in 1696 the Swedish King, Charles XI, enjoined the Archbishop and Consistory of Upsala to look after the needs of the American congregations. The next year (1697) three ministers arrived from Sweden, and the Swedish congregations on the Delaware came to life and entered upon a new period of activity. For three quar-ters of a century Sweden maintained a close relationship with the American churches, and the ministers sent out were generally men of high caliber. Altogether twenty-four clergymen were sent from Sweden during the next seventy-five years, and it has been estimated that Sweden expended between one and two hundred thousand dollars in carrying on the work of the American mis-sion.[23] Long before Sweden severed her connection with the American churches Swedish had ceased to be the language of the congregations, and gradually they united with others to form Anglican churches. The greatest of all the clergymen sent from Sweden to the Delaware was Charles Mangus von Wrangel, one of the King of Sweden's chaplains, who arrived in 1759 and was recalled in 1768. Broadminded and learned, he cooperated with the German Lutherans, and even corresponded with John Wesley regarding the religious needs of America.

---

[22] *Ibid.*, p. 396.

[23] Israel Acrelius, *A History of New Sweden, or the Settlements on the River Dela-ware*, Translated from the Swedish by W. M. Reynolds (Vol. XI, The Historical Society of Pennsylvania), 1874, is termed by Dr. Bergendoff the chief literary monument of the Delaware Mission. See also the Bibliographical Note in connection with Conrad J. I. Bergendoff, "The Swedish Church on the Delaware." (*Church History*, Vol. VII, No. 3, September, 1938, pp. 215–30.)

V

THE CHURCHES UNDER ENGLISH RULE

FROM THE BEGINNING of the seventeenth century there had developed an increasingly bitter trade rivalry between the English and the Dutch. There had been petty war between the Dutch and English East India Companies in the East Indies, and indeed wherever the traders of the two nations came together there was friction and often fighting. The seizure of New Netherland by the English in 1664 was but a phase of this larger struggle. In May 1664, the English sent an expedition against New Netherland under Colonel Nicolls, and Governor Stuyvesant, following the advice of Domine Megapolensis, surrendered the Fort without a struggle. This was one of the causes of a war that broke out between England and Holland in 1665, ending two years later with the Treaty of Breda, by which New Netherland was ceded to England. The coming of the English to power made certain adjustments necessary for the Dutch Reformed Church. The Duke's Laws (February 28, 1665), to which reference has been made in a previous chapter, were at first applicable only to Long Island and Staten Island, and the first English Governor refrained from enforcing them among the Dutch. Under the liberal terms of the surrender the Dutch could not be classed as dissenters, neither could the Dutch Church be considered on the same basis as the Church of England. Thus its position was peculiar and gave rise to numerous complications.

One of the effects of English control was the cutting off of further Dutch immigration, and the growth of the Dutch Church must, therefore, depend upon retaining the loyalty of the Dutch people and their children. English rule also cut off any further financial support from the Dutch West India Company, so that the ministers' salaries were soon in arrears, as the people were not accustomed to contribute directly for their support. There was, therefore, little inducement for ministerial recruits to come out from Holland, and in 1670 there were but three Dutch ministers to care for ten thousand souls. In a third Dutch war with England (1672–74) the Dutch recaptured New Netherland and for several months the Dutch flag again waved over the Fort on Manhattan Island. The Dutch Church again was established, and the new magistrates were required to be of the Reformed religion, though there was a provision for the toleration of other religious bodies. This, however, came to an end in February 1674, when by the Treaty of Westminster New Netherland was restored to England. This marked the end of Dutch rule in America, but not the end of Dutch influence. Dutch jurisprudence, founded on Roman law, and Dutch customs and religion have left a permanent impress upon American life.

The re-establishment of English rule also marked the beginning of the colonial career of Sir Edmund Andros. He came out as Governor of New York in 1674 and took an intelligent interest in the affairs of the Dutch Church. Under the administration of the Irish Catholic Governor Thomas Dongan (1683) the first New York legislative Assembly was held in which two-thirds of the members were Dutchmen. One of its most important acts was the passage of the *Charter of Liberties and Privileges* which granted entire freedom to all religious persuasions in New York, stating that "all other Christian Churches that shall hereafter come and settle within this province shall have the same privilege." [24] Although the last clause was intended for the benefit of Roman Catholics, the Duke's and the Governor's co-religionists, yet it undoubtedly reflected the will of the Dutch members of the Assembly. These years also mark an increased French immigration to New York. Large numbers of French Walloons had settled in Ulster County, on Long Island, and on Staten Island, and in the very year of the revocation of the Edict of Nantes (1685) at least a fourth of the population of New York City was French. Between 1682 and the end of the century five or six French churches were formed in and about New York City. Their most important leaders were Reverend Pierre Daille, who arrived in New York in 1682, and Pierre Peirot, who came five years later. These were all Reformed churches, in close association with the Dutch.

The overthrow of King James II in 1688 and the consequent confusion in the government of New York led to what is known

---

[24] *Ecclesiastical Records of the State of New York*, Vol. II, pp. 864–65.

as the Leisler rebellion. Jacob Leisler, though a German, was a member and a deacon in the Dutch Church. The delay of the new King, William III, in appointing officials to displace those who had received their authority from King James II, was the occasion for Leisler's rise to power. Instead of being welcomed by the Dutch Domines, as he had expected, Leisler found no friends or supporters among them. His humble origin and his lack of statesmanship, together with his assumption of certain rights and dignities, such as his taking over the Governor's pew in the church, scandalized the first families and with them the Domines, who, it is feared, were more influenced by social considerations than should have been the case. Many members of the Dutch churches were supporters of Leisler, and because of the Domine's rabid opposition to him many refused to attend the churches or contribute to the support of the ministers. The leading Dutch minister, Domine Henry Selyns, was particularly hostile to Leisler, declaring him an incarnate devil and stating that there was no hope for his salvation. On the Sunday after the arrival of the legally appointed Governor, Henry Sloughter, Domine Selyns preached a strong anti-Leisler sermon from the text, "I had fainted unless I had believed to see the goodness of the Lord in the land of the Living."

After the conviction of Leisler on the charge of treason and murder, three of the Dutch ministers demanded the death penalty, an unfortunate example of ministerial vindictiveness. At Leisler's execution a great crowd which assembled in the rain to witness the spectacle was much impressed by Leisler's courage. Even Domine Selyns was compelled to admit that Leisler died like a Christian, praying that "in their graves all malice, hatred, and envy might be buried." [25] The verdict of history has largely vindicated Leisler, and the vindictive Dutch Domines have suffered as a result. This is not the first time nor the last that the clergy have lined up on the wrong side.

The attempt of the early English Governors to obtain the establishment of the Anglican Church in New York has already been

---

[25] *History of the State of New York* (A. C. Flick, Ed.), *op. cit.,* Vol. II, Chapter III, "The Transition from Dutch to English Rule, 1664-1691," by Victor Hugo Paltsits furnishes a good summary and a select bibliography.

considered in Chapter II of this volume. The fear on the part of the Dutch Church officials that the royal Governors would attempt to appropriate their property for the use of the Anglican Church led the Church in New York to attempt to secure a royal charter. In 1695 the Consistory of New York made application for a charter, stating that they had acquired certain properties in New York, including a church, and they sought to guard these possessions. The following year (1696) the Governor, much against his will, signed the charter incorporating the Dutch Reformed Church in New York City, which granted them the right of freedom of worship, the right to hold property, and of choosing their own ministers. The next year the Anglican Church (Trinity) was also chartered. The Trinity charter stated that the Episcopal Church was by law established, which the Dutch knew was not true. But since their charter gave them protection, they made no objection to it, though they did insist on a final paragraph which stated that nothing in the charter should be interpreted as abridging the privileges of any other Protestant Church. Other Dutch churches later obtained similar charters; the Kingston church in 1719; Albany in 1720; Schenectady, 1734; Hackensack, 1750; the five churches of the Raritan Valley unitedly in 1753; Bergen in 1771, and Hillsborough in 1775.

In the year 1695 the Chaplain of the English garrison in New York, Reverend John Miller, prepared a report on the general conditions in the province of New York for the Bishop of London.[26] He had little good to say of the religious character of the people generally and proposed as one of the remedies the sending of a suffragan bishop. Religiously, he stated, the people were much divided. Of the 3525 families in the province, he estimated that 1754 were Dutch, 1355 English dissenters; 261 French; 45 Lutherans; 90 Episcopalians; and 20 Jews. The Dutch he characterized as wealthy, the English in moderate circumstances and the French poor.

---

[26] Miller's manuscript was not published until 1843 (London, Thomas Rood, bookseller). For a brief summary of the progress of the Reformed Dutch Church for the hundred years following 1688, see Chapter II. "The Church, the School, and the Press" by Augustus H. Shearer, in *History of New York, op. cit.*, Vol. II, pp. 49–54. See also *Ibid.*, Bibliography, pp. 88–90.

VII

The Germans Find a Haven in the New World

A NEW RELIGIOUS strain was introduced into colonial America with the coming of the Germans. Though represented by a variety of distinct religious bodies, as Mennonites, Dunkers, Moravians, Schwenkfelders, Inspirationists, the Reformed and the Lutherans, together with those who had separated from all religious organizations, generally speaking may all be classed as Pietists, using that term in its broadest sense. Stressing Christianity as a life rather than as a creed Pietism gave chief place to the devotional side of religion. The Lutherans and the Reformed held to their distinct churchly and creedal traditions, but the principal colonial leaders of both bodies were distinctly pietistic.

As a definite movement in German Lutheranism pietism began in 1670 when, in order to combat the dead orthodoxy in the German Churches and the appalling immorality of the time, Philip Jacob Spener, the Lutheran pastor at Frankfort-on-the-Main, formed from among the more earnest members of his congregation a little group which met twice a week at his home, there to read and discuss the Bible and to engage in prayer and the singing of hymns. Thus arose the *Collegia Pietatis* or the societies of piety. The movement spread to other parishes and soon had permeated every section of the country. It obtained a strong foothold among the Reformed people, swept into the Scandinavian countries and influenced the Methodist movement in England. It became the dominant influence in revived Moravianism through Count Zinzendorf, a pietistic Lutheran, while the Mennonites, the Dunkers and the Schwenkfelders were fundamentally pietistic in their religious emphases. Though, doubtless, the Lutheran and the Reformed Churches would object most seriously to being listed with the German sectaries in any classification, yet there can be no denial that the pietistic strain was common to them all in colonial America. To quote the author of the standard life of the American Lutheran patriarch, Henry M. Mühlenberg,

Pietism was, indeed, the form under which in those years warm-hearted godliness almost exclusively existed in Germany. . . . It was the living source from which then proceeded most works of Christian charity, missionary enterprises, care of the orphans, the spreading of the Bible among the masses of the people, and the instruction of the neglected.[1]

The two great pietistic centers in Europe during the eighteenth century were the University of Halle and Herrnhut in Saxony, the former the home of Lutheran pietism, the latter the fountain-head of Moravian activity. Spener had been influential in inducing the Elector of Brandenburg (later Frederick III, King of Prussia) to found the University of Halle (1694) and Augustus Hermann Francke was called to one of the professorships of theology. Francke became the guiding genius of the University and the Orphan House later established, and from these two institutions pietistic influences spread throughout the German world. Here was inaugurated a new era in theological education in which exegetical theology was stressed, since it was held that the "Holy Scriptures are the sole fountain of our faith, from which all theology must be sought," and it was therefore more important "to be engaged with the fountain than with the stream." [2] During the first twenty-nine years of its history more than six thousand ministers were trained at Halle, and they went out imbued with a warm Christian piety and fervor.

The reorganization of the Moravian Church is directly related to the pietistic movement. Count Zinzendorf, the recreator of Moravianism, had studied at Halle and was Spener's godson. Soon after his purchase of Berthelsdorf he extended to a group of Moravian exiles under the leadership of Christian David the

[1] William J. Mann, *Life and Times of Henry M. Mühlenberg*, 2nd ed., Philadelphia: 1911, p. 393.

[2] James W. Richards, *The Confessional History of the Lutheran Church*, Philadelphia: 1909, Chapter XL, pp. 546–565.

privilege of settling on his estate, where in 1722 the community of Herrnhut was established. From his childhood Zinzendorf had displayed an extreme sensitiveness to mystical religious influences. At the early age of six he thought of Christ as his brother and would talk with Him as a familiar friend. As a student at Halle, he, with a group of fellow pietists, had organized the "Order of the Grain of Mustard Seed" whose members were pledged to walk worthily in the doctrine of Jesus and to exercise charity toward their neighbors. After several unhappy years as an official at the Court of the King of Saxony, he left his duties there in 1727 to take up his residence at Herrnhut, where he identified himself more and more with the Moravian exiles.

A number of German pietists also were attracted to Herrnhut, some of them of liberal education, as Augustus A. Spangenberg and Peter Böhler, both of whom later became important leaders among the Moravians in America. It was Zinzendorf's first intention to encourage the uniting of the Moravians and the Lutherans on his estate, and for a time they worshipped together. The desire of the Moravians, however, to maintain their ancient Church manifested itself with increasing strength, and resulted finally in the complete separation of the Moravians from the Lutherans. Zinzendorf now identified himself with them, and to the end of his life (1760) the increasingly wide-flung Moravian activities were carried on under his direction. Because he was suspected of harboring fanatics and promoting views contrary to the Lutheran Church he was banished in 1738 for ten years. It was during this period of banishment that the Moravians under Zinzendorf's leadership began the establishment of missions in foreign lands. From this time forward Herrnhut became one of the most active missionary centers in the world. The first Moravians to come to America came primarily as refugees and not as missionaries.[3]

---

[3] The principal books on Moravianism in English are J. Taylor Hamilton, *A History of the Church known as the Moravian Church*, Bethlehem: 1900; J. Holmes, *History of the Protestant Church of the United Brethren*, 2 vols., London: 1925; J. E. Hutton, *History of the Moravian Church*, 2nd Edition, London: 1909; Edmund DeSchweinitz, *The History of the Church Known as the Unitas Fratrum*, Bethlehem: 1885.

I

THE MENNONITES

BY THE time of the Declaration of Independence it has been estimated that one tenth of the population of the United States were
people of German blood, one third of whom were living in
Pennsylvania. The vanguard of this great migration was a little
group of German Swiss people of Dutch descent, thirteen families
in all, who had come from the little city of Crefeld in the Rhine
Valley near the Dutch border, where they had found temporary
abode. It seems that most, if not all those who made up this first
body of German emigrants, were Quakers of Mennonite background who had been won to Quakerism through the efforts of
the Quaker missionaries from England who had been active in
that region as early as 1655. Crefeld was the seat of an old Mennonite congregation, although they were only a tolerated group,
and it was not until 1695 that they were permitted to erect their
first house of worship on a back street where it would attract little
attention. The Quakers were even less favored by the city authorities, which accounts for the prevailing religious complexion of
this first group of Germans who accepted the invitation of
William Penn to settle in his great free province.

Through William Penn's agent at Rotterdam the company
secured passage on the *Concord,* a large roomy ship which could
accommodate 180 passengers. They arrived in Philadelphia October 6, 1683. Francis Pastorius, a pietistic lawyer of Frankfort-on-
the-Main, generally has been considered the founder of Germantown. He was an intimate friend of Spener's and was in touch
with William Penn's friends. Devoutly religious, he had become
dissatisfied with his legal profession and at the instigation of a
body of Frankfort Quakers agreed to become their agent to
negotiate a purchase of land in Pennsylvania. Arriving in Philadelphia in August 1683, some two months ahead of the Crefeld
company, by the time of their arrival he had secured some 15,000
acres of land from Penn and took the lead in laying out German-

town.[4] Until his death in 1720 Pastorius was the leading citizen of the town and was its first mayor. He taught in a Quaker school in Philadelphia and during the latter years of his life was the Master of a school in Germantown.

The Crefeld settlers were weavers rather than farmers and were handicapped at first because there was no demand for the product of their looms. Most of the early inhabitants were of Dutch descent and were either Quakers or Mennonites, but after 1707 the great majority were Palatinate Germans representing all the various religious bodies of that region. It seems probable that during the early years the several religious groups in the town worshipped together in a community meeting house which had been built in 1686. Gradually, however, separate congregations emerged and in 1705 the Quakers withdrew to their own meeting house and in 1708 the Mennonites did likewise, though they had carried on separate worship since 1690. In that year the Mennonite congregation in Germantown numbered ninety-nine members, which represented a Mennonite population of some two hundred and fifty souls. The Palatinates were on the lookout for farm lands and passed Germantown by for the rich limestone country in what is now Bucks, Lancaster and surrounding counties. Lancaster county soon became the principal Mennonite center in America as well as the chief distributing point for Mennonite immigration. Large tracts of land were usually purchased in the names of the leading men and were divided up as settlers arrived. In 1710, for instance, a warrant was issued for 10,000 acres to ten persons, "Switzers lately arrived in the province." It had been purchased from the Proprietor for £50 Pennsylvania money, to be paid in six annual installments subject to one shilling quitrent annually for every one hundred acres.

With the opening of the Seven Years' War (1756) Mennonite immigration practically ceased and never again attained the vol-

---

[4] See the article in the *Dictionary of American Biography* on Pastorius. C. H. Smith, *The Mennonite Immigration to Pennsylvania in the Eighteenth Century,* Norristown: 1929, pp. 88–89, holds that Pastorius was not the founder of Germantown. Andrews, III, p. 302, states that Germantown was a Quaker colony and not German nor Mennonite. He also states that Pastorius was a Quaker, but it is nearer the truth to say that he was always more of a Lutheran than a Quaker.

ume of the early years.[5] Some twenty-five hundred Mennonites arrived in America during the colonial period, representing about one tenth of the total colonial German immigration. The importance of the Mennonite immigration, however, is not due to their numbers but to the fact that they blazed the trail to the New World for the vast numbers of their race which were to follow. A few Mennonite families found their way into Maryland and Virginia during the seventeen hundreds, coming down the Cumberland Valley from Pennsylvania, but by and large the great free Province of Pennsylvania was the home of the colonial Mennonites.

The Mennonites shared with other left-wing religious groups a certain body of views. They held that religion was an individual matter; that Church membership could be achieved only on the basis of an inner conviction. Their rejection of infant baptism and their advocacy of baptism upon profession of faith only naturally followed. Their doctrines of non-resistance and separation of Church and State were based on literal New Testament injunctions. This was but a part of their attempt to restore primitive Christianity as set forth in the New Testament. Governments they believed were necessary, and were ordained of God, and it was the duty of the Christian to pray for those in authority. In their European homes they had been forbidden to hold office, for there the magistrate was the tool of the State Church and would be compelled to punish dissenters. In Pennsylvania, however, where Church and State were separated, they did not find it necessary to make the same distinction between the Christian and the world. Some of their number held local offices in Pennsylvania, and in the elections for the Assembly the Mennonite vote was a factor in keeping the Quakers in control long after they had ceased to be a majority. Their refusal to take an oath was based on the literal application of the injunction "swear not at all." The stress laid upon the necessity of separating from the world accounts for their peculiar garb and the forbidding of marriage

---

[5] Smith, *op. cit.*, is the fullest account of Mennonite immigration into the colonies, based on a wide acquaintance with the sources. In 1717, 300 Mennonites arrived in America, the largest number in any one year. *See* Chapter VII.

outside their own group. Their practice of foot-washing, the kiss of peace, the little cap worn by their women in time of worship, all come from the same source a literal following of the New Testament.

Mennonite theology was Biblical rather than philosophical. They considered the making of theological distinctions inimical to the life of the spirit, as it undoubtedly often has been. The Pennsylvania Mennonites, however, brought with them a statement of principles adopted at Dort in 1632, which had been signed by representatives of congregations in Holland and northwestern Germany. In 1660 the Churches of the Palatinate adopted it and from there it came to Pennsylvania. The Mennonites, however, were far more interested in formulating rules for human conduct than in drawing up theological statements.[6]

With almost every phase of human activity regulated, there were as a consequence many cases of discipline. Gross sins were punished by excommunication administered by the elders with the consent of the congregation, and in the more rigid congregations, as the Amish Mennonites, "avoidance" was practiced. This meant that the faithful were neither to eat, drink, visit, buy or sell with an excommunicated person. As prosperity increased among them pride was one of the commonest sins with which they had to deal. Beards were worn universally by all Mennonite men, but though beards were insisted upon, the mustache was banned, as it was considered the mark of a military man.

Mennonite congregations conducted their own affairs with no outside control of any sort. Each congregation had its own bishop, elders and deacons, the bishop possessing the full power to perform all the ecclesiastical functions. All officials were chosen by lot from among the members. With this type of uneducated ministry there was little chance for progress, with the result that Mennonites clung tenaciously to their old European customs.

---

[6] For a convenient summary of the doctrines of the Mennonites and other left-wing bodies see Roland H. Bainton, "The Left Wing of the Reformation," *Journal of Religion*, Vol. XXI, April 1941, pp. 124–134. The Dortrecht Confession of Faith may be found in John C. Wanger, *Glimpses of Mennonite History*, Scottsdale, Pa.: 1940, Appendix III, pp. 84–111.

There was this advantage, however—there was never a lack of a ministry in their frontier settlements. Thus their religious life did not need to wait for any outside authority before beginning its organized existence. Frequently a Mennonite or Dunker Church was the first to be formed in new German settlements and was often the only Church long after the Lutheran or Reformed made up the largest part of the population.

II

THE DUNKERS

THE FACT that the German Baptist Brethren or the Dunkers are known by so many different names has led to confusion concerning them. They have been called Taufers, Tunkers, Tunkards, Dunkards, Dunkers and Dippers.[7] These several names, however, all imply that they are baptizers *par excellence,* for no other religious body insists upon trine immersion, or dipping three times face forward in a flowing stream.

The first congregation of the German Baptist Brethren was formed at Schwarzenau [8] in Hesse-Cassel in the year 1708. Its founder and first pastor was Alexander Mack, a man of considerable means, who had become dissatisfied with the deadness of religion in the Reformed Church in which he had been raised. At the little town of Schwarzenau where he had fled to escape persecution he became friendly with Christopher Hochmann, who as a student at the University of Halle had come under the influence of Francke and had become an extreme pietist. Together Mack and Hochmann formed a little group of pious people who were accustomed to come together to study the Bible and for prayer. Hochmann opposed the forming of anything like a Church organization, fearing the return of the evils which had led him

---

[7] Dunkers, the name commonly in use today, is derived from the German pronunciation of "Tunker" in which the letter "T" is given a soft "D" sound.

[8] The American Dunkers have recently established an official journal and have given it the name *Schwarzenau.*

to withdraw from the Church. Mack, however, saw no other means of carrying on their work, and under his leadership, after the little group had prayed together, they went down to the banks of the river Eder, and there, one of them chosen by lot, led Mack into the stream and baptized him, dipping him three times face forward in the name of the Father, the Son and the Holy Spirit. The other seven were then baptized by Mack and thus was constituted the first Church of the Brethren, a direct offspring of pietism.

It is always a distinct advantage to a religious group working among simple people to lay stress upon a particular spectacular rite such as that of trine immersion. The news of what had been done at Schwarzenau spread into neighboring provinces and other congregations were formed. One was at Marienborn, which later, because of persecution, moved to Crefeld, and it was this congregation under the leadership of Peter Becker which started, in 1719, the Dunker migration to America. Four years later (1723) seventeen Dunkers gathered at the home of Becker in Germantown and there formed the first Dunker Church in America, choosing Becker as their elder. During the day six new converts were baptized in Wissahickon creek, after which they gathered around a long table in the home of another member, the women on one side and the men on the other, where, after a service of song, prayer and scripture reading, they washed one another's feet. They then partook of a meal, followed by Communion, passed the "holy kiss of charity" gave "the right hand of fellowship" and brought the meeting to a close with prayer and hymn. Thus was inaugurated the first Dunker congregation in America with the rites and customs which have been continued among them to this day.

With this beginning other congregations soon were formed in the German communities where the Brethren were settling. One such congregation (1724) was at Conestoga in Lancaster county, over which Conrad Beissel was chosen elder. Five years later (1729) Alexander Mack arrived with some thirty families and at once assumed the leadership of the expanding movement. By 1770 fourteen congregations had been formed in Pennsylvania and one in New Jersey with a total membership of some seven hundred.[9]

The following is Morgan Edwards' description of the Pennsylvania Dunkers within a generation of their coming to America:

> They [the Tunkers] use great plainness of language and dress like the Quakers; and like them will never swear nor fight. They will not go to law nor take interest for the money they lend. They commonly wear their beards and keep the first day Sabbath, except one congregation (Ephrata). They have the Lord's Supper with its ancient attendants of love-feast, washing feet, kiss of charity, and right hand of fellowship. They anoint the sick with oil for their recovery, and use trine immersion, with laying on of hands and prayer, even while the person is in the water; which may easily be done, as he kneels down to be baptized and continues in that position till both prayer and imposition of hands be performed. . . . Every brother is allowed to stand up in the congregation to speak in a way of exhortation and expounding, and when by that means they find a man eminent for knowledge and aptness to teach, they choose him to be a minister and ordain him with imposition of hands, attended with fasting and prayer, and giving the right hand of fellowship. They also have deacons, and ancient widows for deaconesses; and exhorters who are licensed to use their gifts statedly.

Like the Mennonites the Dunkers were strictly congregational in their form of Church government and with an uneducated ministry drawn from among the people. Though the Dunkers state that they have no confession of faith other than the New Testament, yet Christopher Hochmann's Confession of Faith, prepared by him in 1702 and printed by Christopher Saur in 1743, undoubtedly greatly influenced Mack and the Pennsylvania Dunkers in

---

[9] Martin Grove Brumbaugh, *A History of the German Baptist Brethren in Europe and America,* Elgin, Illinois: 1899, is based on sources and is the standard history. It is, however, overlaudatory, lacks any critical appraisal and is without an index. Frederick Denton Dove, *Cultural Changes in the Church of the Brethren,* Philadelphia: 1932; John Lewis Gillin, *The Dunkers, A Sociological Interpretation,* New York: 1906, are sociological studies. Otto Wenger, *History and Doctrines of the Church of the Brethren,* 2nd Ed., Elgin, Illinois: 1920, is useful. Morgan Edwards, the Baptist minister in Philadelphia, 1761–71, planned a comprehensive history of all Baptists in America, treating each colony separately. His *Materials Towards a History of the Baptists in Pennsylvania, both British and German,* 1770, is based on interviews and observations of his own.

their formative period. Before his coming to America Mack had written a treatise on his conception of New Testament teaching concerning the Christian life, which he called *A Short and Plain View of the Outward yet Sacred Rites and Ordinances of the House of God*. Though not creeds in any formal sense, nevertheless these two statements constitute the foundations of the doctrines, beliefs and practices of the German Baptist Brethren.

The reasons given to Benjamin Franklin by one of the Ephrata Dunkers, Michael Wohlforth, why they had not published their articles of belief, were, that since they had discovered that some of the doctrines which they had esteemed truths were later found to be errors, and others which they had thought errors were found to be truth, they had decided that they had not yet arrived at the end of this progression. If they printed their confession they would feel themselves bound to it and unwilling to receive further improvement, and what had been done by the elders and founders before them would be considered sacred and never to be changed. Concerning this statement Franklin remarked, "This modesty in a sect is perhaps a single instance in the history of mankind, every sect supposing itself in possession of all truth, and that those who differ are so far in the wrong." [10] For a religious sect to win the approval of Benjamin Franklin was no mean distinction.

III

THE EPHRATA SOCIETY

THERE IS A close relationship between the colonial Dunkers and the Ephrata society, formed under the leadership of Johann Conrad Beissel in Lancaster county in 1732. Dunker historians, however, rightly insist that the Ephrata society must not be confused with the Dunker Church. Conrad Beissel, the posthumous son of a drunken baker of Eberback in the Palatinate, after the usual apprenticeship became a journeyman baker. In the course of his travels he came in contact with groups of pietists and in 1715

[10] *The Autobiography of Benjamin Franklin* (O. S. Coad, Ed.), New York: 1929, pp. 154–155.

was converted under their influence. In the words of the historians of the Ephrata community, on his conversion "his reason became so enlightened that he could easily solve the most intrically involved matters." Having gained the violent dislike of the wife of an employer at Manheim, it was "deeply impressed upon his heart that a man who intends to devote himself to the service of God must, at the beginning of his conversion, renounce Adam's regenerative work, for which reason he bade good-night to earthly women at the very commencement." [11] From Manheim he went to Heidelberg where he found many pietists who had separated from the churches and as a result were suffering persecution. Here he was arrested and placed in jail. On his release he was haled before the ecclesiastical court and banished. Coming finally to Schwarzenau and Crefeld he came in contact with the German Baptist Brethren and the Inspirationists. With two like-minded companions, Stuntz and Stiefel, he found his way to America and arrived in Boston in 1720. Proceeding at once to Germantown he found there little demand for his trade as a baker, which led to his serving an apprenticeship in the home of Peter Becker, the Dunker elder, to learn the weaver's trade.

Meanwhile Beissel was quietly laying plans to lead a solitary life and when his year's instruction came to an end, he with the two companions who had accompanied him to America withdrew to a solitary cabin in the forest near Conestoga. Their hermit abode and their strange mode of life attracted the curiosity of the settlers in the vicinity and they were also the recipient of visits by numerous pietistic fanatics. The withdrawal of Beissel's companions led Beissel to the conclusion that the life of a hermit was not an end in itself and that no solitary person could be fruitful. He now accepted baptism at the hands of Peter Becker and for a time served as the "elder" of the Conestoga Dunkers, eventually leading most of the members of his congregation into the Ephrata Community.

The community at Ephrata was established on two main reli-

---

[11] *Chronicon Ephratense: A History of the Community of Seventh Day Baptists at Ephrata, Lancaster County, Penn'a,* by "Lameck and Agrippa," translated from the original German by J. Max Hark, Lancaster: 1889.

gious conceptions: first, Beissel's aversion to marriage and the sex relation; second, his insistence on the observance of the seventh day as the day of rest. The other religious observances were similar to those of the Dunkers,—trine immersion, foot-washing, etc. Celibacy was stressed, but it was not required for membership in the community, though the Order of Spiritual Virgins and the Solitary Brethren constituted its backbone. Beissel was a skillful propagandist and converts flocked to the community. Nor were the converts entirely from among the humble people, though they made up the largest proportion. Johann Conrad Weiser, one of the most prominent leaders among the colonial Germans was, for a time, a member of the Ephrata society, as was also the wife of Christopher Saur, Sr., the well-known printer of Germantown. Another convert was John Peter Miller, the German Reformed minister at Tulpehocken, in whose church Weiser was an elder. The story of Weiser's connection with the Ephrata society furnished an interesting illustration of the many and varied religious currents present among the colonial Germans in the eighteenth century.[12] Weiser and Madam Saur eventually withdrew, but Miller remained and succeeded Beissel as its head. Miller's conversion created a sensation and even threatened for a time the actual existence of the Reformed Church in Pennsylvania. He was reputed to be the most learned theologian of the Province. He was also a linguist of note and was engaged by the Continental Congress to translate the Declaration of Independence into several European languages.

Ephrata was a semi-monastic, communistic community. By 1741 separate buildings had been erected for the "solitary brethren" and the "sisters." The *Saal* or the chapel was the largest building of its kind in Pennsylvania and was built without the use of iron, following the injunction given by Moses (Deut. xxvii,

---

[12] For the story of Weiser's connection with the Society see Julius Frederick Sachse, *The German Sectarians of Pennsylvania, 1708–1742: A Critical and Legendary History of the Ephrata Cloister and the Dunkers,* Philadelphia: 1899, pp. 219, 241–248 and scattered references. One of the reasons why Weiser withdrew from Ephrata was because he was reprimanded by Beissel for having four children by his wife during his supposed celibacy. He later was reconciled and returned, but finally withdrew in 1743, supposedly on the advice of his son-in-law, Henry M. Mühlenberg, and joined the Lutheran Church. *Dictionary of American Biography.*

5.) "Thou shalt not lift up an iron tool upon them." The most extraordinary thing about the buildings, aside from their great size, was the extreme pitch of the roof as well as their extreme height. The whole regimen of the Community was strict to the last degree. Both sexes were clothed in unattractive garbs designed to conceal "that humiliating image revealed by sin." In addition the women were veiled. Every week on the evening of the sixth day every one was to "examine his own heart before God in his own cell," after which a written statement was to be handed to the superintendent as to his or her spiritual condition. Later some of these *lectiones* or confessions were published. Much attention was given to singing, and Beissel himself composed over a thousand hymns. By 1745 a printing press, a paper mill, a fulling mill, a bookbindery and a grist mill were in full operation, all of which were conducted on a purely communal basis. Since the purpose of these industries was not to amass wealth all surplus money was given away. A long list of books were published at the Ephrata Press including the Mennonite book of martyrs (*Blutige Shau-Platz*) and the *Chronicon Ephratense* and a large number of hymn books. On Beissel's death in 1768 he was succeeded by Miller as superintendent, but thereafter the community rapidly declined. During the period of its greatest activity Ephrata was one of the two principal cultural centers among the colonial Germans, but whether or not it exercised a helpful religious influence is at least open to question.

IV

THE MORAVIANS

IN DECEMBER 1741 Count Zinzendorf, traveling as a Lutheran clergyman and under the name Domine de Thurstein, arrived in Pennsylvania. By this time the Moravian settlement which had been begun in Georgia (1735) had been transferred to Pennsylvania (1740) and the town of Nazareth established at the Forks of the Delaware. Zinzendorf was still an exile from his Saxon estates and his coming to America was motivated by his desire

to take up land for his followers, to explore the missionary prospect among both the Indians and the settlers, and to bring
together the numerous German religious groups in Pennsylvania
into a single spiritual communion. Believing that all the evangelical Churches were essentially one he was convinced that
they could all be united about the Augsburg Confession, since it
possessed a universal nature characteristic of all Protestantism.
He had united with the Moravians at Herrnhut, but still considered himself a Lutheran. Zinzendorf held that "in each religion
lies a thought of God which cannot be received through any other
religion. . . . Not any religion has the whole; she must take the
best out of other religions to assist her if she wants the whole."
This broad view of the Church and the creeds was generally
shared by the Moravians, and was the basis upon which Zinzendorf now attempted to bring together the Pennsylvania Lutherans,
Reformed, Dunkers, Ephrataites, Quakers, Mennonites, Schwenkfelders and Moravians, into what he termed "the Church of God
in the Spirit."

The net result of the seven synods which Zinzendorf convened
within a half year's time, instead of promoting the cause of
Christian harmony, only intensified sectarian differences and
increased the discordant voices so that religious confusion among
the Pennsylvania Germans became even more confused. The
inability of the Pennsylvania Germans to understand Zinzendorf's
"Church of God in the Spirit" was one of the principal causes of
failure. They could not get it out of their heads that he intended
to form an organic union, with an overhead authority; in other
words to bring them all under "his own hat." His intention, however, was not to unite the groups into a corporate body, but to
bring about an agreement in essentials and thus create spiritual
ties, but not an external association. Zinzendorf disavowed any
intention of using his union movement to promote Moravianism,
yet the constant use of Moravian hymns and the frequent use of
the lot in the synods gave color to the belief that they were simply
a clever bit of Moravian propaganda. Zinzendorf's domineering
personality also stood in the way of his religious leadership in
America, while his deeply emotional nature led him to say and

do things which gave offence both within and without the German groups. Gilbert Tennent, for instance, denounced Zinzendorf's sermons as a "bundle of contradictions and nonsense, damnable errors and heresies, interspersed with passages of truth and sense." [13] Though Zinzendorf's plan for unifying the German religious groups was a failure, it nevertheless was a noble conception and worthy of serious study by those of our own time who would promote Christian unity.

Defeated in his attempt to unite his American brethren into a spiritual unity Zinzendorf now turned his attention to the promotion of Indian missions and to the establishment of the Moravian communities at Nazareth and Bethlehem. He made three journeys into the Indian country and laid the foundation for those extensive Indian missions which were to become the greatest glory of American Moravianism.

Between the years 1741 and 1744 the two Moravian communities at Nazareth and Bethlehem were gradually taking shape. In the latter year the sane and capable Bishop Spangenberg arrived from Herrnhut to become the supervisor. His coming marked the beginning of what is known as the General Economy, which he had carefully worked out under sixteen rules, based upon the experience at Herrnhut. The members were divided into groups called *choirs*. Thus there was a single men *choir,* a single women *choir,* an older boy *choir* and an older girl *choir,* each living together in their own houses while their lives were regulated to the last detail. Marriage was encouraged because it made for larger contentment, and married couples in turn were formed into *choirs*. Large farms were developed about Nazareth; great barns and granaries were erected and industries of many kinds thrived. All of this growing wealth was considered as belonging to the entire unity of the Brethren in all lands; indeed it was not long until the American Moravians were making large contributions to relieve the financial stress of their European Brethren. In 1759 there were 2454 acres of land under intensive cultivation produc-

---

[13] Jacob John Sessler, *Communal Pietism among Early American Moravians,* New York: 1933, is an admirable recent account based upon thorough research. The above summary of the causes of the Synod's failure is based upon Sessler.

ing annually thousands of bushels of all kinds of grain and supporting live stock running into the thousands. There were, all told,
97 buildings which included 17 choir houses, 5 schools, 20 buildings where trades were carried on, 5 mills, 2 inns, and 48 farm
buildings. Among the members of the two communities there were
nearly a hundred different trades represented.[14]

The *choir* organization served as a most useful educational
device. Since the children were already formed into their appropriate *choirs,* the subjects taught were accommodated to each age
group, so that the result was what we would term today graded
schools. In this respect the Moravians were educationally a hundred years and more ahead of their time. In 1755 there were three
hundred children in the various schools, and in their instruction
eighty teachers and helpers were employed.

As the number of married couples increased, with the resultant
children, discontent with the communal manner of living spread.
As soon as children were separated from their mothers they had
been placed in nurseries, and later were removed to the boys' or
girls' boarding schools. By 1760 the demand for family privacy
had become so insistent that some of the buildings were turned
into family apartments, and two years later the General Economy
was abolished. Membership in the communities continued to be
based on membership in the Moravian Church, but the farms and
the industries were conducted as private enterprises. In 1775 there
were some 2500 Moravians in Pennsylvania. In 1752 a body of
Moravians had been sent from Bethlehem to select a place for a
Moravian settlement in North Carolina. A hundred thousand
acres were purchased from Lord Granville and three communities established, the most important being that at Salem.

The Moravians made no distinction between the secular and
the religious, for all work to them was religious. They were a
simple, industrious people whose child-like faith was the most
important fact in their lives. Their preaching and teaching were
almost exclusively Christo-centric with the major emphasis upon
Christ's sacrificial death. The blood atonement was the central

---

[14] J. M. Levering, *A History of Bethlehem, Pennsylvania, 1741–1892,* etc., Bethlehem:
1903, pp. 378 ff.

theme in their hymns and litanies, which made up a large part of their formal worship. As a result their Church music was more highly developed than that of any other Church in colonial America.

Both at Herrnhut and in America the Moravians went through a period of extreme fanaticism on the subject of Christ's atonement, though this was neither characteristic of ancient Moravianism nor Moravianism at its best. The purpose was to present so vividly the picture of the blood and wounds of Christ that the "hardest heart would melt." Zinzendorf, in order to emphasize the closeness of the relationship of Christ to believers, compared it to the conjugal relation. He taught that all souls are female, and married to one "conjugal Lord Jesus," thus the relationship which exists between the saved soul and Christ is the most intimate of all relationships. Out of this emphasis came many sentimental and even sensuous expressions of endearment. The Lord's Supper was spoken of as an "embrace"; Christ presses the communicant to His heart; kisses her with His pale lips. Hymns expressing the marriage relationship were common such as:

> Our husband's side wound is indeed
> The Queen of all his wounds;

or

> My dearest, most beloved lamb
> I who in tenderest union am.

Earthly marriage was considered a preparation for the heavenly marriage, which led to the exaltation of marriage in their hymns particularly. Sex relations were sanctified and childbirth and the pains attending it were considered as having a spiritual significance. These abnormal traits dominated the whole Moravian community to an extent unusual in the Christian tradition, but quite analogous to the symbolism to be found among certain Hindu sects.

It was during Spangenberg's absence in Herrnhut (1746–50) that fanaticism reached its height. On his return there was an immediate check put upon it, though its influence long remained. The American Moravians continued to be controlled from Herrnhut until well along in the nineteenth century, and rigid discipline was maintained in all their communities to the end of the colonial period. Outside their Indian missions Moravian exclusiveness prevented them from having any widespread influence. Though John Wesley was indebted to Moravianism in his early years, he soon rejected it as not big enough for the things he felt needed to be done.

V

THE SCHWENKFELDERS

CASPER SCHWENCKFELD VON OSSIG (1490–1562) was of an ancient aristocratic family in the Duchy of Leibnitz. Spiritually awakened in 1518 he became an early supporter of the Reformation, and though a layman took an active part in propagating Reformation ideas, being influential in its spread throughout Silesia. He had contact with all the leading reformers and carried on a correspondence with Luther. Of an independent and active mind, he soon developed views out of harmony with the Lutheran party and was not backward about making them known. His two main points of difference with Luther were over the view of the Scriptures and the Sacraments. The Scriptures, he held, do not contain everything necessary for salvation, but the *living word* must be added. Man's renewing depends upon "the immediate efficacy of Christ in the Holy Ghost." To him, therefore, the Scriptures did not occupy the same exalted place as in Luther's thought. Nor, he held, were the Sacraments vehicles of grace. Schwenkfeld's views brought him into conflict with Luther, who considered him a dangerous heretic. As a consequence he became involved in numerous controversies and was a prolific writer. Driven from one place to another to escape persecution, he began to gather about himself a devoted following, and secret meetings were held for worship. A century and more after Schwenkfeld's death his followers continued to persist in Silesia and southern Germany. Though having no desire to form a new sect, the treatment they received at the hands of the recognized Churches, both Protestant and Catholic, forced them into separatism. In 1720 the Emperor Charles VI attempted their extermination through a specially constituted Jesuit mission, resulting in a considerable migration of them into Saxony, where they found refuge on Count Zinzendorf's estate. It was this group, in 1734, which began the emigration to Pennsylvania. They settled in Bucks, Montgomery and Berks counties, where five Schwenkfelder congregations persist to this day.

Since the Schwenkfelders had come to America from Zinzendorf's estate, the Count felt himself obligated to them and dispatched Spangenberg to America to attempt to win them to the Moravian fold. This attempt proved a failure. The year following their arrival in America the Schwenkfelders chose George Weiss as their minister and until his death in 1741 he kept religion alive among them by holding services in the homes of the settlers. On Weiss's death Balzer Hoffman was chosen their religious leader, but his efforts met such feeble response that he resigned his leadership in 1749. Concern for the lack of religion among them led five heads of families in 1753 to agree to hold regular meetings in their homes in rotation. Thus religion was kept alive among the Schwenkfelders until 1762, when a general conference was called which proved to be a "heart-searching, prayerful and face-to-face consideration of the sad condition of affairs among them." Out of this came a closer union, a catechism and a hymn book. Systematic religious instruction of the young was begun and a school system was organized. A plan of regular services was agreed upon and continued for twenty years. There was no attempt to form a denomination and there was no official ministry. The leadership was entirely in the hands of heads of families. It was not until 1782 that the American Schwenkfelders were formed into a Church, and not until 1790 was there a church building erected.[15]

---

[15] H. W. Kriebel, *The Schwenkfelders in Pennsylvania: A Historical Sketch,* Lancaster: 1904 (Vol. 13, Pennsylvania–German Society Proceedings), and A. A. Seipt, *Schwenkfelder Hymnology and the Sources of the First Schwenkfelder Hymn Book printed in America,* Philadelphia: 1909, constitute the two principal books in English on the American Schwenkfelders. In 1907 the Schwenkfelder Church in Pennsylvania and the Hartford Theological Seminary began the publication of the writings of Casper Schwenckfeld von Ossig, under the general title *Corpus Schwenckfeldianorum.* Of the 17 volumes planned 14 have appeared.

VI

THE GERMAN CHURCHES

THE GERMAN SECTARIES were the first to form religious organizations among the colonial Germans. As has been noted, this was due to the fact that all of them, with the exception of the Moravians, cut loose from all Old World connections once they had turned their faces to the New World. All of them were also congregational in the Church polity and were therefore independent of all outside control. Both the Lutheran and Reformed Churches, on the other hand, retained their Old World connections throughout the colonial period, and during the early years both were dependent upon Europe for leadership and financial assistance. There were no doubt many people of Reformed and Lutheran background among the earliest German immigrants, certainly enough of them to have established congregations in well populated German communities almost at once, but in many such communities their organizations were delayed because of their dependence upon outside help. The fact that both the Reformed and Lutheran people had been accustomed to a close State-Church relationship in their European homes was a handicap in the New World where the support of their ministry and Church was dependent upon voluntary contributions.

The first stage in the history of the German Churches in the colonies, the Lutheran and the Reformed, have many things in common. Both drew largely upon the Palatinate immigration, made up mostly of refugees from a country ravaged by the armies of Louis XIV. Many were compelled by their poverty to come out as redemptioners. That is, in order to secure passage they sold themselves to servitude on arriving in America for a period of from three to five years. Both received help from the pietistic center at Halle and both were aided by their Dutch brethren in America, while the Swedish Lutherans on the Delaware also rendered valuable assistance to their German co-religionists.

VII

THE GERMAN REFORMED

THE FIRST German Reformed minister to arrive in America was Samuel Guldin, who landed in Philadelphia with his family in the year 1710. He came, however, as an immigrant farmer and not as a minister. He preached to scattered groups in houses and barns and groves, but formed no congregations. John Philip Boehm was the real founder of the German Reformed Church in America. The son of a Reformed minister at Frankfort-on-the-Main, he became the parochial schoolmaster of the Reformed Church at Worms. Attracted to America, evidently by friends who had migrated to the New World, Boehm arrived in Montgomery county in 1720 and settled in the Perkiomen Valley as a farmer. Soon after his arrival his German neighbors persuaded him to conduct religious services for them, and as the meetings grew in size and as the settlers increased he was urged to assume the office of minister among them. Finally after five years (1725) he permitted himself to be persuaded. He now proceeded to form three congregations, one at Falkner's Swamp, a second at Skippack, and a third at Whitemarsh. This done, Boehm was chosen minister and although he was without ordination he assumed the full duties of a clergyman, administering the Sacraments as well as preaching.

The arrival of a German Reformed minister, George Michael Weiss, with a colony of Palatinates in 1727, brought a crisis in the affairs of Boehm and his congregations. Weiss denounced Boehm as a mere farmer, unfit to carry on the work of the ministry, and attempted to take his congregations from him. Boehm's friends, however, rallied to his support and with his leading elder Boehm went to New York to confer with the Dutch Reformed ministers there. They advised that he lay his case before the Classis of Amsterdam. This was done, and in due time an answer was received stating that under the circumstances Boehm's action in assuming ministerial functions was justified, but advised that he now seek ordination. This Boehm gladly did and was ordained at the hands of the Dutch ministers in New York on November 23, 1729. Writing to the Classis the following year Boehm thus expresses his gratitude to them:

We could not receive this (your) letter without tears, because of our surprise and heart-thrilling joy, considering that the Reverend Classis had so graciously listened to the prayers of us poor people.

Boehm's conflict with Weiss bore double fruit. It not only led to his own ordination and the continuation of his useful labors, but it aroused the interest of the Synods of Holland in the German Reformed people in America, and eventually a relationship was formed which continued throughout the colonial period. Weiss also appealed to the Dutch for assistance, and in 1729, accompanied by a wealthy German farmer, Jacob Reiff, journeyed to Holland. They secured both money and Bibles for use in America, but the refusal of Reiff to surrender the money until after ten years of bickering constitutes one of the many scandals reflecting upon the character of too many of the German religious leaders. In 1731 some eight hundred exiled Palatinates passing through Dort to take ship at Rotterdam for America were visited by the Synod of South Holland in a body. After furnishing the emigrants with supplies and medicines, and after prayer and exhortation, the Synod promised them assistance in their new homes. Later a committee of the Synods was set up through which this help for America was administered.

The following report on conditions in Pennsylvania, to the Reformed Synods of Holland in 1732, furnishes a clear picture of the situation which organized religion faced among the German emigrants.

We think there are altogether fifteen to sixteen thousand German Reformed in Pennsylvania, but these people live scattered over more than three hundred miles of territory, and there are no churches in the land. We have thus far only two regularly called ministers, and it is almost impossible to ascertain the actual number of members. The most of those who come here are compelled to sell themselves for their passage money, and also their children, who generally must serve until their twentieth year. Here in Philadelphia some 100 are in service of the English people, but they have the privilege to attend our service. Others in the country who have no opportunity for the exercise of the Reformed religion, resort to other sects, of which there are a great number in the land, or they accustom themselves to live without religion. . . . We have no candidates at all for the ministry, and only a few school teachers, because the people live so far from each other that they cannot send many children to one locality, wherefore the children must be allowed to grow up in the greatest ignorance.

. . . During the past year (1731) nearly 4000 souls arrived in ten ships. By far the smaller number had any means, and the most of them had to be sold for their passage money. . . . When these people have served out their time, they are just as poor as when they first arrived, and it takes a long time until they contribute anything to the church.[16]

The German Reformed Church in the colonies faced a crisis with Zinzendorf's attempt to form his *Church of God in the Spirit*. Boehm led the resistance to this movement and published a series of letters warning Germans in general against the Moravians. We know in considerable detail of Boehm's activities through letters he sent to the Deputies of Holland. Among his letters are several written in 1744, one of which contains a detailed account of the several Reformed congregations in Pennsylvania. The congregations, he states, are increasing but the new members were almost entirely poor people "who arrive every year from all sorts of countries . . . yet they are precious souls and our fellow members (according to their certificates, without which few of them come to us) of the body of Christ." Boehm founded or had a part in the founding of thirteen German Reformed congregations, a record which no other German Reformed minister came anywhere near equaling.[17]

With the close relationship established between the Dutch and

---

[16] From the report of Revs. John B. Reiger and John J. Diemer, March 4, 1732, made to the Synodical Deputies of Holland. Extracts from Daniel Miller, *Early History of the Reformed Church in Pennsylvania*, Reading: 1906, pp. 24–25.

[17] William J. Hinkle, *Life and Letters of the Reverend John Philip Boehm, Founder of the Reformed Church in Pennsylvania, 1683–1749*, Philadelphia: 1916. See also James I. Good, *History of the Reformed Church in the United States, 1725–1792*, Reading: 1899.

German Reformed Churches it is not strange that a union was suggested. The Dutch Deputies in 1738 appointed Peter H. Dorsius, a Dutch Reformed minister in Bucks county to be their commissioner and inspector of the German Churches. Five years later, the Synods of Holland, through Dorsius, proposed a union of the Dutch, German and Presbyterian Churches in the colonies. The Presbyterians refused even to consider the proposition, nor were the German Reformed any better disposed toward it. "We trust," says Boehm in a letter to Holland (March 18, 1744), "that the Reverend Christian Synods will not take it ill of us, that we humbly request to be permitted to abide by our Church order established from the beginning in our churches." He points out that their people do not understand the English language and any divergence from the Heidelberg Catechism and the Church order of the Synod of Dort "would be regarded by most people as a defection from our true religion, which would be very harmful to the growth of our congregations."

The coming of Michael Schlatter [18] to Pennsylvania in 1746 as the special representative of the Dutch Synods marks the beginning of a new period in the history of the German Reformed Church in the colonies. A native of Switzerland, educated at Swiss and Dutch universities and speaking both Dutch and German, Schlatter was an energetic and capable leader well fitted for the task assigned by the Synods. He was instructed to organize the ministers and Churches of Pennsylvania into a Coetus [19] subject to the Synods of Holland; to visit all the congregations and fully inform himself of their problems; to form new congregations where needed; and finally to take charge of a congregation himself. Arriving in Philadelphia, by way of Boston and New York in September 1746, within less than two weeks he had begun his visitation of the Churches. His first disagreeable task was to get the money contributed by the Dutch Churches from the close-fisted and evidently dishonest Reiff. Reiff led off by presenting a

---

[18] *The Diary of Rev. Michael Schlatter* (Journal of the Presbyterian Hist. Society, Sept., Dec., 1905); Henry Harbaugh, *The Life of Michael Schlatter,* Philadelphia: 1857; Good, *op. cit.,* are the principal sources for our knowledge of Schlatter.

[19] The term Coetus means a subordinate body.

report showing that instead of his owing the Pennsylvania Churches, they actually owed him a hundred gulden. There were quarrels in almost every congregation, while many of the ministers were at odds with one another. Indeed as one reads the contemporary records of the personal quarrels, the name calling and the frightful accusations made one against another among the German colonial ministers he is led to wonder how good could possibly come from the ministrations of these men.

Schlatter was indefatigable and within a year after his arrival took steps to organize a Synod, which at the suggestion of the Deputies of Holland was called a Coetus. This was accomplished in Philadelphia in September 1747, when four ministers and twenty-seven elders representing twelve congregations came together at Schlatter's call. The main work of the Coetus was to provide ministers for the Churches and to give general supervision. It never included all the Reformed Churches in the colonies nor all the ministers. The most serious weakness of the Coetus was its lack of authority to ordain men without permission from Holland. When the need for ministers was everywhere so great, the delay necessary in obtaining permission was an awkward and often serious handicap. From the formation of the Coetus to 1775 twenty-eight ministers joined that body; of these twelve were ordained by the Coetus and sixteen were sent out from Holland.

The serious lack of ministers and the continual springing up of independent congregations under unordained men, or of discredited ministers, was the principal cause which led Schlatter to visit Holland in 1751 to lay the situation before the Dutch Deputies. Schlatter prepared an extensive report which, with an appeal, was printed in Dutch and German. So great was the interest aroused that not only did the Synods of Holland promise greater assistance, but the states of Holland and West Friesland granted an annual subsidy of 2,000 gulden for five years. This was renewed in 1756 for a period of three years. Armed with these generous promises Schlatter left Holland for Germany to find six additional ministers to accompany him to America. Disappointed in not being able to find candidates at Heidelberg or at the Swiss universities, Schlatter turned to the little pietistic university at Herborn.

Here he secured six young men who were willing to accompany him to America, of whom Philip William Otterbein was to become the most famous as one of the founders of the United Brethren Church.

The very vigor of Schlatter's leadership led to suspicion and criticism. Some thought he strove for power, while the manner of dividing the subsidies which came from Holland was a constant cause of dissatisfaction. Indeed it is a question whether the funds and control exercised by Holland did not do more harm than good, for they undermined self-reliance, which is an indispensable requisite for the carrying on of any enterprise on a frontier. Growing dissension was evidently one of the principal causes which led Schlatter to withdraw from his leadership in the Church to give his attention to education. In 1753 he sought release from the Synods of Holland to accept the superintendency of schools being established in Pennsylvania among the Germans by an English society. The schools proved unpopular and after a few years Schlatter resigned that position. Meanwhile he had withdrawn from the Coetus and was never again associated with it, though he later served some independent congregations in and about Philadelphia. The loss of Schlatter's leadership was a most unfortunate circumstance for the German Reformed Church in the colonies, for no other leader of equal ability arose to take his place.

VIII

The Lutherans

THE HISTORY of colonial Lutheranism follows much the same general pattern as the German Reformed. Like the Reformed people, the Lutherans came without pastors or school teachers and with meager economic resources. Many came as redemptioners and were scattered widely throughout those regions where Germans were settling. Of all the emigrants to the American colonies, none were more shamefully exploited than were the Germans. Their inability to speak English placed them at the mercy of rapacious exploiters of all sorts. The sufferings endured by the three thousand Palatinates who were settled along the Hudson (1710) to produce naval stores, and their subsequent failure to secure land for farms in New York turned them toward Pennsylvania. From that time forward William Penn's Province was their promised land.[20]

The forerunner of the long line of Lutheran ministers in America and the first to come from the pietistic center at Halle was Justus Falkner.[21] Ordained by the Swedish Lutherans and installed as the minister of the Dutch Lutheran Church in New York in 1703 he remained at that post until his death twenty years later. Falkner had accompanied his brother Daniel to Pennsylvania in 1700, and for a time lived with the band of hermits on the Wissahickon, though he did not share in their fanaticism. He was, however, a sincere pietist and his chief concern was for the religious welfare of the swarming German colonists. Falkner did not confine his labors to New York City, but considered the whole of the Hudson Valley as well as East Jersey and Long Island as a part of his parish. Falkner has been justly called one of the most winsome figures in the history of American Lutheranism. On his death Falkner was succeeded by another German, Wilhelm Christoph Berkenmeyer, a man of character and ability, but completely out of sympathy with pietism. In 1731 his great New York parish was divided when Michael Christian Knoll was secured from Germany to minister to the Lutherans in New York and surrounding regions while Berkenmeyer presided over the northern region. Unfortunately for colonial Lutheran unity the New York and New Jersey ministers, secured through the Consistorium of Amsterdam, belonged to a different theological school than those who came to the leadership of the Lutherans in Pennsylvania and the other colonies.

From 1703 to 1740 scattered Lutheran congregations were gradually forming in the German communities of the Pennsylvania

---

[20] Walter A. Knittle, *Early Eighteenth Century Palatinate Emigration*, Philadelphia: 1937.

[21] Julius Frederick Sachse, *Justus Falkner, Mystic and Scholar*, Philadelphia: 1893. Also A. L. Grobner, *Geschichte der Lutherischen Kirchen in Amerika*, St. Louis: 1902, pp. 89–99.

counties surrounding Philadelphia. Daniel Falkner,[22] the elder brother of Justus, who had succeeded Pastorius as the agent of the Frankfort Land Company, secured a great tract of meadow land in the northern part of Montgomery county which came to be known as Falkner's Swamp. It soon grew into one of the largest of the early German settlements and it has been a tradition that here Daniel Falkner organized a Lutheran church in 1703, but records of his ordination are wanting and there is no proof that he was ever a Lutheran minister. There are dim records of several Lutheran ministers working among the German settlers during the first decades of the eighteenth century, among them Jacob Henkel, the Stoevers, father and son, and John Christian Schulz. The most active of them was John Casper Stoever, Jr., who worked mostly as an itinerant missionary extending his journeys as far south as Maryland and Virginia. Arriving in Philadelphia in 1728 he was listed among the immigrants as a theological student. Always an irregular, the younger Stoever, however, occupies a worthy place in the early history of American Lutheranism. He received ordination at the hands of a fly-by-night Lutheran minister, John Christian Schulz, who arrived in Philadelphia in 1732 and remained but a year. Though a somewhat doubtful character, Schulz served a useful purpose in colonial Lutheranism by founding the congregation in Philadelphia and in persuading the three strongest congregations in Pennsylvania, Philadelphia, New Hanover (Falkner's Swamp), and Providence to unite into one parish and to send him and two laymen to Germany to secure ministers and funds for the erection of churches and schoolhouses. Fortunately, after performing this useful service, Schulz never returned, but his journey bore additional fruit in that it set in motion a set of influences which eventually led to the coming of Henry M. Mühlenberg. And this event marks the turning point in American Lutheranism.

The Salzbergers, an isolated body of Lutheran immigrants, the victims of the intolerant Catholic Archbishop of Salzberg in Austria, had come out to Georgia in four groups between the

---

[22] See the article on Daniel Falkner by G. H. Genzmer in *Dictionary of American Biography.*

years 1732 and 1741. They had been accompanied by two Halle-trained ministers, John Martin Boltzius and Israel Christian Gronau. Boltzius was not only the spiritual head of the Salzberger colonists, but became their business head as well. Few colonies in America achieved economic success in so short a time as did the Salzbergers. Both from the standpoint of industry, high idealism and sincere religion the Salzbergers' Ebenezer was an oasis in the desert. Several Lutheran congregations were formed under the ministry of the devoted pastors, and the order prevailing among them was in great contrast to the confusion which characterized the situation among the congregations in New York, New Jersey and Pennsylvania. This contrast is of course explained in large part by the contrast in leadership.

Previous to the coming of the Salzbergers there had been a considerable influx of German Swiss and Palatinates into the Carolinas. Newbern, North Carolina, took its name from a group of emigrants from Bern, Switzerland, who together with some six hundred Palatinates arrived in the year 1710. There were Germans in Charleston when the Salzbergers arrived and in succeeding years other German settlements were formed on the frontiers of South Carolina. Orangeburg and Lexington counties became strong German communities and served as distributing centers for newly arrived settlers. The first minister to serve a Lutheran congregation in South Carolina was John Ulrich Giesendanner, a Swiss who had arrived in Orangeburg county in 1737. On his death the following year he was succeeded by his nephew, who served the church for ten years, when he left for London to secure Episcopal ordination. On his return in 1749 his church became Episcopalian. Such a transition became increasingly common as the eighteenth century wore on. There were fifteen German churches in the interior of South Carolina in 1788, when they formed a union called the *Corpus Evangelicum*. Of these churches nine were Lutheran, most of which are still in existence; the German Reformed Churches in the union have all ceased to exist.[23]

---

[23] Albert Bernhardt Faust, *The German Element in the United States, with special reference to its political, moral, social and educational influence*, 2 vols., Boston and

The history of colonial Lutheranism after 1742 may be conveniently gathered about the activities of Henry M. Mühlenberg, who in that year arrived in America. The commission headed by Schulz (1733) made their appeal to Rev. F. D. Ziegenhagen, the Lutheran court preacher in London, a devout pietist, and to Francke at Halle, both of whom were interested in helping their American brethren. After a long delay, due to the unwillingness of the American congregations to pledge a definite salary, a call was extended through Dr. Ziegenhagen to thirty-two-year-old Henry M. Mühlenberg to be the minister of the united congregations in Philadelphia and Montgomery counties. Despite the uncertainty of support Mühlenberg accepted the call and in the late summer of 1742 set sail for America.

For nine weeks Mühlenberg was the guest of Dr. Ziegenhagen in London. Here he benefited from Ziegenhagen's knowledge of conditions in America and perfected his English. He was advised by his patron to visit first the Lutheran congregations in Georgia, and accordingly sailed for Charleston, where he arrived in September 1742 after a fourteen weeks' voyage. Due to the long voyage the ship's water supply became exhausted and but for the meeting with two British men-of-war all might have perished. Making his way to the Salzberg settlements he spent eight days among them, learning at first hand of some of the problems he was soon to meet. Of the Salzbergers he wrote:

In temporal matters, it is a real wonder to see how these people have, by the Divine favor, worked themselves up out of their poverty; and in spiritual things a rich harvest may be confidently expected.

Count Zinzendorf's activities made Mühlenberg's presence in Pennsylvania imperative if Lutheranism was to survive, and his arrival in Philadelphia on November 25, 1742, was in the nick of time.

Henry M. Mühlenberg was admirably fitted for the task to which he now gave all his great energies. He combined a robust

New York: 1909. Vol. I, Chapters VII and VIII, contain excellent surveys of religious developments among the Germans in colonial Virginia and the Carolinas. See also Gotthardt Dellman Bernheim, *History of the German Settlements and of the Lutheran Church in North and South Carolina*, etc., Philadelphia: 1872.

frame and a frank open countenance with an unusual degree of common sense and an abounding energy. Coming at a time when quarrels and misunderstandings were the usual thing among the German congregations, Mühlenberg possessed the rare gift of being able to see others' points of view. Not only was he well prepared in theology, but he possessed an unusual language gift which soon enabled him to preach in English and Dutch as well as in German. Among all his qualifications none were more important than his sincere piety and his exemplary life. The three congregations over which he was to preside were all divided over Zinzendorf's union movement, and to make things worse two discredited Lutheran ministers had insinuated themselves upon two of the Congregations. Within four weeks of Mühlenberg's arrival he had rid his parishes of the Zinzendorf influence, had put to flight the two impostors, and had been installed over his churches by the Swedish Lutheran minister at Wilmington.

It required the traveling of at least a hundred miles each week to care for his three churches, but it was not long until he had added a fourth, Germantown. At the latter place he baptized at one time (1743) a mother and her five adult children, and he reports that they were so much affected that "I might have baptized them with their tears." Because of the impossibility of finding a schoolteacher he undertook the instruction of the children in each of his parishes, spending a week in each in succession. Soon also churches at Lancaster, Tulpehocken and York were added to his responsibility. His tact and wisdom were called repeatedly into practice in arbitrating church quarrels, and he was frequently called to handle such cases outside Pennsylvania. One famous case was that of August Wolfe, an unworthy minister of four churches in New Jersey who had alienated his congregations as well as his wife and children. During the latter eight years of Wolfe's incumbency the Lord's Supper had not been administered nor confirmation performed. The situation was rendered more difficult for Mühlenberg's mediation because the New York and New Jersey Lutheran ministers were opposed to pietism and were therefore out of sympathy with Mühlenberg's point of view. Mühlenberg succeeded, however, in ending Wolfe's hold over the churches. This having been accomplished, he returned several times to instruct the young, administer the communion and reawaken interest in religion which had been largely dissipated under Wolfe's unworthy leadership. In 1774-75 Mühlenberg was called upon to arbitrate a serious dispute in Ebenezer. While in Georgia on this mission he took occasion to make an inventory of all Lutheran property in that colony and carefully examined the deeds to make sure that the Established Church could not lay claim to it. He also drew up a form of discipline for the government of the Georgia churches. Mühlenberg's journeys included, besides his many visits to New Jersey and his long painful trip to Georgia, a missionary tour of Maryland, a visit to the congregations on the Hudson, and six different visits to New York of longer and shorter periods.

Six years after his arrival in America Mühlenberg was ready to begin the formation of a Synod. His reports to Halle[24] had brought reinforcements in both men and money. New churches had been built at Providence, Tulpehocken and Philadelphia, while at New Hanover a schoolhouse had been erected. Calls were coming from numerous communities for pastors, asking for the ordination of some of the Halle recruits to serve in this capacity. These were the principal considerations which led Mühlenberg in calling together the ministers and lay representatives of the churches in August, 1748, for the purpose of forming a Synod. Six ministers and twenty-four laymen were present, representing ten congregations. Under the presidency of Mühlenberg a common liturgy was adopted and reports were heard from the laymen on the conditions of the parochial schools and the effectiveness of their ministers. The Synod took the name *United Pastors* and for

---

[24] The history of colonial Lutheranism after the coming of Mühlenberg may be traced in detail through the Halle Reports (*Hallesche Nachrichten*) which consist of a large collection of reports and letters sent to the Lutheran Ministerium of Halle by Mühlenberg and other Lutheran ministers in America. These were first published in Halle in 1787 and were reprinted in German under the editorship of W. J. Mann, B. M. Schmucker and W. Germann under the title *Nachrichten von den vereinigten Deutschen Evangelisch-Luthersichen Gemeinen in Nord-America*, Erster Band, Allentown: 1886. Zweiter Band, Philadelphia: 1895. An edition in English in two volumes with historical and critical notes was published in 1882, translated by C. W. Schaeffer, Reading: 1882.

the next six years held annual meetings. Opposition to it gradually developed, especially among those ministers who held no allegiance to Halle, and from 1754 to 1760 no meetings were held. The coming of Charles Mangus von Wrangle, a devoted pietist, to be the provost of the Swedish churches and his interest in German Lutheranism was a large factor in the revival of the Synod.

Mühlenberg had not come to America as a temporary missionary, and almost at once identified himself as a thorough American. His marriage in 1745 to Anna Marie Weiser, the daughter of Johann Conrad Weiser, the famous Indian agent, was doubtless one of the influences which caused him to make this decision. From this union came one of the most distinguished of American families. Of their six sons the three eldest were sent to Halle to complete their education, and all entered the Lutheran ministry. John Peter Gabriel, the eldest, became one of Washington's most trusted generals; Frederick Augustus Conrad, the second son, became the first speaker of the Federal House of Representatives; Gotthelf Henry Ernst gained a wide reputation as a botanist and served as the first president of Franklin College. Of the five daughters two became wives of Lutheran ministers. In the *Dictionary of American Biography* there are seven Mühlenberg biographies, all of them sons or grandsons of the founder of the Mühlenberg line.

The most serious problem which the German churches faced was that of securing an adequately qualified leadership. Mühlenberg soon saw the futility of depending upon Europe for ministerial supply. Not only were the numbers inadequate but the quality was often low, and as has been frequently noted disreputable ministerial vagabonds too often secured a foothold in congregations and wrought havoc among them. The only solution was in the training of a native ministry under the supervision of the Synod. This, Mühlenberg, with sure insight, attempted to promote. In 1749 he purchased a large tract of land in Philadelphia on which a school was projected as well as a seminary and home for the aged. Funds, however, could not be secured. Again and again in his Halle reports Mühlenberg urged the necessity of schools and a seminary for the training of a ministry, but the Halle fathers failed to respond to his appeal. Though no training school for a native ministry was established in Mühlenberg's day, yet there were a number of native German Americans trained for the ministry under private instruction. Mühlenberg himself trained several successful pastors; von Wrangle privately instructed three young German candidates for the Lutheran ministry, one of them Mühlenberg's son.[25] Thus the pietism of Mühlenberg and von Wrangle was carried over to their sons "in the gospel" so that the general emphasis in American colonial Lutheranism continued to be, at least mildly, pietistic.

By the end of the colonial period there were some seventy Lutheran congregations in Pennsylvania and surrounding colonies, and some thirty in Virginia, the Carolinas and Georgia. There were, however, many German communities without religious leadership of any kind and among all the elements in the colonies the Germans very probably contained the smallest proportion of Church members.

---

[25] Abdel Ross Wentz, *History of the Gettysburg Theological Seminary . . . 1826–1926*, Philadelphia: 1926. Chapters I and II treat of theological education in the colonial period.

VIII

The Presbyterian Irish

COLONIAL PRESBYTERIANISM was the product of the mingling of English Puritans with Scotch and Scotch-Irish Presbyterians. The large Presbyterian Puritan element in early New England after the adoption of the Cambridge Platform conformed to the Congregational-Presbyterian polity as set forth in that instrument. Later Presbyterian outcroppings appeared in the Massachusetts Proposals of 1705 and in the Connecticut Saybrook Platform of 1708, but this was Presbyterianism in embryo, rather than full-fledged Presbyterianism.[1] During the latter half of the seventeenth century a number of Puritan Churches were formed on Long Island, in northern New Jersey, Pennsylvania, Maryland and South Carolina. Most of these were of New England origin. Indeed, the tendency of Congregationalists to turn Presbyterian on leaving New England began almost at once, so that by 1700 from ten to fifteen germinal Presbyterian Churches were found in New York and New Jersey alone. As early as 1690 a Puritan Church was formed in Charleston, South Carolina; five years later another Puritan Church organized in Charlestown, Massachusetts, removed with its minister to Dorchester, South Carolina.

During these years also the Presbyterian and Congregational Union of London was cooperating with Massachusetts and Connecticut in sending to Pennsylvania and Delaware ministers who became pastors of Presbyterian Churches in Philadelphia and Newcastle, Delaware. The Scotch also made some direct contribution to early American Presbyterianism. On the breaking up of the ill-fated Scotch colony on the Isthmus of Darien (1698-99) a majority of its members, with their ministers, found refuge in

---

[1] For a discussion of the Presbyterian element in early New England see Henry M. Dexter, *Congregationalism of the Last Three Hundred Years as Seen in its Literature*, Boston: 1880, p. 431; also C. A. Briggs, *American Presbyterianism, Its Origin and Early History*, New York: 1885, Appendix, Chapter III, pp. xxiii–xxix.

New England. One of the ministers, Archibald Strobo, driven by a storm, took refuge at Charleston, South Carolina, and remained there as pastor of the Presbyterian Church. Other Scotch Presbyterian ministers, ejected from the churches in Scotland by the attempt to establish episcopacy after 1662, came to New England. At the same time a considerable Scotch emigration came to Maryland, Virginia, and South Carolina.[2]

Thus by the opening of the eighteenth century there was to be found a considerable Presbyterian element scattered throughout the colonies, though as yet there were no Presbyterial organizations.

I

ULSTER BECOMES A PRESBYTERIAN STRONGHOLD

FOR THE last two decades of the seventeenth century emigration to the American colonies from England proper steadily declined, while Scotland and particularly Ireland were beginning to furnish a constantly increasing stream. Misgovernment, and especially unwise and unjust economic and ecclesiastical legislation on the part of the English and Irish Parliaments, was the immediate cause of this new emigration. Of the two regions furnishing the bulk of British emigration in the eighteenth century, North Ireland was by far the more important.

During the early years of the seventeenth century a movement was under way to displace the native Irish population of all northern Ireland by colonists from England and especially from Scotland. Lack of effective means of political control in that region, due to the fact that the Clan chiefs were practically a law unto themselves and fomented constant uprisings and violence,

---

[2] Charles A. Hanna, *The Scotch-Irish or the Scott in North Britain, North Ireland, and North America*, 2 vols., New York and London: 1902. Vol. II, Chapter II, "Seventeenth-century Emigration from Scotland and Ulster," furnishes interesting details of Scotch settlement in Maryland, Virginia, New Jersey and South Carolina. A recent study of the Scotch Colony on Darien is T. C. Pears, *The Design of Darien, Journal of the Department of History, Presbyterian Historical Society*, Vol. XVII, 1936.

was the immediate cause of this policy instituted by King James I. The first step in this new policy was the confiscation of some 3,800,000 acres in six counties of northern Ireland. Already private enterprise had brought over numerous English and Lowland Scotch settlers to counties Down and Antrim, but the establishment of the Ulster Plantation was a scheme of vastly larger proportions. The plan for settlement called for the division of the great tract into estates of not more than two thousand acres, which were to be granted to men of wealth and standing who should agree to live on their Irish estate, to bring over Scotch and English settlers, and to build not only houses for themselves and tenants, but also fortifications and churches. The native Irish were to be assigned the poorer lands, while the new settlers were to be kept together to encourage intermarriage among themselves and to discourage intermingling with the native population.

Those sections of Scotland nearest Ireland furnished the greatest share of the colonists, while the great families of that region received the largest number of the grants. In many instances it was specifically stated that the tenants were to come from England or the "inward parts of Scotland," which meant that only the Lowland and not the Highland Scots were wanted. There were three classes of proprietors: the first and most numerous as well as the most privileged were the English and Scotch; the second were military undertakers who were permitted to have Irish tenants; while the third were the native Irish. It is interesting to note that the first class paid the smallest yearly rental; the native Irish paid the highest—a commentary on the Scriptural precept that "To him that hath shall be given, and from him that hath not shall be taken even that which he hath." Special grants were also made to Trinity College, Dublin, and to the Established Episcopal Church of Ireland, while to the City of London was given a large part of the County of Derry.

The immediate result of this careful planning was a tremendous transplantation of population, especially from southwestern Scotland. In the first ten years after 1610 between thirty and forty thousand immigrants came to Northern Ireland, and by 1641 there were thought to be 100,000 Scots and 20,000 English in Ulster. The Scotch colonists were practically a hundred per cent Presbyterian, and were accompanied by their ministers and the entire Presbyterian ecclesiastical organization and discipline. The history of Presbyterianism has, therefore, large significance in the subsequent history of North Ireland.[3]

The general conditions which the colonists faced in North Ireland were not greatly different from those which their descendants met on the frontiers of the American colonies three generations later. For the first several years they lived in the rudest kind of dwellings while the land was being cleared of forests and made ready for cultivation. Nor were their grandchildren in greater danger from Indian forays than they were from the half-wild and mistreated native Irish. Among the colonists were many described as "the scum of both nations" and fugitives from justice. A majority seemed to be fleeing from God, and at first cared little for the Church or religion. On all hands atheism and disregard of God increased. Iniquity of all kinds, contention, fighting, murder, thieving, and adultery abounded.

Under the preaching of the emotionally unstable minister at Oldstone, Mr. Glendinning, a great spiritual concern began to be awakened among the people. His emphasis upon "the wrath and the terrors of God for sin" aroused a growing "anxiety and terror of conscience," and more and more men and women began to ask, "What shall we do to be saved?" Under such preaching many were stricken and swooned "with the Word." Some of the strongest and most wicked men were "carried out of doors as dead, so marvellous was the power of God smiting their hearts for sin." "Multitudes of such men had no power to resist the word of God," and many "who had sinned and gloried in it because they feared not man, are now patterns of sobriety fearing to sin because they fear God." This revivalistic religion of fear

---

[3] Hanna, *op. cit.* The best single work on the subject; contains also a large number of sources in Appendices, Vol. II, pp. 133–525. W. D. Killen, *Ecclesiastical History of Ireland,* 2 vols., London: 1875. James Denton Reid, *History of the Presbyterian Church in Ireland,* 3 vols., Belfast: 1867. The Killen and Reid volumes are condensed in Samuel D. Alexander, *History of the Presbyterian Church in Ireland,* New York: 1860.

spread through the country as a contagion. But under the leadership of Rev. Robert Blair of Bangor, one of the most level-headed of the early Presbyterian clergy in Ireland, a better prepared and more constructive ministry was attracted to the country from Scotland, "Then did love enter instead of fear; the oil of joy for the spirit of heaviness, and withal . . . a great desire in many to walk in the ways of God." [4]

This is not the place to recount the religious history of North Ireland during the seventeenth century, though some knowledge of it will be necessary if we are to understand all the factors which contributed to the great migration of the Presbyterian Irish to America. By 1688 the Irish Presbyterian Church had eighty ministers, about one hundred congregations and five Presbyteries, while its communicants outnumbered those of the Irish Episcopalians, in that region, fifty to one. The toleration policy of King William's reign led to the rapid increase of immigration from Scotland which greatly enlarged Irish Presbyterianism, and congregations numbering a thousand each were not unusual in the vicinity of Londonderry. By 1702 the total number of churches had increased to 120, formed into nine Presbyteries, with three sub-Synods and a general Synod which met annually. In 1717 there were 140 congregations and a membership of some two hundred thousand.

---

[4] A striking account of the early moral and religious conditions in North Ireland, and of the religious awakening which swept through the region is found in Andrew Stewart's *History of the Church of Ireland*, printed in Hanna, Vol. I, *op. cit.*, pp. 549–555, from the MSS found among the Wodrow MSS, Advocates Library, Edinburgh. It was evidently written 1670–71. Stewart was the minister at Donaghadee, County Down, 1645–1671.

Reid suggests that Stewart's picture of moral and religious conditions in North Ireland is "probably a little over charged." Rev. Robert Blair, however, in an autobiographical fragment begun in 1663, supports Stewart's account. He states:

"The parts of Scotland nearest to Ireland sent over abundance of people and cattle that filled the counties of Ulster that lay next the sea; and albeit amongst these, Divine Providence sent over some worthy persons for birth, education and parts, yet the most part were such as either poverty, scandalous lives or, at the best, adventurous seeking better accommodations, set forward that way. . . . Little care was had by any to plant religion. As were the people, so for the most part were the preachers."

For a detailed discussion of this whole question see Henry Jones Ford, *The Scotch-Irish in America*, Princeton: 1915, Chapter III.

II

SCOTCH-IRISH EMIGRATION TO AMERICA

ECONOMIC HARDSHIPS have generally been considered to have furnished the principal incentives for the great Scotch-Irish exodus in the eighteenth century. Long leases at easy rentals had been one of the principal attractions to the Scotch colonists; now when they expired they were renewed at double and even treble the old rates. This caused widespread discontent. Added to this were the restrictions imposed on importations into England of Irish livestock of all kinds, as well as of beef, mutton, pork, butter, and cheese. Ireland was also shut off from all colonial trade, as well as all direct trade with Europe. As a climax to this restrictive legislation was the Woolens Act of 1699 which destroyed the Irish woolen industry; altogether enough to create an atmosphere of gloom in every Scotch-Irish household. But all this might have been borne had not religious restrictions and actual persecution been added. The fact that the emigration to America was almost a hundred per cent Presbyterian would seem to indicate that the restrictions imposed upon Irish Presbyterianism acted as the last straw.

From the beginning Irish Presbyterians had been assessed for the support of the Established Episcopal clergy. With the opening of Anne's reign the Irish Parliament, dominated by the Episcopal bishops in the upper house, passed an act (1704) which made office holding impossible for Presbyterians, since to hold even the most humble office it was required that the Sacrament be received according to the rites of the Episcopal Church. This the sturdy Irish Presbyterians refused to do. Even in regions where Presbyterians made up an overwhelming majority of the population the lowliest offices were closed to them. To add to their grievances it was made illegal for Presbyterian ministers to perform marriages, a measure which struck at the happiness of every Presbyterian home. Eighteenth-century Ireland has been described as "wretched and broken hearted," where "chronic scarcity alter-

nated with actual famine," with little commerce and no manufacturing, "save the slowly increasing linen industry in Ulster."
Under such conditions was it any wonder that the most energetic,
the most active-minded of those of Presbyterian faith began to
look for a new place of refuge? In the great emigration which
now began from Northern Ireland to the English colonies in
America, there were no Catholics and few if any Episcopalians;
it was in fact a transplanting of Irish Presbyterians to the New
World.[5]

The year 1710 marks the beginning of the great migration; ten
years later it had become a steady stream, averaging from three
to six thousand emigrants a year. In 1718 the first large body,
consisting of from six to eight hundred, arrived in Boston with
two ministers. They soon discovered that New England was not
as hospitable as they had anticipated. Though they were not permitted to remain in the vicinity of Boston, they were encouraged
to settle on the frontiers to form buffer settlements against Indian
depredations. Consequently they divided into several groups. Some
two hundred or more went to the Province of Maine where they
formed settlements near present-day Portland; others went to
southeastern New Hampshire and founded Londonderry, while
a third body found their way to Worcester, Massachusetts, then
a frontier region. At Londonderry a Presbyterian Church was at
once formed with the Rev. James MacGregor, who had accompanied his congregation from Ireland, as the minister. By 1724 a
church and a parsonage had been built, and by 1730 there were
four flourishing schools in the township.

The Maine and New Hampshire settlements were unmolested
by the civil authorities, but the Worcester colonists experienced
some unpleasant examples of Massachusetts' intolerance. They
had been unwelcome at Worcester from the start, though for a
number of years they cooperated with the Congregationalists in
maintaining a common Church. When, however, the Presbyterian
Irish determined to build their own meeting house (1740) they

---

[5] H. L. Osgood, *The American Colonies in the Eighteenth Century,* New York: 1924,
Vol. II, pp. 513 ff. See also Hanna, *op. cit.,* Vol. I, pp. 618–623; Ford, *op cit.,* Chapter v,
"Emigation to America."

met opposition and open violence. Before the building was completed a mob levelled it to the ground and burned or carried off the timbers. The next year many Presbyterian families left Worcester and established two new towns farther west, Pelham, N. H. and Coleraine, Mass., which became distributing centers for Scotch-Irish colonists moving into Vermont, western Massachusetts and eastern New York. In 1741 an attempt was made to found a Presbyterian Church at Milford, Connecticut. Samuel Findley was invited to be their minister. No sooner had he arrived than he was arrested, fined as a vagrant, and sent out of the country as a disturber of the peace. Some years later this Connecticut vagrant was elevated to the presidency of the College of New Jersey. Of the Presbyterian Churches that were formed in New England most of them eventually became Congregational, so that "Scotch-Irish emigration tended rather to furnish recruits to Congregationalism than to spread Presbyterianism." [6]

Thanks to New England's lack of hospitality Scotch-Irish emigration turned southward, and the Delaware river towns of Lewes, Newcastle and Philadelphia became the landing ports of the great majority of the Ulster colonists. At first the newcomers spread out from these ports of entry and established themselves in the southwestern section of Pennsylvania, some of them moving across into Maryland. James Logan, himself a Scotch Quaker, the Secretary of the Province of Pennsylvania, writing to John Penn in 1727, speaks of the swarms of Germans and Scotch-Irish pouring into the Province. In another letter, written in 1729, he complains:

It looks as if Ireland is to send all its inhabitants hither, for the last week not less than six ships arrived, and every day, two or three arrive also. The common fact is that if they thus continue to come they will make themselves the proprietors of the Province.

Even the Indians, he continues, are alarmed, and he fears a "breach between them—for the Irish are very rough to them." He complains also of the "audacious and disorderly manner" in

---

[6] For the clash between the Scotch-Irish Presbyterians and the New England Congregationalists, see Ford, *op cit.*, Chapter xii, "On Stony Ground."

which they take over any unoccupied land, defending their action by insisting that

it is against the laws of God and nature that so much land should be idle while so many Christians wanted it to labor on and to raise their bread.

This disregard of the Scotch-Irish settlers for the great land reservations which had been sold by the Penns to absentee land-lords, was, according to Ford, quite largely responsible for frustrating the establishment of the tenant system in colonial Pennsylvania. Once settled on these lands, the Irish settlers refused to be dislodged, and the authorities were forced to make terms with them. Their experience in Ireland had made them wary of rents, and they refused to pay them, however small they might be.

No single racial group coming to the colonies scattered so widely as did the Scotch-Irish, and by the middle of the century (1750) they were to be found in every colony in sufficient num-bers to make their influence felt, culturally as well as economically and politically. From southeastern Pennsylvania they pushed out in all directions. Following the Delaware River northward they arrived in Bucks county in 1720; the same year another stream reached the Susquehanna, founding numerous settlements up and down that majestic river; thence across the Susquehanna into the great unoccupied Indian country, now Cumberland county. By 1732 they were pouring into the Shenandoah Valley, and by 1740 Scotch-Irish settlements were being established along the Carolina frontier from the Virginia line to Florida. After the middle of the century Charleston, South Carolina, became increas-ingly important as a port of entry for Scotch-Irish settlers. Pushing into the back country from tidewater, one stream turned south-ward into Georgia, another northward to meet the tide of Scotch-Irish migration coming down from Virginia and Pennsylvania.

During the years immediately following the defeat of the Pretender at Culloden (1746–47) a large Highland-Scotch emi-gration set in to North Carolina. Many Highland-Scotch who had been taken captive after the collapse of the uprising were pardoned on the condition that they go to the colonies. This flow of Scotch Highlanders continued until the opening of the Revolution and was the origin of the Scotch settlements along the Cape Fear River.[7] As late as 1770 fifty-four vessels loaded with Scotch Highlanders sailed for North Carolina. Hanna estimates that all told there were more than five hundred distinct Scotch and Scotch-Irish communities in the American colonies at the end of the colonial period, and they constituted the stuff out of which American colonial Presbyterianism was chiefly made.

III

Scotch-Irish Contributions

The future of American Presbyterianism was largely dependent upon the effectiveness of the leadership with which these swarming Scotch-Irish emigrants were to be supplied. It is to Francis Makemie, more than to any other single individual, that credit is due for the furnishing of this initial leadership. Fortunately the foundations of Presbyterian organization in the colonies had been laid already before Scotch-Irish emigration had reached flood proportions.

Francis Makemie, a native of North Ireland, was born of Scotch parentage in Donegal county in 1658. His boyhood covered the period of the Anglican crusade against Scotch Presbyterianism, when the boot, the thumb screw and the scaffold were used to enforce submission to bishops. Of his childhood we know little, although we learn from his own testimony that "a work of grace and conversion was wrought in my [his] heart at fifteen years of age by and from the pains of a godly school-master." Vivid conversion experiences were doubtless common in those times of great emotional stress, and it was probably at this early age that

---

[7] Considerable material on the Scotch settlements on the Cape Fear River are contained in William Henry Foote, *Sketches on North Carolina, Historical and Biographical*, etc., New York: 1846, especially Chapters x, xi, xii. The major portion of the volume deals with the Scotch-Irish Presbyterians in the colony.

his mind was made up to enter the ministry. As Presbyterian students were barred from the Irish colleges, young Makemie turned his face toward the University of Glasgow. On the completion of his studies he returned to Ireland where, after a trial sermon before the Presbytery of Laggan in 1681, he was licensed; a year later he was ordained for missionary work in America, and in 1683 we find him in Maryland.

Makemie's early missionary labors were spread over a wide area. Before 1698 traces of his activities are found in North Carolina, Virginia and Maryland; in 1692 he visited Philadelphia and is credited with planting the seed of Presbyterianism there; in 1696–1698 he was in the Barbadoes. During these years he was evidently combining business with preaching, as there seems to have been no other provision for his support. His missionary activity on the eastern shore of Maryland and Virginia led to the formation of four or five churches, with two of which, Rehobeth and Snow Hill, his name is most intimately connected. His marriage some time before 1698 with the only daughter of a wealthy landowner in Accomac county, Virginia, probably determined his permanent settlement as minister of the Rehobeth Church. This, however, did not localize his interests or his energies, and for the remainder of his life (d. 1708) he continued his promotion of colonial Presbyterianism from Virginia northward. In 1704–05 he visited England and succeeded in interesting the Presbyterian Union of London in furnishing support for two missionaries, and John Hampden, a Scotch-Irishman, and George McNish, a Scotchman, both graduates of the University of Glasgow, accompanied him to America. They were immediately set to work in Maryland as ministers over four of the churches Makemie had formed.

Makemie's outstanding achievement, however, was the formation of the Presbytery of Philadelphia. That his was the moving spirit in bringing together the scattered Presbyterian ministers in Maryland, Delaware and eastern Pennsylvania for the purpose of forming this first American Presbytery there can be little doubt. At his call seven ministers came together at Philadelphia in the spring of 1706 and there the Philadelphia Presbytery was formed on the Irish model. Of the seven ministers, all were Irish or Scotch except Jedediah Andrews of Philadelphia, who was a New Englander both by birth and education. As Briggs points out, this first American Presbytery was not called into being by any outside authority; neither the General Assembly of Scotland nor the Synod of Ulster had anything to do with it; rather it was a voluntary association of American Presbyterian ministers, coming together on their own responsibility, to form a body to meet the peculiar needs of American settlers. From henceforth the Presbyterians in the colonies had an agency enabling them to license and ordain their own ministers, as well as furnishing them a medium of cooperation, just as the great Scotch-Irish emigration was getting under way. It was, as Briggs states, "a master stroke," giving Presbyterians at once an advantage over Anglicanism, in that the latter were compelled, throughout the entire colonial period, to look to the English bishops for the ordination of their clergy.[8]

The arrest, imprisonment and trial of Makemie on a warrant issued by Lord Cornbury, Governor of New York, for preaching without a license in that Province, has significance in the struggle for toleration of dissenters in the colonies. After the adjournment of the Presbytery in October 1706, Makemie and John Hampden set out from Philadelphia bound for Boston, probably to consult with the Boston ministers. Arriving in New York both were invited to preach, Makemie in a private house, after the Dutch Church had been closed against him, and Hampden at Newtown, Long Island. Arrested and brought before Lord Cornbury, one of the most despicable of all the colonial governors, Makemie defended his right to preach in New York on the ground that the law permitting liberty of worship in that colony had no limiting clause. Cornbury replied that their certificates were from Virginia and Maryland, which were not valid in New York. When required to give bond and security for good behavior, Makemie replied:

---

[8] Briggs, *op. cit.*, pp. 139–143. Also see Guy S. Klett, *Presbyterianism in Colonial Pennsylvania*, Philadelphia: 1937.

If your Lordship require it, we will give security for our behaviour; but to give bond and security to preach no more in your excellency's government, if invited and desired by any people, we neither can nor dare do it.

To this the Governor replied, "Then you must go to the gaol." Whereupon they were imprisoned. Hampden was soon released, but Makemie was confined for six weeks, finally gaining his release on bail, to stand trial in June 1707. Defended by three of the ablest lawyers of the colony, Makemie was acquitted. But notwithstanding his acquittal he was required to pay all costs of the prosecution as well as the defense, amounting to the large sum of more than £83.

The whole story of Makemie's arrest, imprisonment, and trial, together with the documents bearing on the case, was immediately brought together by a "Learner of Law, and a Lover of Liberty" and printed in Boston (1707) under the title *A Narrative of a New and Unusual American Imprisonment, of Two Presbyterian Ministers, and Prosecution of Mr. Francis Makemie, one of them, For preaching One Sermon in the City of New York*.[9] One of the principal charges against Makemie was that he had violated the Queen's instructions to Lord Cornbury in that he had preached in the colony without his certificate of permission. To this charge one of the defense attorneys, Mr. David Jameson, replied that while the Queen's instructions may have been law to Lord Cornbury, they were not "law to any Body else" (p. 28). Further, he states, these instructions to the Governor were private, "and can be no law to others" since it is "Promulgation . . . which gives the finish-stroke to a law." To the argument that Makemie's and Hampden's preaching without licenses from the New York Governor was a violation of the Act of Toleration, the answer was made, that since there was no Established Church for the whole Province "from which we should be tolerated" the Act of Toleration was not, therefore, in force in New York, for, said Mr. Jameson, "We have had Liberty of Conscience another Way, and by an Act of Assembly." He ends his able defense with,

---

[9] Reprinted in New York, 1755.

This Province has not been much more than forty years in the Possession of the Crown of England, and is made up chiefly of Foreigners and Dissenters; and Persecution would not only tend to the disuniting us all in Interest and Affection, but depopulate and weaken our strength, and discourage all such Adventurers for the future. Therefore as this Prosecution is the first of this Nature or Sort, ever was in this Province, so I hope it will be the last.

The Makemie trial was the culmination of a long series of tyrannical acts by Lord Cornbury, who though a "spendthrift, a 'grafter,' a bigoted oppressor and a drunken, vain fool," had shown great zeal for the Church of England, and his interference with the spread of Presbyterians was in the interest of the Anglican Church. The publicity given his tyranny in the Makemie case was evidently responsible for the charges of bribery and encroachment of the liberties of the people brought against him at the next meeting of the New York Assembly, and shortly afterwards he was recalled. Cornbury's version of the case is given in a long letter to the Lord Commissioners of Trade and Plantations in which he describes Makemie as a "Jack-of-all-trades: . . . a preacher, a doctor of physic, a merchant, an attorney, a counselor-at-law, and which is worst of all, a disturber of governments." He entreats their protection against this malicious man "who is well known in Virginia and Maryland as a disturber of the peace and quiet."

The palpable injustice of compelling a man, who had just been declared innocent by the court of the charge brought against him, to pay for his own prosecution was doubtless mitigated, somewhat, in Francis Makemie's mind, by the fact that he had been the means of achieving a victory for freedom of worship for all dissenters in New York, and the reverberations of that victory had echoed throughout the colonies. The fact also that he had prospered in business and had married a rich wife made the fine seem less onerous.

Whether the long and arduous journey from Virginia to Boston together with the six weeks' imprisonment and the worry and excitement of the trial were contributory causes to his death, we have no way of knowing. They well might have been. We do know that the following year (1708) he died, leaving a widow and two daughters, and was buried on his farm in Virginia. Though Francis Makemie was not a genius of any kind, he was a man of courage, energy and true piety, "well fitted by his good judgment and executive ability to be a leader in what his practical churchmanship discerned as a growing necessity of the times—the more effective organization of the scattered Presbyterian congregations" in the colonies. More truly than any other man he merits the title, the Father of American Presbyterianism. In the year 1906, when American Presbyterianism was celebrating its bi-centennial in America, a part of the old Makemie farm in Accomac county, Virginia, was set aside as a park, including within its bounds the old family graveyard. Here a stone was erected at the grave of Francis Makemie. At its dedication Henry van Dyke contributed a sonnet, ending with:

> Oh, who can tell how much we owe to thee,
> Makemie, and to labors such as thine,
> For all that makes America the shrine
> Of faith untrammeled and of conscience free?
> Stand here, gray stone, and consecrate the sod
> Where sleeps this brave Scotch-Irish man of God!

IV

GROWTH OF COLONIAL PRESBYTERIANISM

BY THE year 1700 twelve Presbyterian Churches had been formed in the American colonies—five in Maryland, two in Virginia, two in Delaware, and one each in Pennsylvania, New York and South Carolina. The first two decades of the eighteenth century saw the establishment of twenty-five additional congregations, seventeen of that number being located in Pennsylvania, New Jersey and Maryland. Some of this increase was due to the coming into the Presbytery of several of the Puritan congregations in New Jersey and Long Island, and "ere long the Presbytery was to embrace the entire Puritan strength of New York and New Jersey." Meanwhile appeals were going out in all directions for aid. The

Presbyterian ministers of London were asked to furnish additional ministers for the Presbyterian colonists in South Carolina, who, at that time, embraced a large proportion of the population of Charleston and James Island. In response to this request two Scotchmen, William Pollock and William Livingston, both educated at the University of Edinburgh, were dispatched in 1706. Other ministers came out in response to appeals of individual congregations, while the Presbytery of Dublin, the Synod of Ulster and the Synod of Glasgow all helped with men and money. New England was also interested in helping the cause, especially Increase and Cotton Mather, and from there came four additional ministers. Three Welshmen also joined the Presbytery, two of whom had come to Pennsylvania as Congregational missionaries among the Welsh settlers, but soon sought admission to the Presbytery. Thus the first American Presbytery was made up of a union of diverse elements: New Englanders, English, Scotch, Irish, and Welsh, and as a consequence began its life as a broad, generous and tolerant body.

The next logical step in the organizational development of American Presbyterianism was the formation of the Synod of Philadelphia in 1716. It was composed of four Presbyteries, the Philadelphia, the Snow Hill [Maryland], the Newcastle [Delaware], and the Long Island, later to be called the New York. Almost at once the Synod acquired a missionary fund, called the *Fund for Pious Uses,* which originated through an appeal to the Synod of Glasgow by James Anderson, then the minister at Newcastle, made in August 1716. Read before the Synod at Glasgow in April 1717 it resulted in the appointment of a Sabbathday's collection for the use of their brethren in America, which was sent over in 1719 mostly in the form of goods.

With the formation of the Synod, Jonathan Dickinson and John Pierson, the ministers of the Puritan churches at Elizabethtown and Woodbridge, New Jersey, respectively, threw in their lot with the Presbyterians. Both were graduates of Yale College, the latter the son of the first President. The coming of Dickinson into the Presbyterian Church was an event of major importance to its future development. His leadership in the Synod was immediately recognized. Intellectually superior to any of his Presbyterian contemporaries his moderation and calm judgment were of inestimable value in the formative years of the infant Church when conflicting views were causing controversy and strife. In Professor Briggs' phrase, he was "the symbol of all that was noble and generous in the Presbyterian Church."

The year following the formation of the Synod marks the beginning of the Presbyterian Church in New York City, when James Anderson of Newcastle was called to be the first minister. While a church building was being erected the little congregation worshipped in the City Hall. In building the church the cost of the ground as well as the building was much greater than had been anticipated and a large debt resulted which it seemed impossible for the congregation to carry. Unfortunately the whole situation was further complicated by a division which developed among the members, and for a time the half-completed walls stood, "a monument of ridicule to the enemies of our profession," as Dr. John Nichol, the leading New York Presbyterian layman, expressed it in a letter to the General Assembly of the Church of Scotland. Appeals to the Synod of Glasgow and the General Assembly, however, brought liberal contributions from Scotland and the church was completed. The minister, however, became increasingly unpopular with a considerable proportion of the congregation who could bear neither him nor his sermons. Accordingly the disaffected group withdrew and formed a separate congregation in 1722 and called the eighteen-year-old Jonathan Edwards, just out of Yale College, to be their minister.

This call to Jonathan Edwards to serve the little Scotch Presbyterian congregation in New York was not strange in the light of what had taken place in Connecticut Congregationalism in 1708 in the adoption of the Saybrook Platform.[10] In fact, there was on foot at the time a movement to unite the Connecticut Presbyterianized-Congregational Churches with the Presbyterian

---

[10] The advice of the Connecticut ministers and the trustees of Yale College, by whom Edwards had been sent to New York, had been sought by the New York church. E. H. Gillett, *History of the Presbyterian Church in the U. S. A.*, 2 vols., Philadelphia: 1864, Vol. I, pp. 44–47.

Synod. The Synod had already absorbed the Puritan Churches in New Jersey and New York and there seemed to be no reason why the Connecticut ministers and churches should not unite. Though such a union was not consummated, the very fact that it was considered seriously at this time presaged the union that was to take place less than a century later. Edwards' pastorate was terminated in eight months, and the little church over which he had presided was absorbed by the older congregation.[11]

The Synod did not include the churches in South Carolina, nor those in New England, but in both sections independent Presbyteries were formed. The first Presbytery in South Carolina was that of James Island, constituted in 1722. The first New England Presbytery was the Londonderry, organized in 1730, the year following the death of Rev. James MacGregor, the first minister at Londonderry. During his entire ministry frontier conditions had prevailed in southern New Hampshire and danger from Indian forays was never absent. It was his custom to go into his pulpit with his gun loaded and primed, while all the able-bodied men in his congregation likewise came armed. As population increased, due largely to continuing Irish emigration, a new parish, the West Londonderry, was formed in 1737 which called Rev. David MacGregor, the son of the first Londonderry minister, as their pastor. He had been educated for the ministry by his father's successor at Londonderry, and was one of the first if not the first Presbyterian minister in America to be educated under private tutelage. Two years later (1739) an East Londonderry parish was formed. Thus Londonderry township became a strong and active Presbyterian center.

A second New England Presbytery was formed in 1745 composed of churches in and around Boston, and was called the Boston Presbytery. Later others were formed, the Eastward, composed of the Maine Churches, and the Grafton, of which Dartmouth College was the center. By 1755 thirty-six Presbyterian Churches had been organized in New England, and of these fourteen were in Maine, eleven in New Hampshire, six in Massa-

---

[11] Briggs, *op. cit.*, pp. 181–183. For a brief account of Jonathan Edwards' New York pastorate, see Elizabeth Winslow, *Jonathan Edwards, 1703–1758*, New York: 1940.

chusetts and one in Connecticut. By the opening of the Revolution New England's Presbyterian strength consisted of one Synod of three Presbyteries, numbering all told fourteen ministers, beside two independent Presbyteries.[12]

V

DOCTRINE AND DISCIPLINE

THE PASSAGE of the *Adopting Act* by the Philadelphia Synod in 1729 gives to that year a special significance in American Presbyterian history. The importance of this action will be understood when it is stated that its adoption gave to American Presbyterianism its first definite constitution. Before this time there had been no stereotyped form of procedure developed in America and the Churches and Presbyteries had been more or less a law unto themselves, and had dealt with their peculiar problems as the circumstances seemed best. The impetus for the adoption of uniform standards of doctrine and discipline in America came from Great Britain, as a result of the appearance of radical and heretical opinions among the Presbyterian clergy of Ireland, Scotland and England. The natural result was the erection of ecclesiastical fences in the attempt to keep out the current heretical doctrines such as Deism, Socinianism and Semi-Arianism.

Since the action taken by the Presbyterians in Great Britain had a direct effect upon American Presbyterian action it will be well to review briefly the occurrences there and especially in Ireland. In the early part of the eighteenth century Rev. Thomas Emlyn of Dublin, and a little later Rev. James Pierce of Exeter, England, gave public expression to views opposed to the orthodox doctrine of the Trinity. Emlyn was simply read out of the Presbytery without any question being raised of compelling other members of the Presbytery to subscribe to the Westminster Confession of Faith, the recognized Presbyterian Creed. The excite-

---

[12] Henry D. Funk, *The Influence of the Presbyterian Church in Early American History*, Part I (*Journal of the Presbyterian Historical Society*, Vol. 12, 1924–27).

ment aroused by the Emlyn case, however, caused the Synod of Ulster to pass what was known as the Act of 1705, requiring all persons who were to be licensed to preach the gospel "to subscribe the Westminster Confession of Faith to be the confession of their faith and promise to adhere to the doctrine, worship, discipline and government of this church." In dealing with the Pierce case, instead of simply expelling him from the Presbytery as had been done with Emlyn, the larger question of subscription to the creed became an issue in all the Presbyterian bodies in England. Everywhere there was a division of the ministers into three distinct parties—those who favored subscription, those who opposed it, and those who held to a neutral position. The partisan controversy thus aroused continued for years, and before its deadly course was run English Presbyterianism had almost disappeared.[13]

In Scotland subscription to the Westminster Confession did not originate with the Church of Scotland, but rather with the Scotch Parliament, which in 1693 required subscription to the Confession by all ministers. Before this the Church of Scotland had approved the Westminster Confession "as agreeable to the Word of God, and in nothing contrary to the received doctrine of this Church," but had not required individual verbal subscription. After the passage of the subscription requirement by the Parliament the General Assembly adopted a stricter formula, but this never has been interpreted as meaning verbal subscription.

In North Ireland the subscription controversy centered about charges of heresy (1716–17) made against Professor Simpson of the Theological Faculty of the University of Glasgow, who had been the teacher of many of the leading ministers in North Ireland. Previously a group of Simpson's former students in Ireland had formed themselves into the "Belfast Society." It included in its membership many of the ablest ministers of Ulster, who were in sympathy with the broad Presbyterianism which they had learned in the classroom of Professor Simpson. Members of the Society opposed subscription to any human test of orthodoxy,

---

[13] A. H. Drysdale, *History of the Presbyterians in England: Their Rise, Decline and Revival*, London: 1889.

though they professed to believe the doctrines of the Westminster Confession.[14] In 1720 in an attempt at compromise between those who opposed and those who favored subscription, the Synod of Ulster passed what is known as the *Pacific Act*. Its main feature lay in the permission of persons subscribing to the Confession of Faith to substitute their own expressions for phrases used in the Confession, and if these were judged consistent with the substance of doctrine they were to be accepted. Unfortunately the *Pacific Act* failed to bring peace to the Irish Synod, and eventually it divided into two bodies. The *Pacific Act,* however, had a more lasting significance in America, where it formed the basis of the *Adopting Act* passed by the Philadelphia Synod in 1729.

The movement to tighten up American Presbyterianism both in doctrine and discipline began in 1720, when a vigorous protest was made at the mildness of the Synod's action in dealing with a case of ministerial discipline. From this protest the whole question of subscription finally evolved and parties were soon formed both in the Synod and the Presbyteries for and against subscription. Jonathan Dickinson led the non-subscription party made up of the ministers from New England and Wales, while the Irish and Scotch ministers were almost a unit for subscription, with the Newcastle Presbytery taking the lead.

Dickinson offered the most telling arguments against strict subscription, proposing that instead of requiring subscription to the Confession candidates for the ministry be examined more strictly by the several Presbyteries, and that discipline be administered more firmly in the churches, especially in cases involving scandalous ministers. He held that subscription to a creed, instead of being a bond of union, would be a cause of disunion, and to shut out non-subscribers would be to make the Confession of Faith and not the Bible the standard. He called attention to the heresies which crowded into the Church after the adoption of the Nicene Creed, all of which, he stated, "flowed from the corrupt fountain of impositions and subscriptions." "Subscriptions,"

---

[14] W. T. Latimer, *A History of Irish Presbyterians,* Belfast: 1902, pp. 298 ff.

he concluded, "are not necessary to the being or the well-being of a Church, unless hatred, variance, emulation, wrath strife, sedition and heresies are necessary to that end." The influence exerted by Jonathan Dickinson kept strict subscription from being adopted. If the strict subscriptionists had been triumphant American colonial Presbyterianism would have resolved itself into bitter controversial groups, as had already taken place among the Presbyterians of England and Ireland.

The *Adopting Act* was a compromise measure. The fear of dividing the infant colonial Church was the deciding factor in its passage. The probability is that it was Jonathan Dickinson's hand which had shaped the measure to make it satisfactory to all parties, with the happy result that it was adopted unanimously. The *Act* disclaims any authority to dictate to other men's consciences, yet, it states, in order to keep Presbyterian faith pure and uncorrupt, it is agreed that all ministers of the Synod, as well as all those who shall thereafter be admitted, shall declare their agreement and approbation of the Confession of Faith, together with the larger and smaller Catechisms, "as being in all the essential and necessary articles, good forms of sound words and system of Christian Doctrine." But if any minister or candidate "shall have any scruple . . . with respect to any article or articles of said Confession or Catechism, he shall at the time of his making said declaration, declare his sentiments to the Presbytery or Synod," and "if the Synod or Presbytery shall decide his scruple . . . to be about articles not essential and necessary in doctrine, worship or government," he shall be admitted, or to put it in its simplest form, subscription was required only to "necessary and essential articles." Since the Synod did not define what were the "necessary and essential articles," it meant that there was in every case a large degree of latitude, determined by the theological complexion of the Presbytery before whom the candidate appeared.

Thus it was that wise leadership succeeded in steering American Presbyterianism through the troubled waters which had brought disaster to English and Irish Presbyterianism. The design had been to adapt "the best Presbyterian models to American soil" and not to enforce any one type upon the new Presbyterianism arising in the New World.[15]

VI

TRAINING A COLONIAL MINISTRY

THE INTERCOLONIAL character of Presbyterianism was one of its outstanding characteristics. There was not one of the thirteen colonies, with the exception of Rhode Island, which did not possess a Presbyterian Church by 1763. This was due to the widespread distribution of the Scotch-Irish settlers. Simply the listing of the location of Presbyterian Churches established during any one year in the forties and fifties of the eighteenth century will illustrate this widespread distribution. In the year 1740 there were seventeen new Presbyterian Churches formed—eight in Pennsylvania, two in Maryland, three in Virginia, three in New Jersey and one in Delaware. In 1751 eleven new churches were established—five in South Carolina, one in North Carolina, three in New Jersey and one each in New York and Pennsylvania; and these are typical years.[16]

From the beginning colonial Presbyterianism made strenuous efforts to maintain high educational standards for its ministry. A large proportion of the founders were either graduates of the Scottish Universities or had studied there, while from Harvard and Yale Colleges came some of the ablest early leaders. Even in the face of a continual bombardment of letters asking for ministerial supplies from the new settlements, the Presbyteries consistently refused to send men whom they considered unqualified for the work. The New Brunswick Presbytery within the space of three years from 1738 to 1741, received eighty requests for ministerial supplies. "Desolate places," was the name given communities without ministers, and the problems these communities presented

---

[15] Briggs, *op. cit.,* pp. 216–221. Charles Hodge, *The Constitutional History of the Presbyterian Church in the United States of America,* Part I, 1705–1741, Philadelphia: 1839; especially useful for contemporary documents. A recent appraisal of the *Adopting Act* is Frederick W. Loetscher's article on that subject in *Journal of the Presbyterian Historical Society,* XIII, No. 8, December 1929, pp. 337–355.

[16] Funk, *op. cit.*

were constantly before all of the American Presbyteries. Appeals were being made continually to the Scottish and Irish Presbyteries and Synods as well as to New England.

The impossibility of meeting these demands in any ordinary way led the Philadelphia Synod in 1748 to send regular pastors on preaching tours to the new settlements during certain seasons of the year. At first these tours lasted eight weeks; they were later extended, in some cases, to six months. This, however, was but a makeshift and was not in any sense a satisfactory substitute for a full-time ministry. The scarcity of ministers also led to large parishes, often with two or three churches and as many more preaching places. These somewhat resembled the Methodist circuits, but to have called them "circuits" would have caused a scandal in Presbyterian circles. Unfortunately American Presbyterianism was restricted in devising new methods to meet the peculiar American situation by their rigid adherence to the Presbyterian system of polity set forth in the Westminster Confession.

For more than a generation American Presbyterianism was dependent upon the British Isles and New England for their ministerial candidates. But the lapse of Irish and English Presbyterianism from strict orthodoxy made the American Presbyteries wary of receiving ministers from the British Isles, and threw them more and more on their own resources, which was, in the long run, a fortunate circumstance.

Rev. William Tennent's "Log College" at Neshaminy, Pennsylvania, twenty miles north of Philadelphia, was the first school in which a native ministry was trained. William Tennent was a native of Ireland, and a graduate of the University of Edinburgh. He was raised in the Established Church of Ireland, in which he became a priest. He became dissatisfied with his ecclesiastical relationship, probably because of his inability to find a parish, though the growing Arminianism among the clergy may have had something to do with it. In 1716 he came to America with his wife and four sons, and two years later applied for admission to the newly formed Presbyterian Synod of Philadelphia. From 1718 to 1726 he served churches in New York. In the latter year he went to Bucks county, Pennsylvania, as minister of two churches, one on the south branch of Neshaminy Creek, and the other at what is now Doylestown. Here he remained to the year of his death, 1746.

On a fifty-acre tract of land, granted to him by his cousin, James Logan, William Penn's secretary, he erected a log house, twenty feet square, in which he opened a school. A good language scholar with pedagogic skill, William Tennent was also possessed of an attractive and persuasive personality. At any rate his school became notable for the lasting impress he made upon his students. Gilbert, his eldest son, already had received his training from his father before coming to Neshaminy, but the three other sons, William Jr., Charles, and John, were educated at the "Log College." Among the "Log College" graduates were ten other young men who entered the Presbyterian ministry: Charles Beatty, John Blair, Samuel Blair, William Dean, Samuel Finley, James McRea, Daniel Lawrence, John Roan, William Robinson and John Rowland. And it was this group of American-trained Presbyterian ministers which played the major rôle in determining the development of American Presbyterianism for a hundred years.

The effectiveness of the training received under the elder Tennent is evidenced by the fact that the graduates of his "Log College" not only became the most noted preachers of the next generation but several of them were founders of other "Log Colleges," which to a large degree set the pattern for higher education on the frontier. Thus Samuel Blair established a "Log College" at Fagg's Manor in Pennsylvania from which "graduated" Samuel Davies, John Rodgers, Robert Smith, James Finley, Hugh Henry and Alexander Cummings, as distinguished a group of Presbyterian ministers as can be found in any period of American Presbyterian history. Robert Smith, in turn, founded Pequea Academy in Lancaster county, and Samuel Finley opened Nottingham Academy across the Maryland boundary. Out of this background came the College of New Jersey opened in 1746, of which both Samuel Davies and Samuel Finley became presidents. From the founding of William Tennent's "Log College" in 1726 to the end of the century Presbyterian ministers had established an even hundred schools: "Log Colleges," Academies or Classical Schools, some of which developed into permanent colleges. All of these institutions were primarily ministerial training schools, though none of them were limited to that alone.[17]

---

[17] The following may be consulted on the educational development of colonial Presbyterianism. C. H. Maxson, *The Great Awakening in the Middle Colonies*, Chicago: 1916; Funk, *op. cit.*, Part II, pp. 152–189; Klett, *op. cit.*, Chapter xi, "Education among Presbyterians"; A. Alexander (Ed.), *Biographical Sketches of the Founder and Principal Alumni of the Log College*, Princeton: 1845; George H. Ingram, *The Story of the Log College (Journal of the Presbyterian Historical Society*, Vol. 12), pp. 487–511.

IX

Religion Reaches the Masses:
The Great Awakenings

OR THE first one hundred years organized religion in the American colonies was a matter of the few. In spite of the large influence exerted by religion in the establishment of the colonies, membership in the colonial Churches was relatively small throughout the entire colonial period. This was due to factors peculiar to America. In the first place, in none of the colonies did Church membership come about as a matter of course as was the case in all European countries where State Churches prevailed and where Church membership was almost co-extensive with citizenship. Even in the colonies where there were State Churches, as in New England and the Southern colonies, Church membership was an individual matter. Until the adoption of the Half-Way Covenant, membership in the Congregational Churches of New England could be secured only by the relation of a satisfactory religious experience before the congregation. This was also the requirement in all Churches which held to adult baptism. This meant that Church membership was an exceedingly selective matter and was not easily achieved.

The fact that the Anglican Church did not have an American bishop meant that confirmation was practically unknown in colonial America, for it could be obtained only by going to England. This helps to account for the relatively small number of Anglican communicants. Although under such conditions the Sacraments were not denied unconfirmed individuals, it would mean that only the more earnest would be willing to participate under such conditions.[1] The extreme poverty of the Scotch-Irish and German

---

[1] The rubric in the Prayer Book coming at the end of the Confirmation Service reads: "And there shall none be admitted to the Holy Communion, until such time as he be

immigrants and the fact that most of them came without spiritual leaders greatly delayed the formation of congregations.

As a whole the great majority of the colonists were drawn from the lower economic classes in the Old World where many had had but nominal attachment to the Church. Coming to the New World primarily to better their economic condition, what little interest in religion they had had in their old homes was liable to evaporate or be pushed into the background in the endless struggle to gain an economic foothold.

While in most instances the colonial Churches maintained some kind of Old World connection, nevertheless there were gradually developing certain religious trends and attitudes which were distinctively American. Such Reformation ideas as the universal priesthood of all believers, and the individual's ability to make his own approach to God found more ample opportunity of expression in the New World than in the Old. While this personalizing of religion was characteristic of the small left-wing sects in the Old World, yet for the great majority of people there salvation was an institutional matter rather than an individual concern. In the New World the exact opposite was true. In none of the colonies could religion be said to have become institutionalized, though in New England Congregationalism after the adoption of the Half-Way Covenant there was a strong trend in that direction. In the stress and strain of colonization where the facing of the hardships of pioneering was an everyday affair there was a demand for a type of preaching and a theology that would take account of everyday personal needs. Thus the legalistic theology of Calvinism became in the hands of the colonial preachers a personalized Calvinism searching out the hearts of individuals.

A third factor which helped set the stage for colonial revivalism was the growing awareness on the part of the religious leaders of the decline of religion throughout the colonies. The sermons of

---

confirmed, or be ready and desirous to be confirmed." The last clause in the rubric "or be ready and desirous to be confirmed" was added in 1662 because confirmation had been unobtainable during the Commonwealth period. (W. K. Lowther Clarke and Charles Harris (eds.), *Liturgy and Worship,* London, S.P.C.K.: 1932.) Frequent communion was not customary in the Anglican Church in the latter seventeenth and eighteenth centuries. It is an interesting fact that neither Bishops Seabury nor White had been confirmed.

the New England ministers during the latter years of the seventeenth and the early years of the eighteenth centuries are full of gloomy forebodings as to the future because of the low state of religion and public morals. "O what a sad metamorphosis hath of later years passed upon us in these churches and plantations! Alas! How is New England in danger to be buried in its own ruins," is the plaint of William Stoughton before the Massachusetts Legislature in 1668. Ten years later Increase Mather observed that "Clear, sound conversions are not frequent. Many of the rising generation are profane Drunkards, Swearers, Licentious and scoffers at the power of Godliness." A generation later Samuel Whitman of Connecticut noted that religion was on the wane, and that his generation had "in great measure forgot the errand of our Fathers."

A random survey of the subjects of the election sermons preached at this period show that almost all are of a piece in this respect—they were uniformly denunciatory of the religious conditions of their times. In 1700 Samuel Willard preached on "The Perils of the Times Displayed"; in 1711 Stephen Buckingham's theme was "The Unreasonableness and Danger of a People's Renouncing Their Subjection to God"; William Russell's subject in 1730 was "The Decay of Love to God in Churches, Offensive and Dangerous." The second and third generation Americans had no such stimulus to place religion in the center of their lives as had their fathers, with the result that there was a general cooling off of religion. Such certainly was the case of New England. The Middle and Southern Colonies experienced a crisis in religion in the eighteenth century as a result of the successive waves of new immigration. The feeble religious organizations found themselves entirely unable to cope with the situation, as the many frantic appeals for help on the part of the Presbyterian, Lutheran, and Reformed leaders indicate. Times were ripe for some new emphasis in religion as well as a new type of religious leadership to meet the peculiar situation which the American colonies presented.

I

THE MIDDLE COLONY REVIVAL

COLONIAL REVIVALISM began in the Middle Colonies where German pietism had prepared the way by its emphasis upon inner, personal religion. The first outstanding revivalist was the pietistic pastor of four Dutch Reformed churches in the Raritan valley in the colony of New Jersey, Theodore J. Frelinghuysen. A German, educated under pietistic influences, he came to America in 1720 at the call of three congregations which had been formed among the Dutch settlers in central New Jersey. It was a rough and boorish community, and religiously the people had little desire beyond the outward conformity to accepted religious rites. Their wish was to preserve the Dutch Church as a symbol of their Dutch nationality and of their former independence. The last thing they wanted was to have a religion that would stir the emotions and set up high standards of personal conduct. This was just the kind of religion, however, that Domine Frelinghuysen now began to preach. His impassioned manner of preaching, his advocacy of inner religion in contrast to the mere outward performance of religious duties, and his attempts to bring about conversions soon brought a cleavage among his parishioners. The well-to-do, the kind who generally hold the principal offices in churches, were scandalized; the poorer people and the younger generation were inclined to support their young and enthusiastic domine.

The controversy thus begun in the little frontier communities in central Jersey developed within the next few years into a conflict which had reverberations in every Dutch Reformed church in the colonies and even reached Holland. The officials of Frelinghuysen's churches took their complaints to Domine Boel, one of the Dutch collegiate ministers of New York, who pronounced these doctrines heretical, and Frelinghuysen a schismatic. But the young and perhaps somewhat brash domine was far from being silenced by such pronouncements. He now took to publishing sermons defending his teaching, while Domine Boel answered from his pulpit. Boel even visited the disaffected members of Frelinghuysen's congregations to incite them to resist, and with such success that all Frelinghuysen's churches were disrupted and in commotion. Frelinghuysen, however, continued his direct, pungent, evangelical preaching, and conversions were frequent occurrences until even his elders and deacons, his former opposers, were reached. The revival reached its height in 1726 and was marked by a large ingathering of new members. Nor was the revival spirit confined to the Raritan Valley, but spread to other Dutch communities. At the very start of his ministry Frelinghuysen had introduced, in good pietistic fashion, private prayer meetings. Another innovation was the lay helper, whose duty was to lead the meetings for prayer and, in the absence of the pastor, to conduct the church services. Eventually Domine Frelinghuysen and his revival movement gained the support of the majority of the Dutch ministers, but opposition was by no means at an end, and the division thus created in the Dutch Church was not healed until toward the end of the colonial period.

The Frelinghuysen revival among the Dutch in central New Jersey prepared the way for the next phase of the Middle Colony revival, that among the Scotch-Irish. The principal human instruments in the Presbyterian revival were the graduates of William Tennent's "Log College" at Neshaminy in Pennsylvania.

The elder Tennent was evidently a preacher of power, and extremely evangelical for his day, but his chief claim to fame was as an educator of young men for the Presbyterian ministry.[2] His school had been established primarily to educate his own sons, but later other young men were admitted, which necessitated the erection of a log school building which his detractors called in derision the "Log College." Here in the course of twenty years (1726–46) some sixteen or eighteen young men were trained, a good proportion of whom entered the Presbyterian ministry. That

---

[2] Archibald Alexander, *Biographical Sketches of the Founder and Principal Alumni of the Log College*, etc., Philadelphia: 1851. More recent biographical sketches of William Tennent, Sr., and ten of the graduates are found in *Journal of the Presbyterian Historical Society*, Vols. XIII and XIV, 1928–31.

their preparation was thorough is attested by the fact that a number of them achieved distinction for their scholarly attainments, but their principal distinction, however, was due to their flaming evangelical zeal.

Besides the elder Tennent's sons, other graduates of his school entered the Presbyterian ministry. Gradually a group of Log College men came to be settled over churches in central New Jersey, and under their preaching developed a militant revivalism which swept the whole region. In its beginning the principal leader was Gilbert Tennent, who had been prepared for the ministry by his father previous to his coming to Neshaminy. Called to the Presbyterian church at New Brunswick at the height of Domine Frelinghuysen's revival, he had been warmly welcomed and encouraged by the Dutch minister who recognized in the young Tennent a kindred spirit.

Throughout the seventeen-thirties the Scotch-Irish revival mounted higher and higher, and new congregations were formed as converts increased and new communities were reached. In 1738 the New Brunswick Presbytery was erected, made up of five evangelical ministers, three of whom were Log College men. The principal reason why the revivalists desired to be formed into a separate presbytery was that they might license and ordain men of their own kind. Meanwhile opposition to the revival began to manifest itself among the older ministers who had received their training in the Scottish universities. These men now sought to control the situation by the enactment of laws in the Synod requiring all candidates for ordination to present diplomas either from New England or European colleges. This enactment was obviously aimed at the graduates of the Log College. Other rules also were passed restricting the supplying of vacant churches, an enactment also aimed at the revivalists. But at the very time this was happening, John Rowland, a recent Log College graduate, was licensed by the New Brunswick Presbytery, a challenge aimed at the conservatives.

Such was the situation in central New Jersey when George Whitefield appeared on the American religious scene. Although at the beginning of a career as the greatest evangelist of his time and perhaps of all time, Whitefield had already begun to display certain characteristics which he was to retain throughout his life. One such characteristic was his catholic spirit which made it easy for him to cooperate with any Church or any minister whose central interest was that of soul saving. Landing at Lewes, Delaware, in August 1739, Whitefield immediately began his first American evangelistic tour in the very region where Domine Frelinghuysen and the Log College evangelists had been preparing the soil for his seed. The dramatic results which attended Whitefield's preaching in America on his first tour (August 1739–January 1741) were due not alone to his magnificent appeal, but to the fact that the way had been prepared. There was no need for him to plant; "he merely put in his sickle and claimed the harvest."

As was to be expected, Whitefield found his closest friends and most loyal supporters not among his fellow Anglicans, but among the Presbyterians. This was doubtless helped along by his recent adoption of Calvinistic views. As Whitefield made his way through New Jersey from Philadelphia to New York, the aged founder of the Log College met the young evangelist, "called by the voice of spiritual kinship," and an alliance was formed immediately between them for the continuation of the religious revolution, begun by the young men who had received their inspiration at Neshaminy. Rejoicing in the tremendous impetus which Whitefield's preaching gave to their movement, all of the Log College evangelists gave him full support. But as was to be expected Whitefield's preaching aroused the foes of the revival to a still more bitter opposition. The fact that Whitefield won the support of so many educated and sober-minded men in the Middle Colonies such as Benjamin Franklin, is evidence, however, of the fundamental soundness of the influence he exerted. Franklin on many occasions expressed the utmost faith in him and in a letter to his brother admitted having a deep affection for him. He was employed in publishing the evangelist's Sermons and Journals and their friendship lasted to the end of Whitefield's life.[3]

---

[3] E. P. Cheyney, *History of the University of Pennsylvania, 1740–1940*, Philadelphia: 1940, pp. 17–27. *The Autobiography of Benjamin Franklin, op. cit.*, pp. 139–43.

Another result of Whitefield's visit to the Middle Colonies was the bringing of the New England Churches in northern New Jersey to the support of the revival. Jonathan Dickinson at Elizabethtown and Aaron Burr at Newark, both graduates of Yale College, were revivalistically inclined, but were, nevertheless, hesitant about joining the Log College evangelists. Dickinson's invitation to Whitefield to preach in his church on the great evangelist's return to Philadelphia from New York (1740) thoroughly committed him to the revival. A great revival at Newark the year previous, in which Dickinson had come to Burr's assistance, was doubtless also a determining factor in winning the two Yale graduates to the revivalistic party.

From its very beginning revivalism was a divisive force in American Christianity, and has continued to be so even to our day. The schism in the Dutch Reformed Church as a result of the Frelinghuysen revival already has been noted. A similar division now developed among the Presbyterians. The conservatives were not only critical of the educational qualifications of the Log College evangelists, they were even more bitterly hostile to their invasion of other ministers' parishes uninvited. Whitefield ranged up and down the colonies preaching wherever opportunity offered. The Log College revivalists, especially Gilbert Tennent, followed his example and were in demand far and wide. Even Whitefield's catholicity came in for denunciation. If he, a Calvinist, they asked, could join with the Arminians and Lutherans in religious work, would he not turn Papist at Rome? To these objections Whitefield replied that his only design was to bring poor souls to Christ.

As a rule Whitefield ignored his critics; when he did reply he was inclined to be conciliatory, and not infrequently acknowledged his faults. Not so, however, the fiery Scotch-Irish evangelists, and especially Gilbert Tennent. In the spring of 1740, in the midst of a great revival at Nottingham on the border between Maryland and Pennsylvania, which had begun under the preaching of Samuel Blair, Gilbert Tennent preached his famous sermon on the "Danger of an Unconverted Ministry." Local opposition to the revival had resulted in closing meeting houses in that region against the revivalists, and his congregation was drawn largely from churches whose ministers were opposers of the revival. The situation aroused his combative instincts. He described those who resisted the revival as "moral negroes," who hinder rather than help others "in at the strait gate"; he likened them to caterpillars who "labor to devour every green thing," and advised his hearers to attend the meetings of preachers where they could receive the greatest benefit. He roundly denounced those men who entered the ministry merely as a trade, and who being unconverted themselves had no concern for the conversion of others. Published and widely circulated, this sermon led others to denounce unconverted ministers, and thus the cleavage between the two wings of the Presbyterians became wider and deeper.

The most valid accusation against the revivalists was that too much of their preaching was of a character to terrify the people, resulting in faintings, cries, and bodily agitations. Whitefield, contrary to popular opinion, however, was much less given to this kind of preaching than were the Scotch-Irish revivalists. In fact, Whitefield opposed such manifestations and considered them as having no relation to true conversion. Gilbert Tennent, on the other hand, frightened people into salvation. Whitefield was often tender and persuasive, Tennent "raged, shouted, stamped, roared, and set nerves on edge beyond endurance, and in many instances his meetings were little more than a scramble to safety, and the way led through bedlam." [4] Whitefield knew how to stop as well as to start the groaners. Tennent knew only how to start the noise; he was powerless to stop it. The character and background of the Scotch-Irish were also factors in the appearance of unrestrained emotionalism which developed in the course of the revival.

The division in colonial Presbyterianism came at the meeting of the Philadelphia Synod in 1741, when an anti-revivalistic majority expelled the New Brunswick Presbytery for disregarding the Synod's rule respecting the examination of candidates. Actually the rule was a violation of Presbyterian order, yet it was the conservative majority which accused the revivalistic minority of

---

[4] For an appraisal of Whitefield's and Tennent's styles of preaching see Ola Elizabeth Winslow, *Jonathan Edwards, 1703–1758*, New York: 1940, pp. 189, 194–96.

dissenting from the Presbyterian system of Church government. All attempts to heal the breach proved futile, and the three New Side Presbyteries, which now had been formed, organized the New York Synod in September 1745. Thus, in the very midst of the revival, at a time when the frontier was rapidly filling up with a population overwhelmingly Scotch-Irish and Presbyterian, the Presbyterian forces in colonial America were divided. Neither side had been blameless, but the chief responsibility must be borne by the stiff-backed conservatives, who seemed more concerned about preserving the Presbyterian system than for the spiritual welfare of the new population swarming into the back country.[5]

The new Synod of New York was composed of twenty-two ministers, with the leadership shared between the Log College men and the Yale graduates, thus uniting Calvinism with the pietistic spirit. Its members were generally young men, enthusiastically devoted to the revival, which they regarded as a blessed work of God. The Philadelphia Synod on the other hand was composed of ministers trained in the European universities, who had entered the ministry without experiencing any spiritual crisis in their own lives, and were not concerned in furthering revivalistic religion. The fate of colonial Presbyterianism for the next score or more of years was therefore largely in the hands of the New Side Synod of New York. Under its direction the revival was continued and extended into middle and western Virginia.

The success of the elder Tennent's Log College, as has been noted, inspired the establishment of other such schools by its graduates, thus continuing the stream of young revivalists into the New Side Presbyteries. The greatest educational triumph, however, achieved by colonial Presbyterianism was the establishment by the New York Synod of the College of New Jersey in 1746, less than six months following the death of William Tennent.

---

[5] Charles Hartshorn Maxson's *The Great Awakening in the Middle Colonies,* Chicago: 1920, is a fully documented and understanding study of this phase of the colonial awakenings. The lack of an index is to be regretted. George Whitefield's *Journals;* Thomas Prince, Jr., *The Christian History* for the years 1743–44; Gilbert Tennent's *Sermons;* Alexander, *op. cit.;* T. Murphy, *The Presbytery of the Log College,* Philadelphia: 1889, are some of the principal sources. See also Peter H. B. Frelinghuysen, Jr., *Theodorus Jacobus Frelinghuysen,* Princeton, 1938.

The Log College has been rightly called the mother of Princeton, and the ideals of that humble school were carried over into the new college. Its first five presidents were all great revivalistic preachers and devoted promoters of that movement—Jonathan Dickinson, Aaron Burr, Jonathan Edwards, Samuel Davies, and Samuel Finley; of the five the first three were Yale graduates and the last two the products of Log Colleges.

In the year 1758, to a large degree through the leadership of Gilbert Tennent, the two Synods of New York and Philadelphia were united. By this time the zeal of the revivalists had cooled and they were ready to confess their mistakes. The College of New Jersey had taken the place of the Log College, an institution which met the requirements of both parties. The New Side Synod had increased fourfold, the Old Side body had not even held its own. Opposition to revivalism had resulted in a declining Church, and the Old Side Synod was threatened with speedy death. Under these circumstances they too were ready to unite and to explain away their arbitrary acts of 1741. Thus it came about that colonial Presbyterianism was able to heal its differences previous to independence and were thus enabled to face the problems of the new nation a united body.[6]

II

THE NEW ENGLAND AWAKENINGS

JONATHAN EDWARDS has been called the father of the revivalistic type of Protestantism in America. From every point of view this is an erroneous statement. In the first place the priority of the Middle Colony awakening has been well established. Frelinghuysen's revival in central New Jersey was at high tide at least eight years previous to the beginning of the Edwardian revival at Northampton. In the second place revivalism in America would have become triumphant if there had never been a Jonathan Edwards or a New England Awakening. It was not Jonathan Edwards nor New

---

[6] C. A. Briggs, *American Presbyterianism, Its Origin and Early History*, New York: 1885, Chapter VIII and Appendix XXXI.

England that set the revivalistic pattern for American Protestantism. Rather it proceeded from a situation that was universal throughout the colonies and arose from the necessity of finding a new method of bringing religion to the great masses of the religiously indifferent. In fact New England's need in this respect was far less than anywhere else in colonial America. In the third place, colonial revivalism was rooted in pietism and not in New England Calvinism; it was only by impregnating his Calvinism with pietism that Jonathan Edwards' gospel was rendered effective in reaching the hearts of his people at Northampton. New England Congregationalism became revivalistic only as the clergy centered their interest in a scheme of redemption for individuals, and this was the very heart of pietism.[7] Edwards' book on *Religious Affections,* in which he sets forth the primary place of emotion in religion, is probably more self-revealing than any of his other books, for the emotional experiences which he here recounts he had also shared.[8]

The Great New England Awakening began under the preaching of Jonathan Edwards at Northampton in the fall of 1734, but Edwards was not a revivalist in the usual sense of the term. He never was an extemporaneous preacher, and until Whitefield's example had jarred the New England clergy out of their dreary homiletical rut, Edwards always had taken his entire manuscript into the pulpit with him. As the paper upon which the sermon was written was small, and the writing fine, he must have given far more attention to its deciphering than to the audience before him. His sermon subjects were generally confined to great themes and called for close attention on the part of his hearers. Yet it was under this kind of preaching that the revival began at Northampton. Interestingly enough, the foundation for the revival had been laid by Edwards outside the pulpit, in his work

---

[7] That Edwards was fully conscious of his departure from Calvinism is shown by a statement in his *Preface* of *Freedom of the Will.* He utterly disclaimed "a dependence on Calvin, or believing in doctrines which I hold because he believed and taught them," and he further states that he "cannot be justly charged in believing in everything just as he taught."

[8] A. C. McGiffert, *Jonathan Edwards,* New York: 1930, for an appraisal of this treatise, pp. 68–89.

with the young people to whom he had recommended that on
the day of each public lecture, they assemble in several parts of
the town and spend the evening in prayer and "other duties of
social religion." Their example was soon followed by their elders.
Taking advantage of the rising tide of religious concern which
resulted, Edwards began to preach on "awakening" themes, to be
followed by a series of sermons attacking the easy doctrines of
salvation which were gaining headway in New England and had
even found their way into his parish.

Though these discourses were doctrinal and the language used
the familiar Calvinistic idiom, the preacher's way of presenting
the time-honored themes caused the members of his congregation
to feel singled out. When in his application he called the roll of
the town's sins "which shut men out from God's mercy and
kindled the divine wrath to their destruction"—to use Miss
Winslow's words—it seemed as though he were walking up and
down the village street, pointing his accusing finger "at one house
after another, unearthing secret sins and holding them up for all
to see." [9] Thus the revival of 1734 and 1735 began, and for three
months excitement gripped the town. The number of converts
grew to more than three hundred and the meeting house could
not contain the throngs who came to witness the receiving of a
hundred new members on a certain Sunday morning. Night and
day the parsonage was thronged with agonized sinners seeking
the pastor's help so that they too might join the company of the
saved and the rejoicing. There seems to be every indication that
Edwards managed the unusual situation with common sense. He
encouraged those under conviction to come to him privately, and
used other means of "soothing overcharged emotions," so that
there was actually little to discredit religion in its outward manifestations. Edwards' dignified common sense, however, was not
enough to prevent some sinister consequences. It took several sui-
cides in the spring of 1735 to restore the town to a more normal
way of life.

The ingathering of new members so enlarged the congrega-

---

[9] For a vivid account of the Northampton revival of 1734–35 see Winslow, *op. cit.*,
Chapters VIII and IX.

tion that it became necessary to erect a new meeting house. Nearly twice the size of the old building it replaced, with a gallery and steeple, it was begun in the spring of 1736 and dedicated on Christmas Day 1737. The caring for his increased flock and the multitudinous details which necessarily accompanied the building of a new church must have imposed a greatly increased burden upon Jonathan Edwards' shoulders. Yet it was during these years that he penned the most potent writing of his whole life, if judged by the immediate influence which it exerted. This was a thin volume with the long title *A Faithful Narrative of the Surprising Work of God in the Conversion of Many Hundred Souls in Northampton and Neighboring Towns and Villages, in a letter to the Rev. Benjamin Coleman of Boston,* which appeared under a Boston imprint in 1737. It was the publication of this *Narrative* with its vivid description of remarkable conversions, and emphasis upon the marvels of the Northampton revival, together with the coming of George Whitefield on the first of his five New England tours, which mark the beginning of the religious upheaval which swept like a tidal wave throughout New England. The Northampton revival of 1735 was a gentle shower compared with the tempest which now ensued under the impassioned preaching of the young stranger, George Whitefield.

Just as the Frelinghuysen revival and the Log College evangelists had prepared the way for Whitefield in the Middle Colonies, so Jonathan Edwards and the Northampton revival had done the spade work for his harvest of souls in New England. No public figure of the eighteenth century was more highly praised on the one hand and more vilified and denounced on the other than George Whitefield.[10] As a preacher he was the marvel of the age. Though but twenty-six when he arrived in Boston in September 1740, his reputation had gone before him, and the whole town was awaiting his appearance and planning to hear him at the first opportunity. At Boston he had the support of the leading ministers, although Charles Chauncy of the First Church stood out against

---

[10] The first installment of his *Journal* (from England to Philadelphia) appeared just previous to his arrival and also a publication entitled *Directions How to hear Sermons Preach'd by the Rev. Mr. George Whitefield.*

him. Harvard College welcomed him, though not without some misgivings. The feeling of wonder and expectancy which prevailed among the common people is illustrated by the following account of the excitement occasioned by Whitefield's coming written by a semi-literate Connecticut farmer. He had heard of Whitefield's

preaching at philadelphia like one of the old aposels, and many thousands flocking after him to hear ye gospel and great numbers were converted to Christ, i felt the spirit of god drawing me by conviction i longed to see and hear him and wished he would come this way.

He had heard of his coming to New York and the Jerseys and of the great multitudes which were flocking after him and of their great concern for their souls. Next he had heard of his coming to Boston, then to Northampton and

then one morning all on a suding about 8 or 9 o'clock there came a messinger and said mr. whitfield preached at hartford and weathersfield yesterday and is to preach at middletown this morning (October 23, 1740) at 10 o'clock i was in my field at work i dropt my tool that i had in my hand and run home and run thru the house and bad my wife get ready quick to goo and hear mr whitfield preach at middletown and run to my pasture for my hors with all my might fearing i should be late to hear him i brought my hors home and soon mounted and took my wife up and went forward as fast as i thought the hors could bear, and when my hors began to be out of breath i would get down and put my wife on ye saddel and bid her ride as fast as she could and not stop or slak for me except i bad her and so i would run untill i was almost out of breth and then mount my hors again and so i did several times to favour my hors we improved every moment to get along as if we were fleeing for our lives all this while fearing we should be too late to hear ye sermon for we had twelve miles to ride dubble in littel more than an hour. . . .

As they drew near to Middletown he observed a fog, which he thought was arising from the river and heard a sound like low rumbling thunder, but he soon discovered that what he thought was thunder "was ye rumbling of horses feet coming down ye road" and the fog "was a Cloud of dust made by running horses feet." When they came near to the main road they could see men and horses "slipping along in ye Cloud like shadows" and when they drew nearer "it was like a stedy stream of horses and their riders scarcely a horse more than his length behind another all of a lather" . . . while "every hors seemed to go with all his might to carry his rider to hear ye news from heaven for the saving of their souls it made me trembel to see ye sight."

Arriving in Middletown, he found a great multitude of some three or four thousand had assembled. The river bank was black with people and horses, while "fery boats [were] running swift forward and backward bringing over loads of people ye ores roed nimble and quick every thing men horses and boats all seamed to be struglin for life." He saw Mr. Whitefield arrive and ascend "ye Scaffil" and "he looked almost angellical a young slim slender youth" . . . "with a bold countenance." All this "solumnized" his mind and put him in "a trembling fear" . . . for "he looked as if he was Cloathed with authority from ye great god and a sweet collome Solemnity sat upon his brow and my hearing him preach gave me a heart wound by gods blessing . . . my old foundation was broken up & i saw that my righteousness would not save me. . . ."[11]

Whitefield's first tour of New England lasted but a month, but it was long enough for him, with the help of Edwards' *Discourse,* to set the pattern of New England revivalism for the next four years. Congregational writers have been inclined to place the blame upon Whitefield's shoulders for all the extravagances which occurred, but it must be remembered that such things had occurred under Edwards' preaching before Whitefield appeared on the scene. The novelty of Whitefield's extemporaneous preaching; his impassioned utterances; his marvellous voice and vivid dramatic power must have been a welcome relief to people accustomed to sermons read from closely written manuscripts held in the hand of the preacher, and upon themes as dreary as the droning voice in which they were uttered. It is easily understood why the crowds paid him such extravagant honor, for he "substituted human

---

[11] From a MS. letter in Yale University, printed in G. L. Walker, *Some Aspects of the Religious Life of New England,* etc., New York, Boston, Chicago: 1897, pp. 88–92.

interest stories for logic and gave churchgoing America its first taste of the theatre under the flag of salvation." [12]

Miss Winslow has well pointed out that success came to White-field too soon and too easily, resulting in his stunted growth, for at the end of his career he was preaching the same kind of sermons as in his youth and there was no indication of an enlargement of view or of deepening wisdom. But Whitefield had more to him than mere eloquence. He was devout, sincere, and courageous, and his one great consuming interest and concern was to preach the gospel in such a way as to bring men and women to repentance and to a better way of life. It was but natural that he should have had numerous imitators, and as in the case of most imitators they copied his faults but seldom his virtues. One of his chief weaknesses, especially in his younger years, was his censoriousness and his sweeping judgments of other ministers. At the close of his first New England tour he wrote in his *Journal* that it was his opinion that "many, nay most that preach, do not experimentally know Christ," and on the following page of his *Journal* he records this ungenerous and unjust opinion of the two New England Colleges: "Their light has become darkness, darkness that may be felt." Is there any wonder that on his next visit to New England both colleges closed their doors upon him!

The greatest excesses in the New England revival took place after Whitefield had departed. Soon after his departure Gilbert Tennent was invited to come to New England to carry on the "great work." During his three months' stay Tennent's one theme was hell-fire and damnation, while his rough dress and boorish appearance, together with his roaring and stamping, brought down upon his head a greater flood of criticism than had been bestowed upon Whitefield.

The arrogant Dr. Timothy Cutler, ex-Congregationalist, the rector of Christ Episcopal Church in Boston, characterized Tennent as "impudent and saucy," telling the people that "they were damned." "This," he said, "charmed them; and in the dreadfullest winter I ever saw, people wallowed in the snow day and night, for the benefit of his beastly brayings." On the other

---

[12] Winslow, *op. cit.*, p. 181.

hand, Rev. Thomas Prince, in his *Christian History,* a contemporary record, states that "his preaching was as searching and rousing as any I ever heard while in private he was seen to be of considerable parts of learning—free, gentle, and condescending." The results of Tennent's tour of New England exceeded those of Whitefield's; this was true not only of Boston and New Haven but also of many other towns.[13]

The revivalist, however, who has left the most unsavory reputation for rabble rousing was James Davenport. A graduate of Yale College and a direct descendant of John Davenport, the founder of New Haven, James Davenport at twenty-two became the minister of the church at Southold, Long Island. The reports of Whitefield's triumphs led him to determine to follow his example and he left his congregation to become an itinerant evangelist. Beginning among his own people, he assembled them in his lodging where he addressed them for nearly twenty-four hours without interruption. This led to a near physical breakdown, which seemed also to affect his mind. He now began to make distinctions among the members of his church, calling the converted members "brothers" and the others "neighbours," and the neighbors were forbidden to partake of the Lord's Supper.

He began his travels in 1742 and for more than a year ranged up and down Connecticut, invading parishes uninvited and urging the people to withdraw from the ministrations of their unconverted ministers. It was largely due to his extravagances that the General Assembly of Connecticut passed in 1742 an "Act for regulating abuses and correcting disorders in Ecclesiastical Affairs." He was apprehended by the authorities, judged not fully sane and sent back to his church at Southold, but he was soon again on his travels. On a visit to Boston he preached in the streets with such violent condemnation of the clergy that he was imprisoned by the authorities and again sent to his home. His most

---

[13] The best contemporaneous account of the New England Revival for the years 1743–44 is Thomas Prince, Jr., *Christian History,* published weekly from March 5, 1743, to February 23, 1744. See also Richard Webster, *A History of the Presbyterian Church in America,* etc., Philadelphia: 1857, especially his sketch of Gilbert Tennent, pp. 387–97.

notorious extravagance was his causing his converts at New
London to burn their fine clothes and ornaments to cure their
idolatrous pride. Books of which he did not approve were also
thrown into the flames.[14]

The New England clergy were now divided into conflicting
parties over the revival. The General Convention of Congregational Ministers in Massachusetts adopted a *Testimony* "against
several Errors in Doctrine and Disorders in Practice" in May
1743. As errors in doctrine growing out of the revival they named
the prevalence of "secret impulses upon the mind without due
regard to the written word"; the contention that "none are converted but such as know they are converted and the time when";
that "assurance is of the essence of saving faith," and, finally, "that
sanctification is no evidence of justification." These they term
Antinomian and Familistical errors and contrary to the pure
doctrines of the gospel. As disorders in practice they name itiner-
acy; the practice of uneducated persons without any regular call
"taking upon themselves to be preachers of the word of God";
the ordaining of persons to the work of the evangelical ministry
at large in direct opposition to the Cambridge Platform; the practice of separation from the particular flocks to which they belong;
assuming the prerogatives of God to judge others, and finally the
confusions and disorderly tumults which the revival fostered.
These were the stock criticisms, the substance of which was
repeated in all the numerous indictments.

The adoption of this *Testimony* by a small group of the anti-
revivalists, thirty-eight in number, led the friends of the revival
to call another convention in Boston on July 7 of the same year,
where a *Testimony* favoring the revival was passed. This was
eventually endorsed by 113 ministers from Massachusetts, New
Hampshire, Maine, and Connecticut. Though recognizing that
in some places "many irregularities and extravagances have been
permitted" to accompany the revival, which they "deeply lament
and bewail before God," yet they recognize that a great work of

---

[14] Joseph Tracy, *A History of the Revival of Religion in the time of Edwards and
Whitefield,* Boston: 1842. Chapter xiv, pp. 230–54, is a full and fully documented
account of the career of Davenport.

God has been wrought in New England through the "late happy Revival of Religion."

The Reverend Charles Chauncy, the minister of the First Church in Boston, was, as has been intimated above, the principal critic of the revival. The most influential minister of his time in Boston, Chauncy possessed a powerful and vigorous mind, though in disposition he was cold and prosaic and utterly out of sympathy with all emotional manifestation in religion. It was temperamentally impossible for him to understand, still less appreciate, the benefits which might come through revivals. In his pamphlet *Seasonable Thoughts on the State of Religion in New England* published in 1743, Chauncy had gathered together all the more extreme instances of revival extravagances he could find by combing New England. Though one-sided and unfair—I cannot agree with Miss Winslow that he spoke temperately—Chauncy's indictment of the revival has been generally accepted by recent writers as fairly representing the situation. Rather it would appear that the *Testimony* signed by more than one hundred New England ministers presents a truer appraisal.[15]

Opposition to the revival reached its most extreme form in Connecticut where the General Assembly was called into action to pass legislation aimed at its control. The Act of May 1742 has been already noted. The next year the Assembly repealed what had been known as the "Act for the Relief of sober Consciences," which had been enacted at the time of the adoption of the Saybrook Platform. This act had given legal status to Churches dissenting from the Platform. These Acts resulted in the deposition of several Connecticut ministers, while the Separatists, as the revivalists who withdrew from the regular Churches and formed

---

[15] See Tracy, *op. cit.,* Chapters XVI, XVII, XVIII, for materials on the controversies and opponents of the revival; Chapter VIII in Benjamin Trumbull, *A Complete History of Connecticut Civil and Ecclesiastical,* 2 vols., New London: 1818. Vol. II, pp. 103–218, reproduces many of the documents bearing on Connecticut. Trumbull states (p. 201) that Chauncy collected the "most exaggerated accounts from those who were the most zealous opposers of the work and even condescended so low as to publish accounts from the newspapers relative to it, throwing the greatest odium and reproach upon it." Chauncy tried to prove that the spirit of God could not have been in the revival and that its effects were produced only by wild and extravagant conduct of overheated preachers.

themselves into separate congregations were called, were in some instances persecuted and some of them imprisoned.[16]

There have been various estimates as to the numbers added to the New England churches as a result of the revival.[17] Some have placed it as high as fifty thousand. Benjamin Trumbull, whose *History of Connecticut,* published in 1818, has remained "one of the most important single pieces of writing" on the period of the revival, estimates the number at from thirty to forty thousand. Between 1740 and 1760 one hundred and fifty new Congregational churches were formed, bringing the total to 530[18] besides the new congregations of Separatists and Baptists. Aside from the increase in numbers there was an increase in piety among Church members, some of whom had been previously "dead weights" to the churches. There was also a decided increase in the number of students preparing for the ministry and an appreciable rise in the standard of duty and effort of the ministry. It also secured "a converted ministry for coming times" and raised the requirements of Church membership from the low state to which the Half-Way Covenant had brought it. Trumbull, who personally knew many of the converts, characterized them as "most uniform, exemplary Christians." While recognizing that there was much in the revival deserving condemnation, yet it was his judgment based on a full knowledge of all the facts on both sides, that "it was the most glorious and extensive revival of religion and reformation of manners, which the country ever experienced."[19]

III

THE SOUTHERN AWAKENINGS

IN THEIR broadest aspect the colonial awakenings constitute one great religious contagion sweeping over the colonies like a tidal

---

[16] Isaac Backus, *A History of New England with Particular Reference to the Denomination of Christians called Baptists,* 3 vols., Boston: 1777–96.

[17] For a lengthy discussion of results see Tracy, *op. cit.,* Chapter xx, pp. 388–433; also Trumbull, *op. cit.,* pp. 201 ff.

[18] Tracy, *op. cit.,* p. 389.

[19] Trumbull, *op. cit.,* II, p. 218.

wave. On the other hand the colonial revivals may be best understood when considered as three distinct movements, each with its own peculiar characteristics. The New England awakening was confined almost exclusively to established Congregationalism, though the Baptists and Episcopalians profited indirectly. But it gave birth to no new permanent religious force, for Congregationalism continued to be the dominant religious body. The Middle Colony revival was predominantly Scotch-Irish Presbyterian, though others contributed to it, particularly in its beginnings. But here too the old pattern prevailed.

The southern awakening differed from the Middle Colony and New England awakenings in several respects. In the first place it was more interdenominational in character and requires for its understanding separate treatment in its several denominational aspects. As a whole it bore the stamp of the frontier to a greater degree than did either of the others and more closely presaged the great trans-Allegheny revivals of a generation and a half later. It also forged new and aggressive religious forces in the Baptists and the Methodists and started them on their amazing development, which was soon to make them the most numerous religious bodies in the new nation. In other words it marks the real beginning of the democratizing of religion in America.

THE PRESBYTERIAN PHASE

Generally speaking, religion and education in the southern colonies lagged behind those in the Middle and New England sections. In the South the Episcopal Church was established by law and was socially and politically dominant. Its ministers were, however, with few exceptions second-rate men and some unfortunately were actually scandalous in their lives.[20] The supply was always

---

[20] In a recent article entitled "New Light upon the History of the Church in Colonial Virginia," by G. MacLaren Brydon, in *Historical Magazine of the Protestant Episcopal Church*, June 1941, pp. 69–143, the attempt is made to refute the oft-repeated charges against the Virginia clergy. This he does by referring to the Parish Records, claiming that the record of their activity here shown presents a very different picture from that which has been given by historians. The evidence, however, from Anglican sources on the other side is so overwhelming that the new evidence he presents does not greatly change the picture.

insufficient to meet the needs of the parishes, so that rather than have no minister at all many retained incompetent men. The planter class was in control of the Church as well as the government and the churches were to a large degree maintained for their families and their retainers. Religion as a vital concern of everyday life was foreign to their desires.[21]

A well-recognized social gulf existed between the planter aristocracy and the plain people: Devereux Jarratt, who will be referred to later, states that:

A perewig in those days [his youth] was a distinguishing badge of gentle folk and when I saw a man riding the road, near our house, with a wig on, it would so alarm my fears and give me such a disagreeable feeling that I dare say I would run off as for my life.

He further states that he grew up almost completely ignorant of and indifferent to religion. To the parish church he went not once a year. Nor, said he, would he have received any benefit had he gone, for the clergyman of the parish had no concern for the spiritual well-being of his flock. The church meant little enough religiously to the socially elite; it meant next to nothing at all to the plain people.

A new social order, however, was developing in the back country. Into this region a double movement of population had set in during the early part of the eighteenth century. One stream was coming in from the older tidewater sections; at the same time a second stream was pushing down the valleys from Pennsylvania. This second contingent was composed largely of Scotch-Irish and Germans which rapidly populated the Shenandoah and adjoining valleys. Thus a new Virginia was arising, made up of people of an entirely different racial, economic and religious background. The Germans were pietists, deeply imbued with evangelical ideas; the Scotch-Irish were rigid Calvinists, and, like their co-religionists everywhere in America, were stanchly democratic in politics and

---

[21] W. M. Gewehr, *The Great Awakening in Virginia, 1740–1790*, Durham, N. C., Duke University Press: 1930, is an admirable study. This chapter leans heavily on his researches. See Chapter II for a summary of the social, moral and religious conditions in eighteenth-century Virginia.

devoted to a government by "covenant and compact" in both Church and State. Theirs was a society made up of small farmers and free labor in which no superior social caste existed. The Established Church gained little support in the back country and most of the new communities were far removed from any form of religious activity. They constituted, however, "plastic material for the revivalist" and it was the Great Awakening pushing its way southward which first brought vital religion to this new society.

The story begins with the more or less accidental contact made by the New Side Presbyterians from the Middle Colonies with a peculiar religious movement under way in Hanover county, Virginia. In the winter of 1742–43, William Robinson, a former student in William Tennent's Log College, was sent by the New Brunswick Presbytery to visit communities in western Virginia. Already there were four Old Side anti-revivalistic ministers settled in that region, belonging to the Donegal Presbytery. Robinson's visit, therefore, to this region produced little result. East of the mountains, however, he found the way prepared by a recent visit of Whitefield (1739), but especially through an unusual revival under the leadership of laymen which he found under way in Hanover county.

The most prominent leader of this movement was a certain Samuel Morris, a planter, who seemed to have had no Church or religious affiliation.[22] Morris, with others of his neighbors, having become interested in certain religious books which fell into their hands, began to hold gatherings in their homes where passages from these books were read. Among them were some of Whitefield's sermons, Bunyan's *Pilgrim's Progress,* and Luther's *Commentary on Galatians.* Others now followed Morris' example and a religious concern began to spread throughout the region.[23] The

---

[22] Gewehr, *op. cit.,* pp. 47–51.

[23] Accounts of these happenings may be found in David Rice, *Memoirs,* found in R. H. Bishop, *An Outline History of the Church in the State of Kentucky,* Lexington, Ky.: 1824, pp. 34–35; Alexander, *op. cit.,* Chapter xvii contains a letter from Samuel Davies to Mr. Bellamy (pp. 220–32) giving an account of the beginning of the Hanover revival. This contains Morris' account of his part in the movement. See other references in Gewehr, *op. cit.,* notes, pp. 47–50. W. H. Foote, *Sketches of Virginia* (first series, Philadelphia, 1850; second series, Philadelphia, 1855), contain extracts from contemporary sources.

homes of the leaders now became too small, and "Reading houses" were erected to accommodate the throngs attracted. Morris states that he was invited to read sermons at several places at considerable distances, "and by this means a concern was propagated." This caused such a stir that the authorities began to take notice of it and the leaders were summoned to court to give an account of their activities, and to declare to what denomination they belonged. Knowing little of the denominations except Quakers, and knowing the name of Luther as a noted reformer, and since his books had been of service to them they declared themselves Lutherans. Such was the situation when William Robinson appeared on the scene.

Robinson's visit to Hanover county and his awakening type of preaching started a wave of revivalism among those whose religious concern already had been aroused. This marks the beginning of revivalistic Presbyterianism in the South. Robinson was followed by a succession of revivalist itinerants from the New Side Presbyteries in the Middle Colonies, among them John Blair and John Roan, both Log College graduates. Later also came Samuel Finley, Samuel Blair, and Gilbert Tennent. Roan was an enthusiastic and irrepressible Irishman, and probably being unfamiliar with the religious regulations in Virginia and the provisions of the Act of Toleration, failed to secure a license. His vigorous denunciation of the Established Church and its clergy soon brought down upon him not only the wrath of the Episcopal clergy, but also the arm of the law. Governor Gooch, whose attitude toward the Presbyterians who had settled in western Virginia had been favorable, having promised them protection in the exercise of their religion, now took a strong stand against the New Light Presbyterians and advised the Grand Jury to use all possible means to suppress them.

The Presbyterians in the western counties had little inclination and less opportunity to proselyte Established Church people, since very few were to be found in that region, but the New Lights were making serious inroads among them in Hanover and adjoining counties. To make matters worse for the New Light Presbyterians the Old Side or anti-revivalist Presbyterians now began to send missionaries east of the mountains who joined the ranks of their enemies, denouncing them as deluded men and not true Presbyterians. In spite of all this opposition the revival continued to spread and in 1748 Samuel Davies was called to settle among them as pastor of the congregations in Hanover and adjoining counties.[24]

For the next eleven years (1748–59) the story of revivalistic Presbyterianism in Virginia and North Carolina centers about the name of Samuel Davies. At the time of his coming to Virginia (1748) Davies was twenty-five years of age, a graduate of Samuel Blair's Log College and a member of the New Side Presbytery of New Castle, having been ordained as an evangelist two years previously. Accompanying him as an assistant in his work was John Rodgers, also a graduate of Samuel Blair's school and a licentiate of the New Castle Presbytery. The Governor had issued a proclamation the previous year calling on all magistrates as far as possible "to suppress and prohibit . . . all itinerate preachers. . . ." Previous to entering upon a six-weeks' preaching tour the year before, Davies had secured a license permitting him to preach in four meeting houses in and about Hanover. When, however, application was made for a license for Rodgers, the General Court refused to grant it, and Rodgers was compelled to leave the colony. Inconsistent as it was, within six months after the refusal of a license for Rodgers, Davies was granted the right to add three other meeting houses, each in a different county, to his "circuit." Within this region there were eight Established Church clergymen and, as was to be expected, they put forth every effort in their power to keep the "New Lights" from gaining a foothold within their parishes.

In dealing with this delicate situation Davies displayed a wisdom beyond his years. He made no attempt to win converts by preaching down the Established Church or its clergy. Rather it was irreligion he attacked, stating on many occasions that he had not come "to Presbyterianize the colony" but to advance the cause of Christianity. Likewise he was always careful to keep within the law. As a preacher he soon gained an enviable reputation among

[24] Gewehr, *op. cit.*, pp. 5–67.

all classes and the cause of revivalistic Presbyterianism thrived throughout this large region under his supervision. Davies possessed the unusual gift of appealing to people of widely varied culture and intelligence. Sprague declares that he was "alike acceptable to all, from the most polished gentlemen to the most ignorant African slave." [25] Many things, seemingly extravagant, have been said of his eloquence, until one begins to turn the pages of his printed sermons. Even today they possess persuasiveness, solid content, logical development, and beauty of style.[26] In that time when every-day life was far more precarious than it is today, it was but natural that preachers, and especially revivalists, should dwell upon the imminence of death and the uncertainty of life. As a revivalist it is said that Davies preached "as a dying man to dying men." One brief quotation from a sermon entitled " A Time of Unusual Sickness and Mortality Improved" will illustrate how he utilized such materials:

> As I am a mortal myself, so are my dear people; they are dying fast about me, and dropping into the grave from between my hands. Above twenty that were wont to mingle with us in this assembly, and to hear the word from my lips, have been hurried into the eternal world in a few days. . . . Alas! Is it possible that there should be one vain, trifling, thoughtless mind, in a religious assembly in such circumstances? [27]

The bitter opposition which the New Light Presbyterians met from the Established Church clergy and colonial officialdom made it necessary for Davies to assume the leadership in a fight for religious toleration. The struggle centered about three questions: (1) Did the Act of Toleration of 1689 apply to Virginia; (2) did

---

[25] Sprague, op. cit., III, p. 141.

[26] It has been frequently stated that Patrick Henry took Samuel Davies as his model of eloquence. He was a member of the Episcopal church at Hanover, of which his uncle, Rev. Patrick Henry, was the rector, one of the bitterest of Davies' opponents. As a boy Patrick Henry often drove his mother to hear Samuel Davies preach and when he grew to young manhood he attended Davies' preaching services on his own initiative. Two of his sisters became members of Davies' congregation. He often spoke of Davies as the greatest orator he had ever heard and is said to have ascribed his success as a speaker to Davies' example. (George H. Bost, Samuel Davies [typewritten thesis, University of Chicago, 1942], Chapter VIII, "Preacher and Poet.")

[27] Davies, Sermons, 1864 ed., Vol. III, pp. 229–59; also quoted in Bost, op. cit.

the New Light Presbyterians qualify as a legitimate Presbyterian body; and (3) did the practice of itinerating as carried on by Davies and his helpers disqualify them for receiving a license under the act? The question as to whether the Act of Toleration applied to Virginia was raised again and again in one form or another during the early years of Davies' residence in Virginia. In applying for licenses for three additional meeting houses soon after his arrival, Davies was confronted by the Attorney General of Virginia, Peyton Randolph, who argued that the Toleration Act did not extend to Virginia. Davies was present at the General Court and acted as his own attorney, having made a careful study of the law in preparation for the occasion. He contended that if the Toleration Act did not extend to Virginia, neither did the Act of Uniformity. Both, however, he argued, had been received into the body of Virginia laws, since specific acts had been passed by the Virginia Legislature permitting dissenters to hold meetings according to the requirements of the Toleration Act. His argument convinced the majority of the Court and his point was won.

The next problem was to secure a broad enough interpretation of the Toleration Act as applied to Virginia, so as not to hamper dissenter activity. The Rev. Patrick Henry, the Church minister in Hanover, attacked the New Lights on the ground that they were not a real Presbyterian Church, but a schismatic sect with no claim to any rights under the Toleration Act. This Davies effectively answered. How many meeting houses a dissenting minister might serve, however, was a far more serious question, for the continued success of the New Light Presbyterians in Virginia depended upon how that question was answered.[28] To further his cause Davies secured the assistance of some of the most influential dissenters in England, particularly Philip Doddridge and Benjamin Avery, who gave him not only advice but interceded with the authorities in his behalf. The commissary, Thomas Dawson, was not entirely unfriendly and at least showed on some

---

[28] Letters from Doddridge and Avery to Davies are found in W. H. Foote, *Sketches of North Carolina, Historical and Biographical*, New York: 1846 (first series), pp. 174–75, 213; other letters bearing on the question are found in William S. Perry, *Historical Collections Relating to the American Colonial Church*, Vol. I, *Virginia*, 1873.

occasions an attitude of fairness. Davies also communicated directly with the Bishop of London. In writing to the Bishop of London in 1752,[29] Commissary Dawson stated:

I am not against granting Dissenters a legal Indulgence. If it be asked, "What is a legal indulgence," I answer a Teacher's Settlement within the limits of a parish and a License to have as many Meeting houses, as the convenience of the people within the said limits may require.

In the fall of 1753 Davies, with Gilbert Tennent, sailed for the British Isles on a money-raising mission for the College of New Jersey. Though kept busy with travel and preaching in England and Scotland, Davies found time to give to the cause of dissenter rights in Virginia. One of his most effective helpers was Samuel Stennett, a leading English Baptist minister who seems to have enjoyed large influence at Court. He was advised by an influential dissenter committee to petition the King in Council, and they assisted him in drawing up such a petition which was sent to Virginia to secure signatures. But it was never presented. Davies' principal accomplishment in England in this regard was in gaining powerful friends for the cause and acquainting them with the situation in Virginia.[30]

On his return to Virginia Davies again took up his labors in his Virginia parish. Meanwhile other helpers had been sent to aid in the expanding work, while a third visit of Whitefield to Virginia in January 1755, stirred once more the revival fire. There were now six New Light congregations in Virginia and all of them were increasing in numbers and interest. They were now ready to take the next natural step in organized Presbyterianism and the formation of the Hanover Presbytery followed in December 1755, with Davies as the first moderator. This is appropriately called by Foote the mother of Presbyteries in the South.

---

[29] Perry, *op. cit.*, p. 385.

[30] Gewehr, *op. cit.*, p. 91, states that Davies ·secured from the Attorney General an opinion favorable to every one of his contentions regarding the application of the Toleration Act to Virginia. This is evidently an error, as Davies in his Journal makes no mention of securing such an opinion. John H. Rice, *Memoir of Samuel Davies,* Boston: 1832, is probably the source for the statement. See Bost, *op. cit.,* Chapter v, "To England, Ambassador to Nassau State and Virginia Dissenters."

During the last four years of Davies' residence in Virginia the colony was in a constant state of alarm because of the French and Indian War. The fact that the brunt of any Indian attack would fall upon the predominantly Presbyterian population in the western counties gave poignancy to Davies' eloquent support of the war. That Davies' support in this crisis was appreciated by the colonial authorities is indicated by the fact that in 1758 the Governor of Virginia assured the Hanover Presbytery that he would exert himself in applying the Act of Toleration so as to "secure the peaceable enjoyment of its immunities to all his majesty's subjects who conform thereto." [31] No longer was there denunciation of Presbyterian itinerating, and Davies and the other Presbyterian clergy now preached where they pleased without molestation. Thus the war aided in securing a larger toleration, not alone for Presbyterians but for all dissenting bodies as well.

The French and Indian War sermons of Samuel Davies constitute a body of patriotic eloquence unequalled in sermonic literature. How applicable to the present situation are these words taken from a sermon preached by Samuel Davies at Hanover, Virginia, on January 1, 1757:

Brethren, while we are surrounded by the terrors of war, let us learn our own degeneracy, mourn over it, and cry for the exertion of that power which alone can form us anew, and repair these wastes and desolations. The present war indeed . . . is just, is unavoidable; and consequently our duty. But how corrupt must this world be, when it is even our duty to weaken and destroy our fellow men as much as we can? How corrupt must this world be, when peace itself, the sweetest of all blessings, is become an evil, and war is to be chosen before it? When it is become our duty to shed blood, when martial valor, or courage to destroy man, who was made in the image of God, is become a virtue? When it has become glorious to kill men! and when we are obliged to treat a whole nation as a gang of robbers and murderers, and bring them to punishment? This certainly shows that they are degenerated creatures; and as they share in the same nature with us, we must draw the same conclusion concerning ourselves. Let

---

[31] The MSS. minutes of the Hanover Presbytery covering these years are in the Library of Union Theological Seminary, Richmond, Virginia. See Minutes for 1758.

us therefore humble ourselves, and mourn in dust and ashes before the Lord; let us lament the general depravity of the world.

In the year 1759 Samuel Davies became the fourth president of the College of New Jersey, succeeding Jonathan Edwards, whose death from smallpox inoculation the year before had left the infant college in a precarious condition. Davies had been persuaded with difficulty to accept, having at first declined, stating that he believed his work in Virginia more important. The painful schism among the Presbyterians had been just healed (1758) and it was necessary that a president should be chosen who could receive the united support of the whole Church. Davies seemed to be that man. Though but thirty-six years of age, and in spite of the fact that he had given most of his life to backwoods communities, Davies was probably the most celebrated and without doubt the most eloquent Presbyterian divine in the colonies. His going was sorely lamented by his devoted Virginia parishioners, yet the work he had come to do was now largely done. Southern Presbyterianism was now firmly established, ready to move forward in an orderly way according to the usual Presbyterian pattern. The Presbyterian revival had centered in Hanover and surrounding counties in central Virginia. In the succeeding years its center was more and more shifted toward the frontier following the Scotch-Irish as they pushed their way westward.

THE BAPTIST PHASE

Just five years previous to Samuel Davies' departure from Virginia two Separate Baptist preachers from Connecticut, Shubal Stearns and Daniel Marshall, settled with their families on Opeguoin Creek in Berkeley county, in what is now West Virginia. Both had been converted under Whitefield's preaching and they brought with them the fervor and spirit of that master revivalist. Both originally had been Congregationalists, but having become convinced of the futility of infant baptism they withdrew and joined the Baptists. Neither had had the advantage of a formal education, but they were men of superior natural ability and sound judgment. There were already several congregations of *Regular* Baptists in Virginia, but Stearns and Marshall soon found that they were out of sympathy with their revivalistic preaching.[32] This was probably the principal reason for their leaving Virginia within a year and locating in Guilford county, North Carolina, where they settled on Sandy Creek. The coming of these representatives of the revivalistic Baptists into the Southern Colonies marks the beginning of a new phase in the development of the Great Awakening.

The Presbyterians with their educated ministry and elaborate creedal demands had failed to reach the great mass of the plain people. The *Separate* Baptists, however, with their uneducated and unsalaried ministry, their novel type of preaching, appealing primarily to the emotions, were well suited to the needs and mental capacities of the lower social and economic classes. Extreme emotional revivalism always has succeeded best among people of little education. But the presence of even a few people of higher educational attainments will tend to restrain the emotionalism of a large concourse of the less educated. The Presbyterian congregations usually contained a few people of this type, while the minister himself was always a man of some attainment educationally. Such restraining influences were far more likely to be absent from among the Baptists.[33]

---

[32] The best account of the Baptist phase of the Southern revival is Gewehr, *op. cit.*, Chapter v. See also W. W. Sweet, *Religion on the American Frontier: The Baptists,* New York: 1931, Chapter I. Robert B. Semple, *A History of the Rise and Progress of the Baptists in Virginia,* Richmond: 1810, Chapter I is a contemporary account by a participant. For other sources see Gewehr and Sweet above.

[33] In his discussion of revivalism from its sociological and psychological standpoints Davenport advances three laws. The first is that of *sympathetic likemindedness.* We are all more or less subject to the influences of suggestion, imagination and emotion. When these tendencies are held in check by an educated and cool-headed leadership "we have a population under control." When, on the other hand, the leadership is highly undisciplined emotionally; when, for instance, a revivalist preacher gives way to his own deep feeling; when tears stream down his face as he speaks, shouting and gesticulating wildly, the hearers, if unrestrained, are likely to respond in an equally extravagant way. The second law he suggests is the *Law of Spread.* One weeping individual in a revival will start those around him to weeping until the whole audience is overcome with emotion. From a single center deep emotionalism may spread in every direction. A third law is that of *restraint.* Emotionalism spreads with the utmost abandon unless there is restraint of some kind. A number of controlled individuals, people accustomed to subordinate feeling to rational considerations, will act as bulwarks against the advancing tide of

As Hanover county was the center of an expanding Presbyterianism in the Southern Colonies, so Sandy Creek became the living center of the Separate Baptists. From a church of sixteen members formed by the Stearns and Marshall families at Sandy Creek, the congregation grew within a relatively short time to more than six hundred. Out from Sandy Creek also went Baptist evangelists whose preaching stirred surrounding communities, and new churches were formed in other localities. Daniel Marshall was ordained the minister over the Abbotts Creek church thirty miles away and other preachers were "raised up," such as Dutton Lane, James Reed, and Samuel Harriss, whose itinerating through the back country brought religion for the first time to many a neglected neighborhood. John Waller and Samuel Harriss were among the most successful of the Baptist revivalists. Waller baptized more than two thousand persons, assisted in forming eighteen churches and for many years had the pastoral care of five congregations. Harriss, who had been a man of influence in his community before his conversion and was better educated than the average Baptist preacher of the time, gained such a reputation that people came for miles around to attend his meetings. The long list of men who gave themselves to the work of spreading the Baptist gospel throughout Virginia and the Carolinas, without compensation or promise of earthly reward, is, to say the least, astonishing.[34]

Because of bitter opposition the number of Baptist churches at first increased slowly in Virginia, but in North Carolina where there were no such restrictions their growth was more rapid. Stearns, who remained at Sandy Creek as the minister, itinerated

---

imitation. See F. M. Davenport, *Primitive Traits in Religious Revivals, A Study in Mental and Social Evolution*, New York: 1905, Chapter I. For an excellent brief putting of the Davenport thesis see Elizabeth K. Nottingham, *Methodism and the Frontier, Indiana Proving Ground*, New York: 1941, Chapter IX.

[34] James B. Taylor, *Virginia Baptist Preachers*, Series I and II, 3rd edition, New York: 1860. These two volumes contain short biographies of 228 ministers, few of whom were men of any formal education. The Baptists did not consider learning necessary for the gospel ministry. "Persons endowed with a strong intellect, capable of taking in high and sublime ideas, and prying into mysterious and intricate subjects, and given to know his dear Son, whom to know is life eternal, the ministry may be entered even without learning" (I, 74).

widely throughout the surrounding regions and there were soon several churches, each with its branches in adjoining communities. "Sandy Creek Church," to use the words of Morgan Edwards,

. . . is the mother of all the Separate Baptists. From this Zion went forth the word, and great was the company of those who published it. This church in seventeen years, had spread her branches southward as far as Georgia; eastward to the sea and Chesapeake bay; northward to the waters of the Patomac. It in seventeen years became mother, grand-mother and great-grand-mother, to 42 churches, and from which sprang 125 ministers many of whom are ordained, and support the sacred character as well as any set of clergy in America.[35]

After 1770 the growth of the Separate Baptists in Virginia was little short of phenomenal. At the formation of the first Baptist Association in Virginia in 1771 there were fourteen churches and 1335 members. Two years later the rapid increase of churches led to the division of the Association into Northern and Southern districts with a total membership of more than four thousand. Twenty years later they had become a numerous and respectable body while their zeal "was less mixed with enthusiasm" and their piety more rational.

For a generation or more, however, the revivalistic Baptists were a despised people. The strange mannerisms of their preachers, their odd whoops and whining tones together with the emotional extravagances which took place in their meetings aroused disgust and contempt. One man stated that, "he had rather go to hell than be obliged to hear a Baptist in order to go to heaven." Unlike the Presbyterian evangelists the Baptist preachers gave little or no heed to the law requiring the licensing of dissenting ministers and meeting houses. As a result the heavy hand of religious persecution fell upon them. Often mobs, frequently headed by the law-enforcing officials themselves and encouraged by Anglican parsons, broke up their meetings. The following account is taken from the experiences of Elder David

---

[35] Morgan Edwards, *History of the Baptists in North Carolina*, quoted in David Benedict, *A General History of the Baptist Denomination in America*, etc., New York; 1848, p. 685.

Barrow, a Virginia Baptist preacher who later was to have a large part in the spread of the Baptists into Kentucky. Having been invited by a gentleman to preach at his house near the mouth of the James River, Barrow and another minister arrived at the scene of their appointment only to be met by a gang of "well dressed men" who came upon the stage, which had been erected under some trees, and sang an obscene song instead of the hymn which had just been announced. They then seized Barrow and plunged him into the water, in ridicule of the Baptist practice of immersion, pressing him into the mud until he was almost drowned. The assembly was shocked and women shrieked, but no one ventured to interfere "for about twenty stout fellows were engaged in this horrid business." Without permitting the preacher to change his wet and muddy garments he was driven off "by these enraged churchmen." [36]

Opposition came not only from the "churchmen," but from many rough characters of the lower classes, who joined in it unaware that the Baptist gospel was intended primarily for their uplift. The most serious threat to the Baptists, however, came from the law-enforcing officials. Preachers were arrested and imprisoned on the charge that they were "raising sedition and stirring up strife." It was whispered about among the upper classes that Baptists were dangerous radicals and once they were strong enough they intended to fall upon the inhabitants and take possession of the country. The courts and the arresting officials defended their action, when Baptist preachers were arrested, by stating that they were not molested because of religion but because they were disturbers of the peace and were responsible for calling unlawful assemblies which took the people from the farms and plantations, thereby encouraging "habits of idleness and neglect of their necessary business." These were the same arguments which were used in New England against the revivalists a generation before and indicate that the revival was reaching the lower economic classes.

Since the Baptists held as their first great principle the complete separation of Church and State they could not recognize any right on the part of the civil authorities to regulate their activities.

---

[36] Taylor, *op. cit.*, I, pp. 163–64.

Anything less than complete religious freedom they refused to accept. The fact that the Anglicans were their chief persecutors led them to make unrestrained and exaggerated accusations against the establishment and its clergy. The times, however, favored the Baptists and despite all opposition they continued to grow. The spirit of independence was everywhere on the increase. Throughout the colonies the irksome commercial restrictions were being defied as contrary to the natural rights which belonged to men; for the same reason Baptists refused to heed the laws restraining religion. The Presbyterians in Virginia under Samuel Davies' leadership fought for the rights of dissenters under the law; the Baptists went a long step further and refused to recognize the validity of any law which restrained freedom of religion.[37]

THE METHODIST PHASE

Methodist historians have been prone to consider the beginnings of Methodism in America as an isolated movement, with little or no relationship to, or dependence upon, other contemporary religious forces, a weakness common to denominational historians. They have stressed the contributions Methodists have made rather than the debt they owe to others. But Methodism was far from being an isolated movement. Rather its introduction into the colonies came as the last phase of the great colonial awakenings. Its center was in Virginia, where the Presbyterians and Baptists had prepared the way. John Wesley sent his first missionaries, Joseph Pilmore and Richard Boardman, to New York and Philadelphia in 1769. Of much greater importance from the standpoint of the establishment of American Methodism, however, was the activity of immigrant lay preachers, such as Robert Strawbridge, and the influence exerted by the Anglican evangelical rector of Bath Parish, in Dinwiddie county, Virginia, Devereux Jarratt.

Jarratt was a native of Virginia whose family, like that o. many

---

[37] W. T. Thom, *The Struggle for Religious Freedom in Virginia: The Baptists,* Baltimore: 1900; together with H. J. Eckenrode, *The Separation of Church and State in Virginia,* Richmond: 1909, furnish a full account of the part played by the Baptists in the struggle for religious freedom in Virginia. Gewehr, *op. cit.,* pp. 122–37; 187–218, is an excellent summary.

others in that colony, though nominally churchmen, had slight attachment to the parish church. Like many other Virginians of his class he had been brought up almost completely ignorant of, and indifferent to, religion. Having prepared himself to teach, he obtained a school on the Virginia frontier and there fell under the influence of a New Light Presbyterian family. Here he entered into a definite religious experience and determined to prepare himself for the ministry. Since his conversion had come about through Presbyterian influence he naturally was drawn to that communion. Later the Established Church seemed to offer larger opportunities, and, since his family had been remotely attached to that Church, he sought ordination in that body. This he secured by journeying to England whence he returned to Virginia in search of a vacant parish. Finally in 1743 he was received by the vestry of Bath parish in Dinwiddie county, in south central Virginia, and there he remained, a faithful and indefatigable spiritual shepherd, until his death in 1801.

Jarratt was far from being a typical Virginia parson. Being thoroughly imbued with evangelical zeal he began to preach those doctrines which tended to bring home to the people a sense of their lost condition. He laid great stress upon the necessity of conversion and urged his hearers to rely upon Christ for salvation. More than that he exhorted believers to be careful to maintain good works and to go on to perfection. In other words he was in full harmony with the revivalists, and was himself a successful revivalist. Such preaching brought immediate results. The three churches in his parish were crowded with new hearers and for the first time many of the poorer people were attracted. Some of them had never before spoken to a clergyman. Meetings were also held in groves and in private houses. News of these happenings traveled far and near and his services were crowded with strangers from neighboring parishes. The Lee family furnishes an interesting example of the widespread influence exerted by Jarratt. Though living in an adjoining parish they frequently heard Jarratt preach, and eventually the entire family was converted. Among the Lee children was a son Jesse, who later became one of the most capable of the early Methodist preachers in America, introducing Methodism into New England. In 1800 he came within one vote of being chosen a Methodist Bishop.[38]

Instead of receiving encouragement and help from his fellow clergymen, Jarratt was scorned by them and dubbed "an enthusiast, fanatic, visionary, dissenter, Presbyterian, mad-man." "No man," said Jarratt, "was ever more cordially abhorred than I was by the clergy in general." He was frequently threatened "with writs and prosecutions" for breach of canon law order. One particularly irate clergyman called him to book for the breach of the 71st Canon which prohibited preaching in private houses. To his remonstrance Jarratt replied that,

if to preach in a private house, or even on any unconsecrated ground was a breach of canonical order and regularity, then we were all involved in the same condemnation, for I know not that any clergyman in Virginia ever scrupled to transgress that canon for the sake of forty shillings. This was the legal fee for a funeral sermon. . . . Moreover, I knew that my testy brother was very fond of cards, dice, tables etc., which was expressly forbidden us, by the 75th canon. I made free to ask, if it was not as criminal, and more so, to break the 75th as the 71st canon? From that time I heard no more of the canons.[39]

In 1773 Jarratt had his first contact with the Methodists when Robert Williams, one of Wesley's lay preachers who had come to America with Wesley's consent, called at Jarratt's house. Williams assured Jarratt that the Methodists were "true members of the Church of England"; that "their design was to build up and not divide the church"; that "the preachers did not assume the office of priest" and did not attempt to administer the sacraments, but were dependent for them upon the parish clergy. Their sole object was to call sinners to repentance and to form societies in which vital religion might be cultivated. With such assurances Jarratt from that time forward joined heartily with the Methodists in the promotion of their work and for the next ten

---

[38] L. M. Lee, *The Life and Times of the Rev. Jesse Lee*, Louisville: 1848, pp. 28–32.
[39] Jarratt's *Autobiography*, Baltimore: 1806, pp. 96–97.

years gave them full cooperation. Dating from Williams' visit to Jarratt the revival which had been in progress in Bath parish was merged with that of the Methodists and soon spread throughout the surrounding counties in Virginia and across the southern boundary into North Carolina.

Shortly after Jarratt began his cooperation with the Methodists he wrote John Wesley urging that he send "a minister of the Church of England" to be stationed in a nearby vacant parish in order that the expanding work might have the supervision of Church ministers. Only one other Anglican clergyman in Virginia gave any assistance, and he, a Mr. A. McRoberts, soon left the Church to join the Presbyterians. The fullest account of the revival which now swept through this whole region has been left by Jarratt himself. Francis Asbury and Thomas Rankin also have left contemporary accounts.[40] The high-water mark of the revival was reached in 1775–76. George Shardford, one of Wesley's missionaries, had come to America in 1773 and had been assigned to the circuit embracing Jarratt's parish in 1775. Of all Wesley's preachers in America Shardford was probably the most effective and became the chief instrument in the revival which now swept the region.

During the whole winter [1775–76] Jarratt states, the spirit of the Lord was poured out in a manner we had not seen before. In almost every assembly might be seen signal instances of Divine power, more especially in the meetings of the classes.

Many who formerly had been indifferent to religion and the Church now flocked to hear not only Jarratt and the traveling preachers but the exhorters and leaders as well. The revival spread through most of the circuits and covered a region of between four and five hundred miles in circumference. Through neighborhood after neighborhood the flame spread, and "ran from family to family so that within four weeks several hundred found peace

---

[40] *The Heart of Asbury's Journal,* Ezra S. Tipple (Ed.), New York: 1904, Vol. I, pp. 228–30. The most recent study of the beginnings of Methodism in America, based on all the available sources is W. W. Sweet, *Men of Zeal: The Romance of American Methodist Beginnings:* New York, 1935. This study is fully documented with a bibliography.

with God." The people reached were of all classes and ages and included many blacks.

When Wesley's assistant, Thomas Rankin, visited Virginia in the summer of 1775 he made with Jarratt a tour of the southern part of Virginia and into North Carolina. The great assemblies and the meetings held under the trees were impressive. He speaks of preaching "at a preaching-house near Mr. J's" and remarks "what a work God is working in this corner of Mr. J's parish!" So overwhelming was the demand for preaching that Rankin preached almost to the point of exhaustion. Jesse Lee, who witnessed many a revival scene during this year, wrote that he could not describe half of what he saw, heard or felt. Testifying as to the results of the revival Jarratt stated that he had not heard of one apostate, and many profligates had been "effectually and lastingly changed into pious, uniform Christians."

The tangible results of the revival may be seen by consulting the membership records of the Methodist circuits for those years. In 1774 there were but two Methodist circuits in Virginia, the Norfolk and the Brunswick, with a combined membership of 291; the next year there were three circuits with a membership of 935; in 1776 there were five circuits in Virginia and the adjoining counties of North Carolina, the Brunswick circuit alone having 1611 members. In 1777 there were six Virginia circuits and one in North Carolina with a total membership of 4379. In this year the entire membership of all Methodist circuits in America totalled 6968. This means that two thirds of all the Methodists in America were to be found in the immediate region of Devereux Jarratt's parish. Here indeed was the cradle of American Methodism.

These Virginia and North Carolina Methodists were entirely dependent upon Devereux Jarratt for the Sacraments, for none of the Methodist preachers were ordained men. To meet this demand Jarratt travelled continually, visiting in all twenty-nine counties in the two colonies. At the same time he was preaching regularly in the three churches of his own parish. During the course of the Revolution, when Asbury was unable to visit Virginia because of his refusal to take the oath, Jarratt acted as the superintendent of Methodist activities.[41] Following the close of the Revolution when the American Methodists were in process of being formed into an independent Church, Jarratt felt that he had been deceived and expressed resentment at the separation. But after the lapse of a few years his bitterness was gone and in a letter to Thomas Coke (April 19, 1791) he expressed admiration for Asbury, whom he called "my justly admired friend."

It is of course fruitless to conjecture what might have happened had there been more Devereux Jarratts among the Episcopal clergy of America. Perhaps there might not have been an independent Methodist Church. On the other hand it might be asked, Could Methodism have become the moral and religious force in America if it had remained an integral part of the Protestant Episcopal Church, even if there had been a large number of Episcopal clergymen of Jarratt's kind?

IV

THE BY-PRODUCTS OF THE GREAT AWAKENING

THE IMMEDIATE effect of the Great Awakening on organized religion in the American colonies has been noted in the foregoing discussions of its several phases. That it added greatly to Church membership and strengthened the practical influence of Christianity upon colonial society there can be no doubt. But it also sowed the seed of dissension and controversy. Fortunately the division in Presbyterianism caused by the revivalistic methods of the Log College evangelists was soon healed. Likewise by the end of the century the Regular and Separate Baptists had largely

---

[41] *Minutes of Conference*, I (1782), p. 17. Two recently discovered MSS. letters of Devereux Jarratt's (Dromgoole papers, University of North Carolina) dated March 31, 1785 and March 22, 1788, written to Edward Dromgoole, a Virginia Methodist preacher, show that Jarratt's anger against the Methodists was short-lived. In the first letter, written within five months after the Methodists separated from the Episcopalians, he states: "I have suffered no change at all, I love and honour those who fear the Lord, let their station in life be what it will; but my peculiar attachment has been to the Methodists." Further he states that his not being present at the Methodist Conference was not due to "want of inclination" but to the fact that neither of the Superintendents had invited him.

overcome their differences and, as in the case of the Presbyterians, the revivalistic emphasis triumphed in the union. The same thing may be said, to a limited degree, of the Dutch Reformed controversy caused by the Frelinghuysen revival. The controversy that refused to be healed, however, was that in New England Congregationalism. The reason was that here, though starting as a conflict over revivalistic methods, it soon developed into a battle between two diametrically opposite schools of Christian thought.

Even before the revival began there were evidences that Arminian ideas were becoming more and more current in New England. The Calvinistic insistence that man had nothing to do with his own salvation had by the time of the third generation brought a reaction, and man's part in conversion began to be increasingly stressed. Especially was this true after the widespread adoption of the Half-Way Covenant, and the use of human means as an aid to conversion became a recognized practice. This movement in America was stimulated by a similar trend among non-conformists in England and books dealing with the Arminian points of view began to circulate in the colonies. This "dreadful increase of Arminianism and other Errors in the Land, among ministers and people" aroused the defenders of orthodoxy. The Arminian position was taken very naturally by the extreme opponents of the revival and as their opposition waxed stronger and stronger their doctrinal views became increasingly anti-Calvinistic. The orthodox Calvinists were themselves divided over issues which came out of the revival. The Old Calvinists held that an unconverted man by using the means of grace, such as Bible reading and attending public worship, was thereby placing himself in a position whereby God would the more likely bring about his salvation. The Edwardians, or the New Divinity champions, while admitting that men ought to use the means of grace, held that as long as they remained unconverted while using those means they were growing worse rather than better.[42]

The out-and-out Arminians or Liberals eventually became Unitarian and had their principal following in eastern Massachu-

---

[42] Williston Walker, *A History of the Congregational Churches in the United States*, New York: 1894, pp. 290–92.

setts, particularly in and about Boston; the Edwardians made almost a clean sweep of western Massachusetts and Connecticut; while those representing Old Calvinist views were a scattered remnant. Such was the theological situation in New England following the great revival and, as a consequence, Congregationalism was in a turmoil for more than a half century.[43]

Previous to the Great Awakening there had been established but three colleges in the American colonies: Harvard in 1636, the College of William and Mary in 1693 and Yale College in 1701. The two New England colleges were Congregational foundations; that of William and Mary was Anglican. This gave the two Established Churches a monopoly on higher education in the colonies for the first one hundred years. None of the dissenting bodies made any attempt to found colleges until well along in the eighteenth century for the reason that none of them was strong enough for such an enterprise.

The revival, however, changed the whole dissenter situation and the Presbyterians and Baptists particularly became numerous and widely distributed bodies. As was to be expected the Presbyterians were the most active of the revivalistic Churches in promoting higher education and for the next century they were to be the American college founders *par excellence*. William Tennent's Log College was not only the mother of Princeton, but it was also the precursor of a succession of other Log Colleges conducted by Presbyterian preachers along the line of the advancing American frontier. Many of these academies and classical schools developed into colleges, once colonial ecclesiastical restrictions were removed. Thus what are today Hampden-Sydney College and Washington and Lee University began as New Light Presbyterian academies in colonial Virginia, each sending out its preachers and teachers to spread the revival into new communities. Nowhere did revivalism and education go more consistently hand in hand than among the New Light Presbyterians.[44]

---

[43] Chapter VIII, "The Great Awakening and the Rise of Theological Parties," in Walker, *op. cit.*, pp. 251–308, is the best brief summary of these years in New England Congregationalism.

[44] See Gewehr, *op. cit.*, Chapter IX, "The Founding of Colleges," pp. 219–34.

Of the six eighteenth-century colonial educational foundations the College of Philadelphia was the only one not specifically under denominational control. Its beginnings, however, were definitely related to the revival. On Whitefield's second visit to Philadelphia in April 1740 he found the principal Philadelphia pulpits closed against him and he was forced to preach in the streets and fields. This led a group of his friends and admirers, among them Benjamin Franklin, to start a fund for the erection of a building which was to serve the double purpose of a Charity School and a preaching place for Whitefield and for free preaching generally. By the autumn of that year the building, one hundred by seventy feet, the largest in Philadelphia, was far enough along, though roofless, to permit Whitefield to preach within its walls, and on his subsequent visits it was his principal preaching place in Philadelphia. For a number of years it was used by Gilbert Tennent's New Light Presbyterian congregation. For several reasons the use of the building as a Charity School failed to materialize, and it was not until 1749 that a group of men under Franklin's leadership purchased the building and started the Academy which eventually grew into the College of Philadelphia. Thus it was Whitefield's influence, though rather remotely indirect, which started the movement which developed into what is now the University of Pennsylvania.[45]

Whitefield also played a part in the permanent establishment of the College of New Jersey and Dartmouth College. Both institutions were the legitimate children of the revival. The College of New Jersey was begun by the New Side Presbyterians the very year (1746) William Tennent's Log College ceased to exist as the result of the death of its founder. It was established to carry on the work that the Log College had so well begun, to train a revivalistic ministry. Its founders were the principal revivalists among the Presbyterians, several of them graduates of the Log College. Its permanent location at Princeton was made possible by the funds gathered by Gilbert Tennent and Samuel Davies in England and Scotland. The sum which they thus secured— £3,200—was used for the erection of Nassau Hall. Their success

---

[45] Cheyney, *op. cit.*, Chapter II, "The Foundation."

in that enterprise was partly due to Whitefield's help. Whitefield's wide acquaintance among the nobility of England enabled him to be of great assistance in any money-raising enterprise, a service which he delighted to render.

The deputation sent out by Eleazar Wheelock to solicit funds for his Indian Charity School in Connecticut, made up of the Indian preacher Samson Occom and Nathaniel Whitaker, was probably suggested by Whitefield. On their arrival in London it was Whitefield who, to use Samson Occom's words, "took Mr. Whetaker and I in his Coach and Introduc'd us to my Lord Dartmouth," who "Mr. Whitefield says is a Christian Lord and an unCommon one." It was Whitefield's cooperation which made the mission the most successful one of its kind attempted during the colonial period. Whitaker stated in a letter to Wheelock that "His [Whitefield's] influence was better than all the Presbyterians put together." The net proceeds was £11,000 and enabled Wheelock to transform his Indian Charity School into Dartmouth College, named in honor of that "Christian Lord" whom Whitaker calls "a C^{hh} & a methodist." [46]

In 1764 Whitefield made a serious attempt to transform his Orphanage at Bethesda, Georgia, into a full-fledged college. The Georgia Governor and Council acted favorably upon the proposal and granted two thousand acres of land as an endowment. Whitefield agreed to turn over all the resources of the orphanage and suggested that the charter be modelled after that of the College of New Jersey. When this proposition was submitted to the Board of Trade and Plantations they insisted a provision be placed in the charter requiring that the head of the college be a member of the Church of England, and that all public prayers be according to the liturgy of the Church. To this Whitefield objected, stating that the orphanage funds had been largely contributed by dissenters and that unless the college was established upon a "broad bottom" it would cause a "general disgust" and would "open the mouths of persons of all denominations" against him. Unable

---

[46] The story of the Occom and Whitaker mission to England is told in Leon B. Richardson, *An Indian Preacher in England, etc.*, Dartmouth College: 1933. This is a collection of Occom and Whitaker letters and diaries.

to secure a charter without these restrictions Whitefield abandoned his plan.[47]

The founding of King's College in New York (1754) had no direct relationship to the revivals, other than the fact that they had created a general atmosphere favorable to the establishment of colleges. The Episcopalians and the Presbyterians entered into a bitter controversy over its control; the Episcopalians claimed that a group of belligerent Presbyterian lawyers in New York, of whom William Livingston was the leader, desired to exclude all religious teaching. Livingston contended for a college that would be non-sectarian and catholic. The gift of a valuable tract of land by Trinity Church, on condition that the president of the college always should be an Episcopalian and the services in the college chapel conducted according to the prayer book, was responsible for giving the Episcopalians the major control.

The founding of Queen's College by the Dutch Reformed Coetus at New Brunswick, New Jersey, in 1766 was brought about by the triumph of the American movement within the Dutch Church inaugurated by their great revivalistic leader Theodore J. Frelinghuysen. The opening of the College of Rhode Island in 1764 was the direct result of the large increase of Baptist influence in New England and the Middle Colonies, due both directly and indirectly to the revival.[48] Though none of the colonial colleges required students to subscribe to any religious creed as a condition of becoming members of the institutions, the College of Rhode Island was the only one which specifically stated in its charter that "Sectarian differences of opinions, shall not make any Part of the Public and Classical Instruction." It also imposed no religious tests for members of the faculty.[49]

---

[47] *The Works of the Reverend George Whitefield,* 6 vols., London: 1770–72, Vol. III, pp. 480–82; 573–75.

[48] Herbert and Carol Schneider (Eds.), *Samuel Johnson, President of King's College: His Career and Writings,* New York: 1929, 4 vols., Vol. IV, "Founding of King's College." William H. S. Demarest, *A History of Rutgers College, 1766–1924,* New Brunswick: 1924. Walter C. Brownson, *The History of Brown University, 1764–1914,* Providence: 1914. Also Reuben A. Guild, *Life, Times and Correspondence of James Manning and the Early History of Brown University,* Boston: 1864.

[49] For discussion of the charters of the colonial colleges see Brownson, *op. cit.,* pp. 14–33.

Coming directly out of the revival was a greatly renewed interest in Indian missions. With the death of John Eliot in 1690 and the opening, at the end of the century, of the intercolonial wars in which the Indians played an important part, the old concern for the conversion of the Indians largely disappeared from New England Congregationalism. By the middle of the eighteenth century, however, a new missionary impulse, coming directly out of the revival, sent John Sargent to begin his mission among the Stockbridge Indians in Western Massachusetts, and led Eleazar Wheelock to open his school for the training of missionaries and Indian youth for missionary work among the Indians. The revival also was responsible for starting Presbyterian Indian missions. David Brainerd, a convert of the revival expelled from Yale College because of his revivalism, transferred his Church relationship to the Presbyterians and devoted the remainder of his short life to work among the New Jersey and Pennsylvania Indians. His saintly character and life of devotion as revealed in his diary edited by Jonathan Edwards was a tremendous stimulus in promoting interest in missions. Samuel Kirkland's missionary activities among the Senecas and Oneidas in central New York was also a direct outreach of revival influence. The Moravian Indian missionary activities, begun by Christian Henry Raush in 1740 and continued under the direction of David Zeisberger, are likewise a part of the new missionary impulse that was rooted in the great revival.

A new social consciousness and a broad humanitarianism were also products of the Great Awakening. The emphasis in the Edwardian theology and especially in the Hopkinsian school of the New Divinity upon *disinterested benevolence* started movements in New England whose consequences for good in American life are beyond exact calculation. A part of Samuel Hopkins' theological system was a general atonement—that is, that Christ died for all, for Indians and Negroes and underprivileged people generally—as well as for New England Congregationalists. Here was forged the framework of the first anti-slavery impulse in America, and Samuel Hopkins, student of Jonathan Edwards, was its father. The New Light Presbyterians and the Baptists, as they expanded southward, became open opponents of slavery, and the growing Methodist movement, stressing the infinite love and pity of God, added its influence to the new humanitarianism.[50]

---

[50] Gewehr, *op. cit.*, Chapter VIII, "Contributions to the Rise of Democracy," and Maxson, *op. cit.*, Chapter X, "Conclusion," are excellent summaries of democratic and humanitarian influences coming out of the revivals. In this connection see also Thom, *op. cit.*, and Eckenrode, *op. cit.* For the relation of the revivals to Indian Missions, see Jonathan Edwards, *An account of the life of the Reverend David Brainerd, . . . Missionary to the Indians . . . Chiefly taken from his Diary* (Boston: 1749; later editions, Worcester: 1793; London: 1818); Herbert H. Lennox, *Samuel Kirkland's Mission to the Iroquois* (Typed Ph.D. Thesis, University of Chicago, 1935).

X

America and Religious Liberty

OR THE FIRST three hundred years of Christian history the
Church existed entirely apart from the State; indeed it
had no legal status whatever. But in the year 311 the
Roman Emperor Galerius issued a decree placing the Christian
religion on the same legal footing as the worship of the Roman
gods. This immediately changed the whole status of the Church,
and with the beginning of the reign of Constantine, the first
Christian Emperor, the Church began to gain larger and larger
privileges under the State. At the same time it was becoming
more and more dependent upon the State, and soon was being
diverted from its proper work to serve political ends. As long as
the Empire continued strong there was little chance or inclination on the part of the Church to free itself from political control.
When the great Empire began to fall apart, however, and the
government became less and less effective, and as a consequence
less and less serviceable to the Church, there naturally arose a
desire on the part of the Church to free itself from the control of
weak government.

It was in the midst of this period of declining imperial power
that Pope Gelasius (d. 496) set forth his theory as to the relationship between the Church and State. He stated that two
powers govern the world, the priestly and the kingly. "The first,"
he stated, "is assuredly the superior, for the priest is responsible to
God for the conduct of the emperors themselves." Gradually, also,
the Church began to take over duties which previously the Roman
government had performed, since it was better able to keep order
in this period of growing disorder than were the weak emperors.
Thus there arose the doctrine of Church independence of State
control, and in the great investiture struggle the Church maintained it with success against Roman emperors and German kings.

Once having secured its independence of State control, and having perfected its organization to a high degree, the Church grew rich, strong, and aggressive; it even went a long step further and asserted the right of the Church to control the State. The famous *Dictatus* of Pope Gregory VII asserts that "the Pope is the only person whose feet are kissed by all princes"; that he has power to depose emperors; that no one can annul a papal decree, though the Pope may annul the decrees of all other earthly powers; and no one may pass judgment upon his acts. But even in the face of these historic instances of Church-State relationship, it can be categorically stated that there is nothing in Christianity itself which calls for a close relationship with the State, and that both the control of the Church by the State and the control of the State by the Church are equally foreign to the teachings of Christianity.

I

CHURCH AND STATE IN POST-REFORMATION EUROPE

THERE IS a widespread notion among Protestant groups that the separation of Church and State, and thus religious liberty, was one of the immediate products of the Reformation; that the early Protestants were advocates of a large tolerance and that religious liberty was but the logical development of the principles held by all the reformers.[1] Just where this notion arose is difficult to say, and no reputable historian of our own times would endorse it. Historically, of course, the exact opposite is true. The fact is that the rise of Protestantism was accompanied by an unprecedented outburst of intolerance and cruelty in which both Protestants and Catholics participated. To the Catholics Luther, Calvin, Zwingli and all the other reformers were possessed of devils; to the Protestants the Pope was the scarlet woman of Babylon, the beast of the Revelation, the Romish wolf, the anti-Christ.

One of the most notable outcomes of the Reformation was the

---

[1] Theoretically Luther advocated the separation of Church and State, and his placing the young German Protestant Churches under the protection of the Princes was probably considered by him as a temporary expedient.

rise of numerous National Churches in the several countries of
Western Europe where Protestantism gained the upper hand.
Thus in England, Holland, Scotland, and in the German and
Scandinavian states National Churches were established. These
National Churches were, generally speaking, not only intolerant
of Roman Catholicism, but they were also intolerant of the sects
which arose numerously about them. The terrible severity employed by the German States in dealing with the Anabaptists has
been noted already, as well as the anti-Catholic legislation in the
reigns of Elizabeth and James I which completely outlawed Roman
Catholicism in England. This Protestant intolerance was more
than matched by the many instances of Roman Catholic cruelty
toward, and persecution of, Protestants. The bloody policy pursued
by Philip II in his attempt to suppress the growing Protestantism
in Holland; the persecution of the Huguenots in France, cul-
minating in the St. Bartholomew massacre, are but examples in
the long list of Catholic persecutions of Protestants in the post-
Reformation years. The story of the Spanish Inquisition both in
Spain and in the Spanish dependencies displays a cruelty in dealing with heretics almost beyond comprehension. It is also well to
bear in mind in these days of the renewal of Jewish persecution
that Jews too have been persecutors.

Out of the Reformation there came also, as already has been
noticed, a large number of humble and despised groups, whose
primary emphasis in their religious life was to revive primitive
Christianity in all its forms—in life, in worship, in polity and in
the relation of the Church to the State. The Anabaptist groups on
the continent and the English Puritan sects including the Baptists, are examples and represent what we have come to call the
left wing of the Reformation. All of these groups, with few
exceptions, advocated the separation of Church and State. As
far as the Old World was concerned this idea was pathetically
premature, and had no chance of fulfillment at a time when
in every country in Christendom there was a State Church,
either Catholic or Protestant. Everywhere it was thought that
national safety and political unity depended upon religious uniformity, and this idea was as strongly asserted in Protestant as

in Catholic countries. In Spain, Italy, France, Austria and in Spain's colonies in America Protestants were put to death in the interest of maintaining religious uniformity; in England, Prussia and the Scandinavian countries there were attempts to maintain the same principle, and as a result there were banishments, executions and confiscations.[2]

II

RELIGIOUS MINORITIES IN THE COLONIES

THROUGHOUT THE Christian centuries it has been the minority groups that have been the advocates of religious liberty; never the powerful State Churches. This does not mean that all minorities have always been tolerant. Frequently small sects are exceedingly exclusive, take pride in their exclusiveness and have developed a superiority complex as a result of it. But being minorities they do not possess the power to express their intolerance in violent programs of persecution or in the denial of political and religious rights to others. Outside New England and Virginia none of the colonies ever possessed majority religious bodies, so that the minority attitude toward religious toleration and the relation of Church and State came to be the prevailing colonial attitude.

In the American colonies, for the first time in the history of Christendom, there had come to be a group of civil States in which there was no majority religion. "Tolerance," Professor Garrison tells us, "has often been the special virtue of minorities, if that can be considered a virtue which is a method of getting something rather than a motive for giving something."[3] In all the colonies, among the principal forces working for religious liberty were the minority groups. These bodies can be divided into two classes: first, those which advocated religious liberty from

---

[2] For a concise putting of these facts see Carlton J. H. Hayes, *Historical Background for the Contemporary Problem of Religious Liberty in America*, in pamphlet published by the National Conference of Jews and Christians, *Historical Backgrounds for Discussion of Intergroup Relations*, New York: 1932, pp. 4 ff.

[3] W. E. Garrison, *Intolerance*, New York: 1934, pp. 10–24. See especially Chapter II, "Grounds for Tolerance."

principle; second, those advocating it from policy. The Quakers and all the Baptist groups, which included the Mennonites and Dunkers, were advocates of religious liberty from principle; Catholics, Anglicans, Presbyterians, Lutherans and the Reformed churches were not opposed in principle to a State Church, but where they themselves were not the privileged Church, they were to be found in every instance on the side advocating religious liberty. It needs to be remembered that the principles and practices of religious liberty did not originate among peoples pretty solidly in control, nor under the leadership of men representing any majority religion.

The Middle Colonies particularly were the haven of large numbers of minority sects. In Pennsylvania, due to the liberal religious and land policies pursued by the Quaker Proprietor, there were to be found, besides many of the Proprietor's own co-religionists, Mennonites, Dunkers, Moravians, Schwenkfelders, Lutherans, German and Dutch Reformed, several varieties of Presbyterians, Welsh and English Baptists, Anglicans and Roman Catholics, with no one group having an actual majority. Even if there had been a desire on the part of the Proprietors to establish a State Church the very nature of the population would have made it a practical impossibility. While Pennsylvania presents the best example of the great varieties of religions, yet in every colony south of New England, with the exception of Virginia, much the same diversity was to be found from the beginning, becoming even greater as the colonial period wore on. In 1687 Governor Dongan, the liberal Catholic Governor of New York, made a report on conditions in that colony and in it is a summary of the religious situation,

New York [he states] has first a chaplain belonging to the Fort, of the Church of England; secondly, a Dutch Calvinist; thirdly a French Calvinist; fourthly a Dutch Lutheran. Here be not many of the Church of England; few Roman Catholics; abundance of Quaker preachers, men, and women especially; Singling Quakers; Ranting Quakers; Sabbatarians; Anti-Sabbatarians; some Ana-baptists; some Jews; in short, of all sorts of opinion there are some, and the most part none at all.

The great variety of religious groups in early Maryland may be inferred from the third provision of the Act of Toleration (1649), which promises punishment by fine or whipping and imprisonment for any person within the Province, who in a

reproachful manner or way declare, call or denominate, any psn [person] or psns [persons] whatsoever inhabiting, residing, traffiqueing, trading, or commerceing within this Province or within any of the Ports, Harbours, Creeks or Havens to the same belonging, an heretick, Seismatick, Idolator, puritan, Independent, Prespiterian, popish priest, Jesuite, Jesuited papast, Lutheran, Calvinist, Anabaptist, Brownist, Antinomian, Barrowist, Roundhead, Separatist, or any other name or terme in a reproachful manner relating to matters of Religion.

In Edmund Burke's well-known speech on *Conciliation with America* delivered on March 22, 1775, occurs this remarkably accurate summary of the religious situation in the colonies at the outbreak of the American Revolution:

Religion, always a principle of energy in this new people, is in no way worn out or impaired; and their mode of professing it is also one main cause of this free spirit. The people are Protestants; and of that kind which is the most adverse to all implicit submission of mind and opinion. This is a persuasion not only favorable to liberty, but built upon it.

The type of Protestantism most common in America, he states, was a "refinement on the principle of resistance"; it was the "dissidence of dissent the most extreme Protestantism of the Protestant religion." In their religious beliefs they had advanced beyond all others "in the liberty of the Reformation." Existing in America under a variety of denominations they agree in nothing but communion of the spirit of liberty. When the colonists left England, the spirit of dissent was high and among the immigrants it was the highest of all. Of the stream of foreigners which had constantly flowed into the colonies, the greatest part was composed of dissenters from the establishments in the several countries from which they had come, and they therefore brought with them a temper and a character in harmony with the people with whom they mingled. The colonists had accustomed themselves to the freest debate on all religious questions, and so far had individualism developed in religion that even women were permitted to have opinions and it was said that "every man's hat was his Church."[4]

As Edmund Burke has indicated, the colonial Churches had developed under conditions most favorable for the evolution of individualism in religion. All the largest dissenting Churches in the American colonies were self-governing, as were also most of the smaller bodies. Even the Church of England, though established by law in the Southern Colonies and officially tied to England, was in reality little more than a private sect controlled to a large degree by lay vestries. This not only meant freedom from Old World restraints of many kinds, but also the absence of Church officialdom. Added to this fact were the three thousand miles of tossing seas which rendered the colonials relatively safe from any punishment which Old World authorities, whether in Church or State, might impose for their disobedience. All this tended to produce an attitude of mind favorable to the development of new ways of thinking and independence of action.

This independence of thought which had come to prevail widely in Revolutionary America can be traced also to the fact that in large measure the colonial Churches had been founded by religious radicals. Many before leaving the mother country had already departed the usual and recognized ways of thought, both in politics and religion, and coming to a new land, separated as America was from the restraining influences of the old established customs and institutions, their radicalism would tend to increase rather than diminish. At the very time the English colonies were being established in America, a religious as well as a political revolution was under way in the mother country, and the old ecclesiastical as well as the old political faith was under attack from every quarter. Once having turned their backs upon the old home, the old State, the old Church, the colonists

---

[4] Edmund Burke, *Speech on Conciliation with America, 1775*, edited by J. V. Denney, Chicago: 1898, pp. 50–52. Also E. F. Humphrey, *Nationalism and Religion in America*, Boston: 1924, pp. 20–22.

set their faces toward America to find a new heaven as well as a new earth.[5]

III

THE EXAMPLE OF RHODE ISLAND

FOR THE first time in modern history the complete separation of Church and State and liberty of conscience became facts in the colony of Rhode Island. The principles upon which the colony was established were not original with Roger Williams, but his distinction lies in the fact that he was the first to try them out successfully and to guide others in their application. Not only was Rhode Island a bold experiment, it was even more, it was a successful one; and to the end of the colonial period there was little deviation in practice from the great principles upon which it had been founded.[6] Next to Rhode Island the Quaker colonies came nearer to the practice of religious liberty than any of the others. The political and religious ideas of George Fox and William Penn were based on the principle of religious liberty for all, and Penn planned his colony as an asylum for the persecuted of all faiths. It was unfortunately true that pressure from the English government compelled Pennsylvania to enact restraining laws against Roman Catholics. But in spite of these enactments, which ran counter to Quaker desires, Roman Catholics enjoyed larger freedom in the Quaker colonies than anywhere else.[7] Despite

---

[5] C. H. Van Tyne, *The Causes of the War for Independence*, New York and Boston: 1922, Vol. I, Chapter 1, for a full discussion of this type of influence upon thought and action in the American Colonies.

[6] After the death of Roger Williams Rhode Island passed an ordinance excluding Jews and Catholics from the full rights of citizenship. Williams held that citizenship should be granted "to such as the major part of us should admit into fellowship with us" and eventually the "major part" excluded Jews and Catholics. The religious practices of these two groups were not restricted but their political rights were.

S. G. Arnold, *History of Rhode Island*, 2 vols., 1894, II, p. 491. See also S. S. Rider, *An Inquiry Concerning the Origin of the Clause in the Laws of Rhode Island (1719–1783) Disfranchising Roman Catholics*, Rhode Island Hist. Tracts, Second Series, No. 1, Providence: 1889.

[7] For a discussion of Catholic treatment in the Quaker Colonies see Sister Mary Augustina (Ray), *American Opinion of Roman Catholicism in the Eighteenth Century*, New York, Columbia University Press: 1936, pp. 102–107.

Roger Williams' dislike of Catholics and his many attacks upon them he professed willingness to grant to them the same liberty in religion he claimed for himself and others, and there is no reason to doubt that Catholics would have received equal treatment in Rhode Island had they chosen to come to that colony. Thus in four of the thirteen colonies, Rhode Island, Pennsylvania, New Jersey and Delaware, there were no religious establishments, and there almost complete religious liberty flourished.

In creating a colonial environment favorable to religious liberty the New England colonies made the smallest contribution, while Virginia was only a little less backward in this respect. Massachusetts particularly was little influenced by the new spirit of tolerance and compromise that was gaining ground rapidly after 1660, and held on tenaciously to the narrow religious principles of the founders. The loss of their charter in 1684 and its replacement by the new charter of 1691 destroyed the supremacy of the Puritan oligarchy and thereby opened the way for the gradual development of a larger toleration. In the long run, however, it was the Proprietary colonies, with Rhode Island, which were most important in promoting practical situations in which religious liberty found the most favorable opportunity to develop.

IV

Contributions of the Proprietary Colonies

As has been already shown, landed interest and agriculture and not trade were the dominant interests of the seventeenth-century Englishman of the privileged classes. Manorial organization and possession of the soil were the principal interests in the minds of the landed gentry in the colonizing century. Seventeenth-century England was still a land of manors, although the lords of the manor had lost most of their seignorial rights. In this period of the decay of the manors a new social caste was arising known as the "squire-archy" with habits and convictions of its own. One of the principal characteristics of this class was the desire for more land, to increase both their prestige and income. Some of them secured grants in Ireland under the Cromwellian settlement, others were attracted by the prospect of securing large holdings in America and the West Indies. This was the background for the many proprietary grants made especially after the Restoration, but the earliest date from the first quarter of the seventeenth century.[8]

In the great proprietary grants the Proprietors were not only responsible for the government, but they were also interested in the exploitation of the colony as a business venture. And its success as a business enterprise depended upon the Proprietor's ability to attract colonists. The great Proprietary colonies of Maryland and Pennsylvania usually have been considered as primarily benevolent enterprises. They were of course that, but they were also business ventures. Lord Baltimore and William Penn were liberal-minded gentlemen and were entirely sincere in their desire to establish a refuge in America for people persecuted for conscience, and especially for their own coreligionists, but both had vast tracts of land for sale. If their great landed estates were to prove profitable, people in large numbers must be attracted to take up land, establish homes and pay quitrents to the Proprietors. In no other way could this type of colony have been founded.

Lord Baltimore well knew that as a whole the English Catholics of his day did not belong to the emigrating classes. Belonging generally to the nobility and the landed gentry, their large possessions made them reluctant to leave their old homes even in the face of bitter persecution. Belonging to the higher classes, they had a better chance also to escape the severity of the anti-Catholic laws, and it is well known that these laws were, to a large degree, unenforced, and that the English Catholics were never treated as badly as the anti-Catholic legislation would lead one to believe. For these reasons the Catholic Proprietor of Maryland was all the more dependent upon non-Catholic immigration to bring success to his great landed estate in the New World.

---

[8] Charles M. Andrews, *The Colonial Period of American History*, New Haven: 1934, Vol. II. See especially Chapter VI. An excellent brief discussion of religious toleration in the Proprietary colonies is E. B. Greene, *Religion and the State: The Making and Testing of American Tradition*, New York, New York University Press: 1941, pp. 53–61.

Protestants outnumbered Catholics from the very beginning in the Maryland colony. This fact supports the view that the Lord Proprietor was not only interested in making the colony a refuge for Catholics, but he was equally concerned in making it a paying proposition. In fact it could not have been a successful refuge had it not been made a successful business enterprise. Father Henry More, the Jesuit Provincial in England, writing to Rome seven years after the founding of Maryland, states that "three parts of the people of four are heretics." The instructions given by Lord Baltimore to the first Catholic immigrants indicate his concern that nothing be done by his coreligionists to alienate Protestants, or discourage them from joining his enterprise. He admonished that care be taken by the officials "to preserve unity and peace among all passangers" and "no scandal nor offence" was "to be given to any of the Protestants." They were also directed to "cause all acts of Roman Catholic worship to be done as privately as may be" and that they instruct all Roman Catholics "to be silent on all occasions of discourse on Religion . . . and this to be observed on land as well as at sea." [9]

Lord Baltimore's attempts to curb the Jesuits in Maryland is further evidence of the subordination in his own mind of the purely religious interests to those of business and government. Within five years after the establishment of his colony Baltimore discovered that the Jesuits had acquired secretly Indian lands within the territory defined by his patent. The Jesuits no doubt had a right to expect liberal treatment at the hands of the Catholic Proprietor, but Baltimore considered their acquisition of lands within his grant as repugnant to his chartered rights and their assumption of spiritual independence as a challenge to his authority. The Jesuits disputed Baltimore's title to any lands not ceded to him by the Indians, and they likewise questioned the right of

---

[9] A. P. Dennis, "Lord Baltimore's Struggle with the Jesuits, 1643–49," in *Annual Report of the American Historical Association*, 1900, Vol. I. The position that Lord Baltimore's motives in establishing Maryland were wholly free from mercenary ends is defended in J. T. Scharf, *History of Maryland*, 3 vols., Baltimore: 1879, Vol. I, pp. 151 ff. For a statement as to the relative number of Catholics and Protestants among the first colonists, see W. H. Browne, *Maryland* (American Commonwealth Series), Boston: 1895, p. 22.

the English crown to grant him Indian lands. In his struggle with the Jesuits Baltimore considered that 'the ultimate success of the "dearest design of his life" was at stake. This does not mean that his adherence to the Catholic faith was wavering, but rather his determination to uphold his rights as Lord Proprietor against all comers. The passage of the Toleration Act of 1649, which gives to that year a special distinction in Maryland history, was neither a Catholic nor a Protestant measure, as controversial writers on both sides have sought to prove. Rather it was pushed through the Provincial Assembly under "the lash of the Proprietor's whip," as a part of "a triple scheme to defeat the Jesuits and save the Proprietor's authority in the province." At the same time Baltimore's invitation to the New England Puritans to settle in Maryland was not only a bid for favor to the new power then dominant in England, but it was also an attempt to induce settlement on the part of a particularly hardy and valuable type of settlers.[10]

The same set of influences was present in William Penn's proprietary grants as has been noticed in Maryland. Penn, like Baltimore, was sincerely committed to the cause of securing a larger liberty of conscience to persecuted people both in England and elsewhere. In a letter to a contemporary Penn thus sets forth his purpose in establishing his province in America:

I went thither to lay the foundation of a free colony for all mankind, more especially those of my own profession, not that I would lessen the civil liberties of others because of their persuasion, but screen and defend our own from any infringement on that account.[11]

It may have been from the very nature of the Quaker emphasis that religion played a larger part in Penn's plans for his province than it did in Maryland, but nowhere was the business end more carefully looked after. A study of the early documents relating to

---

[10] E. D. Neill, *Founders of Maryland,* Albany: 1876, p. 109; also Matthew Page Andrews, *The Founding of Maryland,* New York: 1933, especially Chapter x, "Freedom of Conscience."

[11] Penn-Logan correspondence, I, p. 373. H. L. Osgood, *The American Colonies in the Seventeenth Century,* New York: 1930, Vol. II, p. 143. For reprints of early documents of Pennsylvania see Robert Proud, *The History of Pennsylvania,* etc., Philadelphia: 1798, Vol. II, Appendix I to VI.

Pennsylvania shows a large amount of attention given to matters of land purchases, surveys, marketing of livestock and other purely business matters, though of course such considerations would have been necessary no matter how high and unselfish the motives of the founder might have been. Penn's problem in securing colonists was doubtless much less difficult than was that of Lord Baltimore, since the Quakers generally belonged to that economic class which would be more inclined to emigrate. The combination of high-minded benevolence and business enterprise is well illustrated in Penn's advertisement of his provinces in the Palatinate. He had made previously two visits to the lower Rhine, the first in 1671 and again in 1677, and was therefore fully aware of the widespread distress prevailing there. A few years later, having become the possessor of his great American estate, he sent his agents there to solicit settlers, and to further their success he had his pamphlet, "Some Account of the Province of Pennsylvania in America," translated into German, and appended to it was his essay on Religious Liberty, likewise translated into German. Such a combination of appeals—a liberal land policy, liberal government and religious liberty—soon resulted in the coming of great waves of German immigrants to become settlers on the rich lands of William Penn's American province.[12]

The merchant class in England, who were ever on the lookout for new markets, were even less interested in maintaining religious uniformity than were the landed Proprietors and advocated the granting of liberty of conscience to all those going to the colonies as an attraction to settlers. An interesting illustration of how the interests of trade furnished a practical reason for granting religious toleration is found in a letter from the Lords of Trade to the President of the Council of Virginia, dated September 1, 1750. The letter refers to the controversy in Virginia over the question of granting a license to the Reverend Samuel Davies to carry on Presbyterian work in the colony.

---

[12] Smith, R., *F. H. Harrington and his Oceana, a Study of a Seventeenth Century Utopia and its Influence in America*, Cambridge: 1914, contends that Harrington's *Oceana* influenced Penn, as well as Locke and Shaftesbury, "the three greatest prophets of civil and religious liberty in the age of the restoration." Chapter viii. See also Andrews, *op. cit.*, III, pp. 167–68.

With regard to the affair of Mr. Davies the Presbyterian,—as Toleration and a free exercise of religion is so valuable a branch of true liberty, and so essential to the enriching and improving a Trading Nation, it should ever be held sacred in his Majesties Colonies; We must therefore recommend it to your care, that nothing be done which can in the least effect that great point; at the same time you will do well to admonish Mr. Davies to make proper use of that indulgence which our laws so wisely grant to those who differ from the Established Church, and to be cautious not to afford any just cause of complaint to the Clergy of the Church of England, or to the people in general.[13]

It was the growing influence of the merchants, together with the large amounts of land which the great landed Proprietors had for sale in America, that at least helps to account for the writing into the charters of New York, New Jersey, the Carolinas and Georgia the liberty-of-conscience clauses. We have seen the general provisions of the Duke's Laws (1665) for New York (Chapter II). In New Jersey toleration was promised from the beginning and especially notable are the "Laws, Concessions and Agreements" of March 3, 1677, in which full liberty of conscience is guaranteed. The Proprietors of the Carolinas were all courtiers. They were associated with the government of Charles II, and therefore fully committed to the policy of religious uniformity at home, but they evidently saw no harm in letting down religious bars in their far-away holdings in America.

Both the Carolina charter and the later pronouncements of the Proprietors declared that none should be molested or punished for differences of opinion or practice in matters of religion, provided they did not disturb the "civil peace." [14] Later when the Anglican Church was established in the Carolinas it was not accompanied by acts of uniformity, and provisions were made whereby any person or persons were given the liberty "to keepe and Mayntayne what preachers or ministers they please." As Professor Greene has stated there developed in all the proprietary colonies "a prac-

---

[13] William S. Perry (Ed.), *Historical Collections Relating to the American Colonial Church*, Vol. I, *Virginia*, 1873, pp. 379–81.

[14] H. L. Osgood, *op. cit.*, II, Chapter XIII, "The Ecclesiastical Relations in the Later Proprietary Colonies."

tical kind of liberalism usually influenced by business considerations" which permitted "differences in religious faiths and practices." Once admitted, "these variations created a situation which made subsequent intolerant and discriminating policies increasingly difficult." [15]

V

THE BAPTISTS

THE GREAT increase in the number of dissenters as a result of the great colonial Awakenings was still another factor in creating an environment favorable to the growth of religious freedom. The rapid growth of the Baptists in New England and in the Southern Colonies, the two regions where State establishments existed, was particularly important, since they were the most active of all the colonial religious bodies in carrying on propaganda for the separation of Church and State. Their growth was particularly phenomenal in Virginia and North Carolina, where by the opening of the Revolution they were probably as numerous as the Anglicans and were becoming increasingly important politically. In New England they had likewise increased in numbers and influence, and in 1767 the Warren Association was formed, one of its purposes being to urge upon those in authority the granting of religious liberty. Later Isaac Backus became the Agent of the Association and under his able leadership the New England Baptists carried on their propaganda for religious freedom throughout the Revolution and beyond. The Baptists constituted the largest single body fighting openly, in season and out, for the separation of Church and State.[16]

---

[15] E. B. Greene, "The American Record in Relation to Religious Liberty," in *Historic Backgrounds for the Discussion of Intergroup Relations, op. cit.*, pp. 13–29.

[16] The important place occupied by the Baptists in the struggle for the separation of Church and State has been treated in W. T. Thom, *The Struggle for Religious Freedom in Virginia: The Baptists*, Baltimore: 1900; S. B. Weeks, *Church and State in North Carolina*, Baltimore: 1893; S. H. Cobb, *The Rise of Religious Liberty in America*, New York: 1902; Jacob C. Meyer, *Church and State in Massachusetts, 1740 to 1833*, Cleveland: 1930; E. F. Humphrey, *Nationalism and Religion in America*, Boston: 1924.

VI

THE UNCHURCHED LIBERALS

By THE END of the colonial period there had come to be more unchurched people in the American colonies in proportion to the population than were to be found anywhere else in Christendom. This was due to a combination of causes. In the first place, in none of the colonies, even in those where there were State Churches, was Church membership easily achieved, whereas in every country in western Europe, on the other hand, Church membership came about as a matter of course and was practically coextensive with citizenship. In New England, where Congregationalism was the State Church, Church membership from the beginning had been a matter of the few and not the masses. Until the adoption of the Half-Way Covenant in 1662, only those were accepted as Church members who could relate a satisfactory religious experience before the congregation, and in the very nature of the case that would mean few indeed. The Half-Way Covenant permitted the children of unconverted parents, who had themselves shared the Covenant with their parents, to receive baptism, but they were not to receive the Lord's Supper nor take part in Church elections. Thus there was established a half-way Church membership, and with each succeeding generation the proportion of half-way members became increasingly larger, until in the course of time the descendants of the half-way members lost all vital contact with the Church.

Ezra Stiles estimated that in 1760 there were 445,000 Congregationalists in the four New England colonies.[17] These figures, however, were based on the assumption that every person who was not a dissenter was a member of the State Church. There were at that time about 600 congregations of Congregationalists in New England, which would mean, if Stiles' calculations were

---

[17] Ezra Stiles, *Itineraries and Correspondence*, F. B. Dexter, Editor, Yale University Press: 1918, pp. 92–94. According to Stiles' calculations there were 62,420 dissenters in the four New England colonies.

correct, that there were on an average 750 members to each congregation, whereas an average of not more than 150 per congregation of actual communicants was very probably much nearer the truth. This would mean that one person in five at most was a Church member in New England, and there can be no question but that New England was the best churched section of the colonies.

In the Middle Colonies, where there was no establishment and a great variety of sects, the percentage of the unchurched was undoubtedly much larger than in New England. The German element in the population was at first poverty-stricken. They came generally without schoolmasters or ministers, thus delaying the formation of congregations. Many Germans came as redemptioners and on landing were sold as indentured servants and were thus widely scattered. The Scotch-Irish were equally poor and came likewise without religious leaders. Scattered widely in the thinly populated back country throughout the thirteen colonies, Church membership would be difficult to achieve even had there been an inclination in that direction. The Baptists, like the Congregationalists, required the relation of a conversion experience for admission to Church membership, which in itself would tend to keep the number of communicants small. There being no Anglican bishop in the colonies, confirmation was, of course, impossible, and in the Church of England colonies the proportion of churched to unchurched was undoubtedly smaller than anywhere else. Bishop William White is authority for the statement that during all the time Washington worshipped in Christ Church, Philadelphia, he never saw him take communion or kneel in prayer.[18] It is doubtful whether Washington ever considered himself a full-fledged member of the Church and this attitude was fairly typical of Virginians of his class.

---

[18] Bird Wilson, *Memoir of the Life of the Right Reverend William White, Bishop of the Protestant Episcopal Church in the State of Pennsylvania*, Philadelphia: 1839, pp. 188–98.

In a letter dated August 15, 1835, in reply to an inquiry as to whether General Washington was a regular communicant of the Episcopal Church Bishop White stated: "In regard to the subject of your inquiry truth requires me to say, that General Washington never received the communion in the churches of which I am the parochial minister. Mrs. Washington was an habitual communicant." P. 197.

By the opening of the War for Independence there was an extraordinarily large body of religiously indifferent people in the American colonies. Pope Leo XIII was accustomed to say that the principal motive of those advocating the cause of religious liberty was indifference.[19] He was unable to understand how any one could propose that ordinary men be left free to follow their own judgment in religious matters if he had any concern for religion. Few liberal-minded men would accept Pope Leo's statement as an adequate explanation of their reason for advocating religious liberty, but there is undoubtedly something to be said for it. A problem which every liberal-minded Church member must face is how to retain his loyalty to his own Church and at the same time preserve a tolerant spirit toward others whose Church attachments are different from his own. People are naturally more tolerant of those things toward which they have no strong loyalties. Many good people who have no definite Church attachment still believe in religion; they believe in all the Churches, but no one of them holds their especial loyalty. This was Jefferson's position and represents that of many others of his time and of ours. People of this type, believing in all the Churches, are unwilling to give to any one Church special privileges. Thus it may be inferred that this large body of unchurched people in colonial America constituted an important element in the growth of the spirit of religious liberty. The fact that at least half the people in the nation today are unchurched is an important factor in the preservation of our basic freedom—religious liberty.

A considerable proportion of the most important leaders in the fight for religious liberty in America were not Church members; Madison, Jefferson and Franklin serve as good examples. None of them were communicants of a Church; all of them were interested in religion as such; all were philosophical liberals, with little in common with the orthodox Churches of their time. Madison was a graduate of the College of New Jersey and remained a year after graduation to pursue further study in Hebrew and Ethics under the sturdy Presbyterian president John Wither-

---

[19] For a discussion of indifference as one of the grounds for religious toleration see Garrison, *op. cit.*, pp. 21–22.

spoon,[20] who not only presided over his formal studies, but imbued him with his own antipathy for a State-controlled Church. Madison had been reared as an Episcopalian, but was never a communicant. Jefferson had little liking for formal Christianity as expressed in the priesthood and dogma, though he was a believer in deity and accepted the ministrations of the Episcopal Church. He was a liberal contributor to many denominations and many clergymen of various Churches were his friends, but he abhorred any connection between Church and State. A few weeks before his death Franklin in a letter to President Stiles of Yale College wrote the following statement regarding Jesus:

As to Jesus of Nazareth, my opinion of whom you particularly desire, I think the System of Morals and Religion, as he left them to us, the best the World ever saw or is likely to see; but I apprehend it has received various corrupting Changes, and I have, with most of the present Dissenters in England, some doubts as to his Divinity, tho' it is a question I do not dogmatize upon, having never studied it, and think it needless to busy myself with it now, when I expect soon an Opportunity of knowing the Truth with less trouble. I see no harm, however, in its being believed, if that belief has the good consequence, as probably it has, of making his Doctrines more respected and better observed; especially as I do not perceive, that the Supreme takes it amiss, by distinguishing the Unbelievers in his Government of the World with any peculiar marks of his Displeasure.

Like both Madison and Jefferson, Franklin accepted the ministrations of the Episcopal Church, but was never a communicant, while his friendship with George Whitefield and his support of the kind of religious activity in which the great evangelist was engaged, is proof conclusive that he at least believed in various types of religious expression. Certain it is that the principal leaders

---

[20] V. L. Collins, *President Witherspoon: A Biography*, Princeton: 1925, Vol. II, pp. 196 ff. Madison's religious views are discussed in John M. Mecklin, *The Story of American Dissent*, New York: 1934, pp. 291–92. For a summary of the religious views of Jefferson see David S. Muzzey, *Thomas Jefferson*, New York: 1918, pp. 295–300. Franklin's religious views are succinctly expressed in a letter to President Ezra Stiles a few weeks before his death. See *Franklin's Autobiography*, edited by O. S. Coad, New York: 1929, pp. 107 ff., and also Notes, pp. 236–37.

of Revolutionary America were latitudinarian in their religious views, with no strong predilection for any one religious body.

Such men, with no great sense of loyalty to any one denomination, naturally would be the most likely to be influenced by the English and French liberal theorists of the seventeenth and eighteenth centuries. In 1688 the English philosopher John Locke published four long letters on *Toleration,* which had previously appeared in shorter form in Latin, Dutch and French. The Church, Locke contended, was a voluntary society, and no man was bound by nature to any particular sect, but every man joined himself voluntarily to that profession and worship which he thought acceptable to God. The Church had no right to avail itself of force or compulsion, because no such power was granted to it by its founder, and also because no man can be saved by any other religion except the one in which he believes freely. Therefore, Locke demanded "absolute liberty, just and true liberty, equal and impartial liberty" for all dissenters, not as a favor or an act of indulgence but as a right.[21] There can be no doubt as to the influence exerted by Locke upon Madison and Jefferson, since the position both took in the struggle for religious liberty in Virginia is Lockean in its every detail.[22]

Voltaire's views on religion also found wide acceptance among America's colonial liberals, and their opposition to religious superstition came to be quite that of Voltaire. Madison was familiar with the Voltaire position and often quoted Voltaire's aphorism: "If one religion were allowed in England, the government would possibly become arbitrary; if there were two, the people would cut each other's throats; but as there are a multitude they all live

---

[21] *The Works of John Locke,* 10 vols., London: 1801, Tenth edition. Vol. VI.

[22] Locke had been strongly influenced by dissenters, having entered Christ Church College, Oxford, in 1652 when John Owen, the great dissenting scholar, was Dean and Vice Chancellor of the University. For the influence of Locke upon Madison and Jefferson see Mecklin, *op. cit.,* pp. 242–342. There has been an attempt in recent years to credit Cardinal Mellarmine, the seventeenth-century Jesuit theologian, with having exerted a determining influence on the views of Madison and Jefferson on religious liberty. Supporting this view see Gaillard Hunt, "Cardinal Bellarmine and the Virginia Bill of Rights," *Catholic Historical Review,* October 1917; see also another supporting article in the same *Review,* January 1925, by J. C. Rager. The opposing view is set forth most adequately by David S. Schaff, in *Papers of the American Society of Church History,* 2nd Series, Vol. VIII, 1928, in a paper entitled, "The Bellarmine-Jefferson Legend."

happy and in peace." To this Madison added, "security for civil rights must be the same as that for religious rights; it consists in the one case in a multiplicity of interests and in the other in a multiplicity of sects." Thus the political and religious liberalism of seventeenth and eighteenth century England and France was mediated to the American colonies through a group of unchurched leaders, whose unattached position made them the more responsive to these liberal voices.

With the coming of the Revolution, the long struggle for religious freedom and the separation of Church and State in America had been virtually won. Neither, however, constituted a direct issue in the struggle for independence. It is true that there were some instances of the Baptists demanding religious freedom as the price for their support of the patriot cause, and as a result they were successful in winning some concessions in Virginia and Massachusetts, but as a Revolutionary issue it was only incidental. But when independence was declared and it became necessary for the states, and eventually the New Nation itself, to form new instruments of government, in every instance, with the exception of the three New England states, Massachusetts, Connecticut and New Hampshire, where Congregationalism had long constituted a majority religion, separation of Church and State and the great principle of freedom of conscience were written into the new constitutions. It is true that Roman Catholics still labored under disabilities in several of the states, but the principle was everywhere recognized and its complete fulfillment was bound to come in due time.[23] The embodiment of these great principles in the new state constitutions and finally in the Federal constitution itself was simply writing colonial experience into the fundamental law of the land.

---

[23] In only two of the states was full freedom of religion granted at the formation of the Union. These were Rhode Island and Virginia. In six states complete freedom was granted only to Protestants, other states had other restraining provisions. (Cobb, *op. cit.,* Chapter ix.)

SELECTED BIBLIOGRAPHY

The following words drawn from a *Preface* [1] by Joseph Priestly well serve to introduce this bibliography.

"To have compiled such a work as this from original authorities only, without making use of any modern writers, would have been more than any man could have executed in the course of a long life. And what advantage do we derive from the labours of others, if we can never confide in them, and occasionally save ourselves some trouble by their means?"

BIBLIOGRAPHICAL AND ENCYCLOPEDIC

BIBLIOGRAPHICAL

Case, S. J., and Others, *A Bibliographical Guide to the History of Christianity* (Chicago, 1931).

Jackson, Samuel M., *A Bibliography of American Church History* (Confined to works published from 1820–93). *American Church History Series*, Vol. XII (New York, 1894).

Mode, Peter G., *Sourcebook and Bibliographical Guide for American Church History* (Menasha, Wis., 1921).

ENCYCLOPEDIC

Dictionary of American Biography, 20 vols. (New York, 1928–36).

Dictionary of American History, 5 vols. (New York, 1940).

The New Schaff-Herzog Encyclopedia of Religious Knowledge, 12 vols. (New York, 1908–12).

Sprague, W. B., *Annals of the American Pulpit*, 9 vols. (New York, 1866–69).

Weigle, Luther A., *American Idealism* (Vol. X, in *The Pageant of America*, New Haven, 1928).

STATE AND HISTORICAL SOCIETY PUBLICATIONS

All of the thirteen original states have published their colonial records, and in addition their State historical societies have made other colonial materials available through their publications. The most important are the following:

---

[1] *History of the Corruptions of Christianity* (Birmingham, 1793) XXIII.

CONNECTICUT

The Public Records of the Colony of Connecticut, 1636–1776, 15 vols. (Hartford, 1850–90).
Records of the Colony and Plantation of New Haven, from 1638 to 1649 (Hartford, 1857).

GEORGIA

The Colonial Records of the State of Georgia, 24 vols. (Atlanta, 1904–16).

MARYLAND

The Archives of Maryland: Proceedings of the Council . . . 1636–1770, 11 vols. (Maryland Historical Society, Baltimore, 1885–1912). *Proceedings and Acts of the General Assembly,* 7 vols. (Maryland Historical Society, Baltimore, 1883–   ).
Calvert Papers (Maryland Historical Society), 3 vols. (Baltimore, 1889).

MASSACHUSETTS

Massachusetts, Colonial Records.
Massachusetts Historical Society Collection, 78 vols., 1792–1927.

NEW HAMPSHIRE

Provincial and State Papers, 24 vols. (Concord, 1867–   ).
New Hampshire Historical Society Collections, 14 vols. (Concord, 1824–1931).

NEW JERSEY

Documents relating to the Colonial History of the State of New Jersey, 3 vols. (Newark, 1880–1900).
New Jersey Historical Society Collections, 10 vols. (Newark, 1846–1917).

NEW YORK

Documents Relative to the Colonial History of the State of New York, 15 vols. (Albany, 1853–87).
The Ecclesiastical Records of the State of New York, 7 vols. (Albany, 1901–16).

NORTH CAROLINA

The Colonial Records of North Carolina, 10 vols. (Raleigh, 1886–90).

PENNSYLVANIA

Colonial Records, 16 vols. (Philadelphia, 1852; Harrisburg, 1851–53).
Pennsylvania Historical Society Publications: Memoirs, 14 vols. (Philadelphia, 1826–96).

RHODE ISLAND

Records of the Colony of Rhode Island and Providence Plantations in New England, 10 vols. (Providence, 1856–65).
Collections of the Rhode Island Historical Society, 10 vols. (Providence, 1827–1902).
Publications of the Narragansett Club, First Series, 6 vols. (Providence, 1866–74).

SOUTH CAROLINA

Collections of the South Carolina Historical Society, 5 vols. (Charleston, 1857–   ).

VIRGINIA

Hening, William W., *The Statutes at Large, being a Collection of all the Laws of Virginia from the first session of the Legislature in the year 1619,* 13 vols. (New York, 1823).

SEVENTEENTH AND EIGHTEENTH CENTURY

Asbury, Francis, *Journal of,* Vol. I, 1771–86 (New York, 1852).
Associates of Dr. Bray, An Account of the Designs of . . . (London, 1764).
Besse, Joseph, *A Collection of the Sufferings of the people called Quakers for the testimony of a good Conscience . . . 1650 to the . . . Act of Toleration . . . in the year 1689,* 2 vols. (London, 1753).
Bishop, George, *New England Judged, Not by Man's, but the Spirit of the Lord, etc.* (London, 1661).
Bradford, W., *History of Plymouth Plantations,* W. T. Davis [Ed.] (New York, 1908).
Callender, John, *An Historical Discourse on the Civil and Religious Affairs of the Colony of Rhode Island* (Boston, 1739; reprinted Philadelphia, 1886).
Calvin, John, *Institutes of the Christian Religion,* 6th American edition, 2 vols. (Philadelphia, 1928).
[Cambridge Platform] *A Platform of Church-Discipline; Gathered out of the Word of God; and Agreed upon by the Elders and Messengers of the churches assembled in the Synod at Cambridge, in N. E. 1648* (Boston, 1649; many editions).

Chalkley, Thomas, *A Journal or Historical Account of the Life and Christian Experience of* (2nd edition, London, 1751).

Chauncy, Charles, *Seasonable Thoughts on the State of Religion in New England* (Boston, 1743).

Chauncy, Charles, *The late religious commotions in New-England considered: An answer to the Reverend Jonathan Edwards's sermon entitled, "The Distinguishing Marks of a Work of the Spirit of God. . . ."* (Boston, 1743).

Childe, Major John, *New Englands Jonas cast up at London, or, A Relation of the Proceedings of the Court at Boston in New-England against divers honest and godly persons, for petitioning . . . for admittance of themselves and children to the Sacraments in their churches; and in case that should not be granted, for leave to have Ministers and Church government according to the best Reformation of England and Scotland* (London, 1647). Reprinted in Peter Force, *Tracts and Other Papers,* Vol. IV, No. III.

Clap, Thomas, *The Annals or History of Yale-College: In New Haven, in the Colony of Connecticut, from the First Founding thereof, in the Year 1700 to the Year 1766* (New Haven, 1766).

Clarke, John, *Ill Newes from New England: Or A Narrative of New England Persecution, wherein is declared that while Old England is becoming New, New England is becoming Old* (London, 1652).

Cromwell, Oliver, *Letters and Speeches of* . . . 3 vols. (London, 1904).

Edwards, Jonathan, *A Faithful Narrative of the Surprising Work of God in Conversion of many hundred Souls in Northampton and neighboring Towns and Villages, in a letter to the Rev. Benjamin Coleman of Boston* (Boston, 1737). Many times reprinted.

Edwards, Jonathan, *A Treatise Concerning Religious Affections; in Three Parts* (Boston, 1746).

Edwards, Morgan, *Materials for a History of the Baptists in Rhode Island* (Collections of the Rhode Island Historical Society, Vol. VI., Providence, 1867).

Edwards, Morgan, *Materials Towards a History of the Baptists in Pennsylvania, both British and German* (Philadelphia, 1770).

Eliot, John, *The Day-Breaking if not the Sun-Rising of the Gospell with the Indians in New-England* (London, 1647).

Eliot, John, *The Indian Primer: or The Way of training up of our Indian Youth in the good knowledge of God . . . 1669* (Reprinted, Edinburgh, 1877).

Fox, George, *The Journal of,* Edited by Norman Penney, 2 vols. (Cambridge, 1911).

Fox, George, and Burnyeat, John, *A New England Firebrand Quenched,* etc. (London, 1678).

Franklin, Benjamin, *Autobiography,* O. S. Coad [Ed.] (New York, 1929).

Hakluyt, Richard, *A Particular Discourse Concerning the great necessitie and manifold commodyties that are like to growe to this Realme of Englande by the Western discoveries lately attempted, written in the year 1584 (Documentary History of the State of Maine,* Vol. II, Cambridge, 1877).

Holmes, Thomas James, *Increase Mather, a bibliography of his works,* 2 vols. (Cleveland, 1931).

Holmes, Thomas James, *Cotton Mather, a bibliography of his works,* 3 vols. (Cambridge, 1940).

Humphrey, David, *An Historical Account of the Incorporated Society for the Propagation of the Gospel in Foreign Parts,* etc. (London, 1730; reprinted New York, 1853).

Hutchinson, Thomas, *The History of the Colony of Massachusetts-Bay,* 3 vols. (Boston, 1764–1828. Last edition, Cambridge, 1936.)

Jameson, J. F., [Ed.] *Narratives of New Netherland, 1609–1664* (New York, 1909).

Jarratt, Devereux, *A Brief Narrative of the Revival of Religion in Virginia. In a letter to a friend* . . . (4th edition, London, 1779).

Keith, George, *A Journal of Travels from New Hampshire to Carratuck, on the Continent of North America* (London, 1706; Reprinted in Collections of the Protestant Episcopal Historical Society, 1851).

Lamack and Agrippa, *Chronicon Ephratense: A History of the Community of Seventh Day Baptists at Ephrata, Lancaster county, Penn'a* (Translated from the German by T. Max Hark, Lancaster, 1889).

Learner of Law and a Lover of Liberty, *A Narrative of a New and Unusual American Imprisonment of two Presbyterian Ministers and Prosecution of Mr. Francis Makemie, one of them, For preaching One sermon in the City of New York* (New York, 1755). Reprinted in Force, *Tracts,* Vol. IV, No. IV.

Mather, Cotton, *Magnalia Christi Americana: or the Ecclesiastical History of New England,* 2 vols. (1st ed., London, 1702; Hartford, 1820).

Mather, Increase, *Returning unto God* . . . a Sermon (Boston, 1680).

Mather, Increase, *Cases of Conscience concerning Evil Spirits* (Boston, 1792).

Morton, Thomas, *New English Canaan, or New Canaan, Containing an Abstract of New England,* etc. (Amsterdam, 1637); Edited with Introduction and Notes by C. F. Adams, Jr. (Boston, The Prince Society, 1883).

Myers, A. C. (Editor), *Narratives of Early Pennsylvania, West New Jersey and Delaware, 1630–1707.*

Nachrichten von den vereinigten Deutschen Evangelische-Lutherischen Gemeinen in Nord Amerika (Erster Band, Allentown, 1886; Zweiter Band, Philadelphia, 1895; English translation with notes, Reading, 1882).

Norton, Humphrey, *New England's Ensign . . . an Account of the Sufferings Sustained by Us in New England,* etc. (London, 1659).

Norton, John, *The Heart of New England rent at the Blasphemies of the Present Generation* (Cambridge, 1659).

Old South Leaflets, 8 vols. (Boston, N. D.). Contains reprints of many colonial writings.

Perry, William Stevens, *Historical Collection relating to the American Colonial Church,* Vol. I, *Virginia;* II, *Pennsylvania;* III, *Massachusetts;* IV, *Maryland;* V, *Delaware* (Hartford, 1870–78).

Prince, Thomas, *Christian History containing accounts of the Revival and Propagation of Religion in Great Britain and America* (Published weekly from March 5, 1743, to February 23, 1744/45).

Prince Society, *Publications of the* (Colonial History), 36 vols. (Boston, 1865–1920).

Richardson, Leon Burr, *An Indian Preacher in England, Being letters and Diaries relating to the mission of the Reverend Samson Occom and the Reverend Nathaniel Whitaker to collect funds in England for the benefit of Eleazar Wheelock's Indian Charity School from which Grew Dartmouth College* (Dartmouth College, 1933).

Roberts, William H., [Ed.] *Records of the Presbyterian Church in the United States of America, embracing the Minutes of the General Presbytery and General Synod, 1706–1788* (Philadelphia, 1904).

Roberts, William H., [Ed.] *Minutes of the General Convention of Delegates appointed by the Synod of New York and Philadelphia and the General Association of Connecticut,* 1766–76 (Philadelphia, 1904).

Schlatter, Michael, *The Diary of* (*Journal of the Presbyterian Historical Society,* Sept.-Dec., 1905).

Semple, Robert B., *A History of the Rise and Progress of the Baptists in Virginia* (Richmond, 1810).

Sewell, Samuel, *Diary* (Mark Van Doren [Ed.] Abridged edition, New York, 1930; Complete in Massachusetts Historical Society Collections, Series 5, Vols. V–VIII, 1878–82).

Shepard, Thomas, *The Clear Sunshine of the gospel breaking forth upon the Indians in New England.* Reprinted New York, 1865.

Society for the Promotion of Christian Knowledge, An Account of (London, 1769; 1773).

Stiles, Ezra, *Itineraries and Correspondence,* F. B. Dexter [Ed.] 2 vols. (New Haven, 1918).

Story, Thomas, *Journal of the Life,* etc. (London, 1747).

Trumbull, Benjamin, *A Complete History of Connecticut, Civil and Ecclesiastical, 1630–1764* (New Haven, 1818; last edition, New London, 1898).

Tyler, L. G., *Narratives of Early Virginia* (New York, 1907).

Van Laer, A. J. F., [Ed.] *Documents Relating to New Netherland, 1624–1626* (San Marino, Cal., 1924).

Von Rick, Mr. Commissary. *An Extract of the Journals of, who conducted the First Transport of Salzburgers to Georgia; and of the Reverend Mr. Bolzius, one of their ministers, etc.* (London, 1734. Reprinted in Force, *Tracts*, Vol. IV, No. V).

Walker, Williston, *Creeds and Platforms of Congregationalism* (New York, 1905).

Whitefield, George, *Journals of* (London, 1739; Philadelphia, 1740; London, 1741; London, 1744).

Whitefield, George, *Works of,* 6 vols. (London, 1771).

Whitney, John, *Truth and Innocency defended against Falsehood and Envy and the Martyrs of Jesus, and Sufferers for His sake Vindicated. In answer to Cotton Mather, a priest of Boston, his Calumnies, Lies, and Abuses of the People called Quakers in his late Church History of New England* (London, 1702; reprinted Philadelphia, 1885).

Williams, Roger, *The Bloudy Tenent of Persecution for cause of Conscience, 1644* (Publications of the Narragansett Club, III, Providence, 1867).

Williams, Roger, *The Bloudy Tenent of Persecution yet more Bloudy,* etc. (London, 1652; Narragansett Club Publications, Providence, 1870).

Williams, Roger, *George Fox Digg'd out of his Burrows,* etc. (Boston, 1676; Narragansett Club Publications, Vol. IV).

Winthrop, John, *Journal,* J. K. Hosmer [Ed.], 2 vols. (New York, 1908).

Wise, John, *The Churches Quarrel Espoused* (Boston, 1710).

Wise, John, *Vindication of the Government of the New England Churches* (Boston, 1717).

OLDER PUBLICATIONS

Acrelius, Israel, *A History of New Sweden, or the Settlements on the River Delaware,* Translated from the Swedish by W. M. Reynolds (The Historical Society of Pennsylvania, 1894).

Adams, Charles Francis, *Three Episodes in Massachusetts History,* 2 vols. (Boston, 1893).

Alexander, A., *Biographical Sketches of the Founder and Principal Alumni of the Log College* (Princeton, 1845).

Anderson, J. D., *History of the Church of England in the Colonies and Foreign Dependencies of the British Empire,* 3 vols. (London, 1845).

Backus, Isaac, *A History of New England with Particular Reference to the Denomination of Christians called Baptists,* 3 vols. (Boston, 1777, 1796).

Bacon, Leonard, *Contributions to the Ecclesiastical History of Connecticut* (New Haven, 1861).

Barker, J. Ellis, *The Rise and Decline of the Netherlands* (London, 1906).

Barnes, V. L., *The Dominion of New England, a Study in British Colonial Policy* (New Haven, 1923).

Beardsley, E. E., *The History of the Episcopal Church in Connecticut from the Settlement of the Colony to the Death of Bishop Seabury* (New York, 1865).

Benedict, David, *A General History of the Baptist Denomination in America,* 2 vols. (Boston, 1813).

Bernheim, Gotthardt D., *History of the German Settlements and the Lutheran Church in North and South Carolina,* etc. (Philadelphia, 1872).

Blok, P. J., *History of the People of the Netherlands,* 4 vols. Parts I, II, III translated by Ruth Putnam and Parts IV and V by Oscar A. Bierstadt (New York, 1907).

Bowden, James, *The History of the Society of Friends in America* (London, 1850).

Briggs, Charles A., *American Presbyterianism, its Origin and Early History* (New York, 1885).

Brownson, Walter C., *The History of Brown University, 1764-1914* (Providence, 1914).

Bruce, Philip Alexander, *Institutional History of Virginia in the Seventeenth Century,* 2 vols. (New York and London, 1910).

Bruce, Philip Alexander, *Social Life of Virginia in the Seventeenth Century* (Richmond, 1907).

Brumbaugh, Martin G., *A History of the German Baptist Brethren in Europe and America* (Elgin, Ill., 1899).

Burgess, Walter H., *John Smyth the Se-Baptist; Thomas Helwys and the First Baptist Church in England,* etc. (London, 1911).

Byington, E. H., *The Puritan as a Colonist and Reformer* (Boston, 1899).

Byington, E. H., *John Eliot, the Puritan Missionary to the Indians* (Am. Soc. of Church Hist., Papers, New York, 1897, Vol. VIII, pp. 111-145).

Cobb, Sanford H., *The Rise of Religious Liberty in America* (New York, 1902).

Corwin, Edward T., *Manual of the Reformed Church in America, 1628-1902,* 4th edition (New York, 1902).

Cross, Arthur Lyon, *The Anglican Episcopate and the American Colonies* (New York, 1902).

Davenport, F. M., *Primitive Traits in Religious Revivals, A Study in Mental and Social Evolution* (New York, 1905).

Davies, C. M., *The History of Holland and the Dutch Nation,* 3 vols. (London, 1851).

Davies, Samuel, *Sermons on Important Subjects,* 4 vols. (London, 1815).

Dennis, A. P., *Lord Baltimore's Struggle with the Jesuits, 1634–1649* (The American Historical Association Reports, Vol. I, 1900.)

De Schweinitz, Edmund, *The History of the Church Known as the Unitas Fratrum* (Bethlehem, Pa., 1885).

Dexter, Henry M., *Congregationalism of the Last Three Hundred Years as Seen in its Literature* (Boston, 1880).

Eckenrode, H. J., *The Separation of Church and State in Virginia* (Richmond, 1909).

Eggleston, Edward, *The Beginners of a Nation: A History of the Source and Rise of the earliest English Settlements in America with special reference to the Life and Character of the People* (New York, 1899).

Ellis, George E., *The Puritan Age and Rule in the Colony of Massachusetts, 1629–1685* (Boston, 1824).

Faust, Albert B., *The German Element in the United States with Special Reference to its Political, Moral, Social and Educational influence,* 2 vols. (Boston and New York, 1909).

Florey, John S., *Literary Activity of the German Baptist Brethren in the Eighteenth Century* (Elgin, Ill., 1908).

Foote, William H., *Sketches of North Carolina, Historical and Biographical,* etc. (New York, 1846).

Foote, William H., *Sketches of Virginia* (First Series, Philadelphia, 1850; Second Series, 1855).

Ford, Henry J., *The Scotch-Irish in America* (Princeton, 1915).

Gillett, E. H., *History of the Presbyterian Church in the United States of America,* 2 vols. (Philadelphia, 1864).

Gillin, John L., *The Dunkers, A Sociological Interpretation* (New York, 1906).

Gooch, G. P., *The History of English Democratic Ideas in the Seventeenth Century* (Cambridge, 1898).

Good, James I., *History of the Reformed Church in the United States, 1725–1792* (Reading, 1899).

Grobner, A. L., *Geschichte der Luterischen Kirchen in Amerika* (St. Louis, 1902).

Guild, Reuben A., *Life, Times and Correspondence of James Manning and the Early History of Brown University* (Boston, 1864).

Hall, C. C., *The Lords Baltimore and the Maryland Palatinate* (Baltimore, 1902).

Hamilton, J. T., *A History of the Church known as the Moravian Church* (Bethlehem, 1900).

Hanna, Charles A., *The Scotch-Irish or the Scots in North Britain, North Ireland, and North America,* 2 vols. (New York and London, 1902).

Harbaugh, Henry, *The Life of Michael Schlatter* (Philadelphia, 1859).

Hawkins, Ernest, *Historical Notices of the Missions of England in the American Colonies, previous to the independence of the United States; Chiefly from the MS Documents of the Society for the Propagation of the Gospel in Foreign Parts* (London, 1845).

Hawks, Francis L., *Contributions to the Ecclesiastical History of the United States*, 2 vols. (New York, 1836).

Hinkle, William L., *Life and Letters of the Reverend John Philip Boehm, Founder of the Reformed Church in Pennsylvania, 1683–1749* (Philadelphia, 1916).

Hodge, Charles, *The Constitutional History of the Presbyterian Church in the United States of America*, Part I, 1705–41; Part II, 1741–88 (Philadelphia, 1839; 1840).

Hughes, Thomas, *The History of the Society of Jesus in North America*, 4 vols. (New York and Cleveland, 1907–17).

Humphrey, E. F., *Nationalism and Religion in America* (Boston, 1924).

Hunt, Gaillard, *James Madison and Religious Liberty* (American Historical Association Reports, 1901).

Innes, J. H., *New Amsterdam and its People* (New York, 1902).

Jameson, J. F., *William Usselinx, Founder of the Dutch and Swedish West India Companies* (Papers of the American Historical Association, Vol. II, No. 3, New York, 1887).

Janney, S. M., *History of the Religious Society of Friends from its Rise to the Year 1828*, 4 vols. (Philadelphia, 1859–67).

Jones, Rufus M., *The Quakers in the American Colonies* (London, 1911).

Jones, Rufus M., *The Faith and Practice of the Quakers* (London and New York, N.D.).

Killan, W. D., *Ecclesiastical History of Ireland*, 2 vols. (London, 1875).

Kittredge, George L., *Dr. Child the Remonstrant* (Reprinted from the Publications of the *Colonial Society of Massachusetts Publications*, XXI, Cambridge, 1919).

Kriebel, H. W., *The Schwenkfelders in Pennsylvania: A historical Sketch* (Lancaster, 1904, Vol. XIII, Pennsylvania-German Society Proceedings).

Latimer, W. T., *A History of Irish Presbyterianism* (Belfast, 1902).

Levering, J. M., *A History of Bethlehem, Pennsylvania, 1741–1892* (Bethlehem, 1903).

Mann, William J., *Life and Times of Henry M. Mühlenberg*, 2nd edition (Philadelphia, 1911).

Mereness, N. D., *Maryland as a Proprietary Province* (New York, 1910).

Miller, Daniel, *Early History of the Reformed Church in Pennsylvania* (Reading, 1906).

Motley, J. T., *History of the United Netherlands from the Death of William the Silent to the Twelve Years' Truce*, 4 vols. (London, 1869).

Motley, J. T., *The Rise of the Dutch Republic: A History*, 3 vols. (New York, 1870).

Murphy, T., *The Presbytery of the Log College* (Philadelphia, 1889).

Neill, Edward D., *History of the Virginia Company*, etc. (Albany, 1869).

Neill, Edward D., *Founders of Maryland* (Albany, 1876).

Newman, A. H., *A History of the Baptist Churches in the United States* (New York, 1894).

O'Callaghan, E. B. [Ed.], *History of New Netherland: or New York under the Dutch*, 2 vols. (New York, 1848).

O'Gorman, Thomas, *A History of the Roman Catholic Church in the United States* (New York, 1895).

Paschal, George W., *History of the North Carolina Baptists*, Vol. I, *1663–1805* (Raleigh, 1930).

Pascoe, C. S., *An Historical Account of the Society for the Propagation of the Gospel . . . 1701–1900* (London, 1901).

Perry, William Stevens, *The History of the American Episcopal Church*, 2 vols. (Boston, 1885).

Phillips, James D., *Salem in the Seventeenth and Eighteenth Centuries* (Boston and New York, 1933).

Proud, Robert, *The History of Pennsylvania*, etc., 2 vols. (Philadelphia, 1798).

Putnam, Ruth, *William the Silent, Prince of Orange*, 2 vols. (New York, 1895).

Quincy, Josiah, *The History of Harvard University*, 2 vols. (Cambridge, 1840).

Reed, Susan M., *Church and State in Massachusetts, 1691–1740* (Urbana, Ill., 1914).

Richards, James W., *The Confessional History of the Lutheran Church* (Philadelphia, 1909).

Richman, I. B., *Rhode Island; Its Making and Meaning*, 2 vols. (New York, 1902).

Rider, Sidney S., *An Inquiry into the Origin of the Cause . . . (of) disfranchising Roman Catholics* (Providence, 1889, Rhode Island Historical Tracts).

Sachse, Julius F., *The German Sectaries of Pennsylvania, 1708–1742: A Critical and Legendary History of the Ephrata Cloister and the Dunkers* (Philadelphia, 1899).

Sachse, Julius F., *Justus Faulkner, Mystic and Scholar* (Philadelphia, 1893).

Seipt, A. A., *Schwenkfelder Hymnology and the Sources of the first Schwenkfelder Hymn Book printed in America* (Philadelphia, 1909).

Shea, John Gilmary, *History of the Catholic Church in the United States*, Vol. I, *1521–1763* (New York, 1886).

Slater, E. F., *John Checkley*, 2 vols. (Prince Society, 1897).

Smith, R., *H. F. Harrington and his Oceana, a Study of a 17th Century Utopia and its Influence in America* (Cambridge, 1914).

Steiner, Bernard G., "Rev. Thomas Bray and his American Libraries" (*American Historical Review,* Vol. II, 1896).

Taylor, James B., *Virginia Baptist Preachers,* Series I and II, 2 vols., 3rd Edition (New York, 1860).

Thom, W. T., *The Struggle for Religious Freedom in Virginia: The Baptists.* Johns Hopkins University Studies in History and Political Science, Series XVIII, Nos. 10, 11, 12 (Baltimore, 1900).

Thompson, Robert Ellis, *A History of the Presbyterian Churches in the United States* (New York, 1895).

Tracy, Joseph, *A History of the Revival of Religion in the time of Edwards and Whitefield* (Boston, 1842).

Van Tyne, C. H., *Causes of the War for Independence,* Vol. I (New York, and Boston, 1922).

Walker, George L., *Some Aspects of the Religious Life of New England* (New York, 1897).

Walker, Williston, *The History of Congregational Churches in the United States* (New York, 1894).

Walker, Williston, *Ten New England Leaders* (New York, 1901).

Webster, Richard, *A History of the Presbyterian Church in America,* etc. (Philadelphia, 1857).

Weeks, Stephen B., *The Religious Development of the Province of North Carolina.* Johns Hopkins University Studies, 10th Series, Nos. 5–6 (Baltimore, 1892).

Wooley, Theodore D., *An Historical Discourse Before the Graduates of Yale College* (New Haven, 1850).

Zwierlein, F. J., *Religion in New Netherland . . . 1623–1664* (Rochester, 1910).

RECENT PUBLICATIONS

*The books marked with an * contain elaborate bibliographies.*

Adams, James Truslow, *The Founding of New England* (Boston, 1921).

Andrews, Charles M., *The Colonial Period of American History: The Settlements,* 4 vols. (New Haven, 1934–1938).

Andrews, Matthew Page, *The Founding of Maryland* (Baltimore and New York, 1933).

Bainton, Roland G., "The Left Wing of the Reformation" (*Journal of Religion,* XXI, 1941).

Barr, Lillian M., *Status of the Churches of Pennylvania in 1776* (Typed M.A. Thesis, University of Chicago, 1920).

Bates, Ernest Sutherland, *American Faith: Its Religious, Political and Economic Foundations* (New York, 1940).

Beatty, E. C. O., *William Penn as Social Philosopher* (New York, 1939).

Bergendorf, J. T., "The Swedish Church on the Delaware" (*Church History*, Vol. VII, 1938).

*Bost, George H., *Samuel Davies, Colonial Revivalist and Champion of Religious Toleration* (Typed Ph.D., Thesis, University of Chicago, 1942).

Brailsford, M. R., *The Making of William Penn* (London, 1930).

Brayshaw, A. N., *The Quakers: Their Story and Message* (New York, 1927).

Brockunier, S. H., *The Irrepressible Democrat, Roger Williams* (New York, 1940).

Brydon, G. MacLaren, "New Light upon the History of the Church in Colonial Virginia" (*Historical Magazine of the Protestant Episcopal Church*, June 1941).

Cheyney, Edward Potts, *History of the University of Pennsylvania, 1740–1940* (Philadelphia, 1940).

Church, Leslie F., *Oglethorpe: A Study in Philanthropy in England and America* (London, 1932).

Correll, Ernst H., *Das Schweizerische Täufer-Minnonitentum* (Tübingen, 1925).

Crane, Vernon W., "Promotion Literature of Georgia," in *Bibliography Essays A Tribute to Wilberforce Eames* (Cambridge, 1929).

Davidson, Elizabeth H., *The Establishment of the English Church in the Continental American Colonies* (Durham, N. C., 1936).

Demarest, H. S., *A History of Rutgers College* (New Brunswick, 1924).

Dobree, B., *William Penn, Quaker and Pioneer* (Boston, 1932).

*Dove, Frederick D., *Cultural Change in the Church of the Brethren* (Philadelphia, 1932).

Eekhof, A., *Jonas Michaelius, Founder of the Church in New Netherland* (Leyden, 1926).

Emmott, Elizabeth Braithwaite, *A Short History of Quakerism: Earlier Period* (London, 1923).

*Ernst, James, *The Political Thought of Roger Williams* (Seattle, 1929).

Ernst, James, *Roger Williams: New England Firebrand* (New York, 1932).

Faust, Clarence H., and Johnson, Thomas H., *Jonathan Edwards* (New York, 1935).

Flick, A. C., [Ed.] *History of the State of New York*, 10 vols. (New York, 1933–37).

Fox, Dixon Ryan, *Caleb Heathcote, Gentleman Colonist* (New York, 1926).

Funk, Henry D., "The Influence of the Presbyterian Church in Early American History" (*Journal of the Presbyterian Historical Society*, 1924–27).

Garrett, Christine H., *The Marian Exiles* (Cambridge, Eng., 1938).

*Gewehr, Wesley M., *The Great Awakening in Virginia, 1740–1790* (Durham, N. C., 1930).

*Greene, E. B., *Religion and the State: The Making and Testing of American Tradition* (New York, 1941).

Hall, Thomas C., *The Religious Background of American Culture* (Boston, 1930).

*Haller, William, *The Rise of Puritanism, or the Way to the New Jerusalem as set forth in Pulpit and Press, 1570–1643* (New York, 1938).

Harkness, R. E. E., "Principles of the Early Baptists of England and America" (*Crozer Quarterly*, V, 1928).

*Hirsch, Arthur H., *The Huguenots of Colonial South Carolina* (Durham, N. C., 1928).

*Hooker, Richard J., *The Anglican Church and the American Revolution* (Typed Ph.D. Thesis, The University of Chicago, 1942).

Hubner, Leon, "The Jews of Georgia in Colonial Times" (*American Jewish Historical Society Publications*, X, Baltimore, 1902, pp. 65–95).

Ingram, George H., "The Story of the Log College" (*Journal of the Presbyterian Historical Society*, XII, October, 1927, pp. 487–511).

Jernegan, M. W., *Laboring and Dependent Classes in Colonial America, 1607–1783* (Chicago, 1931).

*Jordan, W. K., *The Development of Religious Toleration in England:* Vol. III, *From the Convention of the Long Parliament to the Restoration, 1640–1660* (Cambridge, 1938).

Kittredge, George L., *Witchcraft in Old and New England* (Cambridge, 1929).

*Klein, Walter C., *Johann Conrad Beissel* (Philadelphia, 1942).

*Klett, Guy S., *Presbyterianism in Colonial Pennsylvania* (Philadelphia, 1937).

Klingberg, Arthur J., "Sir William Johnson and the Society for the Propagation of the Gospel, 1749–1774" (*Historical Magazine of the Protestant Episcopal Church*, Vol. VIII, 1939).

Klingberg, Arthur J., *Anglican Humanitarianism in Colonial New York* (Philadelphia, 1940).

Knappen, Marshall M., *Tudor Puritanism; A Chapter in English Idealism* (Chicago, 1939).

Knittle, Walter A., *Early Eighteenth Century Palatinate Emigration* (Philadelphia, 1937).

Lennox, H. H., *Samuel Kirkland's Mission to the Iroquois* (Typed. Ph.D. Thesis University of Chicago, 1935).

Loetscher, Frederick W., "The Adopting Act" (*Journal of the Presbyterian Historical Society*, 1929).

MacDougall, Hamilton C., *Early New England Psalmody.... 1620–1820* (Brattleboro, Vt., 1940).

McGiffert, Arthur C., Jr., *Jonathan Edwards* (New York, 1930).

*Manross, W. W., *A History of the American Episcopal Church* (New York and Milwaukee, 1935).

*Maxson, Charles H., *The Great Awakening in the Middle Colonies* (Chicago, 1920).

*Maynard, Theodore, *The Story of American Catholicism* (New York, 1941).

*Mecklin, John M., *The Story of American Dissent* (New York, 1934).

*Meyer, Jacob E., *Church and State in Massachusetts from 1740–1833* (Cleveland, 1930).

Midwinter, Sir Edward, "The S.P.G. and the Colonial Church in Massachusetts" (*Historical Magazine of the Protestant Episcopal Church*, 1933).

*Miller, Perry, *Orthodoxy in Massachusetts* (Cambridge, 1933).

Miller, Perry and Johnson, Thomas H., *The Puritans* (New York, 1938).

Miller, Perry, *The New England Mind* (New York, 1939).

*Mohler, Samuel R., *Commissary James Blair, Churchman, Educator, and Politician of Colonial Virginia* (Typed Ph.D. Thesis, University of Chicago, 1940).

Morison, Samuel E., *Builders of the Bay Colony* (Boston, 1930).

Morison, Samuel E., *The Founding of Harvard College* (Cambridge, 1935).

Morison, Samuel E., *Harvard College in the Seventeenth Century*, 2 vols. (Cambridge, 1936).

Morison, Samuel E., *The Puritan Pronaos* (New York, 1936).

*Murdock, Kenneth B., *Increase Mather, The Foremost American Puritan* (Cambridge, 1925).

*Nettles, Curtis P., *Roots of American Civilization* (New York, 1938).

Nissenson, S. G., *The Patroon's Domain* (New York, 1937).

*Osgood, Herbert L., *The American Colonies in the Eighteenth Century*, 3 vols. (New York, 1924).

*Osgood, Herbert L., *The American Colonies in the Seventeenth Century*, 3 vols. (New York, 1930).

Parks, George B., *Richard Hakluyt and the English Voyages* (New York, 1928).

Parrington, V. L., *Main Currents in American Thought*, Vol I, *The Colonial Mind, 1620–1800* (New York, 1927).

Pennington, Edgar L., *Apostle of New Jersey, John Talbot, 1645–1727* (Philadephia, 1938).

*Peterson, A. Everett, *The Cultural Heritage from the Dutch in the History of New York*, Vol. I, *History of the State of New York*, A. C. Flick, [Ed.] (New York, 1933).

*Ray, Sister Mary Augustina, *American Opinion of Roman Catholicism in the Eighteenth Century* (New York, 1936).

Rose-Troup, Frances, *John White, The Patriarch of Dorchester* (Dorset) *and the Founder of Massachusetts, 1575–1648* (New York, 1930).

Ryan, John A., and Millar, M. F. X., *The State and the Church* (New York, 1936).

*Schneider, Herbert W., *The Puritan Mind* (New York, 1930).

*Schneider, Herbert W., and Carol, [Editors] *Samuel Johnson, President of King's College, His Career and Writings,* 4 vols. (New York, 1929).

Scholes, Percy A., *The Puritan and Music in England and New England, a Contribution to the Cultural History of two Nations* (London, 1934).

*Sessler, Jacob J., *Communal Pietism among Early American Moravians* (New York, 1933).

Shearer, Augustus H., "The Church, the School and the Press," Ch. II, Vol. III, *History of New York,* A. C. Flick [Ed.] (New York, 1933).

*Smith, C. H., *The Mennonite Immigration to Pennsylvania in the Eighteenth Century* (Norristown, 1929).

Smith, C. H., *The Story of the Mennonites,* (Berne, Ind., 1941).

*Strickland, Reba C., *Religion and the State in Georgia in the Eighteenth Century* (New York, 1939).

*Sweet, W. W., *The Story of Religion in America* (New York, 1939).

*Sweet, W. W., *Religion on the American Frontier,* Vol. I, *The Baptists* (Chicago, 1931).

*Sweet, W. W., *Men of Zeal; The Romance of American Methodist Beginnings* (New York, 1935).

*Sweet, W. W., *Makers of Christianity from John Cotton to Lyman Abbott* (New York, 1937).

Townsend, Henry G., *Philosophical Ideas in the United States* (New York, 1934).

*Townsend, Leah, *South Carolina Baptists* (Florence, S. C., 1935).

Van Loon, Hendrik, *Life and Times of Peter Stuyvesant* (New York, 1928).

Vulliamy, C. E., *William Penn* (London, 1933).

Wenger, J. C., *Glimpses of Mennonite History* (Scottsdale, Pa., 1940).

Wenger, Otto, *History and Doctrines of the Church of the Brethren* (Elgin, Ill., 1920).

Wentz, Abdel R., *History of the Gettysburg Theological Seminary* (Philadelphia, 1926).

Wertenbaker, Thomas Jefferson, *The Founding of American Civilization: The Middle Colonies* (New York, 1938).

*Winslow, Ola Elizabeth, *Jonathan Edwards, 1703-1758* (New York, 1940).

Wright, Louis B., "Pious Reading in Colonial Virginia" (*The Journal of Southern History,* 1940).

Index